Sergio Moravia's *The Enigma of the Mind* (originally published in Italian as *L'enigma della mente*) offers a broad and lucid critical and historical survey of one of the fundamental debates in the philosophy of mind: the relationship of mind and body. This problem continues to raise deep questions concerning the nature of man.

The book has two central aims. The first is to sketch the major recent contributions to this problem from philosophers of mind. Among the thinkers and theories covered are the logical neopositivism of Herbert Feigl; the work of the Australian school (Place, Smart, Armstrong); the functionalism of Fodor and Putnam; the anomalous monism of Davidson; and the positions of certain followers of Wittgenstein (Malcolm,. Bernstein) and those of Rorty, Greene, Nagel, Dreyfus, and Margolis.

Having established this framework Professor Moravia pursues his second aim: the articulation of a particular reading of the mental and the mind–body problem. Moravia criticises some of the most influential doctrines in this field, from physicalistic reductionism to mentalism: the mental can be neither eliminated nor identified with the body nor interpreted as a metaphysical entity. Rather, according to the author, it is more fruitful to see the mind as a complex of pragmatic and linguistic acts through which human beings express themselves.

The book's detailed and systematic treatment of this fundamental philosophical issue makes it ideal for upper-level undergraduate and graduate courses in epistemology and the philosophy of mind. It should also prove provocative reading for psychologists and cognitive scientists.

The enigma of the mind

The enigma of the mind

The mind–body problem in contemporary thought

SERGIO MORAVIA
UNIVERSITY OF FLORENCE

TRANSLATED BY SCOTT STATON

NATIONAL UNIVERSITY
LIBRARY SAN DIEGO

CAMBRIDGE
UNIVERSITY PRESS

Published by the Press Syndicate of the University of Cambridge
The Pitt Building, Trumpington Street, Cambridge CB2 1RP
40 West 20th Street, New York, NY 10011–4211, USA
10 Stamford Road, Oakleigh, Melbourne 3166, Australia

© Cambridge University Press 1995
© Gius. Laterza & Figli Spa, Roma-Bari 1986

First published 1995

Printed in the United States of America

Library of Congress Cataloging-in-Publication Data

Moravia, Sergio, 1940–

[Enigma delle mente. English]

The enigma of the mind : the mind–body problem in contemporary
thought / Sergio Moravia ; translated by Scott Staton.

p.   cm.

Includes bibliographical references (p. xxx–xxx) and index.

ISBN 0-521-40550-5. – ISBN 0-521-40557-2 (pbk.)

1. Mind and body.   2. Philosophy of mind.   I. Title.
BF164.M6713   1995
128'.2 – dc20   94–22174
CIP

A catalog record for this book is available from the British Library.

ISBN 0–521–40550–5 Hardback
ISBN 0–521–40557–2 Paperback

NATIONAL UNIVERSITY
LIBRARY
SAN DIEGO

*To Nico and Daniele
from Dad*

Could a *brain* have thoughts, illusions or pains? The senselessness of the supposition seems so obvious that I find it hard to take seriously. No experiment could establish this result for a brain. Why not? The fundamental reason is that a brain does not sufficiently resemble a human being.

NORMAN MALCOLM, 1985

Men are not machines, not even ghost-ridden machines. They are men – a tautology which is sometimes worth remembering.

GILBERT RYLE, 1949

Contents

Preface to the English edition   *page* ix

The enigma of the mind: Introduction to a
metaphor   1

1 Toward a physical science of the mental: Feigl and
   the (re-)construction of the 'mind–body problem'   30

2 The apogee of physicalism: The identity theory and
   materialism in the Australian school   61

3 The obscure relationship: Problems and debates
   surrounding the identity theory   105

4 Psychology as alchemy: The elimination of the
   mental in the 'disappearance theory'   118

5 The mind as function: The functionalist approach to
   the mind–body problem   130

6 The mind as property and as event: The 'reformist'
   neo-identityism of Kim and Davidson   153

7 The mind as language: The linguistic turn in the
   mind–body problem   176

8 Speaking in many different ways: The pluralization
   of descriptions and explanations in the MBP   195

9 The mind as a mode of subjective experience: An
   interpretive model of the features of the mental   206

Contents

10 The mind as 'subject' and as 'being-in-the-world':
Toward a non-mentalistic interpretation of the
mental   236

   Appendix
   The mental as intentional/'personal' emergence:
   The psycho-personological perspective of Joseph
   Margolis   267

   Bibliography   283

   Name index   317

Preface to the English edition

I am pleased that Cambridge University Press has decided to present *The Enigma of the Mind* to the English-speaking world. In effect, the so-called mind–body problem (MBP), which constitutes the subject of my book, though naggingly present throughout the whole history of Western thought, has been investigated in our time principally in the United States, Australia, and Great Britain. That my approach to this "problem" has attracted the attention of various American colleagues is cause for considerable satisfaction. It is likely that one reason for this interest is simply the fact that the book offers a broad comparative overview of the main theoretical tendencies that have grappled with the MBP since the 1950s and 1960s. In this sense, the essay may serve as an introduction to one of the central issues of the contemporary philosophy of mind; one of the few, despite the extremely vast literature on the MBP published in English, to present the historical-theoretical overview I have attempted to give here.

Actually, my ambitions for the function and significance of this work are also of another nature, and it is my hope that the reader will grasp them (and find them legitimate) without great difficulty. In the first place, it has been my aim not to present an eclectic review of various attitudes toward the MBP but rather to show the logic which, at least from my philosophical perspective, has given a certain direction to the debate on the relationship between mind and body. In this sense, my essay is, so to speak, militant. It is a book which criticizes variously formulated reductive conceptions of the mind and advances a thesis that is not *lato sensu* physicalistic, but at the same time, somewhat paradoxically, not mentalistic either. In fact one of the questions I found most fascinating is this: is it truly inevitable that, when faced with the MBP, the scholar is compelled *either* to cancel out the mental *or* to consider this mental something which exists (self-referentially) *an sich*, a solution which for many reasons lacks credibility, even in its most up-to-date versions?

The research I have carried out might be entirely misdirected, but it is certainly rather different from what is generally done in much of the contemporary philosophy of mind. And the real point of interest in the essay may lie precisely in this difference. In brief, in approaching the MBP I did not unquestioningly accept a whole series of assumptions which might appear to be, but are not, self-evident. Perhaps inspired by the Nietzschean component in my intellectual background (the Nietzsche of the "exercise of suspicion"), I subjected the issue of the relationship between mind and body to a number of somewhat unconventional questions. To begin with, are we quite sure that the MBP addresses, really and exclusively, a psychophysical problem? Or is it not rather the case that it serves mainly to pose problems not so much of a psychophysical nature (though these problems exist, and they are serious), as of an anthropological and epistemological nature? – problems, that is, which concern, on the one hand, the image we have (or would like to have) of the human being and, on the other, the image we have (or would like to have) of the "science" which is most congruent with that being.

It is questions of this sort that underlie the orientation and nature of the investigation developed in *The Enigma of the Mind*. Firstly, I have reserved ample space for the most relevant theoretical positions on the MBP offered by the contemporary *theatrum philosophicum*. Secondly, I have chosen to focus not on empirical issues – which, however interesting, I consider to be of minor importance within certain interpretive contexts – but on the truly crucial issues mentioned above: the character of the mind (and of man) and of the science that studies them.

Finally, there is another aspect of my book which requires a justification and an explanation: the abundance of quotations. The ideal book, Walter Benjamin once wrote, should consist entirely of quotations. I cannot wholly agree with the great German critic and philosopher. Yet I would not like my use of quotations to be understood for what it is *not:* a sort of reluctance to assume clear responsibilities in the first person. On the contrary, the reader will realize immediately that my book is unambiguously committed to the defense of precise principles: the rehabilitation of the subject as the "titular" of mental events, the interpretation of the mental as language, and so on. The wide use of quotations answers two different needs. One is to present the reader with direct proof of the actual existence of the theses I criticize (or support). The other is to draw certain positions out of the very words used to express them. After all, what are philosophical positions if not words organized in forms of discourse intended to be coherent and convincing? Moreover, my quotations are never (in my intentions, in any case) casual. They represent, rather, the road signs I encountered in the course of a long, patient journey that led from the thesis, which I hold to be absolutely simplistic and misleading, that "the mind is the body" (in which, to begin with, it is not at all clear what is meant by such dumbfounding abstractions as 'the mind' and 'the body') to the position that holds that the 'mind' is a metaphoric construct bearing meanings produced by the subject who utters them, and largely independent of the bodily vehicles used to transmit them.

I cannot conclude this brief Preface without begging the reader's indulgence on one important point. *The Enigma of the Mind* was written in the 1980s, and it is clear that the debate on the MBP did not stop there. I am also well aware that various scholars discussed in my book have modified or adjusted their positions in new, important works. If, in the end, I have decided not to take these more recent developments into account, this is for two reasons: in the first place, I have the sensation that many of the theoretical options I was interested in commenting on (especially in light of their overall anthropological and epistemological implications) have remained substantially unchanged; in the second, a different decision would have forced me to write another, *different* book. Perhaps I will write such a book one day: but I do not feel I can renounce *this* essay in its present form. I believe that it is a relatively representative testimony – for better or, of course, for worse – of the way in which a European philosopher and historian of ideas writing in the 1980s interpreted a problem which excited considerable passion among American scholars.

As I present this work to my readers I would like to express my gratitude to those who in various ways helped bring it about – particularly Giulio Barsanti and Franco Cambi for their patient reading of the typescript and of an earlier version of this book. I am also grateful to those who, by inviting me to lecture on my work in progress, stimulated me to further develop certain positions and interpretations. Among the philosophers I would like to mention here Carlo Sini and Franco Bianco (together with the colleagues of the interuniversity group under his direction) and among the psychologists and psychiatrists Riccardo Luccio, Sergio Molinari, Alberto Munari, Fausto Petrella, and Alessandro Salvini. I also owe thanks to my students and collaborators for encouraging me in my philosophical work – and for believing in it. Finally, thanks is due to Scott Staton, translator and collaborator, who adopted the text as his own. This volume was conceived in the United States, given shape in Florence, and completed in Ronchi. As I pen the last page, I discover that the final image (or is it a feeling?) associated with the word 'end' is that of the sky and the pinetrees of Versilia.

Sergio Moravia
Florence University, August 1994

The enigma of the mind

The enigma of the mind:
Introduction to a metaphor

I

Ein Weltknoten, a world knot: this is how Arthur Schopenhauer once defined the problem of the relationship between mind and body. This 'knot' ambiguously binds together what are, or appear to be, the two fundamental dimensions of man. This same knot, however, also calls up a series of figures, questions, and issues which extend well beyond the confines of the mind–body relationship. Not surprisingly, then, the relationship between the mental and the bodily is a theme which has pervaded the whole history of Western thought. It played a central role in ancient knowledge, especially among Aristotelians, and in the field of ancient medicine. It re-emerged, in the most various forms, in the culture of the Middle Ages and in Renaissance humanism. We find it again at the center of seventeenth-century philosophy, from Descartes to Spinoza and Leibniz. It reappeared as the subject of a passionate debate in the Age of Enlightenment, and not only within the medical milieu, one of my preferred haunts. The MBP went on to occupy much of nineteenth-century thought, both philosophical and scientific, as is clear from its central role in the works of Maine de Biran, Alexander Bain, Bergson, James, and many German psychologists and philosophers. Finally, in our century the question has continued to spark intense theoretical interest, even among followers of such divergent currents as neopositivism and phenomenology, to name only two.

A systematic, historical study of the debate on the mind–body problem would certainly pose a fascinating challenge, but one would inevitably run the risk, as N. A. Vesey once noted, of meshing such an investigation with the whole history of philosophy (or

1

science) from ancient times to the present. Fortunately, the following pages are inspired by a rather different ambition. My aim is to reflect upon a story which is far more limited chronologically, as well as thematically and theoretically. This story has a rather precise beginning, and it even has a founding father: Herbert Feigl, the well-known exponent of logical neopositivism. The beginning may be set in 1934 (the year in which Feigl's first article on the problem of the relationship between the 'physical' and the 'mental' appeared), or, as some prefer, in 1958 (with the publication of Feigl's systematic study of the problem). Although other characters and dates may justifiably compete for honors, there is good reason to nominate Feigl's two texts. A broad sector of contemporary thought has recognized Feigl and his work as the frame of reference for a debate which has been conducted in relatively homogeneous terms, since it has been limited to the geographic and cultural area of English-speaking countries and to precise presuppositions and objectives. This debate has gradually come to form a well-defined chapter in the intellectual history of our time, a chapter to which many have given the title *The Mind–Body Problem*. I, too, will abide by this label, though perhaps more out of convenience than conviction, and will generally use the abbreviation MBP.

Despite the limitations noted above, the issue under examination is extremely complex, and the relevant literature overwhelming. Indeed, the manifold questions raised by the MBP have attracted the attention of philosophers and scholars of the most diverse tendencies. The *solutions* advanced to what is felt to be a true *problem* are innumerable. A list, albeit incomplete, would include answers proposed by dualists, parallelists, epiphenomenalists, identity theorists, emergentists, functionalists, mentalists, . . . Needless to say, many of these proposals have been advanced in varying forms, thus further complicating the overall picture. What is more, from the beginning of the dispute the MBP has been dissected into its component parts, its linguistic dimension scrupulously analyzed and its logical structure x-rayed. Psychologists and psycho-physiologists, epistemologists, and philosophers of mind – all have addressed ever more minute issues. Thus, not surprisingly, the debate on the MBP has recorded moments of confusion and fatigue. What should have been (and remained) a "world knot" has all too frequently become a pretext for relatively problem-free micro-studies, if not an excuse for academic exercise. We can't see the woods for the trees, warned Terence E. Wilkerson in the mid-seventies, alluding to the truly decisive content of the vast debate on the relations between mind and body (Wilkerson 1974).

Of course, points of detail may have their importance. And no one questions the legitimacy of those approaches to the MBP which emphasize relevant factual or logical linguistic aspects of the problem at hand. One of the central theses of this essay, however, is that the MBP requires to some extent (one might be tempted to say, above all) an interpretation capable of clarifying certain 'strong assumptions' and implications of the debate. This approach should be capable of revealing the deeper and more general (though occasionally implicit) reasons and meanings that emerge from the discussion. It should, in a sense, tell us *what the MBP is 'really' about.*

This ambition should not disconcert the reader. The literature on the mind–body relationship often gives the impression that the MBP is a sort of elusive metaphor. Many scholars seem to address certain issues while having *others* in mind. The questions raised (directly or indirectly) appear to be quite different from, and more complex and disquieting than, the mind–body relationship in the strict sense. This may explain why the debate is so crucial theoretically and so deeply rooted ideologically. Indeed, from more than one standpoint, the MBP is rather awkward and unreliable as a *problem.* It had its place in certain contexts of classical metaphysical thought and, later, in Descartes's time. It had a central role in the area of nineteenth-century thought which served as a battlefield for the struggle between materialist and positivist currents on the one hand and spiritualist tendencies on the other. But in an age marked by the definitive secularization of the human world, the crisis of the *Substanzbegriff* and the achievements attained by neurophysiology, psycho-personological research and linguistic hermeneutics, the canonical formulation of the mind–body question no longer holds up. Man can no longer be interpreted as *homo duplex* (despite the efforts of neo- and crypto-dualists): the 'mind', of course, does not exist as an *entity;* and the 'body' is an extremely generic concept, itself derived from an out-dated brand of metaphysics (if anything, one should speak of the brain and the central nervous system). "Philosophers", Wilkerson has written, "have been quick to observe that the expression 'mind–body' is decidedly unfortunate, for it suggests quite wrongly that something called a 'mind' is attached to something called a 'body,' and that philosophers are concerned to show how precisely it is attached" (Wilkerson 1974, p. 9).

3

All this does not mean, of course, that any attempt to define the relationship between mind and body is meaningless: many psycho-physiological studies have appeared which, within their empirical limits, show highly interesting results. It only means that, especially when scholars have faced the MBP at an adequate theoretical level, they have often been obliged to raise questions which go well beyond the preestablished scope of their studies, and to enter the fields of epistemology, ontology and psychoanthropology. They have spoken of 'mind' and 'mental' – and the unsettling, *real* question was whether one may admit a human dimension which is autonomous and irreducible in relation to the bodily. They have reflected on the descriptions and explanations of psychology – and the question was whether it is possible, or even necessary, to admit the existence of a descriptive and explanatory language of psychic phenomena which is independent of physically constituted languages. They have referred to the mental as something which calls up not so much a *body* as a *man*, or a *subject* – and the question was whether discourse concerning *mind* is to be regarded as psycho-physiological or, quite differently, as psycho-'humanological' discourse. They have asked themselves what the 'nature' of this 'mental' actually is (although it might be conceivable, as Richard Rorty once wrote, that the so-called mind has none at all) – and the question was whether it might not be better to interpret it not as a *thing*, and perhaps not even as an *event* or a *property* (already something quite different), but as a *mode* or a 'sense-giving' *function:* a *sinngebend* mode of individual experience which serves to express the intimate, irreducible *subjectivity* of this experience and which, by definition, cannot be assimilated into a *fact* presumably referring to some *objective thing.*

The list could continue, but the point is already clear. The curious, old-fashioned problem of the relationship between mind and body (also) raises several crucial questions with respect to knowledge in general and to man and his science:

a) Can one posit something which *exists,* and yet at the same time is *non-physical?*

b) Can physicalist knowledge give an exhaustive description and explanation of all "that there is" (Feigl), or does something exist the cognition of which requires a knowledge which is independent of that provided by the physical sciences?

c) Do the rejection of the 'soul' and the achievements attained by the bio- and neurosciences oblige us to hold that man is *nothing but body?*

d) Even if we grant that man is a bodily entity, does this mean that all the "cognitive interests" (Habermas) which refer to the human sphere can be adequately satisfied by the bio- and neurosciences alone?

e) Can the mental be considered a dimension *an sich* (whether psychological or neurophysical is not important at this point), or is it essentially a symbolic figure that largely refers to 'something else': a 'something else' that might be man himself, considered individually and existentially as a *person?*

f) If the preceding hypothesis is true, should not the question of the mental, rather than being linked and perhaps even identified with that of the bodily, be dealt with and mediated by the question of the human, of personhood, of subjectivity?

These are all problems of considerable weight. It was with questions such as these in mind that Wilfrid Sellars once stated that the MBP, when properly approached, appears not so much as one of the many issues of philosophy, but as "nothing more nor less than the philosophical enterprise *as a whole*" (Sellars and Chisholm 1958, p. 507; italics mine). This statement may appear somewhat emphatic, but it certainly contains an important kernel of truth; and the implicit approach to the MBP it suggests has been a constant companion throughout the writing of this book.

II

The need for such an approach has been felt so much the more since – and the point has not been sufficiently made – the MBP has acquired an important role in a revived debate on the human being, the implications of which can hardly be overlooked. The social psychologist John Shotter rightly argued that in contemporary philosophy and scientific thought, two different images of man are contending against one another (Shotter 1975). One is the image of 'man-as-person', a producer of acts, symbols, and values connected essentially with his historical and cultural nature. The other is the image of 'man-as-machine', or 'man-as-organism', the expression of a finite series of *lato sensu* physical components and properties. There is evidence that the 'man-as-person' image – the subject/

object which requires explanations *by reasons* as well as *by causes,* and *hermeneutic* as well as *empirical* and *analytic* approaches – is finding its way back into our intellectual scenario with new energy and credibility. Indicators of this tendency include what Daniel Dennett has called the "return of consciousness" and the parallel reelaboration of the concepts of intentionality and the person. We must also consider the innovative orientation of action theory developed both in the United States (Charles Taylor, etc.) and in Finland (von Wright and his school). And we should not overlook certain themes in the theoretical work of Apel and Habermas which also move in this direction.

Despite all this, it is the *other* image of man which has been gaining weight and consensus. Of course, one reason for this success may be sought in the efficacy of certain approaches and in the cognitive gains which, when real, will be denied by no one. It would be a mistake, however, to suppose that the success of the 'physicalist' image derives *only* from an increase, albeit ample, in empirical evidence. No mere accumulation of *particular findings* is by itself sufficient to found a *general conception,* as this can only be founded on a *theory.* Indeed, the advances made by the 'man-as-machine' image have been closely connected to a revival of doctrines inspired by naturalistic and realist principles about which, actually, too little has been said.

It is curious (or perhaps not) that this complex of positions is reemerging with renewed vigor and insistence in the human sciences. Writers from the most diverse disciplines seem to find a reassuring hub of consensus in certain principles. 'Things' are given objectively and are independent of hermeneutic schemes and frameworks. 'Science' (always in the singular) can and must capture real data, the laws of nature, and the unvarying structures of the world (Armstrong 1978a and 1980). Mental and behavioral phenomena, far from being viewed as constructs linked to well-defined assumptions and cognitive goals, are considered simply as manifestations of *physical* processes which are in themselves self-evident and beyond question. So, for example, if we speak of 'emotion' we are clearly referring to a precise physiological (or pathological) phenomenon. And yet one might recall that the young Sartre had already suggested that emotion be considered not as an objective *fact* but as a subjective *way of being.* To give another example, some would argue that 'aggressive behavior' refers to a real, objective phenomenon which may be adequately explained by the mechanical effect of a particular nervous excitement. But how can we overlook the circumstance that this excitement is merely *correlated* with aggressive behavior, and that the 'aggressive' act or event is defined and experienced as such only in relation to criteria which have little to do with this correlation? Indeed, what is 'aggressive' in one cultural community may be perceived as something quite different in another. 'Competitiveness' and 'success', to extend our list, are considered by some (in particular by sociobiologists) as phenomena which can be thoroughly reduced to biogenetic processes. And what if, instead of being 'natural' facts, they were the result of symbolic and cultural stipulations, largely independent of an alleged biological matrix?

I have been hinting, up to this point, mainly at a revival of realism. But I should also draw attention to what may be an even greater cause of concern, that is, to a revival of materialism. Despite the warnings sounded by more advanced contemporary thought, materialism, whether explicitly or implicitly, appears to be the general *Weltanschauung* underlying research programs which could quite well do without it. Why is this so? Is there some fear that *if* a materialist conception of the world is abandoned, *then* there is no choice but to embrace spiritualism? The absurdity of this fear should be apparent to anyone who – following Heidegger's invitation expressed in his *Brief über den Humanismus* – is accustomed to thinking independently of a narrow binary logic (or ontology). If one is not a materialist, this does not necessarily mean that he is a spiritualist. On the contrary, in certain respects *materialism and spiritualism appear to share the same metaphysical vision:* a vision that prevents us from interpreting the world according to *plural* meanings and interests connected to our multiple cognitive needs and frameworks; a vision which induces us to think in terms of things which are either this or that, in one way or another. Alberto Oliverio once wrote that the MBP forces us to accept either materialistic monism or a form of dualism which posits that a part of us is "inaccessible to human investigation" (Oliverio 1984b, p. 39). This statement leaves considerable room for doubt. First of all, it is simply wrong to suppose that whatever is not encompassed by a directly or indirectly materialist monism is "inaccessible to human investigation": this would mean reducing human knowledge to solely *physical* knowledge. What is more, the statement does not hold up even with regard to empirical reality. I, for one, am not a materialist, since I do not believe that all our cognitive questions concerning reality are satisfied by materialist answers. And yet I am firmly anti-dualist and anti-spiritualist, since I do not believe that it is legitimate or necessary to admit non-material entities such as those which Oliverio rightly questions. Indeed, it is my opinion that beyond materialism and spiritualism *tertium datur*. This third position involves contesting, firstly, the metaphysical vision mentioned above. Secondly, it deals with problems not in realistic and ontological but in hermeneutic and pragmatic terms: that is, it does not ask 'what realities there are' but rather 'what expressive modes there are', what they 'say', 'for what', and 'for whom.' This path may lead to the conclusion – as the second part of this essay strives to show – that certain *denotata* of our psychic experience are literally *neither 'material' nor 'spiritual'*.

Returning to materialism, one point must be made once and for all. The materialistic *Weltanschauung* no longer has the emancipatory and innovative connotation it undoubtedly had in the past. This is largely due to a fact which confirms the validity of the materialistic message: the great battle against spiritualism and idealism has, at least in part, already been won. But times have changed, and so has the nature of the intellectual (and not only intellectual) problems we are facing. It is no longer imperative to acknowledge, once again, the rights of matter and flesh, of the material world and of empirically verifiable 'facts'. It is now far more urgent to recognize the peculiarities of culture and of man's meta-natural, 'artificial', and symbolic productions. We need to reconsider, in response to materialistic 'monism', the *plurality* of the ways in which we relate to the world, and to embrace the corresponding *multiplicity* of heuristic and interpretive devices which can help us, ideally, to 'talk about' that world. From this standpoint, materialism defends an outdated doctrine.

This does not mean, however, that this view is *weak*. Indeed, for reasons which should one day be examined, it has gradually become the ideology of 'that which exists', of that which can be visualized, grasped, measured, verified, law-ordered, and predicted; in short, of what *there is* and is revealed only to a certain type of knowledge. To be sure, no one denies the validity, in certain contexts, of the criteria entailed in these programs. However, one may well suspect that not all experience can be confined within these reassuring parameters; or rather, that not all the questions we raise concerning reality can be satisfied by answers which are bound to them.

While the range of these questions increases, the materialist view seems to privilege the goal of annexing many cognitive practices to the field of biophysics. Some years ago the sociobiologist Edward O. Wilson predicted – in a radically materialist context – that one day neurobiology would "cannibalize" psychology (and perhaps also the other human sciences) (E. O. Wilson 1975). Beneath this somewhat disconcerting prophecy lurks the aim to *reduce* and *simplify* a varied epistemological panorama, assimiliating it *bon gré mal gré* to the biological-materialist paradigm dominant today. Indeed, at a more general level, contemporary materialism appears to be, above all, this: a program of reduction, assimilation, and annexation. In 1970, the philosopher J. K. Feibleman stated that he firmly believed "that matter as presently understood is capable of supporting as properties all of reliable knowledge" (Feibleman 1970, p. 47). The social scientist Edgar Wilson (not to be confused with the sociobiologist cited above) went even further: "When a physicalist account of events is established, it has frequently proved otiose to sustain alternative competing accounts" (Wilson 1979, p. 38).

The conception implicit in these and similar positions appears so much more gratifying and reliable as it responds perfectly to the twofold need to construct a *unitary* image of the world (i.e., a metaphysics) and to construct it under the cover of *Science*. This point was recently made by Hilary Putnam, a philosopher who is surely not suspect of spiritualist or irrationalist penchants: "the appeal of materialism lies precisely in this, in its claim to be *natural* metaphysics, metaphysics within the bounds of science". But in this way, Putnam continues, materialism "has replaced positivism and pragmatism as the dominant contemporary form of scientism", which is "one of the most dangerous contemporary intellectual tendencies" (Putnam 1982b, pp. 146–7).

It is not surprising that this materialistic orientation has been applied with particular fervor in the field of the human sciences. In fact, in the words of Eric Harth, the 'human' represents the ultimate aim, the "last frontier", of a physicalistically constituted knowledge, in the sense that it is the last part of reality which must be shown to be reducible to descriptions and explanations of a materialist nature (Harth 1982, p. 33). This may explain the frequency and insistence of certain positions, directed at promoting not so much *particular* research programs, as *general* beliefs and conceptions. Some years ago M. E. Levin wrote that his book "defends the ancient thesis that a man is a piece of matter, that all his states are physical states, and that all his properties physical properties"

(Levin 1979, p. vii). Thanks to the success of "metaphysical materialism" and "physicalism", Edgar Wilson has stated, the man–nature dualism has been definitively destroyed and the opposing thesis adopted according to which man ("including mind and mind-directed behavior") "is *entirely* incorporated into nature, and the natural processes of cause and effect". Progress in neuropsychology and cybernetics, Wilson adds, has helped to underpin this conception of man – this, in any event, "is the thesis I have developed and sought to make plausible" (Wilson 1979, p. 355). Another philosopher of mind, P. M. Churchland, claims we are on the threshold of a genuine "intellectual revolution": a revolution that will finally replace the now obsolete theory of the person (i.e., of man as person) with the product of what is defined as *the* "scientific theory" of man, which is in turn identified with neurophysiological interpretation of the human being (Churchland 1979, pp. 4–5 and 114ff.).

The number and intensity of these statements should not surprise us. They express not only a certain *cognitive* ambition, but also a practical, ethical, and even political program. For a large number of scholars, reducing man to his physical nature means increasing control over him. This implies, in fact, that all his functions lie within a field which the neurosciences can 'see' and govern with growing authority. An entirely material (or materializable) subject appears as an entity living in an entirely visible space – an entity without dimensions of expression and action which might elude the public scrutiny of Knowledge. All this provides the foundations of what José Delgado called a "psycho-civilized society" (Delgado 1969): a society in which "psycho-civilization" is founded on the physical control of people's brains achieved by means of chemical agents or of electronic impulses (Delgado 1975). If this is the case, Margaret Boden was right in warning that what is at stake in the contemporary debate on the nature of man is no less than "the power to influence basic presuppositions about human beings and society" (Boden 1981, p. 71). To paraphrase Shotter, there are, on the one hand, those who strive to defend the subject by stressing the dimensions and components of man which cannot be known by the physical sciences. Recognizing the existence of such dimensions, however, does not imply a return to a 'spiritualistic' interpretation of man: rather, it serves as a simple reminder that man has a *modus essendi* and *operandi* (psychosocial and historical-cultural) which presents some cognitive problems distinct from those of the other-worldly phenomena. On the other hand, there are those who would free themselves of this subject and reduce it to a series of processes and functions which can be entirely explained by the operation of bodily organs.

From both the anthropological and moral standpoint, the latter position may have rather alarming consequences. Edgar Wilson, for example, argues that the neo-materialistic and 'scientific' perspective now makes it possible to reduce such dimensions of human action as intention and purpose to mere "physical concepts". Talk about what was traditionally called "moral responsibility" is considered "otiose" (E. Wilson 1979, p. 277) because it now lacks (and rightly so) both *personal* content and *moral* commitment. The whole ethical universe built on what "must be" could be simply rewritten in terms of what "is" – namely in terms of the material facts and natural processes that underlie human acts. Indeed, it is "human nature or, as the physicalist would say, biology" which is the basis and justification of "communal life as well as normal [sic] interpersonal attitudes, altruism, truth telling and the like" (ibid., p. 286). Thus, the physicalization of man prepares the way for what Wilson calls a "scientific ethics", or an "ethical naturalism", capable of objectifying certain norms and of eliminating every arbitrary choice and subjective decision as well as the relativistic plurality of moral beliefs. This goal is considered so inspiring that Wilson (along with a conspicuous area of contemporary thought) has devoted himself with disarming enthusiasm to what could be called the 'physicalization' of the world.

III

It is within the framework of the problems I have briefly sketched above that the debate on the MBP should be examined. Indeed, we must keep in mind what has been outlined so far if we are to understand some of the crucial issues at stake in the controversy on the relationship between mind and body. When Richard Taylor claims that the MBP must be "buried" (Taylor 1969), or when Kathleen Wilkes asserts that it is to be simply "dissolved" (Wilkes 1978a, p. 114), they do not seem to grasp the real substance of the controversy. On the contrary, Feigl was right when he stressed that the MBP "is *not* a *pseudo-problem*" (Feigl 1960). Indeed, any attempt to physicalize man entirely must first deal with that problem. Of this *sui generis* being (or, at least, of this being so capable of soliciting *sui generis* questions) which we call man it is the 'mental' sphere which constitutes the most peculiar and unsettling dimension. If, for whatever reason, we are not able to do without this dimension in its specific aspects, then it will be necessary to abandon every 'pan-physicalist' ambition and admit that we need a *plurality* of languages and types of knowledge concerning the 'human'. If, on the contrary, it is possible in whatever way to materialize the 'mental', then the cognitive and practical ambitions noted above will be judged well-founded. It is no accident that many supporters of the latter view vigorously underline the necessity and usefulness of a link between the materialist *Weltanschauung* and the belief in the *identity* of mind and body. "We materialists", David K. Lewis once wrote, "must accept the identity theory" as a "matter of fact": every mental experience "is identical with some physical state" (D. K. Lewis 1966, p. 63).

Given the stakes, it should not be surprising that what might have been simply an elegant philosophy tournament has turned into a truly concrete and bitter struggle; a struggle in which a large number of contenders, passions, and crucial issues have been involved; a struggle, moreover, which has found expression in an astonishing quantity of books, articles, essays, reviews, rejoinders. Consequently, my first goal has been to collect and organize the extremely complex and interdisciplinary material on the subject, so often scattered through the most distant and diverse publications. From a certain standpoint, this volume could be read as a critical analysis of conceptions and theories that are largely unfamiliar in continental Europe – and that even in English-speaking countries, I might add, have not yet been examined in a unified manner.

However, the scope of this study, as the reader may well imagine, is not limited to this. My second, and more important, aim has been to elaborate a particular interpretation of the mental and of the MBP. And yet, I have not sought to provide an interpretation *in abstracto* of the problem, perhaps disguised as a new 'solution' to the MBP. Instead, I have aimed at a more ambitious target – one which is linked to my (neo)-historicist orientation. If philosophizing (as Hegel once put it) amounts to rethinking one's own time and its problems through its concepts, it seems to me that reflecting on the MBP involves, above all, reflecting on how this problem has taken shape *historically*. The problem, indeed, exists not so much *an sich*, but rather as a product of a specific social and cultural elaboration. Reflecting on the MBP, in other words, necessarily involves grasping the *sense* of the principal theories that concern the mental and its science as they emerged in the course of its taking shape. I am persuaded, in short, that a full awareness of what the MBP has meant, and means, can best be achieved by measuring oneself with the theses of those who have generated and developed the problem itself.

My neo-historicism, on the other hand, can certainly not be identified with that 'legitimation of the existent' – or, even worse, of the strongest – which Nietzsche so radically criticized in his *Vom Nutzen und Nachteil der Historie für das Leben*. Some years ago Joseph Margolis wrote that in the contemporary philosophy of mind, the pro-materialist positions have become so forceful that any claim to refute them, or to contrast them, appears naive (Margolis 1978, p. 213). Nonetheless, I have sought to undertake precisely such a task (as did Margolis, incidentally). My 'rational reconstruction' of the past fifty years of debate on the MBP tends to show the limitations of the positions of the (apparent) winners and to rehabilitate the views of (some of) the defeated: what they say is the 'truth' – even though the truth of a minority.

It is clear from these remarks that the orientation which characterizes *The Enigma of Mind* is markedly subjective and philosophically *engagée*. Not only reasons of space (though these had to be taken seriously into account) but also theoretical choices have led me to exclude certain positions from my discussion and to emphasize others. Thus, for example, the present interpretation of the MBP intentionally neglects neo-dualistic conceptions (which appear irremediably out-dated) while granting considerable space to selected 'personological' perspectives. At the same time, I have devoted substantial attention to certain theses, though championed by often little-known writers, which better represent significant tendencies, while often avoiding nearly obligatory references to recognized authorities. I have not, for example, considered Popper, as I feel that his philosophy of mind, although inspired by worthy intentions, is developed along lines that have no promising outlets and is not very representative of the current debate on our subject. I have also not discussed Mario Bunge and his, admittedly, systematic treatment of the MBP (Bunge 1980), since his arguments do not seem particularly innovative in relation to the materialistic and physicalistic positions with which I deal in considerable detail.

On the other hand, though my treatment may be subjective, I do not believe that it is arbitrary. It stems, hermeneutically, from a close interaction between certain general principles and pre-understandings and the 'things themselves'. In this case, the 'things' are the doctrines, conceptions, and interpretations of the mental and its science which have been developed over the last half-century. Closely connected to these doctrines, my 'theory' emerges from, and yet produces a 'story' which tries to give a sense to, the MBP and to the more significant aspects of the debate on it.

The first four chapters of the book outline what could be defined as the genesis of and the radical turn taken by the physicalist approach to the MBP. I begin with an examination of the philosophy of Herbert Feigl, who deserves considerable attention given the fundamental role he played in broaching the problem I am concerned with. The following pages deal with the leading figures of the so-called Australian school (Place, Smart, Armstrong). This school, as is well known, has worked out theses which are markedly monistic and materialistic and at the same time bear the most far-reaching philosophical and anthropological implications. Following a brief interlude, in which I comment on certain problems concerning the notion of the identity between mind and body, this part of my essay ends with an examination of the so-called disappearance theory. This theory was propounded for a time by philosophers of the rank of Feyerabend and Rorty and has led, as we will see, to the most extreme anti-mentalistic conclusions. The discussion of these positions introduces a series of *theoretical* questions which have found in the disappearance theory one of their most appropriate *historical* referents. Can it be said that the mental *is* the physical? Should this question, and its relative answers, be interpreted ontologically or linguistically? Is the linguistic interpretation really as 'liberalizing' as it might seem? Or does a conception which considers physical language the sole expression of scientific validity prevent an adequate rehabilitation of mental language in its cognitive functions? What meta-criterion must be applied to assess the validity of a language or of a conceptual system: its *adequacy* to a criterion established according to *other* (allegedly more respectable) parameters, or rather its expressive *relevance* in relation to its *own* possible truths? And, shifting from the epistemological level to the anthropological, what model of man corresponds to the psychophysical theories advanced by the materialists?

The fifth and sixth chapters of the book describe and interpret some important attempts to transform (more or less radically) the identity view previously analyzed. I first examine the functionalist theory of Putnam and Fodor, then the so-called event identity of Jaegwon Kim, and finally Donald Davidson's "anomalous monism". All these conceptions are quite sophisticated and extremely significant. Functionalism, in particular, seems to suggest a very innovative view according to which the mind can be identified with the body only in the sense that a *function* can be identified with the physical system which actually puts it into effect. A trap, to give an example often used by the functionalists, is something that can be embodied by an *n* number of possible mechanisms, none of which, however, excludes *other* mechanisms or can advance privileged rights: the *function* of a trap can be carried out just as well by a device made of metal or by one fashioned out of rope. In the same way, the mind can be viewed as a function to which certain neurocerebral organs merely correlate *now* and *de facto* (not *always* and *de jure*). From the conceptual standpoint the functionalist theory represents a change of remarkable importance. It moves away from an interpretation of the mind as *res* toward one which is no longer 'ontological' and opens – or could have opened – the way to a pluralistic conception of the 'ways of being' of the mental. Behind all this it is possible to perceive the influence of recent scientific and epistemological advances (which are taken up in appropriate places in this book) made especially in the field of computer theory with its fundamental (and so 'functionalist') distinction between software and hardware.

As to Kim and Davidson, they too introduce some very notable conceptual innovations which tend toward a less rigid view of the mind–body relationship. Kim elaborates a theory which is present also in functionalism and proposes that the mind be conceived not as a *entity* but as a *property*. Moreover, and more importantly, he calls into question the type of connection between mind and body traditionally defended by physicalists. Instead of speaking of an oppressively binding *identity*, couldn't one speak of a less demanding *correlation*? Davidson also adopts and develops several of the theses mentioned above. In particular, he speaks of the mental from an anti-substantialist perspective as a complex of "events": a complex which, at least at times, takes the form of a "holistic" system in which a mental event *x directly* and *holistically* produces a mental event *y*. He also maintains – what may sound scandalous to some ears – that mental events are "unlawful": that is, they do not satisfy the criterion of lawfulness which is a prerequisite for any attempt to interpret the mind in physicalistic terms.

Smooth sailing, then? Not entirely, I'm afraid – at least as regards the theoretical principles I seek to defend. Functionalism, especially in its 'classical' form, seems sometimes to have been not so much a true revolution as a great opportunity that was lost. The assumption that the mental may present itself in an indefinite number of ways could have admitted many different ways of 'reading' it. Many functionalists, however – Fodor is one – prefer to reduce this assumption to a mere hypothesis, valid only in *theory*. In *practice*, they emphasize, the mental is embodied in *physical* vectors; consequently, only a physicalistic heuristic – if not neurophysiological, then computational – may lay legitimate claim to 'telling' the mental.

Kim and Davidson also seem unwilling to abandon a physicalistic view – or at least a neo-physicalistic one – and they prefer to take on the role of reformers (albeit radical reformers) of the identity theory rather than that of determined critics. That a subtle thinker like Davidson is not entirely comfortable with his own alternative position is betrayed by the label he gives it: "anomalous monism". Is the adjective 'anomalous' sufficient to cancel all the elements of reduction and constriction implicit in a term like 'monism'? Surely not. The historian of the MBP, now acting as philosopher, understands that if we are truly to dismantle a certain interpretation of the mind and its relationship with the body, much more will be needed than what I have reported from the literature so far. What is needed is not some sort of 'revision' of the identity theory, but quite simply its rejection – not a modernization and refinement of physicalism, but its abandonment. It should become clear that the understanding of the mental may imply overstepping the boundaries of what can be described in purely physical terms and categories.

But then, the philosopher asks, what is the 'mental'? Isn't it time we thought this question through? We have agreed that it is not a *thing*. But this is not enough, especially if those who have agreed on this point say that this 'non-thing' must still be described in physicalistic terms. It has been suggested that the mental is a *function*; that it is a *property*; that it is an 'unlawful' *event*. What if it were first and foremost a *word* – a word that has to be decoded and interpreted with a certain *esprit de finesse*, a word which, properly examined, may turn out to allude to experiences that are not

physical but in some sense *'meta*-physical' (symbolic, cultural),
though these experiences are often mistakenly reduced to nothing
but physical data?

Questions such as these have led the philosopher, as he returns
to his historical scrutiny, to discover another stage in his itinerary
through the contemporary philosophy of mind. Paraphrasing an
expression used by Richard Rorty, I have called this stage the 'linguistic turn'. Its central figures are Wittgenstein and several philosophers who directly or indirectly followed him or continued his
work. Chapter 7 illustrates some of their contributions concerning
the issues which interest us. Chapter 8 proceeds to draw certain
consequences from this discussion from a point of view which I
have called "explicative pluralization". These chapters, and even
more so the ones that follow, outline what might be defined, with
a certain boldness, the *pars construens* of my investigation. This is,
in any case, the part of the book which I consider the most significant, especially Chapter 10.

To say that the mental is a 'word' is not a snobbish quip or a
hasty avoidance of a serious issue. It implies, rather, radically transforming the status of the 'object' under discussion. It implies thoroughly deontologizing certain *denotata*. And it gives rise to challenging new questions. What do the terms 'mind' and 'mental'
allude to? What do they imply? Why do we actually employ them?
The philosophy of mind can draw considerable stimulation from
Wittgenstein's 'suspicion' (so reminiscent of Nietzsche) that many
things are *words,* and that these words do not refer (or not always)
to *objective* referents. Indeed, we must say (or repeat) that the mind
is not a *res,* that the mental is not *only* a *function,* a *property,* or an
event, and, above all, that neither the mind nor the mental can be
entirely reduced to physically verifiable correlates. What the word
'mind' alludes to is nearly always something quite distant and distinct from the *denotatum* of 'body'. There exists, as Davidson put it,
a radical "categorial difference" between the mental and the bodily
(Davidson 1970, in Davidson 1980, p. 223). The links between these
two apparent poles or dimensions of the human being are far more
tenuous and problematic than some have been inclined to believe.
If these links have been overly stressed, this is because there was
a time during which man believed he could better understand certain aspects of his experience if he attributed ontological status to
presumed 'organs', 'mechanisms' (and even 'places') of his own
being and acting, and the model for this ontologization (we are

speaking of the scientific revolution in the seventeenth century) was that of physical, material bodies. It is no accident that one of the most singular, and misleading, consequences of this theoretical orientation was the privilege conferred, within the mental universe and its analysis, to elementary psychic events. Indeed, some of these events – sensations, for example – appeared to be objectively more *dependent* on certain bodily correlates, almost to the point that they seemed *identifiable* with them. In my 'culturalism' I am inclined to think that even a simple toothache cannot be exhaustively described and explained in neurophysiological terms. I am willing to allow that in such cases the physical element is particularly important. What I am *not* prepared to concede is *that a toothache can be considered the more or less explicit paradigm of the whole of mental life.* Even the founding fathers of the MBP once distinguished, within the area of mental life, between a sensitive-affective sphere, an intellective-cognitive sphere, and a sphere concerning consciousness and self-awareness. Why, then, have they to some extent forgotten these articulations? Why don't they recognize that the 'mental' is also (perhaps principally) thoughts, desires, feelings, intentions, choices, memories, plans, beliefs, hopes, faiths? Why haven't they underpinned their identitist theses with *these* expressions of the mind?

IV

An analysis of mental phenomena aimed at answering the questions that we consider essential cannot do without a far more complex framework than what the physicalists, both early and recent, have offered us. When I conceive something, for example, there is no doubt that certain neuronal circuits begin functioning. But there is no reason to infer that this belief *is* those circuits, or that it in some sense 'emerges' from them. If I examine these circuits closely, even with the most perfect instruments, what will I actually see? I will see, at best, the *mechanism* that *supports* the belief. But I will not see the *belief*. And I most surely will not see *what* I believe, *why* I believe, or whether it is *right or wrong*. And yet, from the psychological standpoint, the object, the reason, and the rightness are *essential* parts of the belief itself. In other words, *there is no belief without a 'what' and a 'why'*. All this, I should stress, has no realist implications: that is, it does not imply assuming the 'reality' of the belief as an entity. At best the implications may be *phenomenological*. We must recognize, as Margolis argued, that every psychic act is an *intentional* act: namely, it is an act (*in itself* incomplete) which includes a reference to something else. And it is clear that this 'something else' is not 'matter': not so much in the ontological sense that it is an 'other' sort of entity (perhaps a part of Popper's meta-physical "world three"), but rather in the *hermeneutical* sense that it comes to light only if sought and approached with meta-natural instruments. One is reminded, in this connection, of an example given by Margolis. I can give a precise, exhaustive electroacoustic account of a series of sounds. But, still speaking in *cognitive* terms, I can also describe that *same series* as a melody, as a melody com-posed (not randomly but *intrinsically*) according to precise struc-tural and aesthetic principles which are in a sense 'meta-physical'. In the same way, the so-called mental phenomenon, which may appear to be nothing but a particular neurophysiological process, can legitimately be examined also in terms that are not purely neu-rophysiological.

This is true not only for the complex mental processes cited above, such as plans, beliefs, and so on: it is also true for states and events which may appear to be much simpler. When I identify the physical correlate of a particular pain, I have in a sense carried out *one possible* analysis of that pain. This analysis, it should be clear, is not only valuable but also perfectly self-sufficient and complete for a certain research program. However, for *another* research pro-gram it might be necessary to look for something quite different. For example, as a psychologist I might be interested in the way in which pain is experienced and how it fits into a particular existen-tial and moral context. This, once again, means that we must study a largely 'physical' event in the light of other correlates which are clearly not physical. In other words, together with the pain-inducing physical factor we also have to consider some other ele-ments of the 'pain', such as the subject's culture, ideology, religious beliefs, and environmental and social context, which make the state or event of pain what it is.

It has been objected that implicit in the position I am defending lies a confusion between mental *fact* and mental *experience*. The dis-tinction is not entirely invalid. But it is the materialists and physi-calists who are responsible for this confusion, not their adversaries. They were the first to reduce the *experience* 'pain' or the experience 'desire' to corresponding *facts* – often to *physical* facts. The majority of post-behaviorist psychologists, I believe, are perfectly justified in asserting their right to study the mental as *experience*. Indeed, we might well ask what it means to study mental events as *facts*, and what significance this study has. Leaving aside some cruder attempts to reduce these events to 'things', it might mean studying the general features of mental events *an sich: the* features of melancholy, *the* features of choice, and so on. The importance of this kind of analysis is clear to everyone. But is it important because it enables us to understand certain autonomous *realities* (and it is not relevant here whether these realities are 'things' or functions), or because it offers some *interpretive models* for the study of *something else?* I lean toward the second hypothesis. In more than one sense, melancholy and choice *in general* do not exist: there exist only *particular* instances of melancholy and particular instances of choice.

Indeed, even this last claim is questionable: strictly speaking, not even particular instances of melancholy and choice exist in themselves and for themselves. Not even they can be studied as truly *self-sufficient* facts (or modes, or functions). Why is this? In these introductory remarks, only a rather synthetic answer may be advanced. Peter Herbst once wrote that it is impossible to reduce "the experience of a color" to a physical event devoid of *my* perception (Herbst 1967, p. 63). The claim is well made. Its significance lies not so much in the stress it lays on the difference between *fact* and *experience* (the mere visual perception of a color tells me very little about the *psychic* experience of that perception) as in the suggestion it offers concerning what *qualifies* and *characterizes* the mental event. This 'something' is the referent shown to be necessary – by means of the possessive *my* – for an adequate account of the phenomenon of perception in its psychic dimension. In this book I have called this indispensable referent the "titular" of the mental event.

What does all this mean? It means that, to some extent, no mental event exists *alone:* each one always refers not only to the intentional 'something else' mentioned above, but also to *the person who experiences it:* this does not mean, perhaps I should repeat, that the study of phenomena such as hope or intention *in themselves* is meaningless. But this study, apart from its heuristic usefulness, runs the risk of becoming the analysis of an empty structure, of an abstract concept. In our real experience suffering and intention are, rather than autonomous figures, a 'being-that-suffers' and a 'being-that-intends'. What would be the sense, Kurt Baier once asked, of speaking of pain without speaking of someone who suffers (Baier 1970, p. 98)? It would, at most, have the sense of saying what constitutes pain *usually* and *in general*. But probably no one would recognize in this his *own* particular pain. Everyone would immediately add, "Yes, but *I* also felt that. . . ". For the psychologist, the details added at this point would be not *incidental* but *essential*. In any case, there should be a discipline which examines precisely this experience as an *individual, personal* experience.

Baier's question and its theoretical implications deserve serious consideration. What is alluded to is not merely the presence, or the action, of a 'holder' in the mental event. We are also invited to consider that this holder cannot be the *mind* – much less the *body*. Indeed, certain phrases of everyday language, such as "he was absent-minded", may be misleading. After all, it is not my mind that is absent (or 'at ease', or 'confused'), but *I myself*. It is only to the human being that many mental attributes can be meaningfully assigned. This point, which I develop in the final chapter of the book, seems to me to mark a crucial turn in the discussion on the MBP. It involves reinterpreting, to a large extent, the *philosophy of mind* as a *philosophy of the 'human'*, of the *'personal'*, of the *'subjective'*.

At times, this position has indeed been stated in excessively trenchant terms. Drawing on a strong tradition of anti-mentalism in Anglo-American thought, some scholars have employed certain principles and arguments to assert that the mental is an absolutely empty notion: it expresses *nothing* (and consequently psychology has to be simply *eliminated*). I would be more cautious. In the present context, I would like to stress that if the mental cannot be completely reduced to the physical, it also cannot be *totally* absorbed by the personal. I am inclined to think, rather, that at the cognitive level it is legitimate and useful to admit a sort of intermediate area between neurophysiology and 'personology'. The 'mental' raises questions the answers to which must (given certain cognitive interests) emphasize a certain function or event, more than the 'personological' dimension that doubtless gives it substance. However, I also believe that in the above statement there is a truth which needs to be expressed: in large part, those phenomena that we traditionally call *mental* are in reality 'simply' *human*. In other words, they are phenomena which do not concern, or derive from, *mind* (or, still less, from something that can be artificially modelled as a mind), but from *man* as such. One might say, borrowing Ryle's evocative phrase, that the mental is the whole of "*human* actions and reactions"; it regards unspoken and spoken utterances (Ryle 1986, p.302; italics mine).

On close examination, this identification works at all the levels (sentience, sapience, and selfhood) in which the so-called mind is conventionally articulated. A feeling of joy, though it is surely not merely a physical sensation, is most certainly not only the state or product of a particular mental faculty: it is, rather, a certain manifestation of man himself, who constitutes and expresses it through means that may belong in principle to the most diverse and unpredictable aspects of his being. Indeed, the most valid and profitable way to understand a 'joy' is to examine the 'man-who-experiences-joy'. This is so much the more true for phenomena rightly or wrongly considered more complex. Thoughts, intentions, or plans have only in part to do with this or that psychic *function:* they are, rather, particular expressions of man's *personhood*. This does not mean, of course, that there can be no science of *sapience:* it means, merely, that certain assumptions and cognitive modes must be changed. Perhaps the proper understanding of a desire requires examination not so much of a certain *mental mechanism* as of a certain *existential situation*.

All this has extremely important implications. In the first place, we must reconsider the sense and consistency of principles which are far from self-evident. For over two thousand years man has maintained that so-called mental activity, the work of *motors* often called faculties, occurs in a *place* called the mind (or soul, or *cogito*) and that this activity must be studied by a special discipline, in recent centuries called psychology. In spite of the radical objections advanced first by Ryle and more recently by Rorty, this picture of the so-called mental universe holds up well. An eloquent example is given by Jerry Fodor, who has quite recently set out (citing Descartes) a renewed realist and spatial conception of the mind. Fodor proposes a return to the old system of psychic faculties and even argues for the rehabilitation of Gall and his bizarre doctrine of cerebral localization ('bizarre' is indeed the only word to use, as anyone who has truly read Gall will agree) (Fodor 1983). It is in relation to positions of this kind that anti-mentalism and a 'humanological' view take on their meaning. They suggest that it may be possible, and even necessary, to do without the mental as a separate dimension; that sentience, sapience, and selfhood do not refer either exclusively or (often) even principally to distinct 'organs' or functions; and that psychology has to radically redefine its object of investigation, acknowledging that many 'psychic' experiences and acts reveal some of their most peculiar aspects only if they are examined not so much in relation to a sphere called the 'psyche' as in relation to existential, pragmatic, and social referents.

In the second place, some of the remarks we made above can help us better understand the question of the cultural dimension of psychic phenomena. So far, even thinkers inspired by the best intentions have had difficulty in mediating these phenomena with 'culture'. If these phenomena, it has been argued, are the product of specific psychic or psychophysical mechanisms, what role does 'culture' play? This is a genuine problem, and a particularly thorny one for materialist positions: after all, how can the 'cultural' factor be grafted onto a neurophysiological base? But the difficulty can be resolved when it is acknowledged that the subject of so-called mental events is not an unlikely 'mind', and surely not a 'body', but rather *man himself*. If, in fact, the referent of an anxiety or an intention is an anxious and intending *human being*, then I am able to describe that anxiety and that intention in terms such as to include cultural components appropriately. This clearly is possible because one can meaningfully speak of man or of a person as the subject/ object of culture. The prerequisite for this passage, however, is that the philosophy of mind should strive, as one scholar has put it, "to take the *person* rather than the *mind*" as "the central concept" (Grene 1976, p. 124; italics mine).

It is from this standpoint that I have identified in the work of Hubert Dreyfus and Marjorie Grene (discussed in the final part of Chapter 10) a contribution of singular theoretical significance. These two philosophers have never devoted their attention specifically to the MBP. They have, however, redefined in quite stimulating terms the true *denotatum* of the so-called mental, or what this concept is at the same time an expression and a metaphor of. Grene, in particular, has perfectly grasped the need to review 'mental' phenomenology within a broader and more complex system – a 'personological' system. There had been others, as I have sought to show, who also moved in this direction. But too often they were content to refer to a human subject (in the sense of *sub-jectum*) with no further explanation. Grene, on the contrary, tries to give a precise consistency to this *sub-jectum*. It is not, as many think, man in a generic sense: it is, to quote Heidegger, a "being-in-the-world". It is an entity that in itself belongs to a certain social sphere, to a certain historical period, and to a certain context of artifacts, norms, and languages. It is only within *this* theoretical framework that one can understand how and why man's "*mental* existence" is made up also of "social and political institutions, languages, artistic forms, rituals" (ibid., p. 120). It is only within this framework that it becomes clear that the 'psychic' acts of man are composed also of values, beliefs, rules, laws, goals. These are all concepts that are clearly not only meta-*physical* but also meta-*psychic*: without them, however, we would lose (given certain cognitive interests) an *essential* part of 'mental' reality. For this reason, and within these boundaries, it must be said that the mental is in some sense the human – the human *in the world*.

V

What does the mental truly 'speak' about? was the question we raised at a certain point in our discussion. It may now be possible to suggest some elements of an answer (though entirely provisional). The most general refers to what we have just said: the mental, and on its behalf psychological language, *speaks about man*. This man, however, drawing on a distinction dear to Binswanger, is not so much *homo natura* as *homo persona*. Of course, we are fully aware that man is also nature, body, matter. But these dimensions are handled perfectly well by the biosciences and neurosciences. These disciplines seek to understand (and do so with increasing success) the general *mechanisms* at work in the body, the *correlations* and *causal concatenations* that can be ascertained between certain processes and certain events and behaviors, and the possible *laws* relative to the occurrence of certain states and events. In this search they do not limit themselves to describing only aspects or components of the organism: on the contrary, they reveal the physical infrastructures necessary to produce the phenomena we call psychic, mental, and behavioral. Seen from this vantage point, the bio- and neurosciences are (as we have stressed elsewhere) extremely precious and absolutely irreplaceable.

But alongside or beyond (perhaps inadequate adverbs) the *homo natura* there is also the *homo persona*: that is, man as an entity with a role in a system that manifests itself (depending on the varying interpretive contexts) as *existence, subjectivity, culture*. This man-as-person clearly does not sever the links that bind him to nature (after all, how could he?). In many senses he will always remain (though in ways and to an extent to be determined) *instinct-dependent*, or better *natural constraints–dependent*. On the other hand he is also, as Hobbes put it, *homo artificialis*. He is 'artificial' in the sense that many of his feelings, desires, plans, and ideals are demonstrably formed in a context (and in a manner) that is not 'natural', but intellectual, historical, social. He is 'artificial' also in the sense that he thinks, chooses, decides, and acts in ways that are not immediately nor exhaustively deducible from his biophysical structures. The failure, so convincingly illustrated by Georg H. von Wright, of the neopositivist plan (and not only the neopositivist) to reduce intentions, reasons, and goals to physically constituted matrices or antecedents speaks for itself. It bears witness to the fact that it is impossible, when our study of man goes beyond certain cognitive schemes, to do without certain heuristic and interpretive categories. As Rorty has evocatively written, our interests lead us to develop a *multiple* cognitive approach to man: "we need *many different descriptions* of ourselves – some for certain purposes, others for other goals, some for predicting and controlling what we do and others for deciding what to do and for attributing a meaning to our lives" (Rorty 1982b, p. 345; italics mine).

In a sense, the metaphoric voice of the mental – the language of psychology – produces one of these descriptions. Man uses this voice, as Ryle once observed, to react against the horror of a universal pan-mechanism which would dissolve the principles and modes of behavior in which he believes (Ryle 1986, p. 74). If some of these principles and modes of behavior are no longer appropriate, this does not mean that the whole psychological interpretation of man is without foundation. By exploring and giving consistency to some 'psychic' components of his existence, man simply attempts to assign value to a certain (though not the only) dimension of his being and acting. He *decides* not to obey only the determinisms of nature, not to dissolve himself completely into the processes of social serialization and conformity – perhaps through those alienations of the self which Proust called *"les plaques de l'habitude"*. I would argue for various reasons that the 'mental' and the 'psychological' universe should be referred to perceptions and decisions of *this* kind. We 'exercise' the so-called mental (or, as Malcolm says, we *are* the mental) when we, as subjects and as individuals, feel our feelings, think our thoughts, plan our plans – and recognize that we 'exist'. We exercise it when we impose meanings and rules, when we evaluate people and situations, and when we deliberate acts and styles of conduct. It is in the course of such 'mental' experiences that we discover we are people with needs and problems some of which do not stem directly from our material being, and require appropriate characterizations. It is then that we begin to elaborate those conceptual figures, so meta-natural and artificial, as Feeling, Fantasy, Thought, Doubt, Hope, Faith, Falsehood, Utopia, Theory, and Myth. None of these figures, clearly, denotes anything objective or univocal: in a *hope* there is also *faith*, but also *feeling*, and *fantasy*, and *doubt*, and *utopia*, and *thought*, and *myth*, and so on. But it is the very irreducibility of these complex figures that leads me to suspect that they express a true and essential dimension of the human being. It is no accident that we elaborate these figures and utter these words (the words of psychology) when we intend to stress certain *peculiarities* of the *person*, certain *differential specificities* of our being and acting in relation both to other physically given entities (e.g., animals or computers) and to collective ways of being. From this point of view psychology expresses what we are sometimes inclined to consider the primary nature of our *humanitas*.

But the mental and the language of psychology are also something else. They are, or express, the dimension of our irreducible *subjectivity*. It makes little sense, Thomas Nagel once observed, to ask what my (mental) experiences *really* are, "as opposed to how they *appear to me*" (Nagel 1979, p. 178; italics mine). The remark may seem somewhat disconcerting, but what needs to be stressed here is not so much its wealth of phenomenalistic and relativistic implications, as the vigorous reference to the *self's* "point of view" (another expression of Nagel's). What is the mental really? Or rather, how is the metaphor of the mental interpreted and employed? Once again, the answer is that it is interpreted/employed neither as a *thing*, nor as a *property*, nor (at least not principally) as a *function*. It is interpreted/employed especially as a *mode*: as one of the modes of the self – the mode, that is, of *subjectivity*. Indeed, the words that belong to the metaphoric universe of the mental allude essentially to the (subjective) ways in which I act in, and react to, the world that surrounds me. When I say 'desire', or 'expectation', or 'commitment', these signifiers *express first of all my self and its particular attitude toward the world*: indeed, my desire and my commitment might not even appear as such without the testimony (the *Sinngebung*) of my subjectivity. Each of these signifiers, as William James once noted, constitutes the condensation of an *indefinite* series of events and pulsions. It is this indefiniteness (multiplied by the indefiniteness of signifieds that I add when I reflect) which, so to speak, transforms quantity into quality, thus making each psychic *designatum* a sort of irreducible microcosm, which takes on the same appearance as the subject that is delineated in it *en abîme*. In this connection, the terms 'mental' and 'psychological' refer to a manner of relating to the world in which there is a prevailing 'subjective' vision or evaluation and in which the interpretations one elaborates, or the way one attributes sense to things, appear to stem not from one or another 'mental' *faculty* but from the person as a whole, from his entire 'personal' *history:* a history which in various ways extends beyond the bounds of the 'psychic'. From another point of view, 'mental' and 'psychological' allude to the space and the conceptual-expressive means which, respectively, we create and employ when, instead of *describing* events and *obeying* norms, we feel we must *raise questions.* How often is the reproach "Don't play psychologist" addressed to someone who is simply reflecting on different possible assessments of a situation, or on alternative modes of behavior?

We feel even more justified in using 'mental' categories and the language of psychology when we realize that a certain act or thought of ours transgresses apparently habitual or normal sequences and concatenations and appears more understandable in relation not so much to the alleged 'normality' of events that 'objectively' or 'usually' occur (a *normality* that for many implies that these events can be *reduced,* at least in principle, either to physical matrices or to meta-subjective formal models), as to the *subjectivity* of the self acting as an individual agent. 'Psychological', in this sense, is everything that appears *unlawful,* unpredictable (Davidson 1970), and perhaps even inexpressible according to known categories and reassuring linguistic formulations. But, despite all this, *it is there;* and unlawful though it may be, *it is meaningful.* This same language also serves us when we want to stress a specific aspect of the way we consider a person or a situation. In such cases, the reference to certain psychic functions, such as my belief or my opinion, alludes not so much to the functioning of certain *objective* mechanisms that are the same for everyone and each individually describable, as to the particularly marked and 'holistic' (Davidson and Peacocke) participation of our *subjectivity* as such.

Finally, reference to the 'mental' and the adoption of the language of the psyche are singularly pertinent and meaning-laden when we notice (and choose to underline) that the 'subjective' implications of what we feel, think, and desire are far more important than the correlative feelings, thoughts, and desires considered in their presumed 'objectivity' – and perhaps in their presumed materiality. When I speak about my condition of 'being in love', usually I am not interested in describing a particular neurophysiological or biochemical state: what I wish to express is infinitely more personal and subjective. And I shape this particular personal and subjective element of the message by 'overdetermining' my feeling by means of a (subjective) amalgam of references to extremely *sinngebende* affective and symbolic systems, to which I attribute *additional subjective* meanings.

Nor can it be claimed that love – that is, *my* love – exists independently of this complex *Sinnaufbau*, or that it may be subdivided into a hard, 'objective' nucleus and a series of soft, 'subjective' interpretations. That nucleus, in itself, *is not* 'love'. On the contrary, at the 'psycho'-existential level that concerns us here, that same nucleus can set into motion the most diverse psychophysical processes. Thus, from a certain *physical drive* (since the proponents of the 'nucleus' theory have precisely this in mind) there may arise many different sorts of *feeling*. The biochemical attraction often considered the *objective* substance of love can *objectively* generate fear, anxiety, horror, and processes of sublimation, rather than love. The pulsion (the 'nucleus') is essentially the occasion, the springboard for an unpredictable series of developments and possible itineraries in which the *subject* is continuously at work (consciously and unconsciously) producing meaning. In the end, we are always faced with figures or situations that, while preserving precious little of the original physical nucleus, have been considerably enriched by the most diverse semantic elaborations and additions.

Finally, what we are facing are not *facts* but *meanings*. Indeed, 'psychic' states and events take shape primarily as complex semantic constructions, built on the foundations of the most varied metapsychic referents and awaiting multiple decodifications. One could even say that the most specific task of the language of psychology (and even more so of psychology as a discipline) is precisely this continuous *creation* and *interpretation* of meanings concerning the subject, and that the so-called mental is used essentially as one of the *conditions of constructibility* of these conceptions and interpretations. If this is true, we can understand the reductive character of conceptions that view the mind either as nothing else but body, or as a mere function or property of the body itself, or as a dimension reproducible without residues in physical, computational models.

And we can also understand why the discipline traditionally called psychology, that codes and decodes meanings in relation to subjects, should be inscribed not within the area of the *Naturwissenschaften* but rather (as Bruno Bettelheim rightly argues in respect to psychoanalysis) within that of the *Geisteswissenschaften* – or better still that of *hermeneutics*.

Chapter 1

Toward a physical science of the mental

*Feigl and the (re-)construction of
the 'mind–body problem'*

I

*The 'Mental' and the 'Physical': General Positions and
the Concept of Knowledge*

As we said in the Introduction, Herbert Feigl is generally considered the father of the reawakened interest in the MBP in this century. Spanning a period of some forty years (his first article on the psychophysical relationship appeared in 1934), Feigl's concern with the problem found its most extensive and systematic expression in the volume entitled *The 'Mental' and the 'Physical'*, published in 1958. Certain theoretical and historical merits of this work should be pointed out immediately. Feigl approached the question of the relationship between mind and body with a deep awareness of its numerous scientific, epistemological, and ontological implications. He carried out his inquiry within a rather rich and stimulating context of positions and conceptions: logical empiricism, realism, materialism, behaviorism, the problems of reductionism and physicalism, the question of theoretical and observational languages, and so on. He firmly rejected doctrines that in one way or another refused to deal with the MBP out of hand: this is the case, in particular, with behavioral psychology (all too often incapable of considering the mental under any form but that of merely *visible* behavior) and with radical materialism, branded as "crass" by Feigl for its *a priori* refusal to recognize even the existence of anything else but matter. He was convinced, moreover, that a serious treatment of the MBP should provide an adequate account not only of the physical but also of the mental. In this connection Feigl proposed subdividing mental states into three distinct parts (a proposal which has received considerable favor): *sentience* (the sensory dimension of the mind), *sapience* (its cognitive dimension), and *selfhood* (the dimension of subjective awareness). Finally, he devoted particular attention to the identity hypothesis, which especially for a certain scientific and philosophical orientation (but also for many of its critics) was called upon to play a crucial role in the debate on the mind–body relationship.

This last point requires a less cursory formulation. Feigl is doubtless one of the first philosophers to understand that there may exist not one but many notions of identity. In his important essay 'Physicalism, Unity of Science, and the Foundations of Psychology' (published in 1963, but written in the fifties) he distinguishes between three types of identity: one, which he calls "accidental", correlates two facts or events by pure chance ("the woman named Ann E. Hodges (32 years old) of Sylacanga, Alabama, is the person who was hit by a meteorite weighing nine pounds in December 1954"); another is "nomological", that is, governed by a law ("the metal which has a specific heat of 0.24 and a specific gravity of 0.27 has an electrical resistivity of 2.8 microohms per cc."); the third is "theoretical" or "systematic" and is distinguished from the other two "in that it requires a background of scientific theory and of semantical analysis" ('Physicalism', p. 255). In *The 'Mental' and the 'Physical'* (henceforth abbreviated MP) Feigl will affirm that identity is a connection that can be determined empirically and will distinguish this "empirical" identity from purely "formal" identity (MP, pp. 444–5).

Feigl goes further. Along with being *empirical,* the identity sought by those who are concerned with understanding the natural, real world must be *contingent.* That is to say, this identity must assert, within the context of the problems that interest us, not the *a priori*, universal, and necessary existence of a given relationship between the mental and the physical but only that mental and physical states and events (or rather their respective linguistic descriptions) are *de facto* identical or identifiable, although they could also *not* be that way: the question must in any case be verified or refuted empirically. In this connection, a pronouncement on identity requires that the 'judge' ascertain a definite relationship between two different entities (or, again, of 'accounts': we will have occasion to determine whether the nature of the identity in question is 'ontological' or 'linguistic'); and that this relationship be determined – at least in principle – by appropriate scientific inquiry.

From this standpoint, what Feigl states in relation to mind–body identity is not so much a theoretical position that has virtually been accepted, as a research program that has yet to be carried out. It is no accident that at a crucial point in *The 'Mental' and the 'Physical'*, he writes: "Any detailed account of the mind–body identities is a matter for *the future* of psychophysiological research" (MP, p. 457). This seems to reveal, leaving aside for the moment Feigl's attitude toward "the future" of scientific knowledge, an approach to the notion of *identity* (a notion often viewed in a somewhat static and speculative way) in terms of a more dynamic and operative *identifiability* of given mental states and events and given physical states and events.

Feigl's discussion is less convincing, on the other hand, when he deals with certain technical difficulties of the concept (and practice) of identity, especially as regards the problems raised by the so-called law of Leibniz on the identity of indiscernibles (see Chapter 3). The objection has also been raised that Feigl does not adequately verify the possibility of realizing a complete *identification* of two sets of concepts as diverse as those relative to mental and physiological phenomena. More generally, one has the feeling that Feigl tends to develop his positions while shunning, as far as possible, a direct confrontation with the concept of identity in itself. Indeed, some time after the publication of *The 'Mental' and the 'Physical'* he explicitly abandoned the strict identity view and embraced a conception which is not identitist but 'substitutionist' in nature. What seems to concern Feigl is not so much the concept of identity as a philosophy of mind which is physicalistic, anti-phenomenological and (in an explicit self-criticism with respect to certain principles of his book) ultimately pro-materialist.

Of particular significance is Feigl's decision to adopt a physicalist orientation – a decision inspired by some well-known theses of logical empiricism. From one point of view Feigl seems to defend what we might call a 'weak' form of physicalism. In the course of his essay, in fact, he does express reservations about some exaggerations and *a priori* assumptions of certain physicalistic theses. In reality Feigl's defense of a definite theoretical stance is far more engagé than might appear on the surface. "I am inclined to believe strongly", we read at a highly significant point in his discussion, "in the fruitfulness of the physicalistic research program (involving micro-explanations) for biology and psychology" (MP, p. 376). He holds this belief because he is convinced that "physical laws" are (or will be) sufficient to produce a series of tendentially exhaustive scientific explanations. This is why he can count on "future scientific research" to demonstrate the adequacy of "physical explanations" (MP, p. 481). Feigl's discussion, however, is not limited to strictly epistemological concerns. Occasionally, he inclines to intertwine a purely cognitive stand with a far more challenging position. In a passage which summarizes his general position, for example, he stresses that in his system "the 'physical' is interpreted as a conceptual system, *or as the realities described by it*" (MP, p. 474). On the same page we also find that "the fundamental laws of the universe *are physical*".

In Feigl's essay 'Physicalism, Unity of Science, and the Foundations of Psychology', his theses on the physicalist perspective do not change. On the contrary, they become an essential part of an interpretation of science that must be understood in order to appreciate his attitude toward the analysis of mental processes.

Feigl embraces, first of all, a "monistic conception" of scientific knowledge – "and therefore – in a sense – also of the universe" (clearly, a by-no-means negligible metaphysical adjunct: 'Physicalism', p. 266). Fundamentally there is only *one* science, both from a methodological standpoint and from that of the (nomological) objectives to be pursued. It is also *empirical* and *sensory*. It is based, that is, on the "primacy of sensory observation": "sensory experiences are much more reliable indicators of 'external' states of affairs than are thoughts, images, wishes, sentiments or other 'non-sensory' data" (ibid., pp. 229). At the same time Science attributes a crucial role to logical and formal procedures, thus ensuring the necessary rigor of the scientific endeavor. From the explanatory standpoint, Feigl adopts and gives priority to the models provided by the physical sciences because he is well aware of their "impressive success" (ibid., p. 266). This "physicalist" position is also founded on the need for *intersubjective and public control* (peculiar to the physical disciplines) which is felt by any research program worthy of the name 'science'. The indispensable "objectivity" of scientific knowledge coincides perfectly with this control (ibid., pp. 227–47 and *passim*).

But what is particularly striking about Feigl's interpretation of science is its all-encompassing, anti-personal and anti-subjective nature. For Feigl, 'true' *knowledge* cannot be but Science – Science with a physicalistic orientation. A determined supporter of what he (rightly) calls "scientific optimism", Feigl declares explicitly and

33

peremptorily that "there is nothing in the realm of existence which is in principle inaccessible to examination and exploration by the scientific method" (ibid., p. 265). What is required is that Science provide itself with the proper (physicalistic) foundations and free itself of all foreign elements. In this connection, Feigl seems to consider it possible and even indispensable to introduce into his episteme an *analogon* of what Popper had called the criterion of demarcation. Like Popper, Feigl attempts to dig a moat around the walls of 'true' Knowledge. The fortress of this Knowledge grants access only to those statements that are laden with "factual meaningfulness": in this way, it is possible to avoid "unanswerable questions" (ibid., p. 238).

In the second place, Feigl admits only propositions that are open to intersubjective and public confirmation: physicalism, he stresses, "excludes as scientifically meaningless statements which could be confirmed *only* subjectively" (ibid., p. 230). Just as Popper was to write in his autobiography that he constructed his realist and objectivist philosophy of science as a reaction against the risks of "relativism", Feigl, inspired in part by similar ideals, declares that the strict limitations imposed on 'his' Knowledge obey the dictates of protection and "conservatism [*sic*]": a principle "without which scientific knowledge would be unprotected against the dangers of groundless and limitless speculation" (ibid., p. 240).

Subjective and qualitative experience and its science

Given the premises outlined above, it is not surprising that Feigl saw the most intriguing epistemological problem arising from within the sphere of psychology. This sphere refers in fact to a dimension of the human experience which appears to be characterized by the subjective and private (and also the individual and qualitative). The ensuing difficulties seem quite serious: "if there were a domain of immediate experience radically private and secluded, i.e., absolutely isolated and insulated, hence completely inaccessible even through the most indirect routes to test by other individuals, then by this very character such immediate experiences could never be or become a subject matter for *science*" (ibid., p. 236).

Might it then be necessary to accept the existence of a dimension of reality which is inaccessible to rational and cognitive inquiry? Or should we admit the existence of a *non-scientific* psychological *knowledge?* Certainly not. Fortunately, a careful examination of the problem allows us, according to Feigl, to overcome the impasse. The general premise of his position is that "everything that *is*", everything that *happens* in the world, must be referable as such, directly or indirectly, to physical determinations (or must be susceptible to physical inquiry, in a broad sense). Arguably, the human universe cannot be exempt from this principle. Thus all the components and events of this universe must, at least *in principle*, be led back to – or "resolved" in – physical referents (or, once again, must be analyzable in physical terms). It follows, for Feigl, that experiences that are *a priori* beyond the reach of science exist only in the imagination of philosophers who are behind the times, or in the "anguished stammerings of existentialists" (ibid., p. 260).

It is on the basis of these assumptions that Feigl launches his assault on the subjective and the private, as well as on other characteristics, functions, or dimensions of the human sphere which have traditionally been considered impenetrable by the scientific probe: quality and teleology, volition and free will, meaning and intention, and even religion and mysticism.

The nature of the attack is *eliminationist* or *reductionist*. Subjectivity and privacy do not exist in a pure state: "Analytic philosophers ... have in various ways rather convincingly argued that the idea of *absolute* privacy or subjectivity which for some philosophers constitutes *the* criterion of the mental is an idea begotten by confusions and pregnant with unresolvable perplexities" (ibid., pp. 230–1). Qualities can be reduced to quantities; the teleological world of ends can be reduced to the world of causes (ibid., p. 253). Even acts of volition and free will itself must be redefined within a causal framework which highlights the determining functions of our "basic personality" and of the empirically ascertainable "interests" that are self-sufficient causes for action (ibid., pp. 253–4). As for religious and mystical experiences (considered the most distant from the categories and explanations of science), Feigl claims that "the majority of psychologists are rather confident that available evidence points on the whole in the direction of explanations formulated within the current framework of psychological (and sociocultural) regularities and will not risk the introduction of fundamentally different categories" (ibid., p. 227). Finally, meanings and intentions (in the broadest sense of the word), far from belonging to a meta-observational, meta-descriptive, and meta-deterministic sphere, are resolvable into, or identifiable with, *sensory facts* and *causal connec-*

tions. The efficacy of intentions, writes Feigl, must be explained, just as is the case with volition, "in a manner compatible with *physical principles*" (ibid., p. 254). As for the problem of meaning, Feigl admits on the one hand that "physicalist categories" cannot be applied to its "normative aspects", but on the other he emphasizes that if meaning, reference, and intentionality are approached as empirical facts or acts, "then these concepts belong to *descriptive* semiotic and no insuperable difficulties arise" (ibid., p. 251).

To illustrate the possibility of knowing exclusively with the scientific instruments of physical observation and causal concatenation any human reality – even the most complex, in terms of meanings, intentions, symbols, rites, and so forth – Feigl uses a rather significant example: the "Martian super-scientist".

> A Martian super-scientist who did not share any of our human repertory of immediate data could nevertheless (conceivably) attain a perfect behavioral and neurophysiological account of human life. He might not 'know by acquaintance' what colors look like, what pain feels like, what it 'means' to experience 'pity,' 'reverence,' 'regret,' etc. . . . The Martian may be completely lacking in experiences of the sort of human piety and solemnity, and hence unable to 'understand' (empathize) what goes on in the commemoration of, e.g., the armistice – but this would not in principle make it impossible for him to give a perfectly adequate account of the behavior of certain human groups on a November 11th at 11 a.m. (ibid., pp. 257–8)

In the lines omitted from this passage Feigl asserts that "a congenitally blind (human) scientist, equipped with the necessary instruments and intelligence could achieve not only an adequate knowledge of the *physics* of colors", but also a scientific explanation "of color perception and imagination" (ibid., p. 257). Within certain limits this assertion could, in principle, be true. We must be careful, however, not to suppose (as Feigl seems to do) that this means that the scientist attains cognition *in every respect* of the event in question. In response, Howard Robinson noted quite appropriately that although a deaf scientist might know the entire *physiology* of hearing, this does not imply that he would have the *experience* of hearing (Robinson 1982, p. 4). It is quite clear, in fact, that the concrete experience of hearing includes not only a certain neuromuscular process, but also *the ways* (psychological, symbolic, cultural, existential) in which the subject has that experience. Indeed, the *subject* hears, not the *ear:* which, on the contrary, seems to be the only referent of the explanations that interest Feigl. Norman Hanson once observed – in reply to a certain form of reductionism – that it is not the *eye* that sees, but the *person* (Hanson 1958). By this he meant that in general, with all due respect to *physiological* micro-analyses, also *psychic* functions must be examined in their appropriate contexts. When I listen to a Mahler symphony, for example, what has to be taken into account is not only the performance of a certain physiological organ, but also the musical sensitivity and culture with which I listen to that symphony. (It has been claimed, in fact, that even given quite similar auditory sense organs, subjects who lack certain experiences and competences would perceive the *same* acoustic messages *differently.*)

Returning to the passage quoted above, it is clear that the greatest problems arise when more complex psychic functions are taken into examination. "A clinical psychologist completely deprived of certain sectors in the area of emotional experiences", writes Feigl, "would in principle be able to introduce the behavioral and neurophysiological equivalents of such (to him completely unfamiliar) emotions in his 'psychology of the other one'" ('Physicalism', p. 257). This sudden revival of behaviorism on Feigl's part may raise a few eyebrows. To what extent is it possible for a psychologist who is *totally ignorant* of the (psychological) phenomenon of emotion *to grasp something like emotion?* Incidentally, it is precisely this kind of question that Sartre addressed (see his *Esquisse d'une théorie des émotions*) about the time Feigl was conducting his first inquiries into the MBP (Sartre 1939). And, rather evidently, the question is even more crucial for a Martian scientist (no matter how 'super').

The answer can only be the following, or at least so it seems. If I have not the slightest experience of emotion, I quite simply will *not be able* to identify emotion in another person. I will only perceive a set of acts or events from among which it will be extremely difficult for me to recognize something like an 'emotion'. Feigl himself acknowledges that this point is well taken when he declares, to some extent unexpectedly, that "*some* basis of immediate experience" is, in fact, necessary (ibid., p. 257). However, this "basis" cannot be easily incorporated into Feigl's theoretical framework, because it would radically alter the hypothesis in question. A further objection could be one which is commonly raised against behaviorism: how can I, the scientist, no matter how competent in the *physiology* of emotions, understand the *meaning* that emotion has for the person who feels it? And how will I know whether the subject actually *feels* that emotion or is merely *pretending* to feel it? To reach this understanding – crucial, we should stress, for a psychological comprehension of the phenomenon 'emotion' (which otherwise would be reduced to the mere *external vectors* of the emotion itself) – I need cognitive elements that an understanding of the mere behavioral and physiological correlates of the emotion cannot provide.

The final part of our passage deserves particular attention. Feigl seems convinced that it is possible for a Martian "completely" lacking in the experience of solemnity to observe (in the sense of identifying and grasping conceptually a certain event) a civic celebration. This is probably the point at which the limitations of Feigl's "observationism" appear most clearly. In response to positions of this kind it has been objected that observation is far from being nothing but a mere empirical act; that is, it is not enough to have great (even Martian) abilities in the field of perception and so forth in order to single out and comprehend an event X *as an event X.* That is to say, this latter operation requires (among other things) a sort of preunderstanding, a concept of the *observandum* – in a sense a whole *culture.* Indeed, if I do not *know* in some way what I am to observe, how can I observe it? This point seems to be particularly crucial in the case under consideration. To put it rather synthetically, without a meta-observational frame of reference, without a *theory,* without an experience of certain myths and rituals, how will Feigl's scientist, albeit a superscientist from Mars, recognize a civic holiday *as a civic holiday?*

What is more, Feigl also claims that his Martian is able to give a "perfectly adequate causal explanation" of the crowd's behavior on this civic holiday. All this is hardly credible and once again reveals the limitations of a definite epistemology. The thesis Feigl advances, in fact, implies: i) a rather reductive (physical and factual) conception of behavior; ii) an 'objectivistic' and 'univocal' conception of causality. As regards the first point, on the basis of Feigl's assertions, what an individual does should consist *only* of *visible* behavioral components and *immediate physical* causes. Indeed, the Martian cannot, by definition, perceive anything but *observable* physical events. On the contrary, behavior – in the sense of what effectively and phenomenologically happens – also includes something like the *motivations* and the *intentions* which induce the subject to behave in a certain way. Otherwise we would not be dealing with a *behavior* (which belongs to the sphere of psycho-anthropology and action theory), but with a quite different referent: a *movement*, one might say (belonging as such to the sphere of physiology). An example may help clarify the difference between these two 'figures'. When I see a man running, if I confine myself (as the Martian *must* do) to pure *factual observation* I can perceive nothing but a certain motor event. But if I am familiar, at a meta-observational level, with particular habits of life, I reach a different and more sophisticated understanding of that event: the recognition, for example, that the person is *jogging*. To conclude our discussion of this first point: since our Martian is forced to understand only *latu sensu* physical *movements*, he will be unable to understand that he is a witness to a complex *social action* or *ritual*.

The second point requires us to consider whether a Martian equipped with observational powers alone (albeit exceptionally advanced) would be capable of elaborating a causal explanation of an observed event. From a certain standpoint, this might be possible. But it would be an explanation modelled entirely and exclusively on the concreteness of empirical facts and their objective, visible concatenations. As an explanation of cause this would be wanting indeed: how many crucial (meta-empirical) elements of the causal connections at work in the behavior of groups of human beings would in fact be left out? That Feigl does not consider this aspect of the question shows that he nurtures an 'objectivist' conception of causal explanation; a conception which to a great extent does not take into account the selective, interpretive, and pragmatic schemes of the *subject* (meta-empirical, goal-oriented, *sinngebende* schemes which the Martian, of course, does not possess).

As we have said, Feigl's model of causal explanation is not only *objectivistic* but also *univocal*. That is to say, what he proposes is not a set of the *different* causal explanations that could be given for a particular event (a set which might, of course, also include a behavioral, neurophysiological account), but *one single* type of explanation. Indeed, it could hardly be otherwise, as Feigl's model explanation is not an intellectual operation performed by subjects who act according to their different interests and purposes (in the plural). Rather, it is essentially a recording of data and concatenations of data belonging to the *pars objecti:* causality is *there*, embedded in *objectivity*, and it unfolds according to a single plan – that followed, necessarily and eternally, by *natural* phenomena. It is no accident that Feigl declares, in an important essay, that he adheres to "naturalism" (Feigl 1960). In the present context this means he interprets the behavioral events of the individuals present at a November 11 celebration not as complex, goal-oriented, motivationally differentiated *human actions*, but as univocal, law-conditioned, causally undifferentiated *natural phenomena*.

One last remark should be made about the 'perfectly adequate' causal explanation that Feigl's Martian is supposed to be able to provide. The concept of 'perfect adequacy', in fact, raises problems of extreme delicacy. Indeed, when we speak of the 'adequacy' of something it would appear obligatory to determine *for what purpose* and *for whom* that 'thing' is (or is not) adequate, and in what situation, and in relation to what needs and interests. Yet Feigl completely ignores questions of this kind. This neglect seems to be connected both to his unwillingness to include in the explanatory process references to *subjective* contexts and purposes and to his conviction, in relation to human phenomena, that there exists *only one* scientific explanation: that which gives priority to the ultimate "molecular" components of these phenomena, that is, to their physiological "micro-levels". Feigl's notion of explanation, then, is a merely *natural* explanation of 'facts', considered, as we have seen, as essentially *natural*. If this is the case, it is not difficult to understand why he uses a descriptive and 'objective' (rather than an evaluative and 'subjective') notion of adequacy. For him, in fact, a "perfectly adequate" explanation is simply one which, once *the* causal chain externally (physically) responsible for the *explanandum* has been identified, reaches the ultimate, natural basis of the behavior of the *explanandum* itself.

The interpretation of the mental and its identifiability with the physical

Feigl's main concern is arguably not so much psycho-anthropological as theoretical and epistemological. The problem he poses regards, on the one hand, the validity and the legitimate use of a particular concept – the mental – in the praxis of knowing and, on the other, the question of the complex relationship between the mental and the physical (a notion which is not employed without ambiguity, as it is often substituted by terms that can hardly be considered synonyms, such as 'bodily', 'cerebral', 'neurophysiological'). It follows that Feigl needs to defend, at least initially, the relative 'consistency', the relative autonomy of the mental, without which it would be impossible to put the question in this two-part form. Some of Feigl's assertions concerning the mental may be seen in light of this need. Mental states exist. These states must be interpreted as "true realities" denoted "by a (very small) subset of physical concepts" exercising causally effective activity (MP, p. 474). Correlatively, they must not be denied or eliminated *a priori*, but rather subjected to a close examination that will lead, if appropriate, to their identification with physical states.

A more careful scrutiny, however, reveals that Feigl's treatment of the mind is inadequate and extremely reductive. In the first place, his inventory of states and functions covered by the figure of the mental is too cursory and somewhat confused. His list, moreover, offers only a rather sketchy illustration of the peculiarities of these states and functions. But what is particularly unsatisfactory is Feigl's attitude toward the nature of the mental as a whole. Essentially, he simply reexamines the main features that are considered peculiar to the mental (generally drawing on the philosophical and psychological literature of anti-materialist tendency) and tries to demonstrate that they are *not* what they appear to be. In other words, it can be shown that, once analyzed with sufficient rigor, the mental does not possess (or is not alone in possessing) those features that have traditionally been attributed to it, or that their existence does not create the problems that so many have insisted on emphasizing.

Thus, a few pages of *The 'Mental' and the 'Physical'* are devoted to assuring the reader that the mental is not *subjective* because so-called subjective phenomena can now rather readily be objectified in various ways and forms just like the 'other' phenomena (MP, pp. 397–8). It is not *private* since nothing (as we already know) is in principle 'closed' to, or unreachable by, public knowledge. Since, moreover, language is "a vehicle of intersubjective communication", a totally private utterance – that is, with no element transcending the strictly personal sphere – cannot by definition exist (MP, pp. 398–403). The mental is also not *non-spatial*, as Feigl (who introduces an interesting distinction between phenomenal space and physical space, but then does not apply it consistently) seems to feel it possible to speak of a *dimension*, and even of a *localization*, of mental states (*where* I feel a particular enthusiasm?) (MP, pp. 406–9). The mental, he continues, is also not *qualitative*, as opposed to a *quantitative* nature of the physical: not only because the physical also has qualitative properties, but also because it makes sense to speak of "mental quantities", that is, to attribute certain "sizes" to mental phenomena (as when we say one pain is *greater* than another, or that a state of jealousy *increases*) (MP, pp. 409–11). Finally, the mental is not *teleological* (i.e., goal-oriented), *holistic* (i.e., not reducible to its constituent parts), or *emergent* (i.e., having properties absent from its components): or at least these properties are *no more,* or no *differently,* characteristic of the mental than that of certain other natural processes. In any case, according to Feigl, modern science is able to express all these features in physical terms of or according to physical-theoretical constructs (MP, pp. 409–15).

It is not necessary to dwell any further on these claims. What is more important is to grasp the purpose that orients Feigl's position. His goal is to show that the two poles of traditional psycho-physical dualism reveal – if properly analyzed – a substantial affinity. In this connection, Feigl had already stressed that "a general account of mental phenomena in physical terms . . . seems to face no overwhelming 'metaphysical' objections" ('Physicalism', p. 254). If this is true, then it seems possible, at least in principle, to devise a concrete program for the identification of the mental with the physical.

As we mentioned above, Feigl subdivides this program into three distinct parts: the complex of sensory experiences (sentience), that of intellective functions (sapience), and the question of subjective awareness (selfhood). As a matter of fact, both in 'Physicalism' and in *The 'Mental' and the 'Physical'* he examines rather briefly the problems connected with sapience and selfhood. Among other reasons, he was probably aware that the scientific data on these two spheres were too meager. We should stress, however, that this does not prevent him from taking rather clear-cut positions on more than one occasion. Thus, for example, he confidently claims that intelligence, a central function of sapience, is "clearly definable in physical terms" (MP, p. 424) (here one senses an echo of the impressive results attained by cybernetics and other research programs concerning the physical reproduction of some intelligent behaviors). Even more revealing stands are taken on selfhood. On the one hand, Feigl shows little interest in examining the polymorphous features of the self and awareness (indeed, he tends to reject or ignore them). On the other he emphasizes the possibility of a material, neurophysiological interpretation of this dimension. This is especially true as regards his conception of the complex organization of the self. But it is also true, more generally, for all the properties and dispositions of subjectivity, "including those attributed by psychoanalysts to the superego". These properties, we read in a highly significant passage, "very likely 'correspond' to (or, *according to my view, are identical with*) certain relatively stable patterns of cerebral structures and functions" (MP, pp. 460–1; italics mine). Even the unconscious self presents no problem for Feigl: the functions assigned by psychoanalytic theory to the id and the ego, he writes, "may well be interpreted by assuming that certain portions of the cerebral processes are blocked off (this corresponds to 're-pressed') from the areas of awareness and verbal report" (MP, p. 461). Although, of course, it is still unclear to what organic structures the concepts of ego, id, and superego can be reduced, "very likely, the psychological notions will appear only as first crude approximations, once the detailed neurophysiological facts are better known" (MP, p. 481). Once again Feigl seems to propose an 'ontological' version of psychic phenomena and of their interpretation (he tends to speak essentially in terms of *facts* and *processes*). He does not even take into consideration the possibility that in certain cases we may be dealing with theoretical notions or symbolic figures that express not so much *physical realities* as *meanings*. He is inclined *a priori* to turn certain *concepts* into *facts*, and certain *senses* into *physical referents*.

"Sentience" and the identification of "raw feels" with neural processes

Feigl's discussion of sentience also rests more on general theoretical assumptions than on empirical evidence and argumentation. Yet, these assumptions are of considerable significance, since it is here, in this context, that Feigl's conception of identity emerges most forcefully. His basic thesis is that "raw feels" (an expression taken from Tolman, indicating crude, elementary sensations) are "empirically *identifiable* with the referents of some neurophysiological concepts" (MP, p. 445; italics mine). From a realist's perspective, argues Feigl, it is perfectly plausible to explain how a bell determines psycho-subjective sensations (visual, tactile, auditory, etc.) by means of physical and objective phenomena produced by the bell itself (MP,

p. 452). One might object that this example illustrates not so much an *identity* as a *production* (or a *correlation* between a cause and an effect). But elsewhere Feigl comes out much more strongly in favor of identity. He claims, for instance, that "the states of experience that conscious human beings 'live through' . . . *are identical* with certain [presumably configurational] aspects of the neural processes in those organisms" (MP, p. 446; italics mine). Correspondingly, it is true that certain cerebral processes are *identical* with "experienced and acquaintancewise knowable raw feels" (MP, p. 457). "If a brain physiologist", Feigl adds, "could investigate my brain processes and describe them in full detail, then he could formulate his findings in neurophysiological language, and might even be able to produce a complete microphysical account in terms of atomic and subatomic concepts" (MP, p. 450).

These are certainly radical stands. Here, as we anticipated above, Feigl's theory of identity – a theory generated from a markedly reductionistic and physicalistic doctrine – comes forth with all its peremptory energy. From the point of view of scientific cognition, sentience exists – without residues or alternatives – *only* in the form given to it by neurophysiology – and, in the future, by microphysics. A question arises immediately: to what extent are these *theoretical* claims borne out by *empirically verifiable facts?* There can be only one answer: to a very limited extent. The first to realize this seems to be Feigl himself. It is no accident that whenever the development of his argumentation requires support from scientific proof, he systematically invokes an age or state of knowledge located in the *future*. There are many examples that might be cited in this regard. To give but one, the "brain physiologist" mentioned above is not a physiologist of *today*, armed with the knowledge *actually* provided by *today's* science: he is – as we read in a line omitted from our quotation – a physiologist "equipped with the knowledge and devices *that may be available a thousand years hence*" (MP, p. 450; italics mine; see also p. 457).

Now this 'reference to the future' – rather frequently used throughout the literature on the identity theory – is less innocent and legitimate than might at first appear. Not only does it presuppose the significant acknowledgement that here and now, in the context of *present* knowledge, there *is no* empirical verification of certain claims: it also presupposes a sort of preemption, an arbitrary prevision of the state of *future* knowledge. Indeed, it presupposes an authentic 'philosophy' of knowledge and of the times *to come*.

44

The statement that "a thousand years hence" we shall have the empirical means to solve – and to solve in a very precise and predictable way – certain problems we face today implies in fact a view of history as a continuum in which the same questions and answers constantly recur; and a view of science as a homogeneous, unitary machine about which we can predict that once it has entered a certain path it will take no unforeseen detours. In other words, if we state that in some unspecified *time to come* our great grandchildren will find the data that *today* are missing and with them solve our problems, we are assuming that in that unspecified future time *our* problems will continue, unaltered, to occupy future generations (no matter how distant in time) and that the scholars of those future generations will hold that precisely those data that *we today* consider essential are still *the* crucial data. But what if tomorrow's questions are different from today's? Or what if, at least, the most pertinent answers to those questions turn out to be (partially or completely) different from those that we are searching for in today's cognitive context? The history of science is full of similar episodes: episodes in which a change in the questions was so dramatic that it led to the cancellation of a whole discipline or research program. Indeed, nothing really gives Feigl the absolute guarantee that "a thousand years hence" the state of knowledge will couple neurophysiology with psychology so completely as to merge them, or will allow neurophysiology to take the place of psychology. What if it is biogenetics or neurocybernetics that is asked to take the place of psychology? Or if the same request were made not to a *natural* science but to a *formal* discipline like artificial intelligence? Or if the request itself is considered *irrelevant* because people will feel then (as some already feel now) that the interests which motivate psychological research cannot be completely satisfied by the knowledge that physical and formal disciplines can supply?

It is not surprising that Popper has ironized on the "promissory note" offered by those who would adjourn verification to a future date (Popper and Eccles 1977). The fact that Feigl does not appear to have devoted particular attention to the problem suggests that his thought was imbued with the continuistic philosophy of knowledge alluded to above. We should only add that in several passages of *The 'Mental' and the 'Physical'* he even argues that neurophysiology has already demonstrated that raw feels and neural processes are identical. Thus it is *science* that attests to the existence and demonstrability of this identity.

45

II

'Ontological' identity or 'linguistic' identity?:
a pseudo-problem

Is everything settled, then? In a certain sense it should be. But after a careful reading of *The 'Mental' and the 'Physical'* one is left with the impression that several issues of a general, theoretical character remain open: those issues to which Feigl himself was unquestionably more sensitive. I am not alluding here to the question of whether it is possible to express in physical terms *the whole* subjective experience of an act of sentience, nor to the fact that other crucial dimensions of the mental cannot be (as was suggested above) completely identified with bodily correlates. I am referring, rather, to a more fundamental problem: the effective range and the real sense of the identity theory. A question which appears inevitable to many readers of Feigl's essay is the following: is the relationship between mind and body proposed/imposed by the identity theory to be read in *ontological* or in *linguistic-formal* terms?

The question, it should be clear, is in part implicit in the very formulation of the identity theory. In certain passages of The *'Mental' and the 'Physical'* this formulation takes on, or appears to take on, two quite different meanings: a) 'the mental is the physical' in the sense that *what* is usually designated by 'the mental' *is* (substantially, *realiter*) *what* is usually designated by 'the physical'; b) 'the mental is the physical' in the sense that the complex of *linguistic and conceptual expressions* that usually designate the mental is identifiable with the complex of linguistic and conceptual expressions that designate the physical. In other words, does the identity theory show reality as it *is* (*objectively*), or does it only propose the way in which we can *linguistically* define the mental *as* the physical, independently of the *nature* of the two referents?

Although this issue is present at various points in the essay, it is in connection with Feigl's discussion of sentience that it emerges with particular emphasis. Yet his attitude toward the question is far from univocal. Certain claims about the relationship between raw feels and neural processes fall clearly into a non-ontological perspective. Raw feels, Feigl writes, are to be identified neither with the gray matter of the brain nor with molecular chemical structures, but rather with a 'physical' conceived as an "unvisualizable conceptual system" (MP, p. 454). In the same context, Feigl makes certain statements that attest to his sympathy (at least in general terms) for a non-realist, conceptualist theory of knowledge.

Not always, however, does Feigl move in the direction I have just indicated. Often – far more often than is generally admitted – he adopts a rather different conception. A few pages after the passage just cited he does not hesitate to emphasize the existence of a reality *an sich* – a physical (neurophysiological) reality. "According to the identity thesis", we read, "the directly experienced qualia and configurations are *the realities-in-themselves* that are denoted by neurophysiological descriptions" (MP, p. 457; italics mine). Even the ingenious "autocerebroscope" (a purely hypothetical instrument capable of locating the single cerebral microprocesses that take place each time a subject registers a so-called mental event) and the models of the brain that Feigl suggests as possible forms of the mind–body relationship bear (despite appearances) ontological implications that are difficult to deny. Feigl's arguments lead *de facto* to the thesis that mental functions are carried out in particular cerebral areas *realiter* and *completely*: that is, denying that there might be some aspect of the mental event which is independent of its neurophysiological agents. On occasion, in *The 'Mental' and the 'Physical'* the ontological-realist perspective emerges into particularly clear view. For example, speaking of sensory states and processes, Feigl defines sentience as the "basic *reality*", adding that this can be said "ontologically speaking" (MP, p. 474). Elsewhere, the way in which he speaks of physicalism betrays a strong inclination to identify the order of *theoretical elaborations* with the order of *reality*. An example is Feigl's claim that physicalism is a monistic conception of *scientific explanation* – "and therefore – in a sense – also of the *universe*" ('Physicalism', p. 266).

At this point there should be no doubt about the prevalence of an 'ontological-realistic' orientation in Feigl's positions. And yet this may not be the main issue as regards an adequate interpretation of these positions. The truly decisive point is that even an alternative, 'linguistic' reading of his thought *would not modify its basic, essential content*. A close analysis of Feigl's texts reveals in fact that a framing in linguistic terms of the MBP would not guarantee *by itself* a true emancipation of the mental: that is, a recovery of the autonomy and dignity of its science. Let us concede that Feigl's examination of the problem – though at times contradictory and ambiguous – is not so much *ontological* as *linguistic-epistemological*. Let us concede, in other words, that he treats 'the mental' and 'the physical' not as two *res*, but as the complex of linguistic and conceptual expressions which designate, respectively, the mental and the physical. However, this approach admits two quite different interpretations:

a) the complex of linguistic-conceptual expressions generally defined as the 'mental' has *one single* semantic and cognitive value, which is identified with the semantic and cognitive value of the *physical* linguistic-conceptual expressions denoting the 'physical';

b) the complex of linguistic-conceptual expressions generally defined as the 'mental' may, it is true, be identified in certain cases with the complex of linguistic-conceptual expressions generally defined as the 'physical', but this identification is realized only in *one particular* semantic and cognitive perspective, since the semantic and cognitive values of this complex (i.e., of the 'mental') are *multiple;* that is, it operates according to *different* semantic and cognitive *modes* and *uses* (corresponding to the different semantic and cognitive interests of different subjects) that cannot be – or cannot be usefully – reduced to *one in particular,* which would be privileged by virtue of its being identified with the mode and value of the *physical.*

The crucial question, then, may be formulated as follows: To what degree does Feigl assign to the mental a semantic and cognitive vehicle of its own, capable of 'telling' the mental itself (as well as phenomenal, direct experience in general) in a way that is neither subordinate nor reducible to other vehicles? It is no accident that this is one of the central issues faced in Feigl's important essay on physicalism and the unity of science.

On a first reading, the author seems to approach the question from a fairly open and 'liberal' linguistic-epistemological standpoint. Indeed, he admits the existence of not one, but two types of *knowledge:* "knowledge by acquaintance" (sometimes called "direct knowledge") and "knowledge by scientific description" ('Physicalism', p. 258). Feigl attributes to the first form of knowledge the ability to generate meaningful forms of cognition. Knowledge by acquaintance (and its relative language) refers mainly to "qualities", that is, to the phenomenal and qualitative aspects of subjective experience. Also the terms and concepts relating to the so-called unobservables are determined by reference to "items of direct experience" peculiar to knowledge by acquaintance (ibid., p. 249). As to its operative procedures, this kind of knowledge adopts the technique of ostensive definition and the criterion of evidence connected to direct acquaintance with phenomena (ibid., pp. 247–9). It also makes wide use of teleo-logical explanations and statements (ibid., p. 236).

But up to this point we have only a part of the story. In fact, Feigl concedes what we have outlined above and yet presents another stand which substantially empties and demolishes, from all conceivable points of view, the notion of psycho-phenomenal knowledge and language. In particular, cognitive acquaintance is drastically devalued: "One might rightly wonder whether the word 'knowledge' should at all be applied to acquaintance . . . in the sense just explained" (ibid., p. 258). Acquaintance is in fact only capable of ascertaining the mere *existence* of "certain contents of experience", but it cannot determine whether these experiences are true or false. It offers a mere *know 'how*, quite different from the *know that* which alone can produce truth judgements (ibid.). The ostensive definitions employed by direct knowledge are considered "an irritating anomaly": fortunately they may be substituted with the use of far more rigorous symbols, to be incorporated "in our linguistic habit system" disciplined by science (ibid., p. 249). Tele-ological explanations and statements, on the other hand, are con-sidered simply "superfluous" (ibid., p. 236) and replaceable with causal explanations and statements. As to the main referent of knowledge by acquaintance, that is, "qualities" (in the sense given above), Feigl peremptorily *eliminates* the possibility or necessity of 'saying' something in only "direct", phenomenal, and subjective terms: "the empirically assertible uniqueness of the qualities is in-separable from the nomological net in which they have their cognitive, conceptual place" (ibid. p. 261). Only *scientific* knowledge is able to symbolize adequately the qualities – indeed *all* the qual-ities – including those considered the most subjective and elemental like "here", "now", and "I". "In the scientific description of the world", Feigl insists, "the 'now', the 'here', and the 'I' – no matter how poignantly and uniquely experienced subjectively – are sup-planted, respectively, by a moment in time. . . , a point in space . . . and a person" (ibid., p. 260). In conclusion, the phenomenal lan-guage of acquaintance cannot show any cognitive force other than that inherent in a vague "evocative appeal" (ibid.). On the whole subject of psycho-subjective knowledge and language Feigl claims in sum that it can and must be *dissolved*.

Feigl's reasoning is so clear – and radical – that ambiguities and last-minute rescues are virtually excluded. Contrary to the initial hypothesis, there are not *two* kinds of knowledge but *only one:* descriptive knowledge, a knowledge anchored in a publicly verifiable world, the only knowledge whose objective is not idiographic but nomothetic. Any *other* knowledge, on closer examination, is not really knowledge. Not surprisingly, these premises lead to a radical devaluation of every form of non-scientific knowledge or language, beginning with literary knowledge – the subjective and qualitative "reflection in the poets' language" (ibid., p. 242). But even the days of *psychological* knowledge are numbered. In effect, whatever essential and useful things it has to say can (indeed *must*) be said by neurophysiology. "The qualitative features of the raw feels directly designated by phenomenal terms may also be indirectly but (empirically) uniquely characterized by their place in the nomological net of neurophysiological descriptions" (ibid., p. 262). At this point it should be no more surprising that Feigl concludes his remarks with a rather singular prophecy – or wish:

> If in the utopian future of a complete neurophysiology children could be taught to use the appropriate neurophysiological terms on the basis of introspection, these terms would then have the same sort of emotive (pictorial, emotional, motivative) appeals that psychological words have in common language: and there would be the additional advantage of getting rid of the spurious dualism that is essentially linguistic. The incorporation of words which fulfill a phenomenal-introspective function into the total terminology of scientific explanatory terms could thus be achieved. (ibid., p. 260)

This passage, I believe, hardly requires comment. Anyone inclined to consider that the issues Feigl discusses pertain only to a rather rarefied and harmless sphere of problems must now think again. In these lines, in fact, a definite *linguistic and epistemological conception* is joined to a precise *practical* and even *political* orientation. What Feigl proposes is not merely a certain model of ideal language: it is also, though perhaps indirectly, a model of man and human society. This model tends to penalize psychological communication, considered to consist of unreliable subjective and emotional messages, and to give absolute value to the objective, rational communication of science. It also seems (at least implicitly) to mistrust what one might call a 'subjunctive' man, whose *modus loquendi* is 'imprecise' and multi-levelled, and to favor an 'indicative' sort of man, who speaks only in markedly referential and verifiable terms, going straight to the point without taking bewildering detours. One can scarcely help recalling, at this point, that only a few years earlier George Orwell had depicted, as one of the traits of the totalitarian state, the great care with which Big Brother imposed upon his world a language that was to be as concrete, univocal, and one-dimensional as possible.

But also apart from the possible political implications of certain positions there remains in Feigl the conviction that physicalistic (or more precisely, neurophysiological) language is the only reliable instrument for the cognitive analysis of man; and there remains the view that psychological language is merely "pictorial, emotional, motivational". These two positions underpin the no less reductive thesis that the psycho-subjective dimension *can* and *must* be completely reformulated in "appropriate neurophysiological terms". It is all too clear, then, that the approach Feigl champions does not enable us to 'tell' adequately the mental and subjective acquaintance *juxta sua principia*. What Feigl advocates is an epistemological and linguistic universe in which the dimension of the mind and of subjectivity, lacking an appropriate foundation and a space of its own, must be redefined and dissolved in 'another', neurophysiological and objective, dimension.

This conclusion is not only important in and of itself. It also leads us back to the problem of the twofold orientation in Feigl's thought ('ontological' and 'linguistic') with which our discussion began. It brings us back to this point only to show us that we are dealing in large part with a *pseudo-problem:* or at least that the *two* paths take us to *the same* destination. Just as the ontological orientation leads us to admit the existence of only *one* reality, the linguistic approach produces the same result. In fact, if the situation is as I have sought to present it, then the linguistic view also ends up with a *monistic* solution. Indeed, even for 'the linguistic' Feigl there is in any case only *one* reality *since there is only one cognitively legitimate way of 'telling' it.* More precisely, this way is *physicalistic:* therefore that reality is (and is only) *physical* – just as the 'ontological' Feigl had said.

A 'scientific' or a 'philosophic' solution to the MBP?

That Feigl was deeply sensitive to the claim that only *one* language exists for cognitively expressing human reality is evident from his return to this issue, in his *opus majus* of 1958. In this work he seems indeed to acknowledge that the primitive state of psychophysical knowledge means that a unitary language for talking scientifically about human experience is still "in the 'promissory note' stage" (MP, p. 469). But probing the question more deeply, Feigl reaches the conclusion that such a language *can* and *must* in any case be sought or invented. What is essential is that this search or invention be carried out exclusively within the sphere of *philosophy* (MP, p. 461).

It is only natural that this last thesis should raise some crucial questions: questions that at a more general level regard, in a sense, the whole of Feigl's thought. In short, is Feigl's investigation of the mental and its relationship with the physical 'scientific' or 'philosophic'? In other words, does it proceed in harmony with the (actual or *legitimately* foreseeable) indications of science, or is it based on considerations, hypotheses, and prospects which are essentially theoretical and speculative? An adequate answer to this question would take us too far from the issue at hand. Fortunately, Feigl himself raises and, at the same time, marks the limits of the issue under consideration. He does this by relating it to the so-called parallelistic solution to the MBP and to the possibility of going beyond this hypothesis and arriving at a solution in terms of identity.

It should not be surprising that a problem as delicate as that concerning the 'philosophic' or 'scientific' approach to the psychophysical relationship should emerge in connection with the 'parallelist' view. Indeed parallelism, at least in some of its versions, is one of the most sophisticated answers to the MBP. Broadly speaking, this view holds, on the one hand, that psychic phenomena and physiological phenomena can be conceived as conceptually autonomous and, on the other, that they are strictly interrelated, obeying conjointly definite rules. These rules, however, do not express causal constraints (of which we lack sufficiently generalized and rigorous evidence), but simply relations of simultaneity – or parallelism (relations which also make it possible, in certain contexts, to approach the two series of phenomena in relatively independent ways).

What is Feigl's position on parallelism? In his article on physicalism and the unity of science his critique is rather severe. This doctrine, he says, is disappointing. It is a position typical of "cautious philosophers and psychologists", who prefer to speak of mere "correlations" between the mental and the physical while suspending judgement not only on the nature of the two poles but also on the nature of their relationship ('Physicalism', pp. 262–3). Yet, in his 1958 essay his position seems to change, at least to a certain extent. Now he holds the parallelistic conception of the mind–body relationship to be "plausible". More precisely, he considers a parallelistic analysis of "some of the striking and remarkable features of mental life" *scientifically* feasible (MP, p. 461). And here we arrive at the point which interests us. The first question is the following: what validity does this acknowledgement have for Feigl? To what extent can the 'scientific' view proposed by parallelism be sufficient for his purposes? To this question there can only be one answer: this acknowledgement can only be of limited validity, and thus the parallelistic view alone cannot suffice. The reason is that Feigl was not interested so much in identifying (even 'scientifically') *certain correlations* between certain (psychic) phenomena and certain others (physiological), as he was in *generalizing* those results, in showing that these *correlations* are in reality *identities* of an asymmetrical nature (in the sense that 'mind (M) *is* body (B)', but not vice versa), and in concluding that they therefore not only *justify* but *require* an analysis in physical terms. At this point the second question which must be raised (and which Feigl does raise) is the following: how should we proceed in an investigation of the MBP in such a way as to achieve *these* objectives?

This is the point at which Feigl expresses his views concerning science and philosophy – and concerning the need to shift emphasis from the first to the second. He maintains that science – the *organon* of strictly empirical research – cannot take on any task other than that of investigating actually observable and analyzable data. It follows that a pure scientific examination of these data cannot lead beyond the solution outlined by parallelism. Empirically, in fact, what we perceive of our psychophysical states and events is only a given series of correlations that say nothing about the deep *reality* of the presumed M and B poles, or about the general *reality* of their relationships. Consequently, if and when we wish to assign to knowledge additional tasks referring to those realities we have to adopt *another* sort of inquiry. Not science but philosophy – the *organon* of *meta-empirical* generalizations, justifications, and interpretations – can and must complete the final phase of work on the MBP: that is, *the elaboration of a theory of the psychophysical relationship in the form of a general conception which posits the identity between the mental and the physical.* As Feigl himself stresses with extreme clarity, "The step from parallelism to the identity view is essentially a matter of *philosophical interpretation*" (1958, p. 461; italics mine). It is only to philosophy that we must turn when the MBP reveals the existence of an obviously meta-empirical question: the question of the striking differences between the "evidential bases" that underpin psycho-subjective phenomena on the one hand and neurophysiological phenomena on the other (MP, pp. 461–2). It is here that Feigl – Feigl the 'scientist' – shows that he unhesitatingly accepts the meta-scientific 'challenge'. It is here that philosophy is called upon to propose a solution to what is significantly called "the *philosophical* or logical crux of the identity thesis*" (MP, p. 461; italics mine).

How is philosophy to go about solving the problems Feigl poses? In two different ways, which I will call the *hermeneutic-eliminative* approach and the *hermeneutic-propositional* approach. In the first case, Feigl's (philosophical) objective is to show that the great distance which separates the universe of the psycho-subjective and the neurophysiological universe can be bridged through recourse, so to speak, to a 'partial' interpretation: an interpretation, that is, which aims at bringing the two universes together by *eliminating* all the traits that makes *one* of them (the psycho-subjective) different from the *other* (the neurophysiological), the latter being considered – on the basis of a meta-empirical, *philosophical* decision – the truer and more valid. This initial operation leads us to a conclusion we are already familiar with: Feigl claims (rather than 'demonstrates') that the psycho-subjective dimension is not – as is often held – an irreducibly private, a-spatial, qualitative, teleological reality, and that it can be better described in the interpersonal, 'spatial', quantitative, causal language natural to science. Consequently, from a cognitive point of view this dimension can be set in parentheses, or even eliminated.

As for the hermeneutic-propositional method, this is employed to bring to bear certain principles – once again, meta-empirical, *philosophical* principles – on other difficulties of the identity theory, or rather to give the theory a more sturdy underpinning. Indeed, it is Feigl himself who claims that an appropriate theory of identity must adopt (directly or indirectly) certain premises or general theoretical supports. These are the principle of parsimony, the principle of causality, and the monistic principle.

Feigl maintains the principle of parsimony, significantly, in the course of his discussion of the passage from 'scientific' parallelism to the 'philosophical' identity theory. Generally speaking, this principle holds that, all things being equal, it is preferable that a problem be solved with the smallest possible number of elements. As regards the MBP, Feigl's claim is that it is best to avoid duplicating "realities" when this is not necessary. This position clearly favors an identity solution to the problem, and Feigl himself considers the parsimony principle to be a pillar of monism (MP, p. 461). But it is equally clear (both to Feigl and to the reader) that the parsimony principle is not so much an objective-scientific as a philosophical-pragmatic criterion, and that it cannot be applied without being justified by the requirements of certain cognitive problems (a justification which Feigl does not provide adequately).

The causality principle is also mentioned in the same context, albeit indirectly. Feigl claims that the question of causality cannot be decided empirically: once again, a *philosophical* approach is required (MP, p. 464). The allusion to this crucial issue is indeed general and fleeting. And yet a direct connection between the causality principle, philosophically viewed, and Feigl's interpretation of the mind–body relationship is not difficult to find. On the one hand, Feigl's idea of an identity theory requires the replacement of the mere "correlations" proposed by parallelism by stronger, causal links. On the other, he considers this substitution (and the nomological generalization with which it is, or is yet to be, connected) the result more of a *philosophical option* than of *scientific evidence*. Both the principle and the substitution appear to be perfectly legitimate theoretically as well as, so to speak, operatively. We must only keep in mind that the solution is, as we said, *philosophical*. This awareness, however, in no way coincides with an even implicit condemnation of the option itself. Feigl even raises the question explicitly: is philosophy an invalid knowledge? And his answer is not at all. The philosophy proposed by the causally organized conception of the identity theory is anything but "otiose metaphysics" (ibid.). It is a *philosophical* conception, but it is not *bad* philosophy. On the contrary, it allows us to pose a crucial problem – and its solution – in an appropriate way.

The monistic principle, finally, appears to be the only view that supports the identity doctrine on a general level. This explains why, in many passages in Feigl's essay, monism is insistently linked with the identity theory. As to the nature of this principle, Feigl regularly defines it as a "philosophical" conception. Monism, that is, is not empirical but meta-empirical, not particular in application but general and systematic. Of course, from another point of view Feigl would like to build his whole theoretical credo on scientific foundations, but he is aware that only "the future development" of certain inquiries will reveal whether the identity assumptions underpinned by monism can be confirmed empirically (MP, p. 482). He is confident, however, of having adequately demonstrated that his "philosophical monism" is already at present "very plausible" also on scientific grounds (MP, p. 483).

Whether or not this confidence is justified is not essential at this point. What is more important is that in its final part *The 'Mental' and the 'Physical'* seems to lead in a direction which is decidedly more 'philosophical' than 'scientific', and it outlines not so much a balance of the empirical research already carried out on the MBP as the result of a certain philosophical *Weltanschauung*. All this could confirm, once again, that what mainly interests Feigl is not the 'objective', impartial search for an empirical solution to the MBP, but rather the interpretive, 'subjective' construction of a *particular* theoretical solution to that problem – a solution which aims at reinforcing an overall monistic, physicalistic, and causal conception.

In this connection we should recall that in his article 'Mind–Body: Not a Pseudo-Problem' (1960), published two years after his longer essay, Feigl reconfirms his explicitly *philosophical* orientation. The identity theory is "preferable" (a choice, then, which is to some extent pragmatic and not strictly scientific) in that it serves to "simplify our conception of the world" (in *Inquiries and Provocations*, p. 349). This theory gives us, moreover, "one reality" (another witness to Feigl's 'ontological' monism) represented by "two different conceptual systems" (but we know that the contents of one of the two are non-scientific and even non-cognitive, and that they can in principle be reformulated in the terms of the other). Feigl adds he would like to define this position as "metascientific", but he admits that others might even call it "metaphysical" (ibid.). And indeed, who could object to this definition and to what it implies from a theoretical point of view?

*Feigl's self-criticism: toward materialism
and radical 'substitutionism'*

But rather than linger over this article it seems more convenient to move on directly to the important 'Postscript after Ten Years' which Feigl appended to the new edition of *The 'Mental' and the 'Physical,'* published as a separate volume in 1967. Written, as the title indicates, a decade later, this text contains indeed a series of significant corrections and modifications.

The most moderate, though certainly not the least important, of these reconsiderations concerns the crucial question of phenomenal language. Feigl condemns his earlier tendency to consider phenomenal descriptions exclusively emotive (in 1958, we should recall, he had suggested they were "purely evocative"). His new thesis is that this language has a cognitive dimension and even produces truth claims ('Postscript', p. 149).

This position seems to be not only radically new but also quite significant, since it tends to attribute a rational and cognitive efficacy to psycho-subjective expressions. In reality, however, it marks a rather modest opening which is immediately emptied of meaning by Feigl's subsequent observations. Phenomenal language can certainly make truth claims: but it must be recognized that the "truths" they express cannot be confirmed by reliable criteria. But is it at least true that this language can produce some sort of knowledge? Well, yes and no. On closer examination, phenomenal descriptions represent nothing but "the extreme lower limit of cognition" (ibid.). Clearly, we are a long way from explicitly and substantially rehabilitating the immediate, psycho-subjective expression of human experience. Feigl remains a staunch supporter of the priority assigned by logical empiricism to objective scientific language. Not surprisingly, then, despite the 'opening' mentioned above, phenomenal language is elsewhere chased back into the sphere of pure sentiments, the sphere of what Feigl calls "warm familiarity" (ibid., p. 142). Feigl's recognition that it is impossible to eliminate, on a psycho-existential plane, the "aura" that this language possesses – the "colorful, 'Christmasy' pictorial and emotional" appeals of everyday language (ibid.) – frankly seems to be more the sign of an attitude split between opposing orientations than a genuine evolution in his theory.

Of considerably greater importance, on the contrary, is Feigl's criticism of no less than the very notion of identity. Doubts about this concept had already surfaced in the 1958 essay. But they must have grown significantly in the following years if Putnam could write in 1964 that Feigl himself had told him he had abandoned his "well-known 'identity theory' of the mind–body relation" (Putnam 1964, p. 69). This change in position is briefly explained in the 'Postscript'. Feigl states that he is definitively convinced that the identity theory (or practice), while valid for the natural sciences, can be extended to the MBP only if we conceive of psychology as a branch of biology (ibid., p. 141). Indeed, 'phenomenal' concepts (i.e., those relative to direct subjective experience) are too different from 'physical' concepts: consequently, "within the conceptual frame of theoretical natural science, genuinely phenomenal (raw feel) terms have no place" (ibid., p. 141; see pp. 143–4). It follows that we can, and must, no longer speak of an *identity* between phenomenal and physical concepts (ibid., p. 149): this is also true because nearly insurmountable problems arise in relation to Leibniz's law (ibid., p. 145).

But whoever thinks that Feigl's recognition of this irreducible difference is the first step toward the recognition of a relative autonomy of the mental (the phenomenal and the subjective) with respect to the physical is in for a bitter disappointment. In fact the rejection of identity in no sense 'opens' toward this autonomy. On the contrary, it leads the way to a not entirely unfamiliar strategy which is ultimately no kinder to the mental than the identity theory: the strategy of "replacement". The aim, writes Feigl, is to systematically "replace" the psychological and phenomenal concepts as expressed in everyday language with more rigorously precise ones drawn from neurophysiology and, eventually, microphysiology (ibid., p. 141). In other words, the "familiar phenomenal features of the world" as we know it in daily life have to be "replaced, transformed, supplanted by the more rigorous, consistent, and explanatorily more coherent and fruitful features of the world as represented by physical concepts" (ibid., p. 145). According to Feigl, these concepts – called "successor concepts", echoing Wilfrid Sellars, since they 'come after' the others (both theoretically and historically) – are "neutral": that is, free of the "emotional appeal" inherent in the concepts we use in our everyday life and speech (ibid., p. 146).

It would not be out of place, at this point, to make a few observations on Feigl's view of physicalism as expressed in 'Postscript Ten Years After'. "My *entire* discussion", Feigl writes significantly at the end of his essay, "is predicated upon the scientific acceptability of . . . physicalism" (ibid., p. 160; italics mine). Indeed, only a radicalization of the physicalistic interpretation of science (and of reality) could justify the universal 'replacementism' set out in the 'Postscript'. And this is precisely the road Feigl takes. Here too it would not be inappropriate to speak of a true self-criticism of his earlier positions. "I had hoped", writes Feigl, "that my own double-knowledge, double-designation view would yield what is wanted"

58

(ibid., p. 138). For a certain period, that is, he defended the existence of *two* types of knowledge, or at least of two approaches to, or descriptions of, reality. Later (see especially in the 1958 essay), his position on this question became more ambiguous. Now, any residue of doubt (though only latent or implicit) has been overcome. Feigl suggests that "'in principle' a *physical* description of the world is *complete*, i.e., leaves out *nothing*" (ibid., p. 138; italics mine). If it is true that phenomenal concepts are different from physical concepts, it is also true that it is possible to design a physical language capable of 'retelling' psychological and phenomenal language (by replacing it): "a good and complete physicalistic . . . account of the world will contain 'successor' concepts to *all* phenomenal concepts". And he adds: "in the scientific conception of the world, theories of perception, of learning, and of language . . . become the 'successors' to the phenomenological-epistemological account" of the world itself (ibid., p. 144).

Feigl's rallying to the defense of the most radical form of physicalism and his parallel conversion from identity to replacement theory prepare the terrain for what is probably his most striking reversal in the 'Postscript': his self-criticism concerning materialism. We have already pointed out Feigl's initial aversion to "crass materialists", whom he accused of being presumptuous and crude and of nonchalantly dismissing the mental (as well as, by extension, the mind–body problem).

> For many years I opposed materialism, holding that it is illegitimately reductionistic. . . . I felt that not only the radical behaviorists, but also the materialists somehow suppressed the "other perspective"; that they practiced what I called the "Hylas touch" – i.e., they turned whatever they touched into "matter" or physical events and processes. (ibid., pp. 144–5)

Now his assessment of materialism has indeed changed radically. The main reason for this change is that Feigl recognizes his error concerning the materialists' approach toward knowledge of reality. The materialists do not practice the "Hylas touch", after all: that is, they do not effectively engage in a sort of *a priori*, speculative reductionism. What they obey is not *speculation*, but *science*. Their attempt to derive the psycho-mental universe from the physical universe merely corresponds to what "the advancing sciences make increasingly plausible": that is, the real possibility of giving a complete physical account of the world (ibid., p. 142).

Feigl goes further. There is another reason which gives legitimacy to his new opinion on materialism. This reason is epistemological and concerns the logical-cognitive procedure followed by the materialists – more precisely, the procedure of "replacement". We must be careful, Feigl warns, not to confuse *replacement* with *elimination*. The materialists (now no longer called "crass", but "sophisticated" [ibid., p. 139]), as they progress in their task of replacing the concepts of phenomenal, subjective, everyday language, do not simply *abolish* them. On the contrary, they *include* them in a more "comprehensive conceptual system" (ibid., p. 145). The thesis is extremely challenging and ambitious. Feigl suggests that physical language is powerful enough to be able to reexpress, objectively and scientifically, *everything* that is said in phenomenal terms without sacrificing anything truly meaningful. The only thing that is eliminated is the subjective, emotional "aura" surrounding statements made in the phenomenal language.

But the point is, Is it really possible that physical language has such an all-embracing extension? Is it really possible to divide phenomenal language into a 'serious' semantic content – objective and translatable without residues into 'another' – and an emotional, subjective "aura"? Isn't it true, instead, that the 'objective' semantic content is instrinsically constituted *also* by the 'subjective' "aura"? If (to use one of Feigl's examples) I say to myself, "Now is the moment to make my decision", can I truly distinguish an 'objective' temporal and decisional core from what Feigl calls the "existential anguish" that accompanies my thought? And even if I were able to overcome the problems inherent in that task, wouldn't I lose something essential by eliminating the component of existential anguish (considered inexpressible in the scientific language)? Apart from the particular question of anguish, how could I, more generally, make a statement in the physical language capable of expressing all the desires and plans, the symbols and cultural conventions present in my utterance concerning the decision to make? Wouldn't it perhaps be more plausible to suppose that a language composed solely of physical (or neurophysiological) concepts is able to grasp only a part of the experience expressed in a phenomenal and subjective utterance?[1]

---

1. A partial reconsideration of certain pan-physicalistic ambitions, with particular reference to the Australian materialists, appears in Feigl's article 'Some Crucial Issues of Mind–Body Monism' (1971).

Chapter 2

The apogee of physicalism

*The identity theory and materialism
in the Australian school*

PLACE: THE NATURE OF
PSYCHOPHYSICAL IDENTITY

In the preceding chapter brief mention was made of the Australian school of materialists. It was noted that in the later works of Feigl, especially in the 'Postscript' published in 1967, considerable importance is given to the theories advanced by the exponents of this school. Indeed, Australian materialism plays an extremely significant, and aggressive role on the stage of contemporary thought on the MBP and no discussion of the issue can avoid a confrontation with the radical principles it defends. The Australian school, moreover, has the merit of pointing out the extent to which a seemingly 'technical' and circumscribed debate on the relationship between mind and body actually touches on problems far broader in scope: the nature of the mental, the properties of man's higher functions, the method and goals of 'true' science in relation to the psychoanthropological universe.

As Max Deutscher once wrote, the conception elaborated by the Australian school is "physicalism . . . in its most recent incarnation" (Deutscher [1964] 1967, p. 83). When and how did this "incarnation" come about? A firsthand account of the events runs something like this:[1] In 1955 U. T. Place held a series of lectures at the University of Adelaide in which he presented an identity solution to the MBP (or, more precisely, to a fairly restricted part of it). The initial reactions of philosophers like Smart and Martin,

---

1. A clear reconstruction of how the Australian school developed is presented in Presley 1967.

who were working on a theory of mind, were not favorable. Their approach to the mind–body relationship was at the time conditioned by Gilbert Ryle's interpretation of the mental and its functions as purely linguistic and conceptual notions. Thus, it seemed illegitimate to them to identify consciousness (as Place did, though cautiously) with some-*thing* called the 'mind'. The evolution of the reflection and debate on the MBP moved ahead rapidly. In 1957 Smart taught a course on Wittgenstein and Ryle at Princeton in which he argued for positions substantially similar to those of Place. In November of the same year, lecturing at Cornell, he explicitly expounded and defended Place's thesis. At the same time other Australian scholars were examining the validity of the identity solution to the MBP. Some, such as B. Medlin and M. C. Bradley, defended it, while others, including C. B. Martin, D. L. Gunner, P. Herbst, and M. Deutscher, found grounds for criticism. Notwithstanding the importance of the more critical positions defended by certain Australian philosophers, as of the late 1950s and the early 1960s the Australian debate on the MBP had taken a decisive turn toward the identity theory and materialism. The seminal document of this orientation is generally considered to be Place's article 'Is Consciousness a Brain Process?' (1956; rpt. in Borst 1979).

Place's theoretical aim is to show that it is a "reasonable scientific hypothesis" to identify consciousness with a definite brain process (ibid., p. 42). This hypothesis can be considered proven *if* it can be shown that nothing precludes this identification and that it is possible to explain "the subject's introspective observations by reference to the brain processes with which they are correlated" (ibid.). As we see, Place's formulation is quite prudent, and this prudence helps him to avoid overemphasizing the psychoanthropological content and implications of his inquiry, while lending greater weight (at least in a part of his essay) to an essentially logical and conceptual approach to the MBP.

This approach leads Place to carry out a very stimulating analysis of the concept of identity. There are two different versions of this concept that particularly attract his attention: i) *identity by definition* ('red is a color'); ii) *identity by composition* ('his table is an old packing case'). Quite evidently, there are considerable differences between the two types of identity. Whereas in the first case identity is true by necessity, in the second it is true only contingently, and has to be verified empirically. Furthermore, while in the first type of identity whatever is true for the first part of the assertion is also true for the second, in the second type this is not the case: I can maintain the identity between a table and a packing case without all predicates valid for tables necessarily being true for packing cases (ibid., pp. 44–5).

These distinctions are of no small account. They inject a new awareness into an old question: can it be said that consciousness *is* a brain process? Place's thesis is that the two entities share the same identity and that they are identical not by definition but by composition. This second point has at least two crucial consequences for the problem at hand: i) it is *not* legitimate to reject the assertion that consciousness is a brain process on the grounds that not everything that can be said about consciousness can also be said about brain processes; ii) just like the identity between a table and a packing case, so also the identity between mind and body is not analytical and necessary, but empirical, contingent, and factual. This means that the identity in question involves empirical facts, that verification of it must be made, at least in principle, by the experimental method; and that the terms of the relationship must be logically independent and connected to each other in a way that is not formal and necessary: thus their identity exists (or can be demonstrated), but could also not exist. The *demonstrandum* is that, not analytically but factually, the account of a state or act relative to the sentience, sapience, of selfhood of a person is identical with the account of a definite brain process.

PLACE: THE ONTOLOGICAL FALLACY

Place's analysis of the identity between consciousness and brain processes is just getting under way. Now it enters a field of particularly thorny problems. Once the nature of compositional identity has been established, he continues, one might object that, since the terms of the proposition 'consciousness is a brain process' are logically independent and connected not by necessity, it follows that their meanings could also not refer to the same *thing*: in other words, there could be two different things (ibid., p. 45). This 'move' on the part of dualists may appear ingenious, but for Place it is misguided. The confusion, argues Place, derives from an error of considerable consequence: the illegitimate passage from the concept of *logical independence* to that of *ontological existence*. In other words, the dualists are mistaken in believing that if two logically autonomous utterances exist, this implies that there are two autonomous ontological entities as well.

Place gives an enlightening example to support his position. Take a cloud. One can certainly say that a cloud is identical to a mass of water droplets. We are dealing, of course, with identity not by definition (necessary) but by composition (contingent). Indeed, in logical-linguistic terms nothing prevents us from identifying a cloud with a mass of fibrous tissue. And nothing prevents us, in the same terms, from identifying instead a cloud with one of the symbols it embodies in certain fairy tales and myths. This means that "there is no logical connection in our language between a cloud and a mass of tiny particles" and that the terms 'cloud' and 'mass of tiny particles in suspension' "mean quite different things" (ibid., p. 46). And yet we can surely not conclude *from this* that there must be two different things: the cloud and the droplets of water. That we are able to avoid this 'ontological slip', Place argues, derives from the fact that, despite the constant association cloud = droplets, we do not observe, or make statements about, the two phenomena *at the same time*. Indeed, if we were to perceive *simultaneously* both the cloud *and* the droplets of water (which are, moreover, *independent* concepts), we would be forced to conclude that these two independent and simultaneous things must be *different*. What happens instead is that *in one phase* we observe that a cloud is a cloud and *in another phase* we observe that it is a mass of water droplets. Seen from a distance, Place points out, a cloud is a cloud. From close up, when we are inside it, the same cloud appears as something quite different: it is no longer a cloud, but fog, a mass of water in suspension, and so forth. Consequently, we cannot conclude that the existence of two compositionally identical *terms* or *concepts* necessarily implies the existence of *two different things*.

Place is fully aware that the example of the cloud is not without its imperfections. But its purpose is merely to demonstrate what we might call the principle of *ontological fallacy*, to borrow a phrase used by Place himself in another context. Now, this principle appears to be applicable to the psychological question that concerns us. It suggests that in the relationship between consciousness and brain processes the logical-linguistic independence of the two concepts, along with the evident non-simultaneousness of their observation and verification, *does not* allow us to assert the *ontological existence* of consciousness and of a relative brain process.

Place's argument would be perhaps of little theoretical value if it stopped here: it would merely assert that, on the basis of certain premises, there is no foundation for the ontological-dualist position. The question, however, is how one can (or rather, *if* one can) take a step further and posit, affirmatively, the possibility and legitimacy of a monistic-physicalistic theory. This is the crucial issue that is faced in the second part of the article. Place proposes a clear, precise solution to the problem:

> We treat the two sets of observations [namely, the observations of consciousness and those of a brain process] as observations of the same event in those cases where the technical scientific observations set in the context of the appropriate body of scientific theory provide an immediate explanation of the observations made by the man in the street. (ibid., p. 48)

"In order to establish the identity of consciousness and certain processes in the brain", Place adds, "it would be necessary to show that the introspective observations reported by the subject can be accounted for in terms of processes which are known to have occurred in his brain" (ibid.).

These two passages are extremely significant. Here, in fact, two radically different forms of experience and knowledge meet and collide: on the one hand, the immediate, subjective, phenomenal reports provided by the individual; on the other, the mediated, objective, real accounts supplied by science. What comes out of this encounter? We shall see in due course that Place's conclusion is inspired by a strong physicalist conviction, and we shall see how he reaches it. And yet Place's conclusion is far from being inevitable. One could argue that it is by no means self-evident that subjective and phenomenal reports (about consciousness, etc.) can be formulated in objective and scientific terms; indeed, the opposite could be claimed: that is to say, it is not likely that subjective and phenomenal reports, and their corresponding language, can be accounted for in objective, scientific terms (i.e., reduced to, or translated into, those terms). Place, however, does not seem to be entirely aware of this. It is no coincidence that the position he adopts regarding these two forms of experience and knowledge (the subjective-phenomenal and the objective-scientific) clearly reveals the *philosophical* orientation that underlies his *scientific* research.

PLACE: THE PHENOMENAL FALLACY AND THE
REALISTIC AND PHYSICALISTIC ALTERNATIVE

Place's position concerning the two forms of experience and knowledge is centered on what he calls a criticism of the "phenomenological fallacy" (in Borst 1979, p. 48). He considers human beings to be potentially (but also *de facto*) victims of a dangerous phenomenological-idealistic illusion. This illusion rests on the notion that the universe of feelings and thoughts which lies within the realm of consciousness or the self is the first to be activated, is ontologically more coherent and guarantees greater cognitive reliability. In other words, first come our subjective patterns, and then come things conditioned by, or modelled on, our schemes. Place's reaction against this position is inspired by an explicit realist philosophy and takes on an extremely radical form:

> We begin by learning to recognize the real properties of
> things in our environment. . . .It is only after we have learned
> to describe the things in our environment that we learn to
> describe our consciousness of them. We describe our con-
> scious experience not in terms of the mythological 'phenome-
> nal properties' which are supposed to inhere in the
> mythological 'objects' in the mythological 'phenomenal field,'
> but by reference to the actual physical properties of the con-
> crete physical objects, events, and processes which normally
> . . . give rise to the sort of conscious experience which we are
> trying to describe. (ibid., p. 50)

This stand is very important for the issue at hand. Place's intuition is that in order to affirm the primacy of the physical, and the indentifiability of the mental with the physical, one must start by reducing the prominence and autonomy of – and, so to speak, devaluing the phenomenal and subjective side of – man. He is so certain of this that a crucial part of his article is devoted not directly and exclusively to the MBP, but to a reinterpretation of the phenomenal and the subjective. His main theses are essentially those expressed in the passage quoted above and can be summarized in the following general terms: a) the subjective is something that, as it were, comes after the objective events and processes of reality. It is something which does not create or add anything essential in relation to those events and processes; b) the phenomenal is only the most immediate and unreliable level of an experience, which in itself is solidly founded on the physical structure of reality.

If this is true, then not surprisingly realism and physicalism appear to be Place's most peculiar philosophical orientations: i) realism is viewed as the only interpretation of the world capable of establishing the correct relationship between things and phenomenal experiences (the former guide and model for the latter); ii) physicalism is taken as the theory emphasizing, more precisely, the primacy of the *physical* objects and properties – and, correlatively, the primacy of the propositions denoting these objects and properties according to the rules and norms of the language of the physical.

At this point, it seems that the MBP has been somewhat overshadowed in Place's discussion by issues of a higher order. Indeed, it has become little more than an epiphenomenon of a far more complex and radical problem: the reduction of both subjectivity and phenomenality (of which the mental is viewed as a part) to the objective and physical organization of reality (of which the body is viewed as an organic component). Place is convinced not only of the *possibility* but also of the *necessity* of this reduction: a necessity connected with the rigorous scientific goal that all scientific research is supposed to have. In Place's view, the aim of true science is, on the one hand, to give an account of the physical structure of reality and, on the other, to demonstrate that all subjective phenomena are in reality (or are at least translatable into) objective, physical data. The point is illustrated by a clear example. When I call an image "green", I should not suppose that I am describing *my* experience with *my own* means of expression in an effort to communicate this impression of mine in some personal way. What actually happens is something much more objective: something of which the subjective side (i.e., my personal experience and the language used to describe it) is, or can be made to become, irrelevant. In effect, I am simply saying, in this situation, that I am having "the sort of experience which we normally have when, and which we have learned to describe as, looking at a green patch of light" (ibid., p. 50). This is the process of removing the subject and physicalizing sense data that Place considers to be both possible and necessary.

A critic of the identity theory, put on the defensive, should counter that the *experienced, subjective meaning* of a sensation is something different from the event or the correlative *physical* assertion with which Place claims to describe the "whole" sensation. One could also object that the example illustrates, at best, how a simple micro-event – a sensation – can be identified with a particular neurophysiological process. We shall reserve for a later moment our discussion of the first objection. The second merely reminds us that many other phenomenal events may be so complex, so intertwined with subjectivity (which encompasses also culture, society, history), that they cannot be reduced to, and identified with, a physical fact as easily as a sensation can.

Place is hardly bothered by objections of this sort. The delicacy of the question seems merely to underscore the confidence with which he formulates his positions. It should be clear, he writes, that "the problem of explaining introspective observations in terms of brain processes is far from insuperable" (ibid., p. 50). Indeed, Place's argument for reduction and identification goes much further than the simple sensation. It can be applied to virtually the *whole* phenomenal and subjective dimension of the individual. "There is nothing", Place stresses, "that the introspecting subject says about his conscious experiences which is inconsistent with anything the physiologist might want to say about the brain processes which cause him to describe the environment and his consciousness of that environment in the way he does" (ibid., p. 51).

Let no one be misled by the apparent moderation of Place's position. If we link the passage just quoted with Place's claim that the physiologist should be able to reformulate the phenomenal observations and experience of "the man in the street", his ultimate message becomes all too clear. The whole universe of phenomenal, subjective experiences as well as their relative linguistic statements can and must be reduced (with the aid of a realist solution to the "phenomenological fallacy") to a neurophysiological structure and a physicalist use of language capable, respectively, of *naturalizing* and objectifying – and thus rendering *scientific* – that experience and its linguistic expression. Not unlike Feigl, Place begins with a formal recognition of the existence of the phenomenal and the subjective only to work out a conception that identifies both with the physical (an asymmetrical identity, what is more, since 'M is B' but it does not follow that 'B is M'). And not unlike Feigl, Place is careful not to leave room for a plurality of languages, and in particular not to grant adequate cognitive dignity to the language of phenomenal and subjective experience.

SMART: THE IDENTITY THEORY INTERPRETATION OF THE PSYCHOPHYSICAL RELATIONSHIP

Place was more the ground-breaker than the founding father of the Australian school of the identity theory. He published very little, was reluctant (aside from certain exceptions, as we have seen) to take a position on questions of a broader theoretical scope, and perhaps lacked the sort of personality that was needed as a reference point in the animated debate on the mental. But Smart was gifted with precisely this kind of personality. Professor for many years at the University of Adelaide, he wrote a number of important essays and a monograph that made a significant contribution to philosophical and scientific realism (Smart 1963). His truly epoch-making essay on the problems we are concerned with appeared in 1959 (references to this essay, as to the one by Place, are drawn from the reprint, edited by Borst 1979).

The very title of this essay, 'Sensations and Brain Processes,' hints at a kind of research with which we are already familiar. Just as Place had approached the MBP through the issue of consciousness alone, so Smart approaches it only through that of sensation. But this is, in a sense, only a part of the truth. In fact, it becomes quickly evident that what really interests Smart is a much broader and more challenging problem: the possibility of expressing sensorial and conscious experiences in physical and chemical terms, of using the same terms to provide an explanation of the human being, and, in short, of defining the entire world from a physicalistic perspective.

> It seems to me that science is increasingly giving us a viewpoint whereby organisms are able to be seen as physico-chemical mechanisms: it seems that even the behavior of man himself will one day be explicable in mechanistic terms.
> There does seem to be, as far as science is concerned, nothing in the world but increasingly complex arrangements of physical constituents. ('Sensations', p. 53)

Clearly, Smart's sights are set on a target lying far beyond the confines of the MBP as such.

Smart argues that the physicalistic view is not merely sufficient, but exclusive. Indeed, the very idea that one might employ non-physicalistic terms to describe sensations (the 'official' subject of his essay), when "everything should be explicable in terms of physics", he considers "frankly unbelievable" (ibid., p. 54). It might almost appear that Smart is on the verge of pronouncing the problem of the relationship between sensations and brain processes closed even before it is opened. But if this is the case, it is due not so much to some sort of philosophical impatience as to Smart's conviction that certain general assumptions are simply self-evident. He expounds them – in his own words – as a "confession of faith" (ibid.). Later in the essay he explicitly declares his allegiance to a "materialistic metaphysics" (ibid., p. 60): a daring statement indeed when used by a proud supporter of Science and empiricism, and an eloquent witness to the *meta-empirical* premises constituting the basis for his discussion of an (apparently) empirical problem. Smart's aim is to fit his observations on questions such as that concerning sensation and its relationship with certain brain processes into the more general framework of a suitably dramatic meta-problem, which revolves around the central issues of reality versus appearance, matter versus spirit, objectivity versus subjectivity, epistemic publicity versus experiential privacy.

As we have said, the subject of Smart's article is the nature of sensation and its relationship with definite neurophysiological events. His main thesis certainly cannot be faulted for ambiguity: "sensations are brain processes" (ibid., p. 56). Attempts have been made to deny the 'ontological' nature of Smart's theory, but they are hardly convincing. Even if, for the moment, we leave aside certain other aspects of Smart's thought, there is no question that his formal definition of sensation is ontological in nature: "sensations are nothing over and above brain processes". And again, "in so far as a sensation statement is a report of something, that something is in fact a brain process" (ibid., p. 56).

"In fact" simply means that Smart (like Place) conceives the relationship between the mental and the bodily as empirical and contingent, rather than analytic and formal. But Smart does not follow up on the theoretical implications of this point (that, for example, the relationship between sensations and brain processes could *in fact* be, or become, *something different* from what it has so far appeared visibly and constantly to be). His main 'message' continues to be physiological and proclaims a categorical refusal to accept any dimension of sensation that is not purely neurophysiological. One could object that, certainly, sensation is a brain process, but is it *only* a brain process? Is it really not possible to consider it from a

different point of view? Smart's answer is simply no; an answer
that precludes a *priori* any other approach (phenomenological, e.g.)
to sensation itself.

This same position emerges in the course of Smart's discussion
of the concept of identity. Although he properly distinguishes between identity in a 'broad' or 'weak' sense and "strict" identity,
this distinction is not applied convincingly. Indeed, Smart's point
of departure is already determined by his "faith" in the *strict* identity between sensation and brain process. In strict identity, what is
more, the predicate says *objectively* and *univocally* what the subject
is: it expresses ontologically "the true nature" of the *thing* being
examined (ibid., p. 57). Thus, just as in the statement 'lightning is
an electrical discharge', the predicate denotes (for Smart, necessarily and invariably) *the nature* of lightning, so in the statement 'sensation is a brain process' the predicate denotes *the nature* – unique
and invariable – of sensation. Clearly, the *ontological* perspective
reinforces the *physicalistic* perspective of Smart's conception: the
neurocerebral definition of sensation is not the result of a cognitive
analysis (as opposed to other *equally legitimate* analyses): it is *the
only* definition that a form of knowledge able to grasp the essence
of things can arrive at. Smart's ontological realism virtually closes
out any hermeneutic alternative. The science founded on this realism is indifferent to the changing cognitive interests of the subject:
it is able to, and required to, give an account exclusively of what
reality is like *a parti objecti*. Moreover, this ontological realism does
not permit, or at least discourages, an analysis of the possible *plural*
meanings of the *singular* thing examined. Indeed, a *distinction* between the thing and its meanings, while not excluded *de jure,* is
excluded *de facto.* In analyzing *the thing,* realist/ontological thought
ultimately designates *its basic meaning.* Any hypothetical *other*
meaning would be *unscientific* (as it would result from another procedure than *the one* procedure which is scientific) and *non-objective*
(the result of the arbitrary, and thus unscientific, action of the subject).

In discussing his example of lightning, Smart gives a clarification
which in reality only serves to underline the reductionist and physiologistic nature of his position. He points out that he speaks of
lightning as a physical object, not as a sense datum (ibid., p. 58).
Certainly, the distinction may be valid. Yet, what Smart does not
seem to understand is that *a sense datum is also 'something':* it is a
psychic experience that we can legitimately – at least sometimes –

71

aspire to understand psychically (not physically), following procedures and with results that are *cognitive,* autonomous, and not subordinate to other ways of knowing. Smart seems so unaware of this that he can view a sense datum as *only* "a brain state *caused* by lightning" (ibid.). What we call into question here, as elsewhere, is not so much whether it is possible to explain a sense datum in *that* way, as whether this can be the *only* way (and it would be the only way since sense data, for Smart, have no components that are not strictly physiological).

SMART: SUBJECTIVE SENSATIONS AND
TOPIC-NEUTRAL LANGUAGE

Smart, then, proposes a straightforward solution to the MBP: sensations are to be considered 'strictly' identical with definite neurophysiological processes. However, the adversary of the identity theory, Smart recognizes, could raise another intriguing hypothesis. Even supposing that the *objective reality* of a sensation is as described, it remains that certain of its properties might be different: that is, they could exist "over and above" the brain processes (in Borst, 1979, p. 59). For Smart, this is indeed a thorny problem: if these qualities did exist autonomously, the conclusion that the psychic (or its science) is not completely reducible to the neurophysiological would appear to be unavoidable. The problem becomes even more difficult when properties (at least certain properties) are viewed as the *qualitative and subjective ways* in which individuals perceive events. In fact, the admission of these properties seems to imply the existence of a subjective dimension of human experience: a dimension independent of its objective (physical) correlates. It is no coincidence that others who picked up on the substance–correlate–property distinction (if only to substitute an identity between 'things' with a 'property-identity') moved in just that direction (see Chapter 6).

Smart, however, follows another path. A convinced realist and physicalist, he has no intention of calling into question the privileged ontological status of events by admitting that there might be *another* dimension. While not entirely denying the existence of properties and qualities, he simply claims that these properties and qualities, even in the 'subjective' sense indicated above (namely, as personal modes of sensory experience), can be reduced to mere

72

objective, observable, rule-governed data. Smart's well-known example of the yellowish-orange after-image sums up his position in
a nutshell:

> When a person says, 'I see a yellowish-orange after-image,'
> he is saying something like this: "There is something going
> on which is like what is going on when I have my eyes
> open, am awake, and there is an orange illuminated in good
> light in front of me, that is, when I really see an orange".
> (ibid., p. 60)

The sense of what Smart is after here will not escape the reader.
What he proposes to do is to neutralize, in some way, the qualitative and subjective content of certain properties. His aim, in effect, is to 'de-subjectify' and 'de-qualify' those properties. In this
way, the so-called phenomenological properties of a visual micro-
experience can be bracketed off or, even better, translated into
something else. Into what? Smart is quite clear on this point. In
place of *qualitatively* and *subjectively* connoted properties, we
would have an account of the *objective* events which are alone responsible for the manifestation of those qualities. This operation
can be carried out rigorously, according to Smart, thanks to the
use of what he calls, following Ryle, a "topic-neutral" language
(ibid., p. 60).

Topic-neutral language is a means of expression that is considered capable of translating assertions of quality and statements on
given phenomenological events into an account that represents the
'state of things' in its naked, objective essence, without assuming
any further ontological commitment. In other words, this language
on the one hand lists only the purely factual properties of phenomena, and on the other does not say if they belong to one or another
sphere of being (e.g., if they are 'bodily' or 'psychic'). The implications of this thesis for the philosophy of mind are immediately
evident. Smart's assumption is that the universe of so-called mental
events can be described using a language that eliminates, or rather
'replaces', a certain component of that universe by translating its
substance into more appropriate, rigorous expressions. Thus, for
example, to say adequately that a man suffers does not in the least
imply, for Smart, admitting the existence of particular phenomenal
and subjective qualities or experiences. It only implies the recognition that *"there is pain"*. In the suffering man, as Keith Campbell
has written, there simply exists "a certain state, which arises from

his sensory system and emerges in certain models of behavior" (Campbell 1967, p. 185).

Smart's conception is open to criticism on more than one point. Here, it will suffice to raise two objections that seem particularly important for the present discussion. In essence, the strategy of 'translation' and 'replacement' rests on two undemonstrated assumptions: a) that subjective and qualitative properties can preserve and reveal their inner core, without significant loss, when reformulated in topic-neutral language; b) that it is reasonable to admit something like a topic-neutral language, capable of expressing things 'as they objectively are', and yet devoid of any subjective features and ontological pre-judgements.

On the first point, it has been observed that sensation as Smart describes it is purely and simply a *physical* event: an event that requires *sine qua non* the list of facts indicated in the quotation above. But does it make sense (say, in the fields of psychology or anthropology) to speak about an event like a sensation *only* in this way? Is it not more reasonable to say that the real, phenomenological sensation, far from being the result *only* of "good light" and "open eyes", is *constitutionally* made up *also* of those *subjective* and *qualitative* connotations that Smart seeks to eliminate? Ultimately, Smart's thesis is unacceptable even in its most basic form: *a (generic) 'yellowish-orange sensation' is not my (specific) 'sensation-of-orange'*. This is all the more true for those who, in their inventory of necessary and sufficient preconditions for the production of the *specific* sensation, lack the pre-understanding of what an orange is. If someone has a "yellowish-orange after-image" without knowing what oranges are, his sensation will be the same as that of someone who perceives oranges in exclusively *neurophysical terms*. But in these terms *oranges are not oranges:* they are at most yellowish-orange after-images. From a *psychological* point of view, on the other hand, which considers a particular perception event in terms of its actual phenomenological constitution, what was initially the same sensation would be considered more complex, and *different*. In fact, the (real) sensation of an orange is never *solely* a "yellowish-orange after-image". The topic-neutral language that in whatever way sought to 'translate' or eliminate my sensation's subjective and qualitative components would transform my *real* sensation into an *abstract* sensation, that is, into an unreal zero-degree (or almost zero) sensory pattern.

The notion of topic-neutral language is clearly a residue of the old neopositivistic and physicalistic belief in a means of expression capable of freeing itself of all theoretical and ontological implications and of any relationship with what it designates. Much of contemporary epistemology and language philosophy has debunked this model, or at least many of its claims. Every statement is theory-laden. Every statement prefigures the *designandum* in its *own way*. In a sense, even Smart's list of the 'objective' data necessary and sufficient to produce a sensation really presents an *individual* interpretation of sensation itself. In Smart's case, this interpretation is physiologistic and, despite his defense of a supposed ontological neutrality, far from neutral. Indeed, it rests on a very definite point of view, while more or less tacitly excluding every other interpretation that could be given simply by changing the conceptual framework in which it is defined.

It is now time to point out more precisely the kind of interpretation of the sensation (and more generally of the mental life as a whole) provided by Smart. We could term this interpretation as physiologistic. In fact Smart, in his discussion of psychic functions and phenomena, does not limit himself to rejecting *a priori* every reference to non-material experiences and figures. He also considers it possible and necessary to base apparently psychic functions and phenomena on physiological structures. In psychology, Smart writes in his *Philosophy and Scientific Realism* (1963b), one must reject any form of "phenomenism" or anthropocentrism and strive to reach a 'lower' level: "the neuronal level or even below it" (ibid., p. 62). This dual choice is unavoidable since, as Smart observed in an article published in the same year, "the internal goings-on . . . are brain processes" ('Materialism', 1963a, in Borst 1979, p. 164, italics mine). "What is important in *psychology*", he writes, "is what goes on in the *central nervous system*" (ibid., p. 167; italics mine). In discussing the concept of topic-neutral language, Campbell points out quite rightly that Smart's refusal to take a position, linguistically, on the *nature* of certain phenomena follows a line of reasoning which is *de facto* extremely committed in ontological terms – ontological terms which ultimately reflect a *physiologistic* ontology (Campbell 1967, p. 185). If it is true (to come back to an example we used before) that for Smart the statement 'a man suffers' does not imply an interpretation of pain that is *in any sense* metaphysical, Smart himself interprets pain as – and *solely* as – "a state of the central nervous system of his organism". It must be admitted that it is not easy to claim that the promises made by the theory of topic-neutral language are perfectly congruent with such an explicitly ontological position.[2]

SMART: PRIVATE EXPERIENCE AND ''COLORLESS WORDS''

The criticism we have leveled against Smart's theory brings us back to a question we have already raised: Smart's apparently circumscribed treatment of the MBP often seems to serve as a backdrop to problems of a much vaster range. Crucial epistemological issues are raised and positions advanced that might be called psycho-anthopological. In this regard, it should be emphasized (or repeated) that high on Smart's agenda is *the systematic elimination or 'substitution' of the subjective dimension.* The science of the mental (and of the human in general) is worthy of its name only insofar as it can claim to be a science of *objective* facts and relationships – and so much the better if this objectivity turns out to be in some way synonymous with a 'materiality' that can be analyzed in exclusively physical terms.

As evidence that this is one of his principal objectives, one could cite Smart's critique of so-called private experiences and how they are expressed. In answer to the objection that private experiences can hardly be voiced using a public medium, Smart takes a highly significant stance on the (subjective) *modus loquendi* one adopts when speaking of a strictly subjective experience. This *modus loquendi* undoubtedly exists and has some very common and apparently unproblematic expressions, like 'it seems to me that...' and 'I feel that...'. But for Smart, as a way of talking about things, it is inappropriate and imprecise. Indeed, it is an ''uninhibited'', impressionistic, reprehensible way of expressing oneself. It is just such subjective, spontaneous reactions, Smart adds, that ''one normally suppresses because one has learned that in the prevailing circumstances they are unlikely to provide a good indication of the state of the environment'' ('Sensations', in Borst, 1979, p. 64).

What is striking here is not only the curiously quasi-moralistic attitude of censorious disapproval that Smart adopts toward ''un-

2. The most important critics of the theory of topic-neutral language (and of Smart's positions in general) are Beloff 1965, Rollins 1967, Bernstein 1968, and Cooper 1970.

inhibited" speech. Even more, it is the reduction of subjective expressions to mere para-behavioral "reactions": almost as though an individual's phenomenal and subjective statements could not rise above the level of instinct. But one is also struck by the unambiguous call for the repression and even elimination, once again, of subjective expressions as a whole: "normally" (an adverb dear to those behaviorists who give preeminence to the *abstract average* of 'normal' cases over the concrete experiences of *real individuals*) these expressions can be "suppressed" (ibid., p. 64).

All this, finally, is justified in the light of a metacriterion of efficiency. Smart supposes that a speaker's goal cannot be but to provide "a good indication" of the state of things, that is, of the environment or of the 'world' (ibid.). There is considerable room for discussion here on the concept of a 'good indication' (Good *for whom?* Or is there some sort of objective, self-evident 'goodness'?). And one might well ask whether it is really so certain that in describing a situation a 'subjective' statement necessarily starts out with a handicap with respect to 'objective' statements. Indeed, this position would seem prejudicially to assign greater value to physical, natural situations (often more accurately describable in 'objective' terms) than to those we might call psychosocial (certain aspects and meanings of which may be better rendered by subjective statements). But questions such as these are not to the point for a scholar who, like Smart, *has already decided* not only that objective descriptions enjoy cognitive priority in any circumstance, but even that, in the final analysis, *"there is no language of private qualities"* (ibid., p. 65; italics mine).

Smart argues, for example, that "to say that something *looks* green *to me* [subjective statement] is simply to say that my experience is like the experience I get [and, for Smart, normally everyone gets] when I see something that really is green [objective description]" (ibid., p. 64; italics mine). This identification, however, is (or can often be) illegitimate. It is not necessarily true that *my subjective* experience of green is *completely* equivalent to the *normal, objective* experiences people have when they see things that are "really green". In fact, not all experiences that are *similar* are actually *identical*. It is this dissimilarity between apparently analogous different experiences that makes room for the subjective dimension. It is precisely *my subjective* experience of a certain shade of green that, while part of a *relatively* known and objective experience structure, *qualifies* that *specific* experience and makes it *mine* and *subjective*. Unless, of course, Smart – who is talking about *experiences* here, not *perceptions*, or much less *physical facts* – intends to discuss the perception of green in its *strictly physical* dimension. This might be possible: but in that case it would be a question for the physicist and physiologist, not for the psychologist, whose object of study is not so much physical systems as individual people, not so much physical *facts* as psychic *experiences*.

Elsewhere Smart stresses his preference for what he calls, significantly, "colorless words" (ibid., p. 65). His dream is that one day there will be a whole colorless linguistic system. In this connection, another of Smart's illustrations comes to mind: the suggestion that it might be possible to describe a certain situation by saying 'there is someone in the room' and leaving unsaid *who* it is. This is certainly a topic-neutral, colorless way of describing a situation. The problem is whether a statement of this sort, which clearly contains a minimum amount of information, transmits the, as it were, indispensable messages about the situation. Let's say, for example, that 'someone' was a doctor, and I had been anxiously waiting for him. How can it be said, then, that certain information can be eliminated without compromising the description of the *true, objective* state of things?

To conclude, Smart proposes a strategy that is forced to pay a high price to reach its goal. Feigl at least allowed that direct experience and subjective language had an evocative value and even a (modest) cognitive meaning. For him the 'colorful' words had, if nothing else, a 'warm familiarity' that was difficult to do without. There appears to be none of this in Smart. He radicalizes the situation to the point of *inhibiting* the individual from employing subjective language and from expressing private experiences while imposing on him an exclusively objective, descriptive usage. And this is the only usage that appears to be functioning according to Smart's physicalistic theory of man, language, and knowledge.

SMART: MATERIALISM AS A ''CONFESSION
OF FAITH'' AND THE INTERPRETATION
OF THE HUMAN

There can be no question that Smart's thought rests firmly on the foundations of materialism. In Smart's view, materialism *is science* – and science is the reservoir that so often provides decisive empirical support for some more general theory. And yet, we might ask, what is the relationship between the two terms? In other words, to what extent is Smart's materialism underpinned by scientific knowledge? The disconcerting answer, given the ambitious claims of Smart's argument, is that this support is minimal. Indeed, at more than one crucial point in his discussion materialism is defended *independently* of scientific knowledge and advocated for reasons that are not really scientific. We have already noted that, at the beginning of his essay, Smart describes his adherence to materialism as a "confession of faith" ('Sensations', in Borst 1979, p. 54). The question reappears at the end of the article as well. Two points are made. The first is that there is no "conceivable experiment" that could decide the issue for materialism (ibid., p. 65). The second is that the only two arguments that favor a monistic and materialistic solution to the MBP are that this solution follows "the principles of parsimony and simplicity" (ibid., p. 66).

This is hardly a satisfying conclusion. It is disappointing to find that Smart's principles are clearly more pragmatic than truly cognitive (a 'simple and parsimonious' interpretation of psychophysical reality may be *useful* – and perhaps even 'elegant'; but by themselves simplicity and parsimony can scarcely guarantee the *validity* of a given conception). It is, moreover, quite disconcerting to discover that Smart's confident, peremptory tone is based not on conclusive *proof*, and much less on *facts* (Smart even admits that both the identity theory and dualism "are equally consistent with the facts"; ibid., p. 66), but merely on the need for a 'parsimonious' cognitive construct. But what if the nature of psychophysical reality, or rather certain cognitive interests bound to that reality, suggested that parsimony was not the most reasonable and productive approach to that reality? The conclusion would appear to be that Smart's materialism is not so much the (empirically verified) *answer* to a definite scientific problem, as the *premise* for a certain *philosophical* conception, which makes room *also* for the MBP. Ultimately, it seems that Smart focuses his attention more on the question of materialism than on the MBP. The latter is merely an illustrative case study (albeit marred by theoretical inconsistencies and by a shortage of supporting "facts") that serves to confirm Smart's materialist creed.

Not surprisingly, Smart's next important article is devoted not to the MBP but to materialism. Published in 1963, the same year as his book *Philosophy and Scientific Realism*, this essay is particularly sig-

nificant as a witness to Smart's ultimate concern with psychoanthropology (in the broadest sense). It shows, that is, that Smart
regards the debate on the relationship between the mental and the
physical as a sort of prelude to the more general and fundamental
issue of human beings and the science that studies them.

For Smart, materialism generally tends to coincide with physicalism: it admits "nothing in the world over and above those entities which are postulated by physics" ('Materialism', in Borst 1979,
p. 159). No exceptions are allowed: not even those accepted and
justified by emergentism. Smart was well aware of the lively debate
on emergence theories in the early 1960s. But the presentation of
his theory is not so much guided by circumspection and caution,
as it is launched with a certain ideological militancy: "I am concerned to deny that in the world there are non-physical entities and
non-physical laws" (ibid., p. 160).

Clearly, a philosopher of mind like Smart finds a direct, explicit
application of this materialism to the MBP as well as to the field of
psychology in general: "In particular, I wish to deny the doctrine
of psycho-physical dualism" (ibid.). A statement as broad as this
(directed against *one particular* anti-identity version of the MBP)
could still leave room for debate on the question of the status of
mental phenomena – since in addition to identity theory monism
and neo-Cartesian dualism *tertium datur* (as we will have occasion
to see later). But Smart dispels any illusions in this sense. Just to
give an example, on the question of a *lato sensu* mental state like
love he does not hesitate to claim that "it can be analyzed as a
pattern of bodily behavior or, perhaps better, as the internal state
of the human organism that accounts for this behavior" (ibid.).

It cannot be emphasized enough that the appropriate reply to a
declaration of this sort consists not so much in denying the existence of a physical component of a state like love, or in denying
that in order to respond to certain cognitive interests (those of the
biochemist, e.g.) one can and must opt for a purely physical approach to the phenomenon of love. The proper reply consists,
rather, in insisting on the existence of *other* cognitive interests tied
to love; that in order to answer one may legitimately work out
different analytical strategies capable of highlighting *other* aspects of
the phenomenon 'love' – these too, we must stress, of *cognitive* (not
merely emotive or impressionistic) relevance.

Coming back to Smart, we should add that his discussion of materialism touches on another important mental state: pain. "What

is going on in me", Smart says about pain, "is like what goes on in me when I groan, yelp, etc." (ibid., p. 162). It may be worth repeating here that attempts to 'translate' personal accounts of subjective experience into impersonal statements (whether using topic-neutral language or not) can only give unsatisfactory and insufficient results. This quote is also further proof of Smart's heavy debt to orthodox behaviorism: pain can only be ascertained and defined if it is physically and ostensively manifested in behavior. Naturally, the anti-behaviorist will reply that pain is *not* solely a physical fact, and that it is not necessarily accompanied by (much less coincident with) sensorially perceptible manifestations like groans and whimpers. Nothing could be more wrong than to suppose that suffering is always visible and audible. As for the emphasis on the physical, objective, and public dimension of pain over its phenomenal, subjective, and private side, this should not surprise us too much since Smart, following up on Place's discussion of the phenomenological fallacy, declares quite clearly that "our talk about immediate experiences is derivative from our language of physical objects" (ibid.).

Smart's next discussion of abstractions also has a para-behaviorist flavor. The existence of something like 'pain' *an sich* (Smart's 'achiness') is rejected out of hand. The individual does not possess a 'form', a *Gestalt*, a psychocultural preconception of what pain is which might help him identify and define actual pains. No, for Smart the individual can only a) record *what* happens to him and report (translate) it in topic-neutral language; b) link this with analogous events and/or processes; c) construct a *class* (in the epistemic-formal sense) – "and this class of processes constitutes the aches" (ibid., p. 163). From the cognitive and anthropological point of view this approach a) makes pain a mere *fact*; b) presupposes that pains are relatively alike – enough, that is, to constitute a class (which could be the case, but only on certain levels – i.e., physical – *never*, however at the psycho-existential level); c) erases the whole *subjective* dimension of pain (yet the *way* pain is experienced by A and B is phenomenologically relevant, or rather crucial – since *the same* [in the physical sense] pain can be felt *differently* by two *physically identical* but *culturally and emotionally different* subjects).

Given all this, it is not surprising that on a general theoretical level Smart reaffirms his earlier position in univocal terms: "the internal [psychic] goings-on in question are brain processes" (ibid., p. 164). The statement, we might note, is highly ontological, heavily

81

committed to the materialist cause, and, consequently, hardly topic-neutral. It is almost superfluous to add that the treatment of psychic events as brain processes leads naturally to the drastic elimination of psychology as a *human* science: "what is important in psychology", Smart writes, "is what goes on in the central nervous system" (ibid., p. 167). No room is left for any other way to investigate the human sphere. One can hardly expect Smart to imagine a truly alternative approach to the mental, to think of the mental, that is, not as a 'thing', but as a 'figure', as a conceptual construct that may be useful to give expression and emphasis to certain parts of human experience which resist being reduced to physical terms (culture, norms, symbols). Smart, the intransigent naturalist and realist, takes into consideration only *facts* – physical, natural facts. Consequently, he is convinced that it is possible to exclude the existence of a mental sphere with arguments such as the following: "How could a non-physical property or entity suddenly arise in the course of animal evolution? . . . What sort of chemical process could lead to the springing into existence of *something* non-physical?" (ibid., pp. 168–9). Clearly, the question has no answer since it itself is badly put. What the adversaries of the identity theory are talking about, in fact, is not "some*thing* that is non-physical". The point is that there exist not only 'things' but also 'ways', 'rules', 'values', 'ideologies'; it is these ways, rules, values, and ideologies that constitute the referents – not given as *things* – for certain cognitive interests within the philosophy of mind.

We will come back to all this in due time. Suffice it to add for the moment that Smart concludes *Materialism*, much as he did in *Sensations and Brain Processes*, on a twofold note of uncertainty and authority. No epistemological overconfidence is sufficient to close Smart's eyes completely to the difficulties surrounding a monistic/materialistic solution to the MBP. We must recognize, he says, that it is impossible "to reconcile *all* of ordinary language with a materialist metaphysics" (ibid., p. 169). In other words, Smart admits – though without clarifying in what sense and why – the existence of a linguistic dimension (corresponding to a precise experiential dimension) which resists translation into physicalistic terms. Yet, this admission does not prevent him from claiming that "the attempt to reconcile the hard core of ordinary language with materialism is worthwhile" (ibid.). Here speaks the voice of authority. On the one hand Smart recognizes that the arguments in support of the overwhelming dominance of materialism are in some respects inadequate and imperfect. On the other, he *wants* to defend the materialist cause despite everything. So, faced with the impossibility of presenting *conclusive* proof of the validity of materialism, he draws on a *pragmatic, subjective* argument: the materialist cause appears to be at least "worthwhile".[3]

SMART: THE MATERIALIST PERSPECTIVE AND THE RELATIONSHIP BETWEEN MIND AND MACHINE

Smart's militancy – not only theoretical and scientific but also pragmatic and ethical – in the ranks of the materialists is based on strong motives and inspired by clear goals. He is convinced that this is the decisive battle for contemporary thought. He also feels that philosophy (i.e., materialist philosophy) can contribute to the acceleration of an identifiable process involving contemporary intellectual endeavor as a whole, and psychoanthropology in particular. In other words, only materialists are in a position both to impose a certain world view and give credibility to a certain image of man. Part of Smart's *Philosophy and Scientific Realism* is devoted precisely to achieving this twofold aim. At this point in our discussion, we will limit our comments to Smart's treatment of the psychic and human spheres and the science that studies them. Within this context, Smart has some extremely interesting things to say that touch upon important current issues, such as the relationship between man and machine and what robots are actually capable of doing (or what they will be capable of doing in some unspecified future).

Smart opens with a merciless representation of psychology. In the course of even its most recent history, he says, this science – so essential to a complete understanding of man – has committed several cardinal errors. The myth of introspection and many other "wrong ideas about methodology" have significantly slowed down progress. In its behaviorist phase, the emphasis on the stimulus–response relationship proved to be unilateral and misleading, and the stubborn insistence of many scholars on working "at the

---

3. In an article published a few years earlier, Place took a different position, arguing that materialism "should be treated as a straightforward scientific hypothesis" (in Borst 1979, p. 86).

molar level" of human behavior has made things even worse (*Philosophy*, pp. 161–2). Now the time has come to bring about some radical changes in theory – the first step toward the birth of a truly scientific psychology. These changes can be summarized in the following three points, or rather imperatives: a) psychology is and must be considered a *biological* science; b) it must pass from the *molar* to the *molecular* level; c) more generally, psychic phenomena – and human phenomena in general – must be studied in the same way that science studies any other natural phenomenon (ibid., pp. 62–3).

Smart is well aware that the resistance of many thinkers to this "physicalistic" interpretation of psychology is linked to the idea that there are certain aspects of the psychic and the human that cannot be reduced completely to natural facts. For this reason he devotes some central pages of his essay to an ideal research program based on hyper-materialist principles. We will limit our comments to the theses that develop the position Smart presented in his earlier articles.

This first thesis addresses the problem of the so-called secondary qualities. The question may have been cause of considerable concern to philosophical and scientific thinkers over the past three centuries, but for Smart it is quite straightforward. Secondary qualities must be taken out of the subjective and introspective context in which they have been left far too long, and put back into a realist, physicalist framework, the only one capable of grasping their true nature. Above all, they must be analyzed "in terms of the reactions of organisms (in particular, human beings) to stimuli" (ibid., p. 64). It might be surprising that Smart returns to such a typically behaviorist motif. But it is more interesting to note that this interpretation of secondary qualities is explicitly linked with what he presents as the central conception of his book: the idea that all living organisms (including human beings) "are simply very complicated physico-chemical mechanisms" (ibid., p. 65).

What are the possible implications of this view of secondary qualities? Of the many we might mention, let's begin with the following: that the terminology used to name and organize these qualities will have to be radically changed – in the direction of "science". Perfectly in line with Feigl and with his own two earlier articles, Smart advocates a systematic 'de-subjectification' and a corresponding 'objectification' and 'naturalization' of human language. Why, for instance, should we continue to say, "This is a nice smell"? The expression is subjective, private, and imprecise. Wouldn't it be better to say, "This is the smell of jasmine"? The objectivity tf the latter statement would guarantee that it could be both understood interpersonally and verified scientifically (ibid., p. 65). In the same vein, not only on sentience but also on consciousness Smart advances some very bold theses: "conscious experiences are simply brain processes" (ibid., p. 88). Later he says: "If consciousness is a brain process, then presumably it could also be an electronic process" (ibid., p. 106). The first observation to make here concerns, once again, the unambiguously ontological nature of Smart's conception. If Feigl oscillates between an 'objective' and a linguistic perspective, and if Place takes into consideration, at least in principle, different ways of affirming identity, doubts such as these are essentially absent in Smart: "conscious experiences *are simply* brain processes" (ibid., p. 88; italics mine). The adverb, so reductive and peremptory, not only reinforces the ontological statement, but it also implicitly advances what Donald Hebb has called the 'nothing but' principle (or fallacy) in psychology (Hebb 1980). Smart does not only say that conscious experiences *are* brain processes; he claims that they cannot be anything else but brain processes. The significance of this thesis for the physicalist program becomes all too clear when linked to another of Smart's more demanding positions (also based on the 'nothing but' principle), this time on the brain: "I shall be concerned to argue for the plausibility of the view that the human brain is no more than a physical medium, that no vitalistic or purely psychical entities of laws are needed to account for its operations" (ibid., pp. 8–9).

It is at this point in his argument that Smart proposes one of his most radical theses: that on the relationship between mind and machine. The ground is prepared in the passage quoted above, which suggested that consciousness could presumably also be an electronic process. No tentative modal, no cautious adverb tempers Smart's blunt affirmation of the principle he stands by. The principle is, quite simply, that the mind, or rather man himself as a thinking and acting being, *is a machine.* After all, once the basic principles of physicalism have been established and consciousness identified with a brain process, what should hold us back from accepting the total identification between man and machine? In particular, "is there any reason why a machine should not have the sort of purposefulness, appropriateness, and adaptiveness that is characteristic of human beings?" (ibid., p. 107).

This is not the place to review the quite animated debate which, beginning in the 1960s, has surrounded the issues Smart touches on. We should note, however, that the author of *Philosophy and Scientific Realism* goes a significant step further and paints a confident picture of the future of "robots" (in the 1990s he would speak about computers).

> If the brain-process theory is correct, then it is in principle possible that an appropriately constructed robot might be conscious, *i.e.* have sensations. If in its (perhaps electronic) brain there were the right sort of processes, analogous to those that go on in us when we are conscious, then this robot would be conscious too. (ibid., p. 105)

This passage is highly significant for at least two reasons: a) Smart posits an explicit connection between a specific theory of brain processes and the theory of robots; b) with disarming nonchalance he attributes to robots those functions of sentience and consciousness which, by all accounts, appear to be the farthest removed – for well-founded theoretical reasons – from the capabilities of machines. It would be irrelevant to object that Smart's reasoning is purely theoretical here, since it is precisely at a theoretical level that certain proposals, interpretations, and perspectives must be evaluated. And it is at this level that Smart appears unconvincing. At the very least, the claim that an electronic apparatus can be sentient and conscious would require a redefinition of what it means to feel and to be conscious. In the absence of this redefinition, Smart's claim remains empirically unprovable and, in some respects, conceptually debatable.

Not surprisingly, much of Smart's account of the amazing, human-like things robots can do are formulated in terms of an unspecified future (the old promissory-note routine). What is surprising, it must be admitted, is that in his technological utopia Smart even sees the possibility that "machines" might one day be so complex and "evolved" (a curious word indeed since, properly speaking, it is not the machine that *evolves* but the technology responsible for its construction) that they could have "rules of behavior" and a "legal and moral terminology" by which to keep each other in check. These machines will not only be able "to sign documents", Smart continues, but they might even pose not only "physical questions but legal ones" (ibid., pp. 110–11).

Here we have a rather impressive example of what we incline to call the *anthropomorphization of the 'machine'*. It is a common procedure for robot and computer mythographers to single out man's most complex functions and attribute them ('in principle', of course) to physical devices. The principal flaw in this operation lies in the *interpretation* of these functions. In man they are characterized not only by a whole series of intentions, contents, and meanings, but also by their being integrated into his intellectual and practical background – so much so that a real mental function is not separable from its specific psychic, affective, and cultural context. If it is 'separated out' – so as to assign this function to a computer, for example – what is identified is not the *function* as it actually exists but a *final applicative segment* of the function (as though a religious belief or behavior could be identified with the sole act of attending a Sunday church service). In this sense, what we have called the 'separation' of the function leads to its *reduction* or *factualization*. The computer, then, takes on not so much the *function* as the so-to-speak *'factuality'* of the function. And this factuality will never play the same role in the *physical* realm of the hardware as it does in actual human *experience*.

This is one reason why it is often said – correctly – that the computer does not so much *carry out* certain human functions as it *stimulates* them. In other words, the computer is at best capable of generating a mere *analogon* of human performance: an *analogon* that reproduces only the organizational skeleton of the semantic and functional contents which characterize the far more complex human system. Smart claims that the robot (today we would say the computer) will one day be able to pose not only physical but also legal questions. But a computer, insofar as it is a 'machine', will never be able to perform anything other than *physical actions*. Its builder (its programmer) may be able to make it do certain things that are ostensibly similar to those connected with 'posing a legal question' or 'signing a document'. But such acts will always remain mere *simulations* of what we call 'posing a legal question' or 'signing a document'. Indeed, we attribute such acts to the only beings who, in carrying them out, imbue them with the countless meanings and intentions appropriate to our linguistic and cultural context. After all, some computer fans (whether knowingly or not) number among the most naive of behaviorists. They are convinced that the mere presence of a physical gesture embodies the 'substance' and meaning of a particular human act or experience. To refute this belief it is sufficient to point out that a human act may *appear* to be one thing and *be* (i.e., *mean*) another. I can, for example, 'pose a legal question' with meanings and intentions completely opposite to those apparently (and objectively) present in the physical, visible content of my words. And, of course, I can sign a document having already decided that tomorrow I will violate the terms to which I have subscribed.

The computer is not capable of this. The computer is different from us because it is a machine which is not only *stupid* but also *dependent* on the software loaded by an external subject. In contrast with man it has a pathetic and disarming 'virtue': it never acts in bad faith and is never malicious. What is worse, it cannot grasp and correctly interpret the bad faith and maliciousness of human beings, which are far too varied and unpredictable to be programmed into a machine.

ARMSTRONG: REALISM, PHYSICALISM, REDUCTIONISM

The scope and aim of this essay do not allow us to go further into the relationship between computers and human beings. Our discussion of the Australian school has so far neglected a figure of considerable prominence: David M. Armstrong. Armstrong is a professor at the University of Sydney and has for years been among the most eloquent and authoritative voices of the lively philosophical and scientific milieu in Australia. Although he has written extensively on many subjects, he is best known for his essays on the philosophy of mind. Among his publications we might recall his early (and controversial) volume on perception (1961), his book on bodily sensations (1962), his major work *A Materialist Theory of Mind* (1968, henceforth abbreviated MTM), and the collected essays published under the title of *The Nature of Mind* (1980). As David M. Rosenthal has written, these books, along with a number of articles published in a wide variety of journals, present the most ambitious, comprehensive, and detailed treatment of mind–body materialism ever undertaken (Rosenthal 1984, p. 79). Of course, a systematic reconstruction of Armstrong's thought should also include other important works, particularly his study of universals. Here, however, we shall examine only a few of the general principles that underlie Armstrong's approach to the MBP and, at least in outline, his interpretation of the human in general and of psychology.

We should clarify from the outset that Armstrong's philosophy of mind, or rather his psychoanthropology, does not derive in the first place from an empirical consideration of certain questions concerning mental phenomena. Rather, it represents a sort of inflexible (direct or indirect) deduction from a system of ontological and epistemological assumptions. The basis of this system is realism. Things, that is, 'come before' words and concepts, and are independent of them. It follows that thought must concern itself not with *words* but with *things* (Armstrong 1976, p. 18). As to what these 'things' are, Armstrong gives a rigorously one-dimensional answer: all things are solely *natural and objective* entities. Reality in general "consists of nothing but a single all-embracing spatio-temporal system" made up of physical, natural things (Armstrong 1977, p. 149). This emphasis on what is not only *real* but also *natural* is not to be neglected. Indeed, Armstrong also defines his philosophical orientation as "naturalistic". From *Naturalism, Materialism and First Philosophy* (1977) to the more recent essay, significantly entitled (in the German edition) *Naturalistische Metaphysik* (in Bogdan 1984, p. 299), Armstrong stresses that "naturalism" is the only right way of viewing and interpreting reality. In answer to the question "But might it not be necessary to admit non-natural entities or figures?" (Armstrong gives as examples universals, values, numbers, possibilities) he responds flatly: no, it is not necessary. In fact, since the first requisite of existent entities is causal power, and since only spatial and temporal (i.e., natural) things have this power, the conclusion is that only these things exist. Contemporary science, moreover, also makes the opposite thesis implausible (Armstrong 1977, pp. 154ff.).

It is a short step from realism/naturalism to materialism/physicalism. In Armstrong's view, "The world contains nothing but the entities recognized by physics" (ibid., p. 156; note the 'nothing but' principle mentioned above); "everything there is is wholly constituted by such entities, their connections and arrangements" (ibid., p. 157). Consequently the "modern materialist" tries to give "an account of the world and of man purely in terms of physical properties" (Armstrong 1976, p. 29). These premises lead to an epistemological priority conferred to physics, the "supremacy" of which – or rather, its paradigmatic value in the context of knowledge – constitutes an incessant refrain in Armstrong's writings. Nor should this surprise us. *Physics*, for Armstrong, means *science:* or rather, *Science* with an upper case 'S'. This Science, in turn, is *tout court* Knowledge: no knowledge exists but scientific knowledge. Rejecting the "irrationalist philosophies of science" inspired by different sources (beginning with Feyerabend and Kuhn: Armstrong 1966, p. 4n), Armstrong himself calls his conception "scientism" (ibid., p. 4). He also claims to be able to present abundant historical and theoretical proof in support of the validity of this "scientism". At least from the seventeenth century on, Science (mathematical and physical science, of course) has acquired, in Armstrong's view, such moral and intellectual "authority" to deliberate and decide on the most disparate issues – including those concerning man – that a 'scientistic' view of knowledge may be considered fully legitimated.

One of the intellectual strategies correlated to this conception of science is the reductionist approach. Reductionism is in fact another of the crucial factors that underpin Armstrong's epistemology, and it has two faces: one cognitive and another ontological. From the cognitive point of view, the reductionist procedure is seen as the only one capable of transferring notions, concepts, and theories *from* other scientific fields *to* the field of physics, taken as a paradigm. But Armstrong, not content with this kind of reductionism, also hints at a reductionism that is, so to speak, *a parte objecti*. Some things can be reduced ontologically to other things. Natural reality is so compact and unitary that it is not necessary – indeed, it would be misleading – to admit the existence of parts of it characterized by properties or laws that cannot be reduced to the elementary properties and laws of physics. In this sense Armstrong also rejects emergentist materialism, which, without abandoning a monistic, materialistic conception of the world, admits the existence of certain planes or aggregates as distinct from others (MTM, p. 358).

ARMSTRONG: MAN AS A ''PURE PHYSICAL OBJECT'' AND THE CONCEPT OF IDENTITY

Predictably, Armstrong's general assumptions deeply influence his analysis of the human and the mental. "Man", we read in *A Materialist Theory of the Mind*, "is one with nature" (p. 366). In Armstrong's *Weltanschauung*, then, man's *cultural* component is at best latent; at worst it is simply absent. The opening assumption of his major work is that the human being is *"nothing but* his material body" (MTM, p. 1; italics mine). The *cognitive* implications of this *ontological* claim are just what we might expect. Man, "including his mental processes", should be treated "as a purely physical object, operating according to exactly the same laws as other physical things" (ibid., p. 366). In the article entitled *The Causal Theory of Mind*, Armstrong specifies that "the body and brain of man are constituted and work according to exactly the same principles as those physical principles that govern other, non-organic, matter" (Armstrong 1976, p. 19). This is a very radical claim indeed. We may wonder, however, whether it adequately prepares the reader for the bombshell that follows: "the difference between a stone and a human body appears to lie solely in the extremely complex material set-up that is to be found in the living body and which is absent in the stone" (ibid.).

It is on the basis of this theory of man that Armstrong takes up more specific psychological issues, and in particular the MBP. Here, along with the philosophical positions summarized above, his direct referents are behaviorism and the conceptions of Place and Smart. Armstrong reveals a deep sympathy with behavioral psychology (a result, in part, of direct contacts with various proponents of behaviorism [Armstrong and Malcolm 1984a, p. 20]). In his view, the validity of the orientation introduced by Watson and subsequently developed by various scholars lies in its rejection of metaphysical entities, such as consciousness and the self, and of methods of investigation – introspection, for example – that he considers entirely unreliable. In its *pars construens* as well, behaviorism is rich in issues deserving our attention. It is no coincidence that some of its key notions (like stimulus and response) crop up frequently, often with a crucial role, in Armstrong's philosophical and psychological universe. It is perfectly understandable that the behaviorist view should appear "attractive" to the philosopher of mind who believes only in a "scientific" approach to the human sphere, and no less to "any philosopher sympathetic to a Materialist view of man" (Armstrong 1966, p. 4). From another point of view, however, Armstrong considers behavioral psychology irredeemably 'speculative' and of little use since it does not describe what *really*, effectively happens within the human being. To the extent to which it stops at man's physical appearance and does not take into account the *real* (not merely dispositional) "inner states" having "causal powers", behaviorism is "a profoundly unnatural account of mental process" – and must therefore be abandoned (ibid., pp. 4–7).

We shall see shortly that Armstrong's rejection of behaviorism is not as definitive as these last lines might seem to suggest. But first let us consider his attitude toward the positions of Place and Smart. From one point of view, he expresses great admiration and overall agreement in their regard. Indeed, as for the problems faced by the identity theory, little or nothing need be modified in what the two scholars have already said (MTM, p. 355). From another point of view, however, he reprimands them, especially Smart, for having imposed limitations on their field of investigation. In his opinion, they should not have been content with an identity-oriented analysis of exclusively sensorial phenomena. Armstrong's explicit aim is to extend this analysis to "cover *all* sorts of mental processes" (Armstrong 1973, p. 35; italics mine). What must be demonstrated – far beyond the occasional claims hinted at by Smart – is that not only sentience but also sapience and selfhood (and all human phenomena in general) can be systematically identified with definite physical states.

As William Kneale has observed (1969, p. 295), Armstrong does not give one of the key concepts of the MBP – that of identity – the attention one might have expected. Initially, he limits himself to adopting an interpretation of identity not in logical, analytic but in empirical, contingent terms: the only terms, he is convinced, in which the issue of identity can be addressed scientifically (MTM, p. 355). In a more personal contribution he specifies that identity should be conceived and verified not between mind and body, but between mental and physical (or neurocerebral) *states* (ibid., p. 12). Armstrong's purpose seems to be twofold: on the one hand he seeks to avoid treating mental and physical poles incorrectly as entities; on the other he insists on an investigation procedure that is as empirical as possible. In the third place, he stresses that the identity is between *types*, not between *tokens*. Identity occurs, that is, not merely with events that are only *de facto* and *at a certain moment* identifiable with physical states (but in principle could also not be identified with those states), but rather at the level of *unvarying* structures and process, which guarantee *constancy* and *necessity* to the identity relationship.

We should add that in recent years, in the wake of functionalist contributions to the debate (see Chapter 5), Armstrong, unlike other supporters of orthodox identity thought, has at least in part revised his positions. He has sought, that is, to temper somewhat the rigidity of the type–type identity. In one of his latest essays his position on this issue is presented as follows. Certainly type–type identity is too binding and demanding a concept. Yet, to claim a mere token–token identity does not seem enough – and it is, in a certain sense, rather 'cowardly' from an epistemological point of view, since it implies that one "retreat[s] too far in the face of the difficulty" (Armstrong and Malcolm 1984a, p. 162). Thus Armstrong's new position tries to hold a middle ground between the two 'classic' conceptions of identity. We must reject as too ambitious and 'all-encompassing' a conception that claims, for instance (as type–type identity does), identity between pain in *general* and a specific neurophysical correlate; but this identity is to be replaced by a conception that simply places a *partial* limit on this 'generality': one that speaks, that is (to continue with the previous example), not of pain *in general*, but of the pain of the sole class of human beings. Once this limit is accepted, the identification of the 'type'-pain with "some single neurological process" becomes, for Armstrong, "perfectly plausible". This position takes on even greater importance since he insists that token–token identity, if interpreted in a strict sense (as indeed it should be), is absolutely indefensible. Indeed, "the idea that the physiological nature of pain in human beings changes from one occasion to another or even from one person to another seems truly bizarre, although it could be a logical possibility" (ibid.). A number of scholars have replied that the 'bizarreness' Armstrong refers to is anything but evident. They point out that the physical correlates of certain pains can change effectively (and not only 'logically') – especially in the quality and intensity of their manifestations – under different circumstances and in different human subjects. Moreover, the adoption *a priori* of any principles of invariance or necessity in interpreting specific phenomena risks giving a too rigid and impoverished description of the manifold forms in which these phenomena can occur. We shall have occasion to return to issues connected with the different relationships of identity. Here our investigation must concern more directly Armstrong and his conception of the mind and mental phenomena.

ARMSTRONG: THE INTERPRETATION
OF THE MENTAL

In some regards it appears as though Armstrong is concerned to defend the dimension of the mental. He seems to be searching for a concept of the mind that will protect it from the neglect or even cancellation that heavy-handed materialists and blind behaviorists reserve for 'non-observable' phenomena. Thus, in his major work Armstrong defines the mind as "an internal state bringing about outward behavior" (MTM, p. 80): that is, it is what determines the response to certain stimuli. Ultimately, mental states have to be describable in terms of the behavior for which they are causally suited (MTM, p. 83). The concept of the mind, Armstrong insists in one of his most recent publications, is "the concept of that which intervenes between the stimulus and the response" (Bogdan 1970b, p. 281). In this respect, Edgar Wilson is certainly not mistaken in pointing out the strong behaviorist heritage ascertainable in Armstrong's positions (Wilson 1979, p. 70); a heritage curiously entwined with non-behaviorist principles: the existence of internal states, their ability to act causally and productively, and others.

But in the present context the relationship between Armstrong and behaviorism is not the crucial point. What is more important is to ask whether the interpretation of the mental as just sketched out does in fact give it real independence from the physical. And the answer can only be negative. On closer examination, in fact, Armstrong's theses stress not so much the autonomy of the mental state *as a concept* as the *modus operandi* of such a state – which, as we have seen, is *causal* in nature. But if this is the sort of *modus operandi* we are dealing with, then there are definite consequences involved for the problem at hand. Indeed, from Armstrong's pan-physicalist point of view everything that produces something causally cannot be anything other than *physical*. Consequently states that, like the so-called mental states, produce a causal action can only be (or can only be identifiable with) physical states. As Patricia Kitcher has observed, the conclusion of all this is that when we use *mental* terms and concepts "we are (unconsciously) talking about *physical* states that, in fact, play causal roles" (1982, p. 214).

It is not surprising, then, that Armstrong's main goal appears to be not so much to defend the autonomy of the mental (which is untenable) as to search for a matrix (real and physical) for the class of states and actions we traditionally call mental. In the light of the knowledge provided by Science, this goal can be reached without excessive difficulty: the matrix is located in the central nervous system (CNS). The CNS constitutes the "central state" of humans as sentient, conscious, thinking beings and is conceived, naturally, as materialistic and causally active and productive. Armstrong prefers to refer to his conception not as 'identity theory' – the usual expression in contexts like this – but as "central-state materialism theory" (MTM, part 1, chapter 6). Accordingly, Armstrong sets out to demonstrate that in some way all the phenomenology of the psychic – and of the human in general – can be simply reduced to the diverse operations of the CNS (MTM, part 2).

We shall not examine step by step Armstrong's systematic reduction of man to a neurophysiological being. Thomas Nagel once complained that although Armstrong embarks on an apparently revolutionary undertaking, his conception of the psychological organization of the individual is essentially the same as that handed down by an increasingly unreliable speculative tradition (in Block 1979, pp. 200–6). It has also been observed that the analyses of mental states presented by Armstrong tend primarily and *a priori* to lend support to the claim that "mental states are brain states" (Kitcher 1982, p. 225). But this claim is no more than a hypothesis: a hypothesis derived essentially from (physicalistic) assumptions of a *theoretical* and *speculative* nature. Indeed, notwithstanding explicit professions of scientific and empirical faith, Armstrong's analysis is *de facto meta*-empirical and *meta*-scientific and is largely lacking in adequate experimental proofs of its claims. No differently from that of Smart, his commitment is essentially *theoretical* and *prophetic:* he is committed to the position that *in principle* (and/or in some undetermined *future*) all psycho-anthropological states and events might and should reveal themselves as being fundamentally neurocerebral in nature. Commenting on this commitment, Richard Rorty, a philosopher who is certainly not sympathetic to 'metaphysical' leanings, has observed that "whatever the MBP is", it surely cannot be reduced to a "feeling-neuron problem" (Rorty 1979, p. 23).

Armstrong's references to the mind as a series of internal states and causes determining forms of behavior should not be misunderstood. Although he speaks of conditions, states, and causes, he always has in mind *things:* things in the most realistic and physicalist sense of the word. Clearly, then, his claims about these states and causes scarcely prove that he advocates the existence of the mental as a relatively autonomous *dimension.* For Armstrong the mind is an internal state or cause, but as a *thing:* a thing whose existence, in the *realist* sense of the term, must be *defended* (from the behaviorist tendency to ignore it) and at the same time *identified* with something physical.

Yet, the first requirement is no less firmly sustained than the second. In other words, Armstrong's *realist* conception of the mind – of the mind as a *res* – is by no means negligible. This is why – and the paradox is only apparent, as Joseph Margolis has pointed out (1978, p. 31) – Armstrong can be associated with Cartesian positions. It could even be argued that he *is* a Cartesian: one whose allusion (direct or indirect) to Descartes's substantialistic doctrine recalls certain seventeenth- and eighteenth-century French *matérialistes*. Just as they could embrace Cartesianism simply by interpreting the *res cogitans* in a materialistic way, so can Armstrong. A *realist*, like certain philosophers of the *res*, and a *materialist*, like those who did not hesitate to define as *res materialis* even the *Cogito*, Armstrong feels he can legitimate this last definition by invoking the (alleged) authority of Science.

This attitude, though traceable in a number of Armstrong's writings, is particularly evident in a long review essay on Popper and Eccles's *The Self and Its Brain* published in the *Times Literary Supplement* (February 17, 1978). In the light of what has been said thus far, it would be superfluous to add that Armstrong is unyieldingly critical of the authors' attempt to give not a monistic and materialistic, but a materialistic and 'tripartite' description of the human universe (cf. Popper's theory of the "three worlds"). It is more relevant to our purpose to note that Popper and Eccles are defined as neo-Cartesians, and that this characterization of the two scholars leads the reviewer to formulate his own interpretation of Cartesian thought.

For Armstrong, Descartes's ontological dualism and his philosophy of mind are, to use an expression which he refers mainly to Cartesian epistemology, "quite mistaken". (It follows, of course, that all those who, like Popper and Eccles, have embraced certain positions are also mistaken.) Yet, it is truly a pity that Descartes's general principles were wrong, since in other respects he had some brilliant insights. Perhaps the most important of these is that reality obeys a "unified set of laws": a thesis, Armstrong points out, that has been taken up again today and confirmed by what is significantly called the "scientific orthodoxy". But if it is true that reality – *all* reality – is subject to (physical) laws, then why not think that also the "realm of the mind" obeys these laws? And since in order to obey physical laws reality must also be physical (or reducible to physical states and processes), why not identify mental processes with purely physical processes in the brain, processes in the central nervous system? This and only this, Armstrong claims, is the correct way to interpret Cartesian thought: its *proper* historical and theoretical evolution is toward " a thorough-going Materialism or Physicalism".

Armstrong is particularly severe in his criticism of Popper's theory that human reality can be divided into three "worlds". The existence of "World Three" – the world of theories, scientific problems, beliefs, and so forth – is in his view no less than "incredible". Ideas, theories, and values have in fact no autonomous reality. There is only some*thing* (a mind, which we will discover later is the brain) that "encodes" some other *thing*.

> What need to postulate the World Three object? The encodings will do all that is necessary causally. Each encoding will reflect, or fail to reflect the world There seems no need to postulate in addition a World Three object standing over against all the encodings. The World Two "graspings" of the alleged World Three object seem to do all that is necessary. . . .I believe, therefore, that we should reject World Three as a gratuitous piece of metaphysics. (Armstrong 1978b, p. 184)

Nor is this all. "World Two" – the world of mental states and events – seems superfluous to Armstrong as well. In his view, Popper's claim that it exists is based not on empirical evidence but on an "*a priori* argument". The truth is, on the contrary, that "each individual mental process is in fact a brain-process": a process that "has in fact *nothing but* physical properties" (ibid.; italics mine). In other words, sensations and perceptions, images and memories, consciousness and self-consciousness are identifiable with neurophysiological correlates that can be rigorously verified empirically (or in principle) by scientific knowledge.

Many of the assumptions and positions peculiar to Armstrong's thought reappear in one of his most well-reasoned essays, entitled 'The Nature of Mind' (1966; reprinted in the volume of the same title published in 1980, the source of our quotations). Having established that the mind is the cause of behavior, Armstrong immediately dismisses the possibility that this cause can be seen as a mere logical or linguistic model, or as a mere condition which renders a definite class of phenomena thinkable. In his hard-core realism, he conceives it rather as a *substantial* cause: as a cause that necessarily corresponds to the action of some*thing* that exists – indeed, that exists *physically*. And, inasmuch as it must be a *thing*, he raises an *ontological* question about this cause: what is its "intrinsic nature" (*The Nature of Mind*, p. 8)? Armstrong's realistic query receives a scientistic response. It is in fact Science (in the singular) that furnishes the answer, or rather, as Armstrong significantly puts it, the "verdict". And the verdict is that the mind *is* – is ontologically, completely, without residues and (especially) without alternatives – "the physico-chemical workings of the central nervous system". The conclusion, therefore, is that "we can identify these states with purely physical states of the central nervous system" (ibid.).

His most recent writings provide eloquent confirmation of his unwavering faith in this realistic and physicalistic conception of mental states. In the 'Self-Profile' that introduces a volume of essays dedicated to his work (Bogdan 1984), Armstrong reaffirms his conviction that the mind *is* the neurocerebral system and that the mental state is – in a renewed tribute to behaviorism – "that which intervenes between the stimulus and the response" (*Self-Profile*, p. 281). What is more, he also claims that the model of identity between the psychic and the physical is offered by the relationship between the gene and DNA. It is worth pointing out, we might add, that this comparison links two uncontestably *physical* concepts and can, therefore, hardly serve as a valid formulation of the issues involved in the rather problematic relationship between mind and body.

ARMSTRONG: CONSCIOUSNESS, INTENTIONALITY, 'PURPOSEFUL' BEHAVIOR

Just as the mind *is* the brain (or the CNS) – a definition which cannot be altered by any other cognitive approach, as it captures *scientifically* the *real* essence of the mind itself – so too consciousness is interpreted in physicalistic terms. Yet, even the most orthodox champions of the identity theory expressed some perplexity in this regard. Whether it was interpreted as the mere *consciousness*, or more significantly as *awareness* of something, or even as *selfhood* (and it goes without saying that Armstrong and others would have done well to explore more carefully the similarities and differences between these concepts), human consciousness raised a number of intriguing problems. While many were convinced that sentience and sapience could be identified with definite neurophysiological processes, not a few betrayed some reluctance to identify consciousness (or awareness, or selfhood) with some 'other'. Indeed, both the *modus essendi* and the *modus operandi* of this component of the human make-up appeared extremely *sui generis* – perhaps too *sui generis* to be reduced to mere neurocerebral states and events. What relationship of identity can possibly be established between such states and events and that dimension of existence in which the subject is aware of its *self*, of its being – and thus of its historical and temporal 'background', its environmental and social condition, and of the sum of desires, values, and purposes that characterize it? As to Armstrong, he does not seem to be overly sensitive to the problem. His attitude toward the 'reality' of consciousness is, again, essentially reductionist and physicalist. He views consciousness as something exclusively material, nothing but a product of the CNS. More precisely, it is considered "the scanning of one part of our central nervous system by another" (Armstrong 1966, p. 15). Actually, what is interesting here is not so much the definition itself as the procedure adopted to arrive at it. Armstrong's approach is clearly set out in a relatively recent debate with the Wittgensteinian philosopher Norman Malcolm (Malcolm and Armstrong 1984). Here he begins by admitting that consciousness – understood in a wide, multi-levelled sense (as self-awareness, inner meaning, introspection) – is "a very mysterious phenomenon". Immediately afterwards, however, he assures us that the mystery can be cleared up. To his mind, this solution can (and must) be generated by "a *demystifying* and *naturalizing* model" (ibid., p. 110).

Of these two modifiers the second is probably the most significant. The first – the 'demystifying' component – takes on, and intends to demolish, the claim that consciousness can be interpreted as a reified, *sui generis* entity. The second – the 'naturalizing' component – is more indicative of the peculiarity of Armstrong's thought. It consists in reducing consciousness from the rich theoretical figure outlined above to a mere natural – that is, physiological – function. In other words, instead of being considered a multiform, heterogeneous, and complex sphere of the human being (and, as such, requiring appropriate hermeneutic instruments), consciousness is reduced to a far more elementary, homogeneous, and 'thing-like' *bodily organ*. Consciousness, in Armstrong's view, is substantially an *analogon* of the senses. Indeed, one might well say that it is a sense itself. It is a sense, one might admit, with a rather particular *modus operandi,* turned more inward than outward – but, nonetheless, still *a sense.* It is true, Armstrong admits, that as a sense it is not easily located. And it is also true that it acts differently from the other senses: but this "does not seem to be a big enough difference to justify the restriction of the expression 'sensory perception' to the operations of the five traditional senses" (ibid., p. 111). This is, for Armstrong, so evidently true that he has no hesitation in considering consciousness *a particular variety of bodily perception:* that variety labeled by some scientists (and Armstrong with them) "proprioception".

In his reply to Armstrong's essay, Malcolm noted how simplistic it is to connect what we generally call consciousness to a more or less peculiarly sensitive piece of living matter. But it is likely that the initial reaction to Armstrong's conception is another: a reaction of epistemological uneasiness with this particularly trenchant application of a procedure at once 'speculative' and 'absolutist': 'speculative' because Armstrong does not bother to present any empirical evidence to support his interpretation of consciousness (indeed, explicitly speaking only *in principle*); 'absolutist' because he tends to define consciousness according to the 'nothing but' principle already familiar to us. This approach seems particularly misleading in this case. For although it is *possible* that in a certain scientific (e.g., physiological) context consciousness may be as Armstrong defines it, it is *certain* (certain in our experience) that for us it is *also something else.* Put somewhat differently, Armstrong inclines, perhaps, to confuse the 'thing' (but we prefer to say the function, or the 'figure') with its 'bearer'. Indeed, the scanning of one part of the CNS by another is not so much what our actual and effective consciousness is (i.e., what man immediately feels when he is conscious) as the *physical* condition (necessary, but not sufficient) for its existence.

Armstrong's general positions and purposes should be clear by now. We cannot ignore, however, a series of considerations on an issue that has become particularly important in contemporary philosophy of mind and man: the question of intentionality and purposeful behavior. Armstrong is well aware of the influential current of thought (the names of George von Wright and Charles Taylor come immediately to mind) that views as essential to the make-up of human action and behavior certain peculiar components of a cultural, 'metaphysical' nature. But just as in the epistemological debate Armstrong took sides against the anti-realists Kuhn and Feyerabend (whom he called, summarily but significantly, "irrationalists"), here too his position is radically antagonistic toward certain well-defined ideas and tendencies.

What is puzzling about Armstrong's position on intentionality is that he does not discuss it *iuxta sua principia*. Indeed, he reacts to the problems it involves in a way that, to a large extent, begs the question. It is often claimed (so, in sum, runs Armstrong's argument) that intentionality expresses the subject's ability to manifest its beliefs and attributions of sense in a relatively free way; that it does not follow rigid norms and laws; that it is not (or not always) bound to observable and univocal facts. All this, if true, could have dramatic implications: if the intentionality doctrine is right, Armstrong stresses, "then Materialism is false". The reason is that "such an irreducible characteristic has no place in physics as we now conceive physics" (Armstrong 1977, p. 158). But it is *not* true. It would, in fact, imply the existence of phenomena that occur according to rules different from the usual (physical) ones, and we already know that for Armstrong this is impossible. Moreover, while the intentionality theory does not create insurmountable "conceptual difficulties", it is nonetheless "scientifically implausible". There is no proof that the brain, which houses these intentional properties and norms, "obeys any different laws from any other physical object" (ibid., p. 159).

What can we make of Armstrong's stance? The least one could say is that his position is captious and reductive. On a theoretical plane, it simply reaffirms, without adequate argumentation, a pure form of physicalism, admitting of no exceptions (whereas this is exactly what intentionalist doctrines contest), and concludes from this that intentional entities and intentionalistic *modi operandi* cannot exist. Empirically, Armstrong takes for granted a privileged relationship between the brain and intentionality. And yet this relationship is far from self-evident. Indeed, it is precisely the *demonstrandum* contested by the majority of proponents of intentionality theory. They hold, in fact, that intentionality is not a *physical* but a *psychic* phenomenon, and that it is not a property of the *brain* (which, if anything, is only the 'vehicle' of intentionality), but of consciousness.

As for purposeful behavior, Armstrong grounds his argumentation on the same rigidly physicalistic assumptions and follows a line of reasoning similar to that developed in his discussion of intentionality. Without devoting excessive space to the ideas of those who propose a different approach, he reduces this behavior to a mere variant of the physical processes that occur in nature. "There is", in fact, "no reason to believe that what it is for an organism to have a purpose involves anything more than the *operation of purely physical processes* in the organism" (ibid., p. 151; italics mine). If this is the case (but it goes without saying that this *cannot* be conceded without adequate proof), then it is perfectly legitimate to propose "an account of purposes . . . in terms of processes that do not themselves involve purpose". Significantly, this conclusion is identical to that advanced (as early as the 1930s) by the most reductionist strain of logical positivism and appears unperturbed by the objections raised over the course of some twenty years of literature on action theory. Armstrong's way of thinking is even more clearly revealed in another unsettling passage of the same article, where we read:

1. The cause of all human (and animal) movements lies solely in physical processes working solely according to the laws of physics.
2. Purposes and beliefs, in their character of purposes and beliefs, cause human (and animal) movements.
[Therefore] 3. Purposes and beliefs are nothing but physical processes working solely according to the laws of physics. (ibid., p. 160)

Syllogisms of this sort need not detain us unduly. It was necessary, however, to give a brief sketch of Armstrong's views on human behavior and action, as this enabled us to grasp the connection – the extremely important connection – between a *materialistic identity theory of the MBP* and a *physicalist and anti-intentionalist conception of human action and behavior.* Clearly there is a marked consistency in the positions of those who, believing that the mental can be reduced to the bodily, also believe that (human) *purposes* can be reduced to (physical) *causal mechanisms.* And it should not surprise us to find that Armstrong, one of the most radical advocates of this double reducibility, finds in computers and their admirable capabilities additional, conclusive proof that man is *nothing but* physicality (MTM, p. 357).

A "PHYSICALISTIC METAPHYSICS": ARMSTRONG'S BASIC GOALS

Behind these and other related positions Armstrong harbors an ambition bearing decisive cognitive and ontological implications. His twofold aim is to confirm the universal and necessary validity – without lacunae – of Science (i.e., physics) and to create an image of man that is 'regular' and 'disciplined' (in the fullest sense of the terms). These two goals are closely intertwined. The universality of scientific knowledge as achieved by physics is forcefully confirmed when it shows its capacity to embrace the human world, which is perhaps the most complex and elusive dimension of reality. Moreover, the image of man as a perfectly law-abiding, and thus reassuring, entity is the one that appears to respond most readily to a rigorous paradigm of science.

The passage quoted above gives eloquent testimony of this aim. What is most striking is the extremely radical position Armstrong chooses to assume. To affirm that even "purposes and beliefs" are (not hermeneutically, but ontologically) *nothing but* "physical processes" means claiming that even the apparently less rule-governed and body-dependent human functions can be absorbed into the realm of physical knowledge. It means, that is, making the boldest move possible in order to bring the whole human being within the sphere of what is predictable, controllable, and governable. And *this* is what matters to Armstrong more than anything else. In much the same way as some other currents of contemporary thought (Skinner's neo-behaviorism, Lévi-Strauss's structuralism, Wilson's sociobiology), Armstrong's philosophy tries to achieve what could be called the scientific suppression of human freedom *a parte subjecti*. Indeed, it is for him a pronouncement issued by the irrecusable authority of science that declares that man must obey a system of physical constraints even in his psychic processes (traditionally viewed as the freest). One has the impression that Armstrong strives for this goal for epistemological as well as psychoanthropological reasons. What seems certain is that it responds to an undeniably *meta-scientific* need. In this regard it should be said (or repeated) that – despite declarations to the opposite effect – Armstrong is fully aware that the perspective he assumes is essentially *philosophical*. It is no coincidence that at a crucial point in *A Materialist Theory of the Mind* he admits that his interpretation of the mental should be considered not on its own (empirical) merit but as "a mere prolegomenon to a physicalist metaphysics" (p. 366). In synthesis, *Armstrong's foremost interest lies in the constitution and re-inforcement of a physicalistic conception of the world.* From this point of view, the theories and theses expounded in his work are to be seen as a contribution not so much to the *science* of the mind as to the development of an extremely well-defined (and very ambitious) *metaphysical* project.

Chapter 3

The obscure relationship

Problems and debates surrounding the identity theory

THE CONCEPT OF IDENTITY: MODES AND USES

A considerable variety of positions has already emerged from the debate on the identity theory. Some of these address the more general aspects and implications of the theory, while others touch on specific issues. It is not necessary for our purposes to examine everything that has been written on the subject, but it will be useful to see, through certain selected texts and problems, how identity theorists have brought some of their difficulties into focus.

The issue which has perhaps caused the most animated discussion is the concept of identity itself. Curiously enough, the majority of identity theorists do not seem to be very concerned with this question. Feigl, it is true, does discuss the notion, but in his later works he seems to be so little convinced of its consistency and utility that he puts it more or less explicitly on a back burner. Place contributes a few important distinctions to the problem, but as his investigation progresses he tends to bracket off the issue as secondary. This tendency is even more evident in Smart; and with Armstrong, who deals with the concept of identity in a few meager pages in *A Materialist Theory of Mind*, it becomes disconcertingly conspicuous (see Kneale 1969, p. 295). Many other proponents of the identity theory as well generally ignore the problem or make only passing reference to it.

The claim most regularly made by these theorists is that the identity involved in the relationship between mind and body is not *necessary* but *contingent*. The distinction is important. For only a contingent identity (i.e., the identity involved in the mind–body relationship is not analytical, universal, *a priori*) will lead the investigation back to an empirical plane – a plane of facts and relationships that could be of one type but could also be of another. But is it really true that orthodox identity theorists defend a strictly contingent conception of identity? Some philosophers have expressed well-founded doubts in this regard. Norman Malcolm, for example, has pointed out that in order to demonstrate the identity between mental and physical events, identity proponents (at least those of a realistic leaning) must hold that mental events take place *inside* the skull – that is, they can be located in space. This assumption, however, entails presupposing that such events are *a priori* and *necessarily* physical – in blatant violation of the principle of contingency (Malcolm 1971, pp. 66–8). What is more, even if we admit that some orthodox identity theorists have remained rigorously true to an empirical and contingent interpretation of identity, this interpretation alone hardly clears up all the problems connected with the concept. Why, then, are so many scholars elusive or even silent on the issue? How is it that this notion, so obviously crucial for an identity theory, has been given such inadequate attention?

An answer to these questions may be provided by what we have argued is the true ultimate goal of the identity theory program. Properly analyzed, this program reveals its principal objective as being not so much the 'identification' of the mental with the bodily as the 'physicalization' of the mental. The two aims can be (and in reality are) *contiguous*. They are not, however, *coincident*. At the very least it must be recognized that in the passage from one to the other there is a conspicuous shift in accents, referents, and research orientations.

Behind this reluctance to lock horns with the concept of identity there may well lurk another motive. It has been pointed out quite correctly that this concept is one of epistemology's most complex figures (Hirsch 1982). In its most general acceptance identity is used to some extent as a metaphor for the cognitive act as such: in fact many of these acts seem to be formally expressible in statements of the type 'A is B'. In a more technical sense, however, it presents some rather intriguing difficulties. It has even been claimed that identity is valid as a concept only within the sphere of the exact disciplines: only there, in fact, can it exhibit its most proper meaning and function. This position may be somewhat reductive:

perhaps the concept should also be allowed to embrace the identifications that, *de jure* and *de facto*, are made outside the rigorous
procedures of such sciences as logic and mathematics. A reasonable
strategy could be to distinguish a strict formal identity – an identity
viewed as tautology or synonymy, as has been suggested (Preti
1984) – and a less rigid identity that can be used within the domain
of empirical matters.

Some types of this second version of identity do not seem to
cause great problems. For example, the identity usually called by
definition (e.g., 'red is a color') is fairly easy to accept since it is
not based on a relationship between two entities (which obviously could create difficulties) but between an entity and a character conventionally ascribed to it ('by definition'). The so-called
predicate identity (e.g., 'gold is shiny') is another type that does
not present insurmountable obstacles. Not only does it not link
two entities but an entity and a property, but it also does not
preclude other predicates, that is, other identifications. Problems
definitely arise, however, when A and B, in the statement 'A is
B', are two entities (or two states, or two events), as in Place's
identity by *composition.* In this case many questions are raised by
both proponents and critics of the identity theory. What is meant
by 'A is B'? Does it mean that two given phenomena are identical
a parte objecti? But if they are, how is it that they are *two?* How
do they differ? Or is it the observer who establishes this identity
interpretively? If this is the case, however, the identity is not at
all *a parte objecti* but rather *a parte subjecti.* We are dealing, then,
not with an identity but with an *identification.*

It has been claimed that this second concept is more pliable
and promising than the first. In fact, while identity seems, in
some regards, to be more closely connected with a relatively
rigid, 'objectivist' approach to the MBP, identification suggests a
more 'open', 'subjective', and 'dynamic' orientation (in this concept the stress falls on an event, an operation, rather than on a
state). An orientation, moreover, that could contribute to the development of a rather valid *pragmatic* and *contextualist* approach
to the problem, it could suggest that a given identification is
valid only in relation to certain goals and in the light of certain
premises and conditions. From this point of view, the contextual,
relativistic conceptions outlined by various scholars, for example,
Peter Geach (1957 and 1967), are particularly worthy of attention.

FREGE'S POSITION ACCORDING TO
THE IDENTITY THEORY

Most mainstream proponents of the identity theory, however, flatly reject the 'subjective' interpretation of the identifying act and many opt for an 'objectivist' and realist version of the concept of identity. A host of declarations and positions, both explicit and implicit, could be cited in this regard. Some have already been mentioned, so we will not take them up again. However, a brief review of how certain philosophers of mind have 'read' Gottlob Frege will help identify and shed light on a series of problems pertinent to our investigation. This review is particularly relevant here as Frege is a relatively constant point of reference in the literature on the MBP.

Frege's work on identity was carried out in the context of his well-known doctrine of meaning, based on the distinction between *Bedeutung* and *Sinn* (Frege 1892). Frege contended that the *identity* between two expressions (in the broadest sense of the term) is relatively unproblematic when it can be referred not to their *Sinn* – that is to the sense of the expressions, their *way* of expressing things – but to their *Bedeutung* – that is to the *designatum* of these expressions, their *reference* or *denotation*. In other words, two expressions are identical when they indicate *the same referent*, even though they belong to different *modi dicendi*, that is, to different types or systems of signifying. The classic example is that of the planet Venus. Two different expressions can be used to designate this same 'object': 'the Morning Star' and 'the Evening Star'. According to Frege, the two expressions are identical in that the astronomical *designatum* denoted by both is demonstrably the same, despite the difference between the *two* distinct *ways* of naming it.

It may be worth noting that Frege's conception has provoked a critical response from various philosophers of mind. In particular, Norman Malcolm has observed that this version of identity is not entirely convincing since, apart from other considerations, "the planet that is both the Morning and the Evening Star is not the Morning Star *at the same moment* it is the Evening Star" (Malcolm 1965, in Borst 1979, p. 173). The two *designata*, then, are significantly dissimilar from a temporal point of view.

But what matters in this context is not so much the more or less tenable critiques of Frege's position as the fact that rather diverse interpretations of his theory coexist within the sphere of the MBP.

Some of these interpretations are at once in keeping with the 'doctrine' and yet epistemologically open and 'liberalizing'. Peter Herbst, for example, has argued that M–B identity means, in essence, that there are two expressions (or rather, two linguistic universes: the psychological and the physiological) which, on the one hand, clearly are – and remain – *two*, with their own meanings and characteristics. On the other hand, they refer to, or can be referred to, the same *designatum* (Herbst, in Presley 1967, pp. 48–9). The great advantage of this conception is that this sense of *identity* in no way implies a *reduction* of the mind to the body. Indeed, each of the two expressions has its own semantic, logical, and cognitive consistency, such that it would be unthinkable to *reduce one* to the other (either through *translation* or, even worse, through *elimination*). An approach of this sort also makes it possible to interpret identity in the pragmatic, conventional, and contextual way hinted at above (Polten 1973).

And yet, the majority of orthodox identity theorists tend to read Frege in an entirely different light. Indeed, most of them – and the point is worth highlighting – stress not the existence of *two* expressions, *two* languages, and *two* semantic-cognitive universes, but rather the existence of *one* referent which, in a sense, *unites* them. This shift of attention carries with it two important consequences: a) the 'focus' of the identification is situated entirely in the 'object'; b) the two languages (the psychological and the physiological) are evaluated not on the basis of what they can say, and 'offer', in terms of their own characteristics, but only in relationship to the 'object'. And since the 'object' has already been pre-interpreted physically, it follows that the physiological language is privileged with respect to the psychological one. For the most part, in fact, *identification* is inevitably considered a *reduction/translation,* or a *reduction/elimination,* of one linguistic system to the advantage of the other. For some philosophers of mind the problems that derive from this imbalance are rather serious. Even more serious, perhaps, is that the emphasis laid on the object, combined with the radical *realism* and the equally radical *physiologism* of many identity theorists, often results in an *ontological* interpretation of identity: an interpretation that tends to identify not so much one *designatum* with another *designatum,* as (explicitly or implicitly) one *reality* with another *reality.* In short, the 'mental' reality (whatever this 'reality' is) is – ontologically – the 'physical' reality. The frequent inference (rather obvious, given the point of departure) is that the linguistic universe which 'tells' the mental is – consequently – *reducible* to the linguistic universe which 'tells' the physical.

'ABSOLUTE' IDENTITY AND LEIBNIZ'S LAW

Not all the problems stem from an objectivist and realist interpretation of the act of identification. As we have seen elsewhere, even a linguistic, conceptual approach to the mind–body relationship – which is certainly present in the identity theory – cannot in itself overcome certain difficulties. If I say not that "M is P" (where M and P are two real states or events) but that " 'M' is 'P' " (where 'M' and 'P' are two linguistic expressions), I must be able to call upon strong criteria for a reliable verification of such a radical pronouncement of identity. "What can be meant," C. H. Whiteley rightly asks, "by saying that A is identical to B, or that every A is identical with some B, *when* A and B are non-synonymous descriptions?" (Whiteley 1970, p. 195; italics mine). The crucial question, then, is not whether to opt for a realistic perspective as opposed to a linguistic perspective, but whether it is possible to found and justify the act of identification in the all-embracing way in which the majority of orthodox identity theorists have presented it.

It is essential to understand what an identity like M is P (or 'M' is 'P') truly means, or should mean. Many identity theorists – as well as many of their opponents – have firmly established that the conditions for the existence of such an identity are those indicated by what is called Leibniz's law. Strictly speaking, Leibniz never actually formulated a law of identity. Intent on demonstrating the *principium individuationis* at work in natural reality, he simply set out the conditions under which two (individual) entities are *not* identical. The well-known principle of the identity of indiscernibles states that "in nature there are never two beings that are perfectly alike and in which it is not possible to find a difference" (*Monadologia*, 9). Still, the so-called law can be inferred from a proper restatement of this principle of indiscernibles:[1] two

---

1. On this question see D. Kalish and R. Montague, *Logic Techniques of Formal Reasoning*, New York: Harcourt, 1964, p. 223.

entities are identical when there is no difference, internal or external, between them. Leibniz himself wrote that "A is identical to B" when A can "be substituted" for B in every sense "without changing the truth" (*Ricerche generali sull'analisi delle nozioni e delle verità*). This possibility of intersubstitution, however, seems to imply the existence of an *absolute* identity between the two terms under consideration. The implication, that is, is that not *many* but *all* the properties of an entity A, a candidate for identification with entity B, are the same as those of entity B.

It has been justly pointed out that, interpreted in this way, Leibniz's law can only constitute an ideal rule, at least when applied within the realm of empirical experience. Daniel Dennett, in particular, has shown that it cannot be employed literally in psychophysical identifications (Dennett 1978b, pp. 252–3). But even admitting this limitation, even if Leibniz's law cannot serve as an obligatory frame of reference, many scholars are still convinced that an identity worthy of the name must be 'strict'. And this is where the problems arise. As early as 1960 Quine argued that "if identity is taken strictly as the relation that every entity bears to itself only, [one] is at a loss to see what is *relational* about it and how it differs from the mere attribute of existing" (Quine 1960, p. 116). Eli Hirsch, echoing Quine, has also said that it is highly doubtful that a strict identity could be defined (and practiced) in some useful way (Hirsch 1982, p. 59). Despite these warnings, a whole group of scholars has affirmed the possibility, and even the necessity, of maintaining a conception of identity that is not weak or 'liberal' (see, e.g., M. E. Levin 1979, pp. 3ff.). This thesis has been supported with particular authority by the logician Saul Kripke – and with far-reaching consequences. If identity is identity, argues Kripke, it must be understood in the most binding sense possible. Not only can it not be reduced to something else (e.g., to mere correspondence), but it cannot even be interpreted contingently. Identity must be valid in all possible situations and in all possible worlds. It does not admit exceptions (Kripke 1980). Some years ago, the uneasy situation in which the identity theory found itself given certain premises was succinctly summarized by Richard Rorty in the following terms: if this theory is too 'strict' it is essentially useless, if too 'weak' it isn't what it sets out to be (Rorty 1982a).

PSYCHOPHYSICAL IDENTITY AND
THE PRE-DEFINITION OF M AND P

The difficulties inherent in the 'strict' conception of identity, as employed by some orthodox identity theorists, become even more evident when one considers the *denotata* this identity is supposed to be applied to in the MBP. In this connection, it is worth pointing out, as Thomas Nagel has observed, that it is one thing to identify two relatively homogeneous terms or concepts, whose referents and procedures of verification are known (the case of physical terms), and it is quite another to identify two terms or concepts whose very comparability is so dubious as to become itself the *demonstrandum*. The difficulty is further compounded by the fact that the *existence* and *recognizability* of one of the terms – the mental – are equally problematic and *demonstranda* (Nagel 1974, cited in Nagel 1979, p. 177).

Many philosophers of mind have pointed out the problems that this heterogeneity of mind and body creates for the identity theory. Others have expressed serious doubts about an even more delicate question: the vague notion of the mental in the same theory. After all, how can one carry out a valid empirical investigation into a possible identity between the mind and the body without a clear definition of the mind? And even greater clarity could scarcely dispel all doubts if it is linked to an unconvincing interpretation of the mental. In this respect, critics have complained that some identity proponents assume, without adequate argumentation, a concept of the mind that is from the outset already 'factualized' and crypto-physical. But is *that* mind really a *mind?* Commenting on this tendency, Joseph Margolis has remarked that *specifically mental events* are too often confused with what are rather their *organic vehicles* or *supports*. The fright I get from a nightmare, for example, stems at least in part from psycho-existential (not 'physical') sources, although it *also* requires certain neurocerebral conditions (Margolis 1978, pp. 34–5). Thus, a proper understanding of mental phenomena requires the comprehension of a *relatively* specific aspect of these phenomena, made up of the functions and 'contents' that – independently of their subsequent possible identification with some physical processes – our experience suggests we attribute to the mental phenomena themselves. Peter Herbst's forceful position leans in the same direction: "I myself do think that experiences, and particu-

112

larly thoughts, *cannot* be identifyingly referred to except by reference to their *content*, nor desires, ambitions, hopes, fears and expectations, except in terms of their *objects*" (Herbst 1967, p. 64; italics mine). Of course, these "contents" and their "objects" do not immediately belong to the physiological universe. This is one of the reasons why Putnam once wrote that a substantial part of psychology belongs not so much to the bionatural sciences as to the disciplines that study sociocultural phenomena "and their effects in individual behavior" (Putnam 1973a, p. 146).

We have just spoken of the need for an appropriate definition of the mental as a prerequisite for a possible identification of the mental and the bodily. We hasten to add that in addition to being appropriate this definition should also be *independent* of the definition of the bodily. This second requirement is no less important than the first. Indeed, how can I proceed toward a (possible) identification between pole M and pole B if I have not *autonomously* characterized pole M? This question is clearly crucial to the problem of identity, and it has not escaped the attention of scholars. Thomas Nagel's notion of "independent ascribability", illustrated in a well-known essay on physicalism, represents an important contribution in this regard. Nagel argues that certain attributes of a complex referent are not necessarily referable to its elementary constituents (or to 'other' correlates) and must therefore be "ascribed", at least in a first approach, to the referent itself. Only in a second phase will it be determined if and how these attributes can *also* be ascribed to the constituents (or to 'other' correlates) of that referent (Nagel 1965, in Rosenthal 1971, p. 103). Accordingly, the mental could be interpreted as the referent for a group of "independently ascribable" properties, leaving for a later phase in the analysis the decision as to whether these properties can be attributed to apparently different constituents of the mental.

Indirectly sketched out by Nagel, this need for an independent predefinition of the mental is taken up more explicitly by Grover Maxwell. Maxwell maintains that if the identity theory intends to defend adequately its ultimate goals it must modify some of its starting positions – beginning with its attitude toward the mental itself. In particular, it must recognize the existence of *two* distinct classes of phenomena (physical phenomena *and* mental phenomena), each having some "intrinsic properties". It must then describe the class of mental phenomena (events and states) using cognitive as opposed to physical procedures, as the latter are not always suitable for discerning certain properties of the mental (we can physically open up the brain without being able to "get closer to seeing *sensations* of pain, joy, sadness, and so on" (Maxwell 1976a, p. 319). Only at this point will it be possible to determine whether and to what extent the members of the two classes are identifiable empirically (Maxwell, 1978, pp. 395ff.). This argumentation carries particular weight since Maxwell explicitly advocates a physicalist identity concept – albeit 'critical' and updated – of the MBP.

As might be expected, similar observations and demands have been vigorously advanced by the opponents of the identity theory. Herbst, in particular, stresses on the one hand the need for a relatively autonomous characterization of the mental, and on the other the requirement that this characterization result from procedures as far as possible independent of those used to analyze the bodily. Indeed, it would be incorrect to define the mind following procedures similar to those used in the physical sciences, since otherwise what is to be *demonstrated* in the course of the investigation would actually be tacitly conceded at the outset. It follows, then, that the mental must be defined beforehand *juxta sua principia* (Herbst 1967, pp. 57ff.).

But is it really possible to define the mind preliminarily and independently of 'other' referents and principles (physical ones, e.g.)? Some scholars, such as Max Deutscher, have not concealed their perplexity. For Deutscher, an attempt to satisfy this demand would risk running up against some intriguing contradictions. In fact, if a human being describes his mental state as he feels it, "and *before* physicalism identifies it as a brain state, then "that state must be allowed to have the properties by which the subject identified it", and those properties will most likely be *sui generis* and *distinct*. But if they are *truly distinct*, how can I later demonstrate that they are *identical* to something else? (Deutscher 1967, p. 70). The objection raised by the 'neo-identity theorist' Jaegwon Kim, to whom we shall return, is in many regards similar: "if we define 'mental event' by a certain property . . . and then define 'physical event' as those events lacking it, or conversely define 'physical event' by a certain property . . . and 'mental event' as those lacking it, then the identification of the mental with the physical becomes hopeless" (Kim 1972a, pp. 323–4).

IDENTITY BETWEEN MENTAL AND PHYSICAL 'PROPERTIES' AND THE M–P ASYMMETRY

It should not be overlooked that in both Deutscher and Kim a sort of conceptual shift has taken place. Deutscher, in particular, no longer speaks of the mental but of "mental properties". The difference is important as it signals a transition in the discussion from the plane of *entities* to that of *properties*. We shall come back to the significance and implications of this change in due time. What matters here is whether it solves the problems connected with a 'strict' identification of the mental with the bodily.

The answer does not seem to be in the affirmative. Already in the 1920s Charles Broad had pointed out that it is impossible to identify the properties of physical entities with those of mental entities:

> About a molecular movement it is perfectly reasonable to raise the question: "Is it swift or slow, straight or circular, and so on?" About the awareness of a red patch it is nonsensical to ask whether it is a swift or a slow awareness, a straight or a circular awareness, and so on. Conversely, it is reasonable to ask about an awareness of a red patch whether it is a clear or a confused awareness; but it is nonsense to ask of a molecular movement whether it is a clear or a confused movement. (Broad 1925, pp. 622–3)

Some forty years later James Cornman was forced to repeat Broad's remark almost word for word:

> We can talk about intense, unbearable, nagging, or throbbing pains. And yellow, dim, fading, or circular after-images. And dogmatic, false, profound, or unconscious beliefs. On the other hand we can also discuss publicly observable, spatially located, swift, irreversible physical processes. Thus if the Identity Theory is correct, it seems that we should sometimes be able to say truthfully that physical processes such as brain processes are dim or fading or nagging or false, and that mental phenomena such as after-images are publicly observable or physical or spatially located or swift. (Cornman 1962, in Borst 1979, p. 127)

We have said that Cornman was "forced" to take a certain position. In the early 1960s, in fact, many proponents of the identity theory supported the 'strict' identity between mental and physical properties, thus leading inevitably to the conclusion voiced by Cornman in the passage quoted above. What is more, alongside the notion of 'strict' identity another position, also based on the figure of *properties,* enjoyed equal favor: that of radical 'substitutionism'. Richard Rorty, for example, claimed that mental properties could correspond perfectly well to correlative neurological properties, to the point that "the terms signifying these properties would take over the roles of these latter terms just as 'stimulation of the C-fibers' took over the role of 'pain' " (Rorty 1970a, p. 224). Replies to this sort of position came from the most diverse theoretical orientations. Sellars, for instance, asked: "How can a property which is in the logical space of neurophysiological states be identical with a property which is not?" (Sellars 1965, pp. 443–4). Borst essentially reiterated the argument suggested by Broad and Cornman. We can say that "beliefs are true, false, well-founded or absurd; afterimages are yellow or green or hazy; but no brain process could intelligently be said to be any of these things" (Borst 1979, p. 26).

Of the many other questions raised in the debate on psychophysical identity we shall mention only one more: that which could be called 'the knot of symmetry'. The most lucid explanation of the problem is presented in C. V. Borst's introductory essay to his classic collection of readings on the identity theory. If the identity between M and B is to be truly rigorous, Borst argues, then it is not clear why it should be interpreted, so to speak, in just *one* direction: in the direction that identifies M states and events with B states and events. Why, he asks, shouldn't the opposite be true as well? In other words, if M = B, why not also B = M? (Borst 1979, p. 21). One of the most telling answers to Borst's question is probably that given by Richard J. Bernstein in another well-known collection of essays on the mind–body relationship. For Bernstein, to admit a *symmetrical* identity, as would seem correct from a formal point of view, means admitting a possible solution to the MBP not only in materialist terms ('M is B') but also in mentalistic terms ('B is M'): terms that cannot be accepted by orthodox identity theorists (Bernstein 1968, in Rosenthal, 1971).

Bernstein is perfectly right. We might merely add that if identity theorists reject such a possibility *a priori* it is not only because of certain implications (idealistic, etc.) of the statement 'B is M', but also because they champion an interpretation of M that subjects it to the cognitive principles of a *definite* science (i.e., physics, in its broadest sense). Accordingly, as was pointed out at the beginning of the preceding paragraph, their most pressing goal is not to establish first and foremost the *identity M–B* but to *materialize and physicalize M*. And we have already suggested that this priority may in part explain why they have not always delved too deeply into the problems connected with the concept of identity.

Whether this hypothesis is correct or not, one thing is certain: identity – as it has been treated by orthodox identity theorists – seems to have created more problems than it has solved.

Chapter 4

Psychology as alchemy

The elimination of the mental in
the 'disappearance theory'

THE 'DISAPPEARANCE THEORY' AND CRITIQUES OF THE IDENTITY THEORY

It is in part due to the difficulties inherent in the identity theory discussed in the preceding chapter that in the 1960s there emerged a new conception of the MBP, known as "eliminative materialism" or "the disappearance theory" (henceforth DT). Although it has not attracted a great number of followers, DT enjoys considerable prestige among students of the problem that interests us: this is due mainly to the impact of some of its undeniably brilliant arguments and to the renown of its two principal proponents: Paul K. Feyerabend and Richard Rorty.

DT has its strongest appeal within a clearly defined group of philosophers of mind: supporters of a materialist, physicalist, and reductive solution to the MBP. In fact, the approach outlined by Rorty and Feyerabend is oriented in precisely that direction. Feyerabend, in particular, holds a radically materialist view not only of the mental but also of the human in general: "the only entities existing in the world," he writes in his important essay *Materialism and the Mind–Body Problem*, "are atoms and aggregates of atoms" (in Borst 1979, p. 142). And the essay closes with the peremptory declaration that there is "not a single reason why the attempt to give a purely physiological account of human beings should be abandoned" (ibid., p. 156).

If this is the DT perspective, how does it differ from that of the orthodox identity theory? The most immediate answer is that DT does not propose the *identification* of the mental with the bodily, but its *elimination* (hence, the term 'eliminative materialism'). In the

118

second place, DT proposes to solve, or to avoid, certain difficulties inherent in the identity theory. This is particularly evident in Rorty, who in various ways appears to be the most authoritative voice of this new theory of the mind–body relationship. (For this reason we shall refer more to his positions than to Feyerabend's, which are different in some respects and less pertinent to our discussion.)

Some of Rorty's criticisms of the identity theory have already been mentioned, the main one being that it proposes a conception of identity that is either too strong (thus empirically unprovable or sterile) or too weak (thus bordening on banality). Arguably, his most radical observations are directed against the strong or 'strict' version of the identity theory. Rorty points out that this kind of identity implies, among other things, that brain processes can be *false* and that mental phenomena can be *located in space:* and both propositions are manifestly absurd (Rorty 1965, in Borst 1979, pp. 188ff.). But Rorty's principal criticism of the orthodox identity theory is another one. When considering the MBP (and, more generally, every sphere of knowledge) we cannot and must not speak ontologically, that is, about *entities* in the realist sense of the word. The mind is, in fact, not some-*thing* that can be identified with some other *thing*. Indeed, the mental, like the bodily, is merely a definite *expression*, a definite *linguistic and conceptual world*. Smart had also come close to a position of this kind when he suggested the possibility of a general "translation" of psychological sentences into a "topic-neutral" language. But Rorty quickly dismisses Smart's 'translationist' form of identity: "The disappearance form holds that it is unnecessary to show that suitable translations (into 'topic-neutral' language) of our talk about sensations can be given – as unnecessary as it is to show that statements about quantities of calorific fluid, when properly understood, may be seen to be topic-neutral statements" (ibid., pp. 189–90).

The 'linguistic' approach Rorty uses is essential to the main assumption underlying DT. Briefly, this assumption might run as follows: certain statements, containing references to definite *denotata*, can and must under certain conditions be simply *eliminated*. This occurs if and when science establishes that the basic presuppositions and cognitive objectives that justified the use of those statements are proven to be, respectively, *false* and attainable in a *different way* (the *true* way) by another set of statements. If and *when*, it was said. In effect, it is not Rorty's aim to deny absolutely – that is, independently of historical circumstances – the legitimacy of certain statements. It could well be that even for a lengthy period of time these statements – and with them their reference to definite phenomena – have an (apparent) plausibility and meaning. But as human knowledge progresses we can sometimes prove that those phenomena quite literally *do not exist*. It is at this point that the purposes which were served by our referring to these phenomena can and must be answered by new conceptual and linguistic expressions designating new phenomena, new *denotata*.

One of Rorty's favorite examples is the case of caloric. As is well known, this concept was in use for a relatively long period of time, and undoubtedly satisfied definite cognitive needs. At the end of the eighteenth century, however, it was shown that it did not actually correspond to any empirical referent or phenomenon. Later, it became possible to answer the 'question' which up to then had been answered by the notion of caloric with the new notion of 'mean kinetic energy of molecules' (ibid., p. 189). At this point, says Rorty, we must conclude that caloric does not exist and that the theory and 'explanation' built on that basis are, literally, empty. More generally speaking, it can be said that 'non-existing entities' such as caloric are concepts linked to doctrines that have been, or are in the process of being, left behind. Not only, then, do these concepts have no further right to exist, but there is also no reason to preserve them in any way or form. Far from being more or less captiously *identified* with something different (as when one says that 'the mind', which in truth does not exist, 'is the brain'), they must simply *disappear*: they must be *eliminated*. We should no longer say something like 'A is B', but rather something like 'today there should only be B, and A must be suppressed' – where A is both the referent and its corresponding universe of discourse which the current state of knowledge has shown not to exist.

THE "ELIMINATION" OF PSYCHOLOGY

Up to a certain point Rorty develops his concept of elimination in general terms. Then he applies it specfically to the issue of the mental and psychology. To this purpose he introduces a couple of suggestive analogies, the most striking being that between demons and sensations (ibid., pp. 191–3). It could happen (and indeed *has* happened and continues to happen), Rorty argues, that certain primitive peoples attribute diseases to the action of evil "demons". More advanced civilizations know that these diseases are caused instead by germs, viruses, and so forth. Demons are mere mythological figures and serve no cognitive purpose. Thus they can, indeed must, be eliminated – as has, in fact, happened, at least as far as possible. The same thing could, in principle, happen to sensations. "Sensations", says Rorty, "may be to the future progress of psychophysiology as demons are to modern science. Just as we now want to deny that there are demons, future science may want to deny that there are sensations" (ibid., p. 192).

Rorty is well aware that the first objection to this analogy is that while *certain* things can be eliminated, *other* eliminations seem implausible. How can we deny or 'make disappear' sensory (or mental) phenomena? But his reply shows no trace of uncertainty: "The absurdity of saying 'Nobody has ever felt a pain' is no greater than that of saying 'Nobody has ever seen a demon' ". Of course, this will be true only when I have "a suitable answer to the question: 'What *was* I reporting [i.e., *really* reporting, from the perspective of events that are *scientifically verifiable*] when I said I felt a pain?" (ibid., p. 193). In other words, the hypothetical elimination encouraged and predicted by Rorty is heavily dependent on the discoveries and progress of scientific knowledge. It will be the "science of the future" that one day will answer the above question by saying: "You were reporting the occurrence of a *certain brain process*" (ibid.). On that day, Rorty writes in another article, it could happen that sensation "might lose its reporting role as well as its explanatory role, just as 'demon' had lost both its roles, and that both of these roles might be taken over by reference to brain-processes" (Rorty 1970a, in Rosenthal 1971, p. 223).

Rorty's argument is striking indeed. Just as caloric or phlogiston have been replaced by other concepts, so is there every reason to believe – and hope – that the same thing will happen to mental events. And if alchemy has disappeared, psychology may one day meet the same fate. We are moving toward a future world where no one will say, "I'm in pain", but rather "My C-fibres are firing" (Rorty 1965, p. 193).

As we said earlier, Rorty is fully aware that at least some 'eliminations' appear rather bizarre and even unacceptable. It is this difficulty that leads Rorty to stress a crucial point of his theory: the apparent unacceptability of certain eliminations stems not from the fact that they would be *false*, but that they would be highly "impractical" (ibid., p. 194). Let us take the example of a table. Science tells us that it is made up of an aggregate of molecules. So why not eliminate 'table'? For Rorty, "the only answer to this question which will stand examination" is that "although we could *in principle* drop 'table', it would be monstrously *inconvenient* to do so" (ibid., p. 196; italics mine). Rorty, in short, approaches the issue from a *pragmatic* perspective. It is no coincidence that at certain crucial points of his discussion he introduces the principle of *simplicity,* the criterion of *convenience, and the notion of efficacy.* Thus, when he speaks of primitive tribes he surmises that their reference to demons has a *raison d'être* connected with one or another practical goal. In spite of this the fact remains that scientific explanations which exclude the existence of demons have an "efficacy" and a "simplicity" that other explanations do not have, and this is "an excellent reason for saying that there are no demons" (ibid., p. 192). Similarly, it is "simpler" and easier to say that "my C-fibers are firing" than to speak of a vague and metaphysical 'pain' (ibid., p. 193). More generally, Rorty claims elsewhere that "mental predicates" should disappear "given the superior explanatory ability of neurological theory" (Rorty 1970a, in Rosenthal 1971, p. 231).

It would be tempting to examine Rorty's theory in greater detail, but here we will limit ourselves to only one further point. Rorty seems to warn fellow eliminationists that in order to eliminate the mental it is not enough to persuade science: it will also be necessary to convince ordinary people to change certain "linguistic practices" (Rorty 1970b, p. 423). In this connection, Rorty had already written that he was more concerned about the right and duty to eliminate one language and replace it with another more valid and useful one than with the prediction that the neurological language would inevitably win out. Indeed, for him even introspective language is, at least for the moment, not completely "illegitimate" (Rorty 1970a, in Rosenthal 1971, pp. 227 and 234).

Actually, the overall tone of Rorty's discussion is far more peremptory than appears from these quotations. This is evident in what remains one of the key texts of DT, the essay 'Mind–Body Identity, Privacy, and Categories' (1965); but it is also discernible in the article 'In Defense of Eliminative Materialism' (1970), where the author openly declares: "the materialist predicts that the neurological vocabulary will triumph", making other vocabularies gradually disappear (ibid., pp. 229–30). On more than one occasion Rorty also claims that it is possible, indeed necessary, to encourage a generalized use of neurophysiological language – what Feyerabend called "materialese" (Robinson 1982, p. 89). Here Rorty echoes the hopes expressed by Feigl and others that future generations will one day be taught to speak not 'psycho-phenomenologically,' but physicalistically – that is, scientifically. The allusion to Feigl is hardly out of place if we recall that the author of *The 'Mental' and the 'Physical'* had also approached positions that were eliminationist in character.

SCIENTISM AND PROPHETISM IN THE 'DISAPPEARANCE THEORY'

Not surprisingly, the radical nature of the theses advanced by DT – which Popper labels "bizarre" (Popper and Eccles 1977), Robinson "strange and counterintuitive" (Robinson 1982, p. 81), and Armstrong "spectacular" but full of flaws (Fløistad 1983, pp. 54ff.) – has provoked vehement objections from all sides. Since an analysis of the entire corpus of these criticisms would take us too far afield, we shall limit our considerations only to the most relevant.

From the epistemological point of view, DT assumes an attitude which might be called scientistic, at least in that some of its formulations tend – as Richard Bernstein has observed – to present mental language as the "language of appearance" and neurological language as the "language of reality" (i.e., the language that tells us how things *really* happen). This implies that science is "the measure of what is that it is and of what is not that it is not", which is precisely one of the possible definitions of scientism (Bernstein 1968, in Rosenthal 1971, p. 220). The scientistic nature of certain aspects of DT is confirmed by the evident priority given to "scientific" language as such: a preference unaltered by various declarations in defense of the "legitimacy" of other languages (such as introspective language). Declarations of this sort, moreover, appear considerably weakened by the persistent tendency on the part of some eliminationists – as Wilkerson points out critically – to identify *tout court* mental language with a-scientific language (Wilkerson 1974, p. 181). Nor can one ignore, in this context, DT's strong leaning toward physicalism: a propensity that seems to contradict the apparent pluralism of some of its epistemological principles.

Two further aspects of the eliminationist hypothesis that have drawn criticism from MBP scholars concern the attitude of Rorty and others toward empirical facts and what could be called the 'futurism' of their proposal. On the first point, while it is difficult to endorse (fully) Howard Robinson's radical critique of Rorty's anti-realism, one can hardly help agreeing with him that there is, after all, a big difference between a demon and a table (Robinson 1982, p. 87) – and, we should add, between a demon and *a sensation*. What is true for a concrete object like a table or a mythological figure is not necessarily true for a phenomenal and subjective experience like a sensation. It is one thing to eliminate a demon, in the sense of dissolving it because no verifiable phenomenon confirms its existence, and it is quite another to eliminate a sensation. In fact, even if what I feel may be reducible to some*thing* different" from the scientific point of view, on the experiential plane it remains true (phenomenologically true) that in having a sensation I feel a definite psychic state – and it is precisely *this* feeling that a non-eliminationist philosophy of mind would like to preserve.

Secondly, it has often been observed that the proponents of DT pay scant attention to the *current* status of knowledge about the MBP. On the one hand they seem to pass over the undeniable fact that there is very little available evidence to support certain theses; on the other, they incline to describe a situation that could exist only in the *future*. In this connection, DT theorists are open to the same accusation of 'prophetism' (i.e., making statements dependent on only *possible* future discoveries) that Popper levelled against radical materialism, and Rorty's claim that "materialism *will triumph*" is a clear example of what the co-author of *The Self and Its Brain* dismissed as a "promissory note". From a different viewpoint, moreover, DT all too often seems to rest on purely hypothetical arguments, true only in principle and based on merely theoretical or analogical reasoning, that are quick to sidestep the difficulties inherent in the eliminationist doctrine.

THE CONCEPT OF ELIMINATION AND THE INTERPRETATION OF THE MENTAL

Leaving aside the 'prophetic' epistemology adopted by the eliminationists, another point that should be emphasized here concerns the conception of knowledge which underlies DT: a conception that at times appears to be somewhat simplistic and one-sided. Is it really true that a new, more 'convenient' theory is destined (and rightly so) to *eliminate* all competitors? Is it really true that a *complex* theory (perhaps even in part *inexact*) can and must be substituted, without risk of loss, by a *simpler* theory? Can we really be sure that this simpler (and maybe more exact) theory is able to satisfy all our cognitive requirements? These questions require more than non-chalant answers. While it is true that one theory may be preferable to others, this certainly does not mean that it has grasped an objective truth, valid *für ewig* and from any possible point of view. But if its 'convenience' cannot be absolute, neither can the elimination of rival theories. There is no doubt that in some cases a simpler theory (or one more directly connected with physicalist principles) can efficaciously replace other theories. But whether this replacement is entirely possible must be decided on a strictly empirical plane and can in no way be guaranteed *a priori*. One should also keep in mind that our "cognitive interests" (to use Habermas's phrase) are not always fully satisfied by one single set of answers, no matter how exact and 'simple'. Consequently, we may find that a new theory responds more effectively to certain cognitive needs whereas it appears less convincing to others, which are better satisfied by some previous or alternative doctrine.

The thesis advanced by DT (and by certain advocates of the identity theory) that a physicalistic language could eliminate the language of psychology has met with the perplexity – and, at times, the sarcasm – of many philosophers of mind. "What a marvelous solution!" quips Norman Malcolm: Marvelous but, unfortunately, totally impractical – and, more importantly, erroneous on a theoretical level. The error (or rather, for Malcolm, one of the errors) consists in identifying the communicative function of linguistic events with their overall nature and action. Besides being a vehicle of information, language is also an expression of intentions and beliefs, memories and habits, all this being intimately connected with definite uses and traditions. As Malcolm observes, a "stripped-down expression will not *take the place* of the familiar expression *unless it is used in the same way*". Thus, the 'elimination' of a certain *proposition* through its 'replacement' with another is not in itself sufficient to reproduce (in the only 'correct' way) what appears to be something extremely complex: a reality which is truly a linguistic behavior or experience whose most significant aspects are linked to the whole *modus essendi* and *agendi* of the speaker as well as to the context in which he acts linguistically. It is not very clear what would be required to carry out the 'correct reproduction' (the 'replacement') under consideration. But it would certainly be something not foreseen by the general program and methods of DT, since it would involve affecting not so much the linguistic enunciation *ut sic* as its socioanthropological dimensions and presuppositions (Malcolm and Armstrong 1984, pp. 98–9).

This discussion of the concept of elimination calls to mind Rorty's analogy between demons and sensations. Is it really possible to hold that the latter can be *eliminated* in the same way as the former have been? More basically, is it really possible to hold that 'demonological' discourse is analogous to 'psychological' discourse? For many scholars the answer is an emphatic 'no'. Wilkerson, in particular, has observed that psychological language speaks – admittedly in an often 'inexact', or partially 'private and subjective', way – of states and events that can be concretely experienced: awareness, pain, desire. Demons, witches, and spirits are instead 'things' that appear to be to the highest degree abstract, literally '*meta*-physical' and '*meta*-empirical' (Wilkerson 1974, p. 181). Giacomo Gava pointed out that while we *deny* the existence of demons, what we tend to do with sensation is, at most, to *identify* them with something else. It is easy to see that these are two completely different operations, implying different attitudes, different judgements, and different linguistic and epistemological practices. Furthermore, Gava continues, to speak of sensations is 'wrong' ('might be wrong', we would say): but it is surely not wrong in the same way as it is to speak of demons (Gava 1983, pp. 121–2).

Actually, what underlies the formulation of certain more or less provocative analogies is something rather serious. Those who compare psychological to demonological (or astrological, or alchemical) discourse share a highly questionable conception of the mental and of its *modus operandi*. Why, Joseph Margolis rightly asks, and on the basis of what real evidence should the mental be viewed (*a priori*) as something fictional, mythical, and 'non-existent' (Margolis 1978, pp. 45 and 58)? It has also been remarked that not only does DT not offer adequate argumentation in support of the alleged *non-scientific nature* of mental language (in fact, there are those who would be satisfied with simply defending its *cognitive* nature): it does not even offer a satisfactory reply to the objection that in certain instances people *really* need to use this, and only this, *mental* language – for example, when they want to describe states or events at the affective or at the symbolic level.

Probably the most convincing and suggestive treatment of these questions has been provided by Richard Bernstein. His main thesis is that in one way or another DT (as well as the identity theory) tends to favor one language over all others, whether by subordinating the latter to the former, or by declaring that other languages can in principle (or in the future) be replaced or eliminated, or by demoting them to the function of mere vehicles of emotional expressions. This tendency could have serious consequences: we risk losing, Bernstein warns, "an entire mode of discourse including its *entire descriptive vocabulary*" (in Rosenthal 1971, p. 219).

THE CRITERION OF 'CONVENIENCE' AND THE NEOEMPIRICIST SOURCES OF THE DISAPPEARANCE THEORY

It was already suggested that in elaborating some of its principles DT seems to approach pragmatist positions. No doubt this is, or rather might have been, a rather stimulating direction to take. In fact, if properly developed, it could 'liberalize' the attitude of DT proponents toward the physical and psychic languages of the 'mental'. Indeed, the adoption of a pragmatist orientation could encourage eliminationists to view the two languages not as (respectively) a true and a false (or inexact, misleading, etc.) expression of definite phenomena, but as a flexible instrument to voice different, yet equally useful, ways of expressing these phenomena in relation to different goals.

Unfortunately, for a large part of DT this does not happen – or it happens only to a rather modest extent. In particular, the promising criterion of 'convenience' appears to be separated from the *contexts* and *aims* that alone can give a fruitful sense to this notion. Indeed, the issue that should have been raised is convenience 'for what', in relation 'to what' – and perhaps also 'for whom'. While not completely ignored, these crucial questions do not receive (with rare exceptions) the truly 'pluralistic' answers that might have been expected. *De facto*, and sometimes even *de jure*, DT considers the criterion of the *right* convenience essentially from the standpoint of the advancement of science – or, even more restrictively, of the advancement of a *definite* type of science. The objection to be raised is that there are states or conditions for which *other* criteria of convenience are valid. Thus, for instance, if I make a statement which is intended to be mainly *my* subjective and emotional statement (in the sense that it is an assertion concerning mainly what *I* feel in relation to a definite situation), this statement may reasonably expect to be understood and judged according to criteria of convenience that do not coincide with those adopted by science in its usual meaning.

One possible conclusion that emerges from what has been said so far is that DT remains, at least in certain respects, bound to a fundamentally neoempiricist epistemology: an epistemology, in any case, that in speaking of *knowledge*, refers essentially to *science*, and in speaking of *science* refers essentially to *physics;* an epistemology, further, that gives precedence to the criterion of simplicity, the process of reduction in an eliminative sense, the principle of the existence of one language that is *a priori* and in general more reliable than others. These are all assumptions and positions which rather clearly originate in neoempiricist tradition. Indeed, it would not be difficult to find many texts belonging to that tradition which appear surprisingly in line with some of the 'eliminationist' programs of DT. Even the key concept/term 'elimination' itself has a neoempiricist origin. Otto Neurath, in particular, used it as early as in the 1930s precisely within the context of the philosophy of mind. And, just like the proponents of DT, he linked an *eliminationist* program to a *physicalist* one. Deriving the psychic phenomenon of perception from the physical event of "neural modification', Neurath issued a sort of epistemological linguistic proclamation: "we must continue to *free* the 'clots' of our language of metaphyscial appendages and define everything that remains physicalistically" (1931, p. 401). Elsewhere, widening his discussion to include the whole dimension of the human, he also wrote:

> The elimination of all such [metaphysical] expressions in sociology and psychology, as in all fields, must be pursued not only with the aim of *freeing* these disciplines of superfluous affirmations and avoiding meaningless verbal combinations. . . , but also, and most importantly, for its precise scientific utility, consisting in the *elimination* of possible occasions for certain false correlations in the field of empirical investigation. (Neurath 1931, p. 412)

A final summing up of DT cannot help but lay stress on its materialistic and physiological components. To this end, an article by Rorty on functionalism bears eloquent testimony. Not only does he strenuously defend materialism in the sphere of the philosophy of mind, but he also predicts that we will all be inevitably "converted" to this creed not through philosophical reflection but through the science of the body: "Just as it took modern science to make us atheists – despite all the clever conceptual analyses of the ancient skeptics – so *will it take physiology to make us materialists*" (Rorty 1972, p. 219; italics mine). Certainly, it is not necessary to dwell on issues that have already been explored in the preceding chapters. We shall only point out that it is primarily the presence of this materialistic inspiration that has made it appropriate to analyze DT in close connection with the identity theory. It is no coincidence that the most acute critics of a materialistic and physicalistic interpretation of the mental – Bernstein, Wilkerson, Malcolm, Margolis, Robinson – have associated the two doctrines in many respects.

But before directing our attention to the writings of these and other philosophers of mind who have elaborated an alternative approach to the MBP, we must consider two attempts at a reform – a radical reform, to be sure, but not (as we shall see) a thorough and convincing transformation – of the materialistic conception of the mental and of psychology. We are alluding on the one hand to functionalism and on the other to several positions that cannot easily be grouped under a single heading, but for which we shall in time try to find a common denominator.

Chapter 5

The mind as function

The functionalist approach to the mind–body problem

PUTNAM: THE ATTACK ON MATERIALISM AND PHYSICALISM

In the debate engaging the contemporary philosophy of mind the functionalist movement has proved to be an extremely lively, complex, and epistemologically formidable contender. Functionalism has addressed themes and issues of crucial importance to the mind–body relationship: the nature of mental states, the structure of psychological explanation, the possible autonomy of psychology as a science, and the problems of reduction and nomology in psychological analysis. Its investigation covers epistemological and (meta)psychological terrain and is carried out on different levels at once. We shall limit ourselves, however, to examining certain theoretical points of particular pertinence to our present concerns and to consider two philosophers who have emerged from a variety of currents as the foremost champions of functionalism: Hilary Putnam and Jerry Fodor.

The most striking quality of the output of Putnam and Fodor is the theoretical breadth. Unlike many MBP specialists, neither Fodor nor much less Putnam (whose foreground role in contemporary philosophy scarcely needs underscoring) confines himself to a 'technical' approach to the question of the relationship between mind and body. On the contrary, both carry out their investigations within a much broader context and assume clear positions on the far-reaching psychoanthropological and epistemological implications of the problem. Not surprisingly, then, Putnam and Fodor take determined stands on issues of general concern to philosophy such as materialism, physicalism, and reductionism.

Putnam began his investigation of the relationship between the brain and behavior in the early sixties, calling into question the theoretical foundations of both behaviorism and materialism (Putnam 1961). A few years later he published an important essay on certain problems connected with robots in which he took a firm stand against the identity theory (Putnam 1964). Further fleshed-out and refined, this position was developed in the well-known article 'The Mental Life of Some Machines' (1967). Here Putnam observed that "materialists" – equivalent, for him, to "identity theorists" – hold mental acts (like preference) to be essentially physical. This implies that 'preferring A to B' is identical to having certain physical features of brain processes, since the "is" appropriate to a mental concept like preference is quite different from the "is" appropriate to other types of states or events (in Castañeda 1967, p. 190). He goes on to say:

> We *cannot* discover laws by virtue of which it is physically
> necessary that an organism prefers A to B if and only if it is
> in a certain physical-chemical state. For we already know
> that any such laws would be false. They would be false be-
> cause even in the light of our present knowledge we can see
> that any Turing machine that can be physically realized at all
> can be realized in a host of totally different ways. Thus there
> cannot be a physical-chemical structure the possession of
> which is a necessary and sufficient condition for preferring A
> to B. (ibid., p. 204)

In subsequent writings on the problems under consideration, Putnam has radicalized his anti-materialist stance. Materialism, he argues in an article already referred to in our Introduction, basically presumes to define how the world (*the whole* world) is made. Seen in this light, it is a *metaphysics:* but a metaphysics that has the ability to present itself as a *science.* One could indeed suggest that materialism has taken the place of positivism and pragmatism "as the dominant contemporary form of scientism". And scientism, for Putnam, is "one of the most dangerous contemporary intellectual tendencies" (Putnam 1982b, p. 147).

Putnam's 1982 article also argues that materialism and physicalism are essentially the same thing. Even aside from this judgement, it is undeniable that Putnam's reflection on the philosophy of mind and the MBP has led him to adopt an increasingly overt anti-physicalist orientation. In his article on robots he had argued that psychological investigation has shown that an organism can exhibit states which are *not* specified in physical terms (Putnam 1964, p. 71). Actually, Putnam's foremost concern is not so much ontological as epistemological and cognitive. One of his basic assumptions in this regard is that it is one matter to presume to know how things *are made a parte objecti,* and quite another (much more serious and practicable) to examine *the explanations* that knowledge can give *about* things. Are we sure that physical things can have only physical explanations?

Putnam's answer to this question is an emphatic 'no'. This emerges most forcefully in his essay entitled 'Philosophy and Our Mental Life' (1975). Here Putnam argues that Descartes and Diderot were mistaken in maintaining that *if* we are made of matter, *then* there can be one and only one explanation (a *physical* one) for our behavior (in Block, 1980–1, p. 137). More generally, it is false that "if something is made of matter, its behavior must have a physical explanation". Putnam's key intuition is that a sharp distinction must be made between *an entity* and its *behavior.* The former can certainly be a physical thing, but the latter could imply, from a cognitive point of view, the reference to something 'other' than pure 'physicalness', for example, rules, symbols, values. Moreover, Putnam insists, not every explanation "must be at the level of the ultimate constituents" – which could indeed be physical – of the *explanandum.* Rather, the explanation "might have the property that *the ultimate constituents don't matter,* that *the higher level structure matters*" (ibid.; italics mine).

We shall have occasion to return to this important principle, which recognizes the full legitimacy of an irreducible, holistic "higher level" of explanation. Here we shall only highlight the important implications that the theses outlined above have for the philosophy of mind. In a clearly anti-physicalist vein, Putnam holds that one can emphasize perfectly well-founded and illuminating differences between a "possible psychological theory of a human being" and its "physical or chemical description" (ibid., p. 135). He even goes so far as to say that "whatever our mental functioning may be, there seems to be no serious reason to believe that it is explainable by our physics and chemistry" (ibid., p. 139). This statement may indeed sound too radical: it seems in fact questionable to deny the mental some sort of (perhaps partial) physical or chemical explanation, referring at least to its material conditions or supports. What is to be denied is not that this is *possible,* but that it is the *only possibility* considered valid, the only one that can answer *all* the cognitive questions that arise from the investigation of mental life.

It has already been observed that on a general level the advocates of functionalism criticize reductionism as well as materialism and physicalism. Paradoxically, in the 1950s Putnam had co-signed with Paul Oppenheim one of the most determined and striking hyper-reductionist manifestoes of contemporary thought (Oppenheim and Putnam 1958), and in several subsequent publications his support of reductionist principles continued unabated. If Putnam's philosophy underwent a substantial transformation in the course of the 1960s, this may well be due largely to his intense investigation into the problems of the mental and of the human sphere. In 1973, in an article entitled 'Reductionism and the Nature of Psychology,' he wrote:

> A doctrine to which most philosophers of science subscribe
> (and to which I subscribed for many years) is the doctrine
> that the laws of such 'higher-level' sciences as psychology
> and sociology are reducible to the laws of lower-level sci-
> ences – biology, chemistry, ultimately to the laws of elemen-
> tary particle physics. Acceptance of this doctrine is generally
> identified with the belief in 'The Unity of Science' (with capi-
> tals), and rejection of it with belief in Vitalism, or Psychism,
> or, anyway, something *bad*. In this paper I want to argue that
> this doctrine is wrong. (Putnam 1973a, p. 131)

Following in the path suggested by this trenchant, admirable self-criticism, Putnam has on various occasions embraced radical anti-reductionist positions. Not surprisingly, his new orientation has injected innovative force into the debate on the philosophy of mind: he has fought with determination in favor of the autonomy of the mental, the independence of psychology from the biophysical sciences, and the irreducibility of certain human features (or of the sciences that study them). He has also made the striking claim that an interpretation of psychology in biological and/or physical terms is "under-determined". "People's psychology", he writes in the same paper, "is partly a reflection of deeply entrenched societal beliefs" (ibid., p. 141). This implies that special attention must be reserved for the connections between psychology and sociology (ibid., p. 146). If scholars stopped concentrating their efforts on the more elementary psychic states (those most conditioned by biological factors) and spent more time studying more complex cases, then they would be "thinking of the parts of psychology which study mainly societal beliefs and their effects in individual behavior" (ibid.). This would be a way both of giving proper attention to areas of psychology which have been unjustly neglected and of recognizing the value of an anti-reductionist and sociocultural approach to psychology itself.

FODOR: ANTI-REDUCTIONISM, ANTI-PHYSICALISM, AND THE AUTONOMY OF PSYCHOLOGY

The anti-reductionism of Putnam was preceded by that of the other leading advocate of functionalism, Jerry Fodor. In 1968, referring specifically to the MBP, Fodor had written: "Psychological entities (sensations, for example) are not readily thought of as capable of being microanalyzed into *anything*, least of all neurons or states of neurons" (in Rosenthal 1971, p. 144). In *The Language of Thought* (1975), one of the classics of the contemporary philosophy of mind, he extended the range of this anti-reductionist orientation. Reductionism, he writes, has positivist roots and tends to identify the progress of what he calls the 'special sciences' with the reduction of their theories to the theory of what is considered Science *par excellence* (at present, physics). The striking popularity of this view is linked to the desire for (or the myth of) the unity of knowledge. Moreover, if taken seriously, this aim of unification and reduction would inevitably lead to the paradoxical conclusion that the more the individual sciences progress, the closer they come to dissolving voluntarily into a single Super-science – at the moment, as we have said, physics. The attempt to reduce 'everything' to physics, Fodor continues (in agreement with Putnam), cannot avoid the fact that if certain entities and phenomena belong to the physical world this does not mean that everything that can be said about them can be said in physical terms. For instance, the phenomena of a 'high-level' science like economics are certainly referable (at least in principle) to the action of physical beings. But it does not follow from this that "the typical predicates of economics" can be reduced to the typical predicates first of psychology and then of physics. On the contrary, while the former refer to realities such as monetary systems, and so on, the referents of the latter are quite different in nature. Indeed, the idea that notions such as "consumption", or "work force", can be reduced to psychophysical constituents is patently absurd (ibid., p. 16n).

The same line of reasoning can be employed in the sphere that concerns us, that of psychic phenomena and psychology. Even if psychic events were physiological events, this would not imply *tout court* "the reducibility of psychology to physiology" (ibid., p. 9). Indeed, the (hypothetical) physical 'nature' of psychic events would not imply that they are *only* physical. More precisely, it is a fact that psychic phenomena are also inextricably linked to highly personal situations: the elimination of this factor would result in the exclusion of "the most complex experiences of daily life". Even if it were possible to demonstrate that every psychic event was physical, not even this would guarantee that physics "can provide an appropriate vocabulary for psychological theories" (ibid., p. 17). The target of constant reductionist attacks, psychology plays, in Fodor's view, an irreplaceable role in contemporary epistemology and in the philosophy of man: it starts, as it were, where psychophysics leaves off (ibid., p. 201).

Given these premises, it is only natural that in *The Language of Thought* Fodor should often take a critical stance toward physicalism – or at least, 'strict', radical physicalism. Physicalism is a sort of metaphysics, a world view rife with all sorts of risks and dangers. What is physics, after all? It is simply a conceptual and explanatory system that wields considerable power today. But this in no way means that it can presume to offer the *only* possible language, the *only* interpretation, the *only* set of answers concerning the world and, above all, the way we relate to it. Physics, writes Fodor, works out its own classification, its own taxonomy of 'what there is': but this is not the only one that can (and must) be sought if we wish to give adequate answers to the *different* purposes of knowledge.

PUTNAM: CRITICISM OF THE IDENTITY THEORY AND OBSERVATIONS ON ROBOTS

It is along the general lines sketched above that Putnam and Fodor formulate their criticism of the identity theory and develop their conception of functionalism. In 1967, in an essay entitled 'The Nature of Mental States', Putnam launched a direct attack on "brain-state theorists". The core of Putnam's argument is essentially logical and theoretical. The brain-state theorist maintains that mental states can be identified with physical-chemical states of the brain (Putnam 1967b, in Rosenthal 1971, p. 157). This implies, for example, that an organism can feel pain if and only if it possesses a brain with certain physical and chemical features. More generally, the brain-state theorist claims that *every* psychic state must have a physical-chemical correspondent in the brain with which it can be identified. But if this is the case, then in order to refute the theory it is sufficient to find "even one psychological predicate" that is *identical* for two organisms whose structures are *completely different* (ibid., p. 158). And this is far from impossible. Take the predicate 'hungry', for example, and refer it to a mammal and an octopus. It is obvious that the two animals can both be hungry; but it is equally obvious that the 'hungriness' corresponds to two *completely different* physical states. The necessary conclusion is that there is a clear-cut difference between psychological predicates and their material correlates (ibid.).

Then what, in the end, is for Putnam the "nature" of mental events? The first answer is that it is *not* neurocerebral. Pain, for example, is not *identical* to any physical state, since it is "another *kind* of state entirely" (ibid., p. 154). But there is another answer that is much more important, because in a sense it challenges the validity of the question itself. *Mental states do not have a 'nature'*, in the ontological sense of the term. They are, instead, *states* – or more precisely, *functional* states.

Putnam has recently claimed – probably alluding to Fodor – that he was the first to introduce the crucial concept of function into the MBP debate. The facts – that is, the texts – seem to support this claim. Putnam had, in fact, employed the concept of function in the early 1960s (see e.g., Putnam 1964). But rather than embarking on a philological hunt for 'who said it first', we should try to discover and understand the conceptual origin of the notion of function. This search leads us once again to robots and reveals the singular role that they have played in the MBP debate.

As the reader may recall, the first to introduce robots into the debate on the psychophysical relationship was Smart (see Chapter 2). Subsequently, they were brought into the discussion by Armstrong and other physicalists. For these scholars, the robot (today

we would say the computer, but for our present purposes the distinction is irrelevant), which in some way 'thinks' and 'acts' in a
human-like way, provides conclusive proof that mental states *are*
physical states. After all, what is a thinking robot if not a *physical*
machine? And yet this machine 'performs' (some of) the events and
processes that we call *mental*. The mental, then, as future scientific
and technological process will demonstrate on an ever-widening
scale, is nothing but the physical. Now Putnam takes up the same
theme, but completely inverting both its interpretation and implications. In a nutshell his argument runs as follows. The construction
of robots demonstrates not that men and/or their mental states are
physical but that certain functions and performances can be repro-
duced (or rather imitated, or better still simulated) by *different* entities, organs, or materials (Putnam 1964 and 1967). This is similar
to the point made about mammals and octopuses, but here the
argument is of far greater consequence as it concerns specifically
man and his mental processes and acts.

Even admitting, in other words, that robots act (or will one
day act) in a human-like manner, for Putnam this means essentially that intelligence and memory, beliefs, and intentions are
able to 'be' independently of some *univocal* and necessary link
with *definite* physical states. They are not then *identifiable* with
neurocerebral processes, as identity theorists have argued. What
is more, the 'strict' identity theory (the Australian version in
particular) does not explain how a mental state or act like intelligence can be manifested, at least in terms of behavior, by
an entity (a robot) *that has neither a brain nor a nervous system.* It
follows that, as we have said, a mental state is a function that
unquestionably presupposes physical correlates, but that is at the
same time *completely distinct from them:* so distinct, in fact, that
the same state can be realized "in a series of completely different ways". It also follows that "(physically) different structures"
can not only act in the same way, but they can "obey the same
psychological theory". This means – once again in contrast to
the identity theory – that psychology *cannot be identified with, nor
can it be reduced to neurology* (Putnam 1964, p. 69). Finally, it follows that "descriptions of the functional organization of a system are logically different in kind either from descriptions of its
physical-chemical composition or from descriptions of its actual
and potential behavior" (in Castañeda 1967, p. 200).

FODOR: THE REINTERPRETATION OF
THE IDENTITY RELATIONSHIP

The scope of our analysis impels us to leave Putnam aside for the moment and move on to the functionalism of Jerry Fodor. The latter's contribution to the debate on the one hand helps clarify the theoretical basis of the functionalist program and the far-reaching significance of its proposals; on the other it also reveals the ambiguities and possible limits of functionalism itself.

Fodor attacks the identity theory on several fronts. All too often, he says, identity theorists tend to postulate the existence of processes and connections that have not been verified empirically (Fodor 1968c, in Rosenthal 1971, p. 129). They also have a propensity to simplify psychic reality arbitrarily and inaccurately. A telling example of this is the off-handed way in which they try to do away with the so-called *qualia* – that is, qualitative features of psychosubjective experience. No less disconcerting is the elimination – or at least the reductive interpretation – of a key concept like consciousness. What is more, identity theory ignores the fact that psychological language often employs notions that are conditioned, and motivated, by definite cultural conceptions (ibid., p. 130). And finally, how is it possible not to take into account the fact that the principles generally used to distinguish neurological states differ from those used to distinguish psychological states (ibid., pp. 147–8)? Fodor also points out that *identical psychological phenomena* can derive from *different neurological mechanisms,* and vice versa. Indeed, it seems absurd to deny *a priori* that "the nervous system may not sometimes produce indistinguishable psychological effects by *radically* different physiological means" (ibid., p. 148). Consequently, for both theoretical and empirical reasons the materialists' claim that "for each distinguishable psychological state there must be one and only one corresponding brain state" must be firmly rejected (ibid.).

Of particular interest is Fodor's criticism of the explanatory structure that identity theorists use to carry out operations of physicalistic reduction and identification. This structure is modelled along the following lines: (a) 'X consists of parts that. . .'; (b) 'X is reducible to physiological microstructures that. . .'. Fodor's observations make a significant contribution to the interpretation of psychic phenomena. His answer to (a) is that not everything can be broken down into parts. This is particularly true of many psychic phenom-

138

ena: the experience of pain, for example, cannot be analyzed into hypothetical and abstract 'parts'. As for (b), as we have seen, Fodor replies that mental events and states "are not readily thought of as capable of being microanalyzed into *anything*, least of all neurons or states of neurons" (ibid., p. 144).

Fodor is also not convinced by the way in which identity theorists describe the act of identification itself. In his view, "no statement of the form '*x* is *y*' could be significant where *x* is a mental term, *y* is a physiological term, 'is' means identity", if for no other reason than that it regularly violates Leibniz's law (ibid., p. 135). Fodor then goes on to introduce a distinction between two kinds of identification, which takes us to the heart of his interpretation of the identity theory.

It is essential, for him, to distinguish between what he calls "type–type identity" and "token–token" identity. The first indicates relationships in which a certain class of events or phenomena is identified *always, a priori* and *necessarily* with another class. If I say, for instance, 'Lightning is an electrical discharge', this identity admits of no exceptions: all lightning has among its general and constant characteristics the fact that it coincides with the equally general and constant type of phenomenon that is an electrical discharge. The second form of identity, on the contrary, merely admits the possibility that a definite event or process may be identified with another event or process. This may occur frequently, or even quite regularly, but *never necessarily:* that is, it could in principle never occur. Returning to this distinction in another essay, Fodor points out that "token–token physicalism" is concerned with "individual mental events", while "type–type physicalism" is concerned with "the nature of mental properties": in other words, "while the former claims only that all mental particulars that there happen to be are neurological, the latter makes that claim about all the mental particulars that there *could* be" (Fodor 1981b, p. 7).

FODOR: THE CONCEPT OF FUNCTION AND FUNCTIONALIST EXPLANATION

We have now reached, as we said, the heart of Fodor's conception of identity. And at the same time we have unearthed the foundations of his functionalism. Beneath the basic distinction between "type–type identity" and "token–token identity" lies the elemental distinction between *things* (or *essences*) and *functions*. A *thing* is a univocal entity: it is always *that* thing and cannot be anything else or exist in any other way. If, following proper scientific procedure, I am able to establish the identity between one entity and another, this identity is to be considered "typical": in the twofold sense that it will be true *always* and *without exception*, and that it will be true for *all* entities of the same kind – that is, for all those things belonging to the same class as the one examined. A *function*, on the contrary, is *not* something *univocal*: that is, something that reveals itself – and cannot not reveal itself – *always* and *necessarily* in one *single* form. We are dealing, rather, with a concept, an operation that can be performed or realized in *n* number of different ways. In this connection, Fodor gives the illuminating example of a trap. Considered not as a *thing* (a particular concrete object) but as a *function*, a trap can be built in any number of ways, using a variety of techniques, materials, and the like: and yet it remains a trap. Another example is that of irrigation: a function that can be performed in many different ways – with a rubber hose, a metal watering can, an electric sprinkling system, and so forth. The principal theoretical consequence of all this, in Sidney Shoemaker's words, is "the fact that functional states are 'multiply realizable' implies that a functional state cannot be *identical* to any *particular* physical realization of it" (1981, pp. 97–8; italics mine).

At the same time that he adopts this first conclusion (at least in part), Fodor develops another point that shows even greater promise. Faced with a *thing*, it is perfectly legitimate to ask: what is it? What is it made of? Faced with a *function*, on the other hand, such questions become ineffective or, at the least, extremely 'weak'. In fact it would seem that meaningful questions about a function will be of the kind: how does it work? What does it do? How is it used? (in Rosenthal 1971, p. 145). We can say, in synthesis, that while an *entity* can be *physically identified* (in the sense that one can say that it *is*, materially, a *definite entity*), a *function* cannot, because, as we have seen, it can take on different material forms and perform according to equally different operating procedures. Fodor concludes, then, that whereas explanations and identifications referred to an *entity* – such as, 'water is H_2O' – imply that we can say *what* physical features are shared by all entities of a certain type, when we explain a *function* we are not committed to describing in physical terms what all the members of a particular class of functions have in common. This sort of explanation is questionable both because having some-*thing* physical in common is not a necessary condition for membership in that class, and because that function can be performed by any mechanism as long as it is *used* in a *certain way* – and it is precisely this *use* and this *way* that allow us to understand the function (ibid., p. 146).

The importance of these positions for the philosophy of mind cannot be overestimated as the functionalists hold that *mental phenomena* are ultimately *functional phenomena*. Accordingly, when we refer to them we must ask not what they are in physical terms – much less to what 'thing' they can be reduced, or what parts make them up – but what is the specific *way* (in this case a psychological way) in which they are performed. Thus, for example, melancholy *is not* (or *is not identifiable with*) a univocal, unchanging physical structure: it is rather a *way* of being that materializes *juxta sua principia* and can take on *n* different physical forms.

At the risk of digressing slightly, it is worth pointing out that Fodor extends his analysis of mental processes and events to the more general level of human behavior. Indeed, he regards behavior as a function too. It cannot be identified with physical *movements* (as Armstrong holds) but has its own autonomy and *modus operandi*, analyzable only according to specific procedures. Moreover, the identity or correspondence between (physical) *movement* and *behavior* is not 'type–type' – that is, general, univocal, and necessary. The proof Fodor claims lies in the fact that "not every occurrence of a given movement or muscular contraction is an instance of the same behavior". Conversely, "two *quite different* patterns of motions ... may be instances of the *same* behavior" (Fodor 1964, pp. 169–70; italics mine).[1] Predictably, in pursuing his reflection on behavioral states Fodor reaffirms the distinction between 'being' and 'acting' that served him to separate things from functions. An analysis of these states in purely *physical* terms would give us only the description of certain "biochemical and electrical" conditions of behavior: it would *not* give the *modus operandi* of behavior as such:

To put it succinctly, a complete psychological explanation [of behavior] requires *more* than an account of what the neurological circuitry *is*: it requires also an account of what such

---

1. An analogous statement, in reference to the relationship between the brain and behavior, was made recently by the eminent neurophysiologist Norman Geschwind: "Similar behavior can be the result of underlying brain mechanisms that are completely different from each other" (Miller 1983, p. 134).

circuitry *does*. This second sort of account is given in terms of the familiar constructs of psychology: drives, motives, strategies, and so forth. (ibid., p. 177)

Having established an explicitly functionalist perspective, Fodor now returns to the issue of the autonomy of psychology and of its language. Psychology cannot and must not be reduced to physiology (or neurology); physiology can only provide knowledge of mechanisms that in some sense support psychic phenomena. This support, it must be stressed, is not univocal: it is in fact conceivable that "*identical* psychological functions could sometimes be ascribed to anatomically *heterogeneous* neural mechanisms", and vice versa (in Rosenthal 1971, p. 146). There are, then, *two* different orders of cognitive referent: psychic phenomena and neurophysiological phenomena. But if this is true, it is absurd to suppose that neurophysiology can by itself express everything that man wants to know about psychic states or events. Fodor rehabilitates the terms and concepts of psychology. 'Drives', 'motives', and 'strategies' are not just empty names: they denote "internal states postulated in attempts to account for behavior, perception, memory, and other phenomena in the domain of psychological theories" (ibid., p. 145). And it must be clear that these terms, as well as the functional states they refer to, can be neither eliminated nor replaced with *something else*. The former serve in fact a definite linguistic and conceptual purpose (they are "names for *functions*", and are not to be confused with *other* names); the latter, as we know, "are not available for microanalysis and theoretical revision could identify them only with other functions, not with mechanisms" (Fodor 1964, p. 179).

FUNCTIONALISM AND COMPUTER SCIENCE

In our discussion of Putnam it was pointed out that 'intelligent' robots played a crucial role in the elaboration of his functionalist model. The same could be said about Fodor. His reflection on functionalism was in fact strongly influenced by the progress made in artificial intelligence and computer science. Like other scholars, he too sees in the ability of machines to perform certain (often quite sophisticated) intellectual operations the confirmation of not the 'ontological' but the 'functional' nature of mental processes. Indeed, it seems clear to him that if the same acts can be performed by such different 'things' as a human brain and computer circuits, then those operations cannot be identified in the strict sense (i.e., according to 'type–type' identity) with neurocerebral mechanisms.

In an instructive article on the MBP, Fodor gives a lucid exposition of the role computers have played in the functionalist interpretation of the mind. Those machines, writes Fodor, "furnish good examples of two central concepts of functionalism: the concept that mental states are interdefined and the concept that they can be realized in many systems" (Fodor 1981a, p. 106). Computer software, in fact, can in principle be written in a hundred different ways. For example, the program for a soft-drink dispensing machine "does not logically require that its concrete realization come about using gears, levers, and diodes". Similarly – and this is the point that interests us here – "the description of the mind's software does not logically require neurons" (ibid.). Fodor's basic idea is that if functionalism is open to computer science and can grasp the special relationship between the concepts of software and hardware (on the one hand closely linked, and on the other completely independent one from the other), it will be in an excellent position to make full use of the principle that "the character of a mental state is independent from its physical realization" (ibid., p. 107). If properly interpreted, in short, computer science can suggest the following solution to the MBP: the mind is to the body as software is to hardware.

Sketched out fairly cautiously by Fodor, these principles and what we shall call for convenience's sake the philo-computational approach to the philosophy of mind have been developed with far greater assurance by other scholars. One who has made particularly brilliant contributions to the MBP debate is Daniel Dennett. Dennett does not limit himself to reaffirming the leading role of disciplines like artificial intelligence and computer science in the "more abstract investigation of the principles of psychology" (Dennett 1978a, p. 112). He also claims that artificial intelligence provides the most sophisticated analysis "of the possibilities of intelligence or consciousness" (ibid., p. 119). Moreover, he is persuaded that the neurophysiology of the brain is essentially irrelevant to the MBP. Indeed, *the mind is ultimately a computer* – or rather, computer software (see also Hofstadter-Dennett 1981).

But the philosopher who is most thoroughly convinced that computer science has a decisive role to play in the philosophy of mind is probably Margaret Boden. In Boden's view, computer science provides nothing less than the most "rigorous formulation and testing of the psychological hypotheses about the mind's contents and functions" (Boden 1981, p. 31). The empirical premise of this bold declaration is that computers "can already do some things that are sufficiently similar to human mental processes" (ibid., p. 33). But the factual grounds for this statement are far less evident than Boden seems to think. And the key concept of resemblance (which is anything but empirical) begs a number of questions: 'resemblance' in what sense, within what limits, with what implications, and (above all) on the basis of what criteria? Not only does Boden not even ask these questions, but she is so convinced of the homogeneity of the mind and 'machines' that she claims that in speaking about computers she is fully legitimate in using characteristically psychological terms such as 'plan', 'represent', 'reason', 'deduce', and 'choose' (ibid., p. 34). Thus her defense of the autonomous nature of psychology and of psychological language against the hegemony of biophysics (ibid., pp. 42ff.) is seriously undermined by the fact that psychology itself becomes in Boden's essay somehow subordinate to a hyper-computational theory of mind. We will not dwell on this point, nor on her even more questionable claim that computer science can "illuminate" the "nature of human subjectivity", the world of individual experience, the dimension of aims and values, and so on (ibid., pp. 31, 42, et passim). What is to be emphasized here is Boden's insistence that computer science has virtually 'solved' the MBP. It is able to demonstrate, in her view, "how it is possible for mind to act on the body during purposive action and voluntary choice" (ibid., p. 31). Computer science, Boden adds, "illuminates the MBP by suggesting *how it is possible* for an immaterial computational process to direct bodily events" (ibid., p. 47). Once again, the basic conclusion – or principle – is that *the mind is a computer*.

CRITIQUES OF MIND–COMPUTER IDENTIFICATION

It will be clear at this point that the role played by computer science in the MBP debate is twofold. On the one hand its theories and applications have made an important contribution to the emancipation of the mental (and its science) from the physical (and its science). On the other hand, however, these same theories and applications risk laying the foundations of a new type of reductionism: no longer the reduction of the mind to the body, but of the mind to the 'machine'. This risk becomes particularly pernicious if an identification of the type 'the mind is a computer' is proposed in ontological and not merely epistemological terms – that is, at the level of strictly conceptual and cognitive models. In other words, if one were to say 'within certain well-defined and well-circumscribed limits it might be useful to *compare* certain aspects of psychic *functions* with certain *operations* of some machines' (keeping firmly in mind that in many other respects minds and machines operate in quite different and incomparable ways), this assertion would be acceptable. Not all scholars, however, adopt this view. Some in fact tend, in varying ways, to claim that 'the mind behaves like a machine' – and even that the mind *is* a machine. Richard Boyd, for example, does not hesitate to declare that "mental events, states, and processes *are* computational (in Block and Fodor, p. 96; italics mine). Both Dennett and Boden argue along the same lines. Boden is so thoroughly convinced of the close analogy, or the quasi identity, between the mind and the computer that she gives a long list of presumed similarities between the two, adding that even the logical-linguistic mechanism of the mind is computational in nature. This sort of reductionism, achieved at the expense of an adequate, autonomous analysis of the mental, is ultimately no less radical than the neurophysiological reductionism proposed by the identity theorists. And it is hardly surprising that this and similar positions have met with the reservations of more than one philosopher of mind. For example, it is obvious, writes Norman Malcolm, that

> anything can be said to be *like* anything else, in some respect or another. People and computers are alike in that people sometimes compute, and so do computers. But the two are also radically unlike. . . .Machines cannot be said to be literally conscious or unconscious, and therefore states of consciousness cannot literally be ascribed to them. This observation alone is enough to dismiss the computer from the philosophy of mind. (Malcolm and Armstrong 1984, p. 100)

In a review of Boden's book, Putnam replies that, leaving aside other questions, the computer performs only factual and causal operations, whereas human beings elaborate thoughts, meanings, and values whose nature is not essentially factual and causal. This is especially important if we consider the process of *evaluation*, such as the evaluation of the 'truth' of human thoughts. It seems untenable, says Putnam, that a machine by merely factual-causal processing can distinguish true thoughts from false ones (Putnam 1982a). What is more, it is not even legitimate to refer to computational operations in terms of truth and falsehood. Strictly speaking, in fact, a machine *is never wrong*. If a computer is shown a circle and draws a cube, *we* are the ones who say "it's wrong": the computer has simply followed its program. It has not *made a mistake:* either it is *broken* or its program is *defective*. If the latter is the case, it is the programmer – a human being – who made the mistake (indeed, only humans properly make mistakes).

The radical differences between the mind (or man) and the computer have also been stressed by John Searle (1980 and 1982; see also Searle 1984). The computer, Searle argues, uses *signs,* not *symbols* (which presuppose the ability to distinguish between 'things' and 'names', or between signified and signifier). Moreover, the computer can follow a *syntax,* but it cannot create a *semantics*. Nor can it express intentions, desires, or value judgements, or take into account backgrounds, contexts, and complex purposes. As for its ability to *understand,* Searle voices grave doubts about the confident claims made by some computer scientists. The cognitive operations carried out by computers, he says, have very little resemblance to human cognitive thought, which develops according to processes – such as pre-understanding, analogy, hypothesis – that are quite different from those employed by computers. And it goes without saying that if one refers not to cognitive operations but to thought in general, the gap between the mind (or man) and the machine widens enormously.

Human thought and feelings, Searle argues convincingly, constitute irreducible specific functions linked to a definite psychophysical structure – and (we would add) to man's symbolic, social, and historical identity. Advocates of a computer-oriented psychology have sometimes replied that their aim is not so much to *identify* the mind with the machine as to *simulate* certain mental acts for heuristic or analytical purposes. There is indeed a certain validity to this answer. It suggests a kind of operation that does not seem to imply an ontological commitment of any sort (I simulate, or cause a machine to simulate, a certain behavior, fully aware that it is in fact only a *simulation:* a mere analogue created *by me* within strictly defined limits). We must remember, however, as Keith Gunderson has pointed out, that it is not always possible to create a faithful simulation of the 'thing itself' (Gunderson 1971). Take a feeling, for example. In principle I can program a computer to simulate a feeling, in the sense that I have it perform the acts that generally accompany and express a certain feeling. The problem is that although a computer can *simulate* a feeling (and this is clearly all it can do) it cannot *experience* that feeling – and consequently it cannot actually *express* it. What it does, in reality, is something quite different: it carries out a series of external, mechanical acts that are similar *in form* to those that are *usually* performed by someone who experiences that feeling (*usually*, certainly not *necessarily:* a feeling can be accompanied and expressed by an infinite and unpredictable number of acts). But the critical responses to behaviorist psychology have convincingly shown that external behavior does not necessarily correspond to definite internal psychic states (I can externally manifest pain without truly feeling it). It follows, then, that the 'behavior' of a computer would not in any case provide us with reliable information about its supposed 'feelings'.

Another general criticism often levelled against computer-oriented psychology is that some of its key terms and concepts are misused. No one objects to the introduction of ontologically uncommitted analogies between the mind and the machine, but it should be clear that certain terms and concepts cannot be employed as though they were *neutral signs,* applicable to whatever entity seems to behave in a given way. Take 'plan'. The notion is not limited to an association with facts or with operative acts, but calls up a host of psychoanthropological and sociocultural meanings with allusions to an evaluation of a particular situation, a more or less tacit knowledge of some values, a desire to achieve a goal. Human beings are 'planning subjects' *par excellence* – indeed, we might suggest that the very notion of 'plan' arose in close relation to them. Computers are another matter. Even if a computer could in principle simulate the acts roughly corresponding to a plan, these acts would remain always and exclusively *physical* operations. No matter how useful and sophisticated they might be, such operations would inevitably lack many of the features we regularly associate with a plan. Although these operations might ostensibly resemble those connected with a plan, they would only reflect the end result of a process which in human behavior has far more complex origins and goals. And it is widely acknowledged that the meaning of an act can scarcely be understood without taking into account its origins and its goals.

THE TWO INTERPRETATIONS
OF FUNCTIONALISM

The questions we have raised concerning the relationship between the 'mind' and the 'machine' – merely alluded to in order to suggest the complexity and importance of a definite field of research within the philosophy of mind – concern a much vaster issue that cannot detain us here. Now we must return to Fodor and to functionalism as a 'solution' to the MBP. It will not be necessary to retrace the steps and arguments illustrated in the preceding pages. What we need to draw attention to is what could be called the underlying ambiguity, or the dual interpretation, of functionalism. What does this 'duality' consist in?

Rorty once wrote that the merit of functionalism is "not to have discovered *the nature* of mental states but to say that they *don't* have a nature" (1982b, p. 336; italics mine). This assessment is rather important, though we would be inclined to interpret it in a different way. 'Not having a *nature*' could mean above all not having *one* nature; it could mean that mental functions have (not only *de jure* but also *de facto*) *many* natures, that is, many different configurations and makeups. Approached from this angle, mental processes appear to be analyzable not only, and not primarily, in terms of physical components (this might be, at best, one of their natures), but also in other terms such as those relative to the memory, symbols, the unconscious, culture, and history. In this sense, a mental state is a state that can be characterized in relation to the most diverse and unpredictable criteria. A desire, for example, while certainly having a physiological correlate and a physiological explanation, will also be explainable from a 'social' viewpoint (no physiologist could explain why the average Italian should yearn for a supercharged compact car while the average American prefers his car to be roomy and with a smoother acceleration rate). In short, a certain version of functionalism vigorously emphasizes that there is no *favored* way to perform a mental function and that, correspondingly, there is an *indefinite plurality* of ways to perform it.

This is not, however, Fodor's approach. Especially in some of the essays following *The Language of Thought* he seems to abandon his controversy with physicalist reductionism and acknowledge the centrality (at least *de facto*) of the physical embodiment of the mental. At the same time he is little inclined to defend the *multiplicity* of the ways in which mental functions can be performed and, ultimately, the autonomy of the mental itself. Fodor now insists not so much on the *independence* of the mental from the physical (in general), as on the claim that there is no logically necessary relationship between the mind and the nervous system (in particular). He conceives this relationship, as we saw, in terms of the distinction between 'type–type identity' and 'token–token identity'. But what does this distinction really tell us about the identity between mind and body? It certainly does not say that there is no identity. On the contrary, an identity does exist, but it is contingent: that is, it exists (*de facto*) in *a certain form*, but it *could* (in theory, *de jure*) exist in *other* forms. Yet, even leaving aside Fodor's tendency to equate '*de facto*' with 'neurological', it is hardly acceptable that the other (hypothetical) forms of identity should also be asked to satisfy a *physical* requirement. As a result, far from using the functionalist conception to emphasize the indefinite *plurality* of the mind's manifestations and to give an 'autonomistic' interpretation of the mind itself, Fodor ends up by proposing what we might call a neo physicalist version of mental states and events. (This neophysicalism can profitably be compared with the positions advanced in Wilkes 1978a; see also Peacocke 1979; Block 1981.)

This conclusion is not the fruit of a personal and isolated interpretation. Michael Martin, for example, argued some years ago that Fodor "has not shown that psychology cannot be reduced to neurophysiology" (Martin 1971, p. 161). For Margolis, Fodor's is ultimately a "crypto-identity" theory (Margolis 1978). More generally, Patricia Kitcher, an attentive student of the philosophy of mind, sees a tendency among functionalists to propose as new what is little more than a particular "version" of the identity theory. In the final analysis, says Kitcher, this sort of functionalism does not deny the physical nature of mental states; rather, it suggests that whenever we are in a certain mental state, we are in a certain physical state, and that "each instance of a mental state is, of course, some physical state". Functionalism merely rejects that an analysis of mental states can *always* be congruent with an analysis of physical states (Kitcher 1982, p. 225). Though Kitcher's comments are directed at a broad range of functionalist conceptions, they are clearly quite relevant to Fodor's.

There is a wealth of commentary on Fodor's theory that runs along the same interpretive lines. If we single out one response for special attention it is because the points made are of particular interest from a theoretical point of view, and because the source is the *pontifex maximus* of contemporary identity materialism, David M. Armstrong.

Considering the objections to the 'Australian' positions raised by many functionalists (and above all by Fodor), one might have expected a defensive reaction on the part of the leader of the Australian school. But this is not the case. In a very interesting article Armstrong has adopted an attitude toward functionalism that might be regarded as lying somewhere between the 'co-optive' and the ironical (Armstrong 1983a). In certain respects, he writes, some functionalist theses were anticipated by Australian philosophers of mind, Smart to begin with. As to the other crucial principles of functionalism, he claims that they are largely reconcilable with the identity theory. What, at bottom, is the functionalists' (and Fodor's) truly innovative contribution to the MBP debate? It is simply the famous distinction between 'type–type identity' and 'token–token identity'. This distinction would seem to help separate the orthodox identity theorists from the functionalists: the former as 'type–type' supporters and the latter as 'token–token' supporters. But is the gap really so wide? Armstrong thinks not. In the final analysis, says Armstrong, the whole MBP boils down to one single question: *the acceptance or rejection of the claim that every mental state is, in fact and with sufficient regularity, a physical state.* Fodor, he continues, accepts this principle when he states (or at least does not deny) that every "mental event" is, *de facto,* "a purely physical event" (ibid., pp. 58–9). As for the more demanding 'type–type' identity, it is very likely that Armstrong continues to believe in its validity more than he lets on (and despite the partial evolution of his views: see Chapter 3). But he declares that he is prepared to keep his more radical views in the closet, so to speak, as long as that even this attack on the identity theory is launched from a position that *does not abandon the materialist and physicalist cause.* (This confirms our thesis that Armstrong's primary concern is not to solve a philosophical-psychological problem, but rather to affirm an overall physicalist *Weltanschauung.*)

How should we reply to Armstrong? We have to admit, at least as far as Fodor is concerned, that he is basically right. A close reading of Fodor's 1981a essay on the MBP will confirm this view. Here, he unambiguously restates the two principles of the *functional* (not *substantial*) character of mental states and of the legitimacy of a psychological sphere that cannot be reduced to neurological constituents. But how does he present these principles, especially the first and most important? They are presented as *hypotheses,* as *logical-theoretical possibilities.* Fodor does not even hesitate to stress that, on a *factual* plane, things could (and in fact *do*) go quite differently from the way they are posited in his *Gedankenexperiment:* "The functionalist would not be upset if *brain* events were shown to be the only things possessing the *functional properties* that define *mental states".* Indeed – as if to clear up any remaining doubts – *"most functionalists expect that it will turn out this way. In other words, functionalism tolerates the materialistic solution of the MBP provided by the central-state identity theory"* (Fodor 1981a, p. 129; italics mine). Fodor states his position with admirable clarity, leaving no uncertainty as to how he conceives the true nature of mental states: and this position is, in the end, not so distant from that of the Australians as one might have thought.

In the collection of essays entitled *Representations* Fodor makes a point of confirming his overall anti-reductionist orientation, develops the question of the autonomy of what he calls the "special sciences," and stresses once again the independence of psychology from neurology (Fodor 1981b). On the other hand, he has telling words of praise for Australian materialism – and for reasons that are clearly open to objection, such as the claim that it has restored (in opposition to behaviorism) an *ontological* conception of the mental (ibid., p. 9). It is certainly true that for Fodor functionalism is not necessarily bound to a neurological interpretation of mental states, and that it holds that these states can be 'conveyed' by non-biological carriers ("at least in *logical* principle", Fodor adds significantly). But we must be careful. Is this enough to suggest a truly new approach to the issues that concern us? Not at all. Indeed, it is one thing to deny the *neurological* (or *biological*) character of the mental, and quite another to deny, more generally, its *physical* character. In order to dispel any misunderstanding in this regard it is Fodor himself who declares he is an advocate of *physicalism* – albeit a "physicalism without parochialism" (ibid., p. 11).

In the light of the preceding remarks, the overall assessment of Fodor's functionalism should be the following. Despite certain encouraging premises, he has not toppled the edifice of the physicalist interpretation of the mental. Even the appeal to computer science has not proved decisive. What has happened, at best, is that he initially connected mental phenomena to certain neurological phenomena (according to the token–token identity), and subsequently speculated on the possibility of linking them with (parts of) computational systems. What remains in any case is the basic assumption that the *mental* phenomenon is identified with something *physical.*[2]

2. A realistic and physicalistic orientation emerges with force in Fodor's *The Modularity of Mind* (1983). The essay (which advances hypotheses and takes up issues rather distant from those treated in the present volume) presents a rather surprising return, given at least *certain* premises of Fodor's thought, to the doctrine of psychic "faculties" and their science. According to Fodor, to explain the "facts of mental life" it is necessary to "postulate" different types of "psychological mechanisms", corresponding to the mental faculties. What must be grasped of these mechanisms are their real features, their "intrinsic" characteristics (p. 1). This research program is particularly urgent since not only the individual psychic functions but all of human behavior is considered the "effect" of a strictly mental "cause" – of a mind, it should be stressed, interpreted not as a *function* but rather as a "structure" (p. 2). What is particularly striking is that the whole investigation is based on a perspective which is not merely *realistic* but also, so to speak, *spatial* (he often speaks of a mental "architecture" composed of "vertical" and "horizontal" faculties). From the same perspective Fodor, who aligns himself with a "Cartesian" conception (the Cartesianism of the *res cogitans*) and debates (though largely in agreement) with the realist Chomsky, does not hesitate to resuscitate phrenology and to suggest a singular rehabilitation of Gall. From behind all this there emerges a, in some sense, 'neo-physiologistic' interpretation of the mental. One of the central referents of Fodor's study is the "neural architecture", the complex of "neural mechanisms" responsible for psychic performance (e.g. pp. 98, 119) – which, we should note, are defined as "natural". Correspondingly, one of the fundamental theses of the book is that every "mental *organ*" is "pretuned" with a "specific sort of [neurocerebral] structure" (p. 120). A similar position appears in Fodor's contribution to the volume *States of Mind*, edited by Jonathan Miller and published in the same year, in which *mental* functions are again presented as neurocerebral "faculties" or "organs", which science is called on to discover and describe.

Chapter 6

The mind as property and as event

The 'reformist' neo-identityism of Kim and Davidson

KIM: THE MENTAL NOT AS BEING
BUT AS "PROPERTY"

Shortly before beginning our discussion of functionalism we made brief mention of another area of thought which has been active in the reform or critical revision of the orthodox identity theory. The terms 'reform' and 'revision' are not chosen casually. Scholars of this orientation do not, in fact, intend to abandon completely the general inspiration and ambition of the identity theory. Their aim, rather, is to reject certain aspects of this theory while modifying (even radically) several of its key assumptions and arguments. We have also said that these scholars do not compose in any way a "school" or an organic, united group. Their positions do, however, share a common line of reasoning which consists roughly in the following choices: a) a strong commitment to an anti-ontological, or anti-substantialist approach to the MBP – this is especially clear in the crucial redefinition of mental phenomena in terms of properties, modes, or events; b) the development of a psychological and epistemological perspective which, on the one hand, is rather more articulated than that proposed by the identity theory and, on the other, retains certain physicalist (albeit 'sophisticated') and monistic (albeit 'anomalous') traits; c) the commitment to maintain some form of connection (perhaps causal) between the mental and the bodily, although this connection is to be given a 'weak', *sui generis* interpretation, or is even to be substituted with the new concept of *correlation*. Keeping to the path we have chosen to follow, it will be best to focus attention on two scholars in particular: Jaegwon Kim and Donald Davidson.

Kim is an important figure in the literature on the MBP and has always been quite clear about his criticisms of the orthodox identity theory. The identity theory, Kim argues, too often neglects to state at precisely what *level* (ontological, linguistic, modal?) the identity between mind and body purportedly exists. Secondly, its advocates never adequately clarify "what kind of physical event a given kind of phenomenal event is" (Kim, in Kim and Brandt 1967, p. 525). Thirdly, many proponents of this view tend not so much to argue for their assumptions on *empirical-scientific* grounds as to appeal to the applicability and authority of certain *general philosophical* principles, such as the "principle of simplicity" and the "principle of parsimony". Leaving aside debatable points of procedure, it is a fact, according to Kim, that the identity theory has never succeeded in reducing, in conformity with these principles, the number of primitive concepts which form the basis of the study of the MBP. A further unresolved problem of the identity theory is linked with its inability (which we mentioned earlier) to predefine the mental autonomously, *before* ascertaining its possible identification with the physical (Kim 1971, pp. 324–5). Nor must we forget that it has proven incapable of going beyond a concept of identity which is too "strict" (and difficult to apply empirically) and one which is reduced to mere correlation or concomitance. And finally, how can we ignore that the predicates used in psychic and physical languages are clearly too different to be applied to a single referent? There is another critical observation which must be made (and which Kim directs at eliminationist materialism as well): even if we allow that the psychic *phenomenon* of pain, for example, could be expressed in physical terms, this hardly means that the *concept* of psychic pain and its corresponding linguistic expression becomes superfluous (Kim and Brandt 1967, p. 537).

What alternative, then, does Kim propose? His position will not entirely satisfy those who, judging by the radical nature of the critique summarized above, might expect a stance which is in clear contrast with the tenets of the identity theory. In fact, as was anticipated above, it is not Kim's aim to propose a 'revolutionary' solution to the MBP problem. At the heart of his thought remains the problem of the type of relationship which connects the mental and the bodily, the general assumptions of this relationship not being open to discussion. There remains another, more burning question as well: the impelling need to be able to express the mental (and, perhaps, the human in general) in physical terms. Given this premise, however, Kim's thought contains a theoretical nucleus of considerable importance which cannot be overlooked (Kim 1966 and 1971).

Reduced to its most general terms this proposal consists in shifting the focus of the MBP from the plane of *entities* to that of *properties* (in fact, the expression "property identity" has been used as a label for the position adopted by Kim and other scholars). The foremost inspiration of this new approach to the MBP is the conviction that a reflection focused on the traditional notion of identity belongs to an ontological philosophy which appears to be in many respects rather outdated. In the second place, and more specifically, if the mind and the body were to be considered two entities, they would be too obviously different to have any organic relationship. Unlike the physical entity, the mental entity has no parts (what are the *parts* of melancholy?), it cannot be univocally located (*where* is happiness?), it is subjective and private (*who* knows or experiences my headache in the way *I* know and experience it?) – moreover, it is qualitative, (often) intentional, and unassailable (Kim 1971). We must, then, give up talking about identity between entities.

Once he has acknowledged the difficulty of an analysis of mind–body identity in terms of entities, Kim moves on to reflect on the possibility of affirming an identity not between *entities* but between *properties* (Kim 1966). Obviously, there is a considerable difference between saying that an *entity* is equal to another entity and that a *property* is equal to another property. We have already discussed some of the problems connected with the identity between entities (see Chapter 3). With the second type of identity what is claimed is only that two definite, partial 'modalities' of two referents have the characteristic of being equal – without requiring that all the 'rest' (their other properties, the possible 'supports' of the properties, etc.) be the same.

Kim gives an illuminating example. When we say that the temperature of a gas is equal to the kinetic energy of that gas, we are not suggesting that a certain *thing* is equal to another *thing*. We are saying that one of its aspects or properties corresponds – and note that this is not (or not necessarily) *always* the case, but only under certain circumstances – to another aspect or property (Kim 1966, in Rosenthal 1971, pp. 86–87). It is clear that this approach de-absolutizes and delimits the boundaries of statements about identity, and it becomes even clearer when Kim stresses that the property he is talking about is not a (presumed) *real, objective* component of something, but a mere "phenomenal property": something quite different from "an *irreducible* kind of property *in nature*" (Kim and Brandt 1967, p. 529; italics mine). In this regard Kim writes elsewhere that "events of course can *have* properties . . . but they do not have *constituent* properties" (Kim 1972, p. 186; italics mine). Obviously, the same argument holds for the mental. In this sphere, Kim does not propose to affirm the identity of *something* called 'mental' with *something* called 'physical': he only says that there are some mental *properties* which in certain contexts can be identified with certain *properties* of brain states (Kim 1966 and 1972).

KIM: FROM IDENTITY TO "CORRELATION": THE CONCEPT OF "SUPERVENIENCE"

Building on what has been said so far, Kim can now deal with one of the problems of major concern to him: the act of identification. His aim is, quite explicitly, to transform, or even give up, the concept of identity. This concept, he argues, belongs to a theoretical framework which is inappropriate for the type of relationship that it purports to describe. Accordingly, in his first contribution to the debate on the identity theory he proposes, as an alternative to the concept of *identity*, the new concept of *correlation*. In a comment on the equation of temperature and kinetic energy which we mentioned earlier, Kim writes with the utmost clarity: "It is sufficient to interpret this equation as asserting a mere *correlation* between the temperature and the mean kinetic energy of a gas," while "it is not necessary to interpret the equation to the effect that temperature *is* mean kinetic energy" (Kim 1966, in Rosenthal 1971, p. 84). As to the psychoanthropological sphere, his claim is that human beings sometimes possess properties of pain that are simply *correlated* to a type of brain state. Indeed, this is even more evident in the case of the mind–body relationship, since the mental and the bodily are not in any way univocally, necessarily, connected. So, in his 1966 article Kim arrives at the following crucial thesis: *within the sphere of the MBP one can and must move from the principle of an 'identity' between entities to the principle of a 'correlation' between properties*. (This thesis, partially outlined by Sellars in 1965, is commented on and in part developed by Thomson 1969, Wilkes 1978a, and Harth 1982. See also Davidson 1970 and Putnam 1981.)

A similar line of thought is pursued in another of Kim's essays, mentioned earlier (Kim 1972). Here his reasoning is centered not so much on the appropriateness of using one term or concept instead of another as on something much more substantial. Certain properties and/or events, he argues, even if usually linked together, cannot by virtue of this connection be considered as necessarily having a mechanical or systematic relationship. Take the example of the statement "Any object that has a color is an object with a shape". The indisputable truth of this statement does not mean, however, that it is true that "for each color there is a shape such that an object has that color if and only if it has this shape" (ibid., p. 185). In other words, color and shape do appear to be 'linked-by-rules', but these rules are not constant, rigid, and exact, and least of all can it be said that color and shape are identical. The same argument, in Kim's view, holds for the mental and the bodily. They are undoubtedly connected, but the relationship that binds them contains discrepancies, voids, and unpredictable possibilities. This should hardly be surprising if it is true that mental phenomena are purely *events* or *properties*. It is in fact obvious that phenomenal figures of this kind – lacking fixed, objective, essential, or constitutive features – can be correlated with many different physical states. Leaving to Davidson the merit of suggesting that certain mental states can also originate *in* – or can be understood through reference *to* – *other mental* states, Kim makes it clear that "we of course should not expect to find a physical correlate for every type of mental event" (ibid., p. 191). He goes on to say: "We cannot . . . be definite about the range of mental *properties* to be comprehended by the thesis of psychophysical correspondence, that is, those mental properties for which we need to find neural correlates to make the thesis true" (ibid., p. 192; italics mine). For Kim, in fact, the principle of psychophysical correspondence – at least in the *strong* sense attributed to it by identity theorists – does not hold (ibid., p. 185). The only identities that can be admitted are not *general* identities, but *particular*, 'local' identities (or rather correlates) (ibid., p. 191).

Along with the key notions of property and correlation another concept that has served Kim well in the elaboration of his non-reductionist, liberalizing approach to the MBP is that of "supervenience". This concept, first introduced in English ethical and juridical discourse (Moore, Hare), suggests that a relationship of determination and dependence may exist between two classes of events and/or properties which does not require what Kim calls "property-to-

157

property correlation": that is, a rigid, exhaustive, term-to-term relationship with no further connections. It has also been the subject of formal analysis (Horgan 1978, Rosenberg 1978) and employed within the sphere of the MBP (Davidson 1970). In this sphere the notion of supervenience can provide initial support for the claim that the mental, while in large part dependent on the physical, is nonetheless not subjected to *exact* and *nomologically organized* correlations.

Kim's application of the concept of supervenience to the MBP is particularly interesting. In an article devoted exclusively to this problem he writes: "There seem to be mental states which are 'nomologically incommensurable' with respect to neurophysiological or, more generally, physical properties" (Kim 1978, p. 150). Let us take, for example, the mental state of 'thinking of Vienna'. This means different things and conjures up different images to different people. Even the same person can think of Vienna in *n* different ways. It follows, then, "that it is exceedingly unlikely that there is some neurophysical state which occurs to a person whenever and only whenever he thinks of Vienna" (ibid.). If I were an identity theorist, I would have to "find for thinking of Vienna a nomologically coextensive physical property". But this is patently impossible. Consequently, "we need a different account of these mental properties which are, or at least appear to be, nomologically incommensurable with respect to physical properties" (ibid., p. 151).

In order to clarify the concept of supervenience, the leading neurophysiologist Roger Sperry used the example (somewhat simplistic, perhaps, but nonetheless effective) of television. The television *program*, although literally unrealizable without a precise *dependence on* and *congruence with* the physical processes that make up television, obeys a phenomenology and *specific* laws that are completely independent from and do not interact with the laws governing the physical circuits of a television broadcasting system: in a certain sense they 'are supervenient on them' (Sperry 1965, reprinted in Sperry 1983, pp. 94–5). Coming back to a more familiar sphere, the observation has been made that when I am with a person, I am in the presence of a system of atoms and molecules and of an individual made up of that system and only that. Nonetheless, although that person is in a sense nothing over and above this system, I cannot refer *precisely* and *nomologically* every single property of his being and action back to single properties of his molecular system. Indeed, the former properties are 'supervenient on' the latter ones.

We should point out immediately that the concept of supervenience is open to at least two interpretations. The one suggested by the two examples above emphasizes the *autonomy* of the two systems to which the concept is applied. In other cases, on the contrary, the stress falls on the close *co-dependence* between the systems (and sometimes even on a *non-symmetrical* co-dependence, leaning toward the operations of *one* of the systems: the physical one). Kim, in the final analysis, seems to opt for the co-dependence interpretation – with an evident bias toward the physical system.

It should be stressed that this slant draws its inspiration from a more general theoretical orientation: physicalism. Kim's physicalism is, without doubt, quite sophisticated and free from the rigid, systematic, and nomological binds of stricter versions. Nonetheless, he clearly emphasizes the role of *one* pole of the psychophysical relationship: that is, the physical in many ways 'comes before' the mental. Once headed down this path, Kim occasionally finds himself not too distant from positions espoused by the identity theorists: or, at least we can say that he does not cut all ties with this area of thought. Nor is it a coincidence that on more than one occasion he adopts a conception of the psychophysical relationship that can only be called unitary – or, to use Davidson's term, "monistic".

Monism, physicalism, and the (neo)identity theory are most clearly intertwined in the article on properties and psychophysical laws which we have already mentioned. "If all mental events are brought under such identities", Kim writes alluding to species-specific identity, "a *monistic theory of the mental* in which the mental is identified with the physical on the basis of empirically discovered mental–physical correlations will have been attained". He points out that while it is true that we should not expect to find a physical correlate for every mental event, this does not deny the fact that "each of these events may have a neural correlate" (Kim 1972b, p. 191). Many new horizons, many openings for further speculation are in this way somewhat abruptly cut off. As we have seen, Kim suggests flexible and subtle ways of approaching the problems involved in the definition of the mental and its relationship with the bodily. But he cannot, or will not, go beyond certain limits. The mental is still, so to speak, 'out on parole'. It is investigated and judged by a court that may be clement, but that is still partial. It is not allowed to present as evidence contents, sources, or *modi operandi* that have not been already examined and accepted by *another* form of knowledge.

CORRELATIONISM AND PROPERTY THEORY IN
AN ANTI-ONTOLOGICAL PERSPECTIVE

Before reflecting on the limits of Kim's views we should stress that his most important 'positive' theses did not fall into a void. Indeed, they reappear, and are often persuasively developed, in many interpretations of the MBP. This is proof that many scholars felt the need both to reject such a limiting conception as the orthodox identity theory and to 'de-ontologize' the psychophysical relationship by employing to the utmost the notion of property; and that this need was extremely widespread, even independently of the assumption of radical stands against a definite approach to the MBP.

One example of this orientation ('reformist' but, as we have said, not 'revolutionary') is offered by an important article by Judith J. Thomson, a scholar whom Popper mentions in favorable terms (Popper and Eccles 1977, 1, p. 82). Thomson, too, firmly rejects any psychophysical view that is *lato sensu* substantialist. Indeed, the problems involved with the relationship between the mental and the bodily concern not so much *things* as *events* or *properties* (Thomson 1969, p. 219). The identity theory has for the most part neglected or slighted the importance of the fundamental distinction between *entities* and *properties*. It is no coincidence that this theory so often compares physical 'bodies' with 'states' or 'processes', which are clearly not *bodies*. So, for example, many identity theorists assume as axiomatic a close analogy between identities of the type 'entity X is entity Y' ('clouds are a mass of water droplets') and identities of the type 'psychic event X is physiological process Y' ('anger is excitement of nerve fibers in the brain'). The error, writes Thomson, lies in building an analogy on incomparable 'subjects'. In the first case the referents are physical objects; in the second case we are dealing with the relationship between a mental *state*, or *way of being*, and a bodily *thing* or *given* (ibid., p. 221). If this is true, it should not be surprising that the type of relationship that can be established between the two different identities must be different. In the case of the relationship between physical objects we can speak of a true *identity* (but Thomson does not go into this aspect of the problem); in the case of the M–B relationship, however, we should speak (as Kim does) of a simple *correlation* (ibid., pp. 221 and 229). This implies on the one hand refusing to consider the mental *state* a *substance* whose essence could be described, and on the other purely ascertaining that two orders of phenomenon are simultaneously present on a more or less regular basis: these phenomena, however, remain totally heterogeneous, and only a "materialist" could presume to *identify* them in a strict sense (ibid., p. 229).

As might be expected, this new theory of properties and correlations has some functionalist advocates as well. In fact, the anti-ontological leaning of the proponents of a *property identity* (or a *property correlation*) is in many respects quite close to the positions of those who choose to reinterpret the mental not as an *entity* but as a *function*. Hilary Putnam, in particular, has argued forcefully for the essential role of the concept of property itself, and stressed that *properties* and *entities* must be considered as belonging to distinct planes (Putnam 1970). It is precisely this difference, he explains in another essay, that allows us to attribute different properties to the same entity. For example, a physical *res* like the brain can easily 'support' an indefinite number of "non-physical properties" – properties, Putnam points out in a radically anti-reductionist and anti-physicalist perspective, "which are definable in terms that do not mention the brain's physics or chemistry" (1981, p. 78).

In more recent years Putnam has continued to investigate the distinction between entities and properties and the peculiar nature of the latter. In an article published in 1982, for example, he underlines that a property is a way of being of something, connected not with the *real* and *objective* being of things but with our *descriptions* of them (1982b, p. 144). This thesis is (or could have been) of considerable relevance to the problems that concern us. Mental 'things' are essentially *properties* that we attribute to a definite physical referent or support: but we shape and describe them – with full cognitive legitimacy – on the basis of *our* existential and cultural interests and models.

Even a scholar of a completely different orientation like Michael Levin has attributed a prominent role to the problem of properties and their possible implications not only for epistemology but also (and most importantly) for psychology and anthropology (Levin 1979). However, despite the wealth of interesting observations that accompany his argumentation (such as those on the non-reducibility of complex psychic properties to the "molecular" level), his position is heavily conditioned by a deep faith in materialism: a creed which has in Levin, as was said in the Introduction, one of its most fervent and committed supporters. But the philosopher who has made the most stimulating and rigorous contribution to the redefinition of the mental in the anti-substantialist terms of properties and events (or, as we shall see, of modes and schemes) and of the psychophysical relationship in terms of non-systematic and non-nomological correlations is Donald Davidson.

DAVIDSON: THE MENTAL AS "EVENT"; ITS "HOLISM" AND "LAWLESSNESS"

Davidson's place within the ranks of critical (or 'reformist') identity theorists is rather peculiar. In fact, while it is true that in a number of significant ways he remains bound to a precise theoretical orientation (see his neo-physicalism, his "anomalous monism", some of his reflections on M–B connections, etc.), it is also true that in some of his writings he comes close to the positions of the most radical innovators, not only with regard to the traditional approach to the psychophysical relationship, but also to reflections on subjectivity, on what it means to be human, and on psychology.

Generally speaking, Davidson has a strong anti-ontological and anti-realistic leaning. Although this orientation is not laid out systematically in the essays which concern us most directly, still it inspires the epistemological analyses that underpin his most important positions; and these positions incline mainly toward a critique of the orthodox identity theory. Like Kim (and some functionalists) Davidson usually speaks not of the *mind* – an *entity* called mind – but of the *mental*. And like his theoretical allies he also tends (and most importantly) toward an interpretation which regards the mental as a general structure, and psychology as the study of objective universal phenomena (Pain, Belief, etc.). In this sense, however, he seems to go well beyond Kim. The latter, as we have seen, considered the mental to be principally a state or a property. Davidson – in a markedly anti-ontological and anti-realistic perspective – speaks of *events* (Davidson 1970). This definition, which also appears in Kim, is more innovative than might seem at first glance. 'State' or 'property' could appear to refer to a mode of phenomena that in some measure belongs to a reality *a parte objecti*, or at least to a constant, regular, and nomological occurrence of the phenomena themselves. 'Event', instead, seems to allude to a referent that is less 'consistent', more individual, diversified, and relatively unpredictable.

Still in general philosophical terms, Davidson's firm anti-reductionism also deserves mention. For him, the procedure of re-duction cannot in any way be generalized or absolutized, least of all in connection with the strategies which characterize the mental and human spheres. Particularly incisive and brilliant is his refu-tation of the often-mentioned 'nothing but' principle. To think of Bach's *The Art of the Fugue* as "nothing but a complex neural event" is for Davidson sheer madness (Davidson 1970, quoted in Davidson 1980, p. 214). He is well aware that the radical materialist is quick to reply: 'if you don't admit that all existing events are physical, then you have to admit the existence of something that is meta-physical'. But Davidson's answer is immediate and convincing. What he calls his "anomalous monism" does in fact recognize that "all events are physical", but it does not accept the thesis that for the particular class of physical events made up of mental events *"purely physical explanations"* can be given (ibid.; italics mine). In this connection, we should note that Davidson, while sympathetic to a *lato sensu* physicalist perspective, firmly rejects all absolutizing physicalism which affirms that all languages and all explanations can be reduced to one single language and one single explanation. (We shall return to this point.)

Given these premises, it is not surprising that Davidson proposes an interpretation of the mental that is not only extremely 'liberal' but also rich in promising implications. He has no intention of ne-glecting, much less of eliminating, the set of events we call "men-tal". Although the delineation of a systematic phenomenology of this set is not one of Davidson's foremost concerns, he does develop a principle of crucial importance to our investigation: the principle of the *peculiarity* and *autonomy* of *mental events*. It is true that what occurs in the sphere that is traditionally called psycho-mental often reveals certain binds of "dependence" on physiological phenom-ena: but this does not mean that *all* that is mental is dependent on the physical, and much less that the two are *homogeneous*. Between the one and the other, Davidson writes, recalling Ryle, there is a "categorical difference" (ibid., p. 223).

But what are the features that make the mental appear (relatively) 'different' from the physical? The 'diversity' that seems most sig-nificant to Davidson regards what he calls the "lawlessness" of mental events (ibid., p. 208). Unlike physical events, mental events are not "lawlike". Claims made about them can certainly be *true*, but they do not obey (nor do they rest on) *laws*. This means that, despite the behaviorists, the class of joys – or beliefs, or expectations

– does not "fall under strict deterministic laws" (ibid.). If this is the case, then it is totally implausible to talk about *psychophysical laws* (an indispensable principle for many identity theorist and materialists). Davidson insists on this point repeatedly and vigorously. It would be a fatal error to confuse mere psychophysical *correlations* with genuine *laws*. The former refer to a simple connection, which may well be causal but does not possess the requisites of necessity and universality; the latter, on the other hand, rigidly require regularity, generality, and predictability. To justify simple correlations *a parte objecti* it is sufficient to appeal to the concept of supervenience. This notion also gives us a rather effective grasp of the interplay of relative autonomy and dependence between distinct phenomena. Laws, on the other hand, imply not only dependence but also congruence and homogeneity: qualities which the categorical difference between the mental and physical precludes. This explains why Davidson begins his 1970 essay with the assertion that it is impossible to capture mental events "in the nomological net of physical theory" (ibid., p. 207) and ends with the conclusion that any nomologism concerning the mental must be rejected (ibid., p. 223). The consequence of all this is radical indeed: if science – or at least *physical* science – cannot do without nomological connections, then *it cannot explain mental events* (ibid., p. 225).

It is not only lawlessness that makes the mental a phenomenal world into itself. There are also other ways in which its peculiarity appears to be self-evident. The most significant is connected with what we would call the *independence* of at least one class of mental events. For Davidson there exist some mental events that are generated not by physical processes but by *other mental events*. Think, for instance, of the relationship between a feeling of joy and a recollection, between jealousy and love, between desire and ambition. In such cases the mental events are surely supported by physical processes, but their salient characteristic is their systematic connection with other mental events. This connection, moreover, assumes mainly forms and modes that are a-physiological and subjective in nature: I feel joy, jealousy, desire as a function of *my* ways of being – and the forms and motivations of these ways of being are not so much *physical* as *existential, cultural, social*. In a word, under certain circumstances certain mental states or events appear inextricably bound together, and even joined in such a way that one leads almost exclusively to another. This is the conception that Davidson often calls the "holism of the mental realm" (e.g., ibid., p. 217).

But if this is the way things stand, then we can expect important consequences on a cognitive plane. In fact, Davidson stresses (or repeats) one point in particular: independent of the *identity* of certain mental phenomena *an sich*, the *explanations* of those phenomena – those, at least, "in which we are typically interested" – relate them "to other mental events and conditions" (ibid., p. 225). So, for example, we explain a person's free actions by linking them not to presumed neurophysiological agents, but to "his desires, habits, knowledge and perceptions". The identity/physicalist position has dismissed all this as mere 'errors' committed by common sense, itself the victim of psychological and cultural prejudices. The truth will be *objectively* demonstrated by the 'things themselves' – revealed by Science. Davidson, as one might expect, takes a very different position. He openly defends the dimension of the mental and its independence from the physical. Moreover he stands by the legitimacy, at least as a program and in principle, of explanatory schemes that do not confine themselves to 'eliminating' mental phenomena or 'substituting' them with something else. What Davidson proposes is a reading of mental events which is not, so to speak, 'vertical' and deterministic (the mental as a dimension that derives causally from an *underlying* physical dimension), but 'horizontal' and relational. This reading encourages a rather innovative approach to the affective, intellectual, and behavioral world of man.

DAVIDSON BETWEEN THE AUTONOMY OF THE MENTAL AND NEO-PHYSICALISM

Davidson has arrived at (or is very near to) theses of capital importance for our inquiry. In the first place, he suggests a non-substantialist conception of the mental that helps us avoid the impasses inherent in the orthodox identity theory. Secondly, he lays the premises for a largely 'autonomistic' interpretation of the mental with respect to the physical, based both on the affirmation of the *heterogeneity* of the two poles of the mind and the body and on the thesis of the "lawlessness" of the first. It should be noted, moreover, that Davidson follows the theoretical implications of these positions well beyond the psychological domain. In a closer examination of the possibilities offered by this new approach to the MBP he vigorously stresses its repercussions on a broader interpretation of man. In fact, the nomological "slack" between mental and physical events opens up and 'complicates' in a positive way the features of the human being. By affirming the 'relative' independence of the mental from the physical, it emphasizes the non-mechanical and non-deterministic aspects of psychic operations. This "nomological slack", Davidson insists, is essential and must be defended "as long as we conceive of man as a rational animal": that is, as a being capable of acting beyond natural limits and constraints (ibid., p. 223). In the same vein, Davidson argues that it is necessary to have an interpretation of man that is *also* 'mentalistic' if we are to preserve the image of man as a free subject and agent: the image that Kant – cited in *Mental Events* as a venerated authority – judged absolutely essential, albeit incomplete without the image of man as an organism, as *homo natura* (ibid., p. 225).

If we consider that elsewhere Davidson also suggests that it is possible to 'read' the mental and the physical in terms of "conceptual schemes" and that *diverse* explanations of the mental can be admitted (see, in Chapter 8, 'Complementary' and 'Different' Kinds of Knowledge'), it becomes clear why his contribution has acquired such importance for an interpretation of the mind in non-substantialist and pluralist terms. One might even ask what is left in Davidson's views of the physicalist and identity positions. Why, in the present 'rational reconstruction' of the debate on the MBP, is he not credited with having promoted a completely new – and unambiguous – way of conceiving the mental, the human, and psychology?

One possible answer to this question is that ambiguities and insufficiently elaborated conceptions are, in fact, not lacking in Davidson's texts on the mental. In the first place, his anti-ontological critique does not appear to be developed to the extent that one might have hoped. Some scholars have pointed out that mental events are sometimes treated, at least *de facto*, as a form of 'reality'. Not only do they 'exist', but they act, produce certain results, establish certain relationships: relationships in which, as Davidson writes (suggesting a somewhat questionable symmetry), "psychological *phenomena* and physical *phenomena* are causally connected" (Davidson 1980, p. xv; italics mine). Whether this observation is valid or not, it is true that we do not find in Davidson's work a satisfactory explanation of the relationship between the mental as an *event* and the mental as a *conceptual scheme*. The two definitions seem to correspond to some extent to two different lines of reasoning, and in the final analysis it is not the second one that prevails.

In the second place, it is true that the mental is granted autonomy. But, at least at the level of actual experience, this autonomy is characterized essentially by the lawlessness of the mental sphere. Besides (with few exceptions), the concrete mental event is *in any case* linked with the physical event, and this link is *causal:* often to the point of determining (as we noted before) a more or less pronounced *dependence* – to use Davidson's own term – of the former on the latter. This may also be one reason why his important thesis of the "holistic" connection and independence of certain mental events is outlined in rather vague terms. Furthermore, Davidson fails to propose not only an adequate analysis of the mental universe as such, but also an appropriate theory of psychological discourse and of its specific referents and contents.

Thirdly, some comment should be made regarding Davidson's ambivalent position on physicalism. While it is undeniable that he rejects the physicalist *Weltanschauung* as an exhaustive (rather, a metaphysical) conception of knowledge, it is equally undeniable that for Davidson there is an overall view which admits (and even requires) the statement that *"all* events are *physical"* (Davidson 1970, in Davidson 1980, p. 214; italics mine). A similar sympathy for physicalism also emerges in more precisely cognitive terms. Despite certain signs of openness, Davidson seems to recognize a sort of ideal primacy of the linguistic and conceptual universe of the *physical.* In a significant passage in 'Mental Events', for example, we read that "every mental event [can] be uniquely singled out *using only physical concepts"* (ibid., p. 215; italics mine). What is more, he suggests another, more demanding thesis: for *"every* mental proposition" we can admit the existence of "an open, co-extensive physical proposition" (ibid., p. 225).

Finally, Davidson is actually quite firm in his rejection of an 'absolutizing' interpretation of the identity theory – the interpretation which posits the *complete* coincidence of the mental with the physical. But he has no intention of pushing his position beyond a certain limit: to the point, for example, of rejecting the identity theory as such. On the contrary, he declares very explicitly that he accepts what could be called a 'weak' version of it. Davidson has in mind an event–event identity which – and this is his only condition – recognizes the inexistence of "strict laws" connecting the mental and the physical (ibid., p. 212; on Davidson's sympathy for the identity theory see Elgin 1980). It is this condition, this further 'slackening' of the mental–physical relationship that distinguishes

Davidson's conception from that of the functionalists. Moreover, at the same time that he reiterates the "lawlessness" of the mental, Davidson stresses that the mental itself (at least the form of the mental which produces a physical event) can be described physically – and, therefore, can *be* "a physical event" (ibid., p. 224). This same thesis returns in another essay, 'Psychology as Philosophy'. Here we read that, "taken one by one", all mental events "are *describable* . . . in physical terms, *that is, they are physical events*" (Davidson 1974, in Davidson 1980, p. 231; italics mine). Especially noteworthy here is not only what one might term Davidson's "physicalistic optimism", but also the questionable identification (which seems to recall certain positions taken by Feigl) between an *attribution of describability* and an *attribution of reality*.

Last but not least, let us not forget that Davidson characterizes his overall views on the psychophysical relationship as "anomalous monism" (Davidson 1980, 214). The "anomalous" quality of this monism is already familiar to us: it lies in the denial that mental events can be *exhaustively* explained in *solely* physical terms. But there is also a noun, and one with precise connotations. This noun, this 'ism', suggests at the very least, if not a commitment to a truly metaphysical bias, certainly a markedly unitary image of the world, which undermines some of Davidson's statements that seem to lead in a very different direction. It should not appear out of place to recall that monism counts among its subscribers many advocates of the most radical kind of physicalism and identity theory. The reference is even less inappropriate if we consider that it is Davidson himself who affirms that his monism "resembles *materialism* in its claim that all events are *physical*" (ibid., p. 214; italics mine). 'Anomalous' or not, this monism undeniably points the overall interpretation of mental reality in the direction of a well-defined path: and this path can scarcely lead us to the reconsideration of psychology and of the human for which Davidson (as we shall see in the following Appendix) has in other ways paved the way.

APPENDIX

Davidson: the perfect robot and the specificity of the human

Davidson's philosophical reflection contains a number of extremely important contributions to the understanding of man and his science. These ideas go beyond the sophisticated neo-physicalism (perhaps even beyond "anomalous monism") examined in the preceding chapter and place Davidson squarely on the front lines of a crucial intellectual battle. For this reason a further analysis of some of his positions seems both opportune and necessary, and more appropriately carried out in an appendix, since they do not directly concern the MBP but address (at least on the surface) the problem of robots and the ambitions of computer science.

The theses in question are presented primarily in an article published in 1973 entitled 'The Material Mind'. Davidson's main concern in this essay is to determine to what extent the cognitive possibilities of the physical sciences are applicable to the human sphere. Davidson begins his inquiry with a hypothesis which he (unlike many others) regards as pure science fiction, but which in its extremism provides the opportunity to make certain crucial observations. We are asked to imagine that an exceptionally refined technology, equipped with a perfect (physical) knowledge of how the brain works and founded on the assumption that the brain works like a computer, can build a sort of mechanical duplicate of a human being. Suppose, further, that the observable behavior of this duplicate – called Art for convenience's sake – is identical to that of a human being. Davidson's 'challenge' is this: if we can demonstrate that the functioning of a robot like Art and the *physical* knowledge referable to him do not eliminate certain *psychic* phenomena and the correlative *psychological* knowledge, then we will have every reason to say (anti-physicalistically) that a psychological investigation of human beings cannot be dispensed with.

The anti-physicalist's first observation concerns the mental. Let us suppose that Art's physical makeup allows him to manifest every possible kind of externally observable behavior. This, as the critique of behaviorism has shown, does not tell us anything about the nature and functions of psychic phenomena as such. The performance of such acts, in fact, "falls short . . . of assuming that we have succeeded in identifying such things as beliefs, desires, intentions, hopes, inferences, or decisions with particular states of the brain or mechanisms of it" (Davidson 1973, in Davidson 1980, p. 247).

Davidson is aware (and so are we, at this point) that the materialist or identity theorist would reply more or less as follows: if we are able to produce and describe physical states that regularly cause mental states (and are able, therefore, to subject these occurrences of causation to constant rules and to predict them without exception), then we can conclude that "psychological events simply *are* (in the sense of '*are identical with*') physical events" (ibid., p. 248). Is this a valid answer or not? For Davidson it is *not*. It implies, in fact, a theoretical concession to the materialist/identity theorist that *cannot* be made. Let us return for a moment to the starting hypothesis. The only supposition we have made with regard to Art and to a 'perfect' physics is that it is possible to give a physical description for every event that is usually called mental. But this does not imply that I have *a priori, absolute and nomologically based knowledge of all mental events*. In other words, no *physical* knowledge can prevent *unforeseen* mental events from happening: events that I can *describe physically* (if and when they happen) but not *predict* in a nomologically guaranteed way.

At the base of all this there lies a differentiation articulated at two different levels: epistemological and anthropological. The first is the difference between mere *generalization* and true *laws*; the second that between man and machine. These two differences are closely interwoven. A man behaves (at a certain level of complexity) according to *generalizable habits* which admit, however, the most diverse *exceptions*. A machine, on the contrary, follows *strict laws*, that do not admit exceptions. A child who has burned himself, for example, will *usually* stay away from fire, whereas a mechanism, if programmed in a certain way, will *always* repeat the same behavior (ibid., p. 250).

For Davidson, then, one of the main limits of physics as it is applied to the psychoanthropological universe is that it works within the sphere of the *describable* (according to precise logical and linguistic paradigms), the *nomologizable* (albeit with reference to a 'liberal' nomology), and the *predictable* (though not necessarily infallible). Now, there is no doubt that the *modus operandi* of physics can be widely applied to the human sphere (just as Art is largely human-like). Yet there are bounds that Davidson feels, rightly, cannot be overstepped. As we saw in 'Mental Events', these bounds are set principally by the impossibility of subjecting mental (and, much less, existential) phenomenology to the pre-requisites of predictability and nomological coherence required by physical science. In 'The Material Mind' Davidson adds two further observations that confirm the inability of physics (even Art's 'perfect' physics) to encompass or replace psychology. The first is, "If a certain psychological concept applies to one event and not to another, there must be a difference describable in physical terms. But it does not follow that there is a single physically describable difference that distinguishes any two events that differ in a given psychological respect" (ibid., pp. 253–4). This is the same as saying that *psychological* articulations and differences are not always and not necessarily referable to *univocal physical causes.*

Davidson's second observation concerns the *different nature* – and, therefore, the (at least) partial untranslatability – of psychological and physical concepts. In particular, the former "are essentially evaluative", and the latter are not (ibid., p. 254). So, for instance, observing that a person suddenly grows red in the face, a physiologist *describes* the neurovascular mechanisms responsible for the physical phenomenon, while a psychologist *evaluates* the same *physical* phenomenon as a (*psychic*) case of shame, shyness, or embarrassment. Shame, shyness, and embarrassment (all *different* mental events which, however, are manifested ostensibly – if we can be forgiven the oversimplification – in the *same physical* appearance of 'blushing', with its neurovascular correlates) are all concepts that single out, qualify, and semanticize definite *physical* events in a *meta*-physical way: a way that is usually called 'psychological', and which it seems we can scarcely do without. But let's now go back to Art and 'perfect' physics.

The basic problem, as we will recall, was this: is Art, the 'perfect' robot, so human-like that he can duplicate a human being in every respect? And again, is physics so 'powerful' that it can replace psychology and all its contributions to cognition? A negative answer to both these questions stems from a new sort of consideration. Let us take as an example the set of operations known as 'information processing' (ibid., pp. 250ff.). It should be pointed out immediately that the example, in a sense, leans toward a physicalist response to our questions. In fact, it is increasingly accepted that what traditional psychology called 'knowledge' is effectively a physically describable processing of information. This processing, what is more, can easily be carried out by a sophisticated robot like Art. So, the example of information processing could provide important evidence in favor of the thesis that Art (read 'physics') is equivalent to, or identifiable with, man (read 'psychology').

But the question that must be raised is this: is Art's information processing the same as man's? Davidson's (negative) answer does not stem from a sort of mystic humanism according to which the Being Man is *a priori* different from the Machine. On the contrary, his rejection of this identification is grounded in a sophisticated and persuasive argumentation – and herein lies its importance. His thesis is that Art's information processing would be identical to ours if and only if it had human features. Can it? The answer is inevitably *no*. Why not? Because Art is by definition a *machine*. Now, if I really wanted to attribute to Art the capacity to carry out a *human* kind of information processing (implying an infinitely complex network of interpretations, references, assessments, etc., but this is not the main point), I would quite simply have to *stop thinking* of Art as a *machine* and start thinking of him as a *man*. Only a *man*, Davidson stresses vigorously, can do *truly human* things. The other 'entities' – robots, computers, or whatever – can at most *simulate* certain performances and behaviors. To be sure, this simulation might be extremely effective. But (as we have observed elsewhere) it is one thing to *simulate* something – *mechanically*, no less – and it is quite another to *actually do* it. To put it somewhat differently: Art, obviously, carries out only *physical* operations. Now, we can easily apply mental *predicates* to those operations. But at this point, either we have strained a metaphor (which is what happens most commonly), or we have to rethink Art from a *new* perspective: psychological, mentalistic, and human. Only if Art becomes to all effects a *man*, a *subject*, can we ask him, for example, what he 'feels' this information processing corresponds to (cognitively, emotionally, etc.). Only at this point – and through, or following, this process of anthropomorphization – can we compare *our* experience of information processing with *his* experience and evaluate the results of the comparison. Before that, no. Before that, we will have in front of us simply a man and a machine, *whose only affinity lies in the operatively and ostensibly identical execution of some operations.* This is no small thing, but it is certainly not enough to bridge the gap between man and machine. Even the most perfect physics cannot reproduce *everything* a man experiences as he processes information. Marcel Proust, in the course of such 'processing', experienced psychic and emotional repercussions that went well beyond any form of nomology or any kind of physical predictability.

A rather similar point can and must be made about the production and comprehension of language (ibid., p. 225). In this case, as well, a careful analysis of the problem confirms the limits of a strictly physical knowledge and the need for a 'different' knowledge. Let us suppose that Art 'talks'. It is evident that this can only mean that he performs all the physical operations connected with linguistic activity. But the question arises immediately, Is the *physical* performance of acts that *simulate* linguistic activity *identifiable* with the *real* (mental) production of speech? Davidson prefers to frame the question in a slightly different way: in order to understand language as *language* is it sufficient to know the *(physical)* capacities responsible for linguistic performance?

The answer, once again, is *no*. If we are to reach a full understanding of language we have to take a sort of *meta*-physical leap. Language (i.e., authentic language) is inextricably bound to an in(de)finite range of assumptions and intentions, the in(de)finite world of the speaker's subjectivity, the *theory* of what language is and the in(de)finite ways in which it can function and act. We cannot simply say that it is all 'very complex' – implying that one day, and in principle, a higher stage of physics will be able to reproduce it. What we have to say, instead, is that *it does not belong on a physical plane*. This is why, if we wish to understand language *not* as an organized physical externalization of sounds, but as the expression of a speaking subject, then we must go beyond the physical plane. After all, either the physical externalization is merely the material *bearer* of the actual mental (or cultural) production of speech, or it is the *simulator* of that production; but if, as we said, we want to understand language *as language* (i.e., a *real* speech act, with all its implications), then we do not want to consider it in its capacity as a mere material-external bearer, nor as a mere *simulator* of something *else*.

When Davidson suggests that it is necessary to overstep the boundaries of the *physical* in the linguistic domain as well, he does not only stress the need to appeal to the mental and cognitive dimension of man if we are to understand language as *language*, but he also introduces the extremely important concept of *interpretation* (ibid., p. 257). Every speech act, far from having one single meaning, is rife with semantic values. Clearly, these different values, 'borne' by one sole *physical* vehicle, cannot be reducible to, or identified with, a particular speech act. It is thus necessary to develop a procedure and a science capable of grasping, with appropriate instruments, those values with their particular features. The procedure required is interpretation; the science is hermeneutics. Both interpretation and hermeneutics operate according to norms and techniques that are considerably different from those proper to a *physical* referent and its correlative *science*. Thus the interpretive or hermeneutic act does not follow rules that can be formalized (like those of physics): it proceeds in ways that are not (or not entirely) preconstituted, predictable, nomological; it does not achieve results that can be considered general or axiomatic; it takes into account the most varied (and, again, unpredictable) references, backgrounds, implied meanings, and purposes – in a word, the subject's entire universe of (*mental, cultural*, but not *physical*) presuppositions and intentions.

At this point the 'limits' of physics should be clear; as is the need for different cognitive approaches to the human sphere. What about Art's limits? We shall conclude these brief comments by returning to Davidson's starting point.

Davidson supposes that Art answers a certain question by saying: 'It's a whale' (ibid., p. 257). The answer, given that Art is a *perfect* robot, is correct. But even such an elementary sentence as this poses unsettling problems of interpretation and understanding (concerning, that is, the comparison of the 'speech' acts of a machine with those of a man). What do we suppose Art 'really' meant? Is there something else 'behind' his answer? At the intellectual level, did he consider the classification of whales as mammals? At the emotional level, did he shiver at the thought of this enormous sea creature? At the linguistic and behavioral level, was there some hidden message he wanted to communicate? Any element of exhibitionism or arrogance or irony in the utterance? And Melville? What about Melville? Even granting that *Moby Dick* had been fed into his memory, could it have occurred to him to associate, by bold analogy, the whale of his answer with Melville's?

These are all, let's admit it, *our* questions. Davidson is content to affirm that Art can certainly say, 'It's a whale', attributing to this statement meanings that are more elementary than, or simply different from, ours. If we want to be more ambitious and ascribe to Art's answer certain predicates, or properties, or mental and cultural implications, we are perfectly free to do so. But we should be fully aware that in order to do this we must be prepared to *pre-define* Art, to *pre*-interpret him *as a person*. For only a completely anthropomorphized, or better, a 'person-ified', machine is able to give certain meanings to certain utterances, to take part in a meaningful comparison with man as regards certain performances, and most importantly, to tell us what experiences, implications, and intentions are connected with its answers. But we must be careful here. *This completely person-ified machine is no longer a machine: it is a person.* And if this is the case, we lose one of the prerequisites for a comparison between a (real) 'man' and a (real) 'machine'. In a word, *either* we *maintain* an appropriate (and for many, self-evident) *difference* between man and machine – and accordingly many of our hypotheses about the possibility of bridging the gap between the one and the other (at least at a certain level of complexity) reveal themselves to be empty and gratuitous – *or* we *humanize* the machine, *preidentifying it* with man – in which case the very possibility of comparing *two distinct* things seems to dissolve.

Everything we have said so far is essentially concerned with the problematic relationship between a human being and a robot. But isn't this also a way – and not a particularly obscure one – of saying something about the relationship between the mental and the physical? Isn't it also true for this relationship that in order to speak of the mental physically it is necessary to have *pre*-defined the *mental* in *physical* terms – thereby cancelling, or underrating, precisely those features which make the mental *mental*, that is, something *distinct* (at least at a linguistic and conceptual level) from the *physical?*

Chapter 7

The mind as language

The linguistic turn in the mind–body problem

THE LINGUISTIC INTERPRETATION OF
THE MENTAL AND ITS VARIANTS

In the preceding two chapters we pointed out the unquestionable merits as well as the limits of the proposals advanced by functionalism and by the other 'reformist' version of the identity theory. These proposals helped 'liberalize' the reflection on the MBP and orient it in new and stimulating directions. They have, however, been criticized by many philosophers of mind. The reservations expressed, more or less explicitly, about the positions of Putnam and Fodor and of Kim and Davidson can be summarized as follows:

a) There are frequent signs of more or less marked sympathy toward physicalism.

b) They show an excessive concern for the problems of the mind–body relationship as they are traditionally formulated. Although these problems have often received innovative answers the assumptions that underlie them have rarely been discussed adequately.

c) There seems to be a certain neglect of the problems regarding the mental *in itself,* that is, of the referents and contents to which it refers and of the *particular* approaches and explanations that it (perhaps) requires.

d) The figures of the physical and (most importantly) the mental have not been adequately thought through in linguistic terms.[1]

---

1. This charge is undoubtedly less well founded in the case of Davidson. And yet not even Davidson provides an adequate linguistic interpretation of the mental,

In a sense, it may be said that it is this last point which most concerns a certain group of scholars who have occupied themselves with the philosophy of mind. As early as 1941 C. I. Lewis spoke persuasively of the need to consider the physical and the mental as two linguistic interpretive schemes (Lewis 1941). A similar thesis was advanced some years later in a well-known article by Percy Bridgman: "There is no agreement here", he writes,

> – some people find it meaningful to talk about the mind of plants. Other people want to talk about mind only when there is a nervous system with which it may be associated. In any event we do not have to decide what mind *is*, but need only decide under what conditions we want to use the word mind. It may be that enumeration of all the specific instances in which one wants to use the word 'mind' will disclose some easily recognizable common characteristic sufficient to justify its retention. (1959, in Curi 1985, p. 262)

Statements like this could be multiplied at will. But it is especially in the 1960s that certain positions were developed and defined in relation to the specific debate on the MBP. In 1974 Wilkerson wrote:

> We should not think of mind–body problems as problems about the way one thing, a body, is attached to another, a mind. 'The mind' is only a convenient label for all those states, dispositions, activities, abilities ascribed by the use of P-predicates. Most particularly . . . it is a convenient label for a series of states of consciousness. (Wilkerson 1974, p. 32)

It has been said, in connection with positions of this sort, that some identity theorists as well have admitted the fundamentally linguistic dimension of the mind and body poles and even the diversity of the languages used to describe them. The observation (though in itself rather debatable) allows us to make an important clarification. What is at play here, what many philosophers of mind demand is not merely that the psychophysical problem take on a substantially 'linguistic' character. It is also the twofold recognition (often stressed in the preceding chapters) that *different* languages

---

nor does he offer a satisfactory rehabilitation of the procedures and language of psychology. This is clear not only from his 'Mental Events' but also from another essay – equally significant, though in part disappointing, especially given its title and initial promises – 'Psychology as Philosophy' (Davidson 1974).

say *different* things, and that they say them, in principle, with equal legitimacy in cognitive terms. And it is the further recognition that there can be two linguistic-conceptual universes which are neither homogeneous nor intertranslatable.

As for the identity theory, it will be recalled that its basic assumption, the point on which it lays the greatest stress, is the affirmation of the singleness of the psychophysical referent (i.e., there is only a B referent), or of the reducibility of the M referent to the B referent; and this affirmation is too rarely accompanied by a reflection on the further dimension of the (psycho-subjective, cultural, pragmatic) *sense* of what is said about the referent itself. Furthermore, identity theorists of a formally or substantially more 'linguistic' orientation do indeed admit the plurality of languages, but they generally hold (and Feigl is a case in point) that certain languages have no cognitive validity and can and must be translated into, or replaced by, *one* precise *scientific* language. Clearly, such a claim largely undermines the significance of recognizing the existence of *different* languages.

It is with the purpose of avoiding this danger that a group of philosophers of mind have chosen an apparently more effective strategy. Although they continue to admit the existence of a single type of referent in psychophysical analysis, these scholars have theorized that the linguistic systems to 'say' it are not only plural but they also are not (or not necessarily) mutually reducible or translatable. Jerome Shaffer, for example, writes that there are *only* "physical phenomena", but that there are nonetheless two different ways of talking about them cognitively (Shaffer 1967a, p. 44). Many other scholars (often moderate physicalists) have espoused a similar conception, among them – at least in part – Davidson. Indeed, Davidson also speaks of two different ways or "schemes" of talking about the world, though he tends to consider the phenomena of this world to be fundamentally physical (Davidson 1970, p. 222). It is worth pointing out that we are dealing with a position which is all the more significant – and pertinent in this context – as it is often assumed from a markedly anti-ontological/realist perspective. Shaffer, in particular, stresses that the thesis he defends has the advantage of avoiding "a dualism of entities, events or properties" (Shaffer 1968, p. 44). As Richard Bernstein writes in this regard (though from a far more radical linguistic perspective), it is not so much an "*ontological* dualism between two types of entities" that is to be constructed as "an *epistemological* dualism between two irreducibly different types of knowledge" (Bernstein 1968, in Rosenthal 1971, p. 207; italics mine).

And yet, on closer examination, even this position has its weaknesses. It is true, as Wilkerson has observed, that it is one thing to affirm the existence of a single (physical) type of entity, and it is another to say (as 'philosophical' physicalism does) that there is one sole mode to talk about it (Wilkerson 1974, p. 68). It is true, that is, that in principle it is possible to admit two or more languages in relation to one single world. But it is also undeniable that an *a priori* pronouncement in favor of the existence of a *single* universe of referents or phenomena – and more specifically of a *physical* universe – makes it objectively difficult to fully recognize the value of a *multiplicity* of languages'– and more specifically of a *mental* language. What is needed, then, is a more radical break not only with the slightest, even vague, commitment to physicalism, but also (and more importantly) with what has been called the primacy – or the myth – of reference. It becomes necessary, in other words, to fully adopt the principle that language comes cognitively 'before' things, in the sense that language defines, categorizes, and baptizes things in manifold, equally 'worthy' ways.

RYLE'S CONTRIBUTION: SOME CONSIDERATIONS

One of the more significant currents of thought committed to this position is, for several reasons, English analytic philosophy and the Wittgensteinian school. Given the focus of this essay, it is not surprising that the first name to come to mind is that of Ryle. Indeed, *The Concept of Mind* was a veritable milestone along the path of a definite area of research. However, from the point of view of the problems that concern us here Ryle's contribution does not appear to be the most significant and innovative. There is no question that Ryle helped promote what has been called the "Copernican revolution" (toward a linguistic orientation) of contemporary thought. But this contribution consists essentially in assigning philosophy the twofold task of investigating notions and concepts by examining "the propositions in which they are wielded" and of analyzing "the ways in which it is logically legitimate to operate with" certain terms (Ryle 1949, p. 4). From another standpoint Ryle does not ground this stimulating redefinition of the task of philosophy (at least in *The Concept of Mind*) on an adequate reconsideration of the relationship between language and reality. Indeed, language is not presented as an (or better, *the*) ordering device and, so to speak, 'semanticizer' of things. Moreover, Ryle's attitude toward things is rather elusive. Although he joins in the attack on the belief in "Enduring Substance" or in a "Thing-in-Itself" (ibid., p. 223), he does not develop certain premises in an overall criticism of the alleged 'consistency' and 'precedence' of the things themselves from a cognitive point of view.

It has been suggested that Ryle was influenced – perhaps in reaction to opposing stimuli – by the realist-leaning philosophy of Moore. That may be. What is certain is that within the realm of the philosophy of mind Ryle does not give an adequate interpretation of the mental and the physical in terms of categorial *modes* and expressive *functions*. In effect, the physical remains, in a sense, a collection of essentially real and natural states and processes. The mental, on the other hand, is radically dismantled and dissolved. The mind, in short, is neither a "thing" nor a "state" (ibid., p. 206); mental events "do not exist" (ibid., p. 164). This latter position is clearly rife with implications. And yet it should be pointed out that Ryle does not examine satisfactorily the possibility of reinterpreting the mental in the alternative terms indicated above. He almost never raises questions as to the possible usefulness or validity – at least from a certain point of view – of a *mental* theoretical and conceptual system. And if he occasionally acknowledges that "mental propositions" can and must legitimately exist (ibid., p. 19), the role – which may be quite important – of these propositions is taken into adequate consideration only on rare occasions. For some this is perhaps the most disappointing point. In a certain sense, Ryle's behaviorist 'prejudgements' on the mind (the *psyche*) impede an adequate reexamination of the possible constitution of an autonomous, self-confident mental (*psychological*) language. This is true even though, in the more general terms of the philosophy of language, Ryle repeats that it is desirable and even necessary to have a plurality of linguistic universes, as when he writes: "I have striven to distinguish *different* types of language" (ibid., p. 313). Consequently those – and there were many – who in the stimulating pages of *The Concept of Mind* hoped to find the justification for a new expressive system that was finally entitled to 'say' a certain dimension of human experience, and to 'say it' according to autonomous (non-physicalistic) principles, were bound to be disappointed.

WITTGENSTEIN AND THE PHILOSOPHY OF MIND

Undeniably Ryle's work does not hold pride of place in the particular phase of the reflection on the MBP that concerns us here. In that phase the notable contribution of analytical philosophy is more significantly represented – at times explicitly, more commonly implicitly – by the specific Wittgensteinian component. "Wittgenstein", Norman Malcolm once wrote, "is easily the most important figure in the philosophy of mind" (Malcolm 1971). This appraisal may be somewhat exaggerated, but there is no question that the struggle to deentify the mental and to recognize the basically linguistic nature of the psychophysical problem owes a lot to the author of the *Tractatus*. Naturally, we will not attempt a systematic examination of the relationship between Wittgenstein and the contemporary philosophy of mind: the question not only goes well beyond the issue of the MBP, but it is still too open and controversial. It will suffice to examine briefly the type of influence that Wittgenstein may have exercised within the context of the problems that concern us here.

In general terms, it is well known that Wittgenstein (the second or 'late' Wittgenstein) was a radical opponent of ontologism and realism, of essentialism and referentialism, of formalism and of linguistic 'monism'. For the author of *Philosophical Investigations* there are no things *an sich*. Nor are there natural and universal structures or essences – in contrast, for example, to the opposite belief expressed by the anti-Wittgensteinian Armstrong, to remain within the realm of the MBP. In the third place, for Wittgenstein it is quite illegitimate, if not contradictory, to admit the cognitive existence of something without considering the linguistic forms through which this 'something' is necessarily acquired. In a certain sense (to repeat a handy image used above), words really 'come before' 'things'. Before 'things', but also before referential *denotata* or *designata*. From a coherently Wittgensteinian standpoint any attempt to give cog-

181

nitive priority (whether direct or indirect) to 'referentiality' must be rejected.

On the other hand it is no less unfounded and misleading to presume that there is a language which is endowed with a greater capacity and legitimacy than others to propose and impose its own *Sinngebung,* its own *Ordnung* of phenomena. Not even physical language, in Wittgenstein's view, can claim to serve as an absolute model of human cognitive experience. And this is true not only for reasons connected with the inherent *limits* of *every* linguistic universe, but also for a further, in part extra-linguistic, reason. Wittgenstein argues that it is not *languages* that baptize the facts of the world but thinking, speaking *subjects.* It is man who 'de-fines', encodes, and reads these facts, or even *constructs* them. Finally, our categories, denominations, and interpretations answer not to universal-abstract meta-criteria but to the particular-concrete interests and purposes of human beings.

All this has many important implications for the MBP debate. The 'mind' and the 'body' appear not as things (or as univocal, rigid expressions of things), but as active, mobile conceptual-expressive instruments indicating – in ways that are not mechanical or objectively preestablished – certain classes of phenomenon or referent in relation to certain (changeable) assumptions and needs of individuals. 'Mind' and 'body', then, are merely the subjects/objects of *different* languages – or of *different* communicative practices, of *different* semantic organizations (the validity of which cannot be judged by a single scale of values) of what is, or passes for, the real world. This explains the reservations that a Wittgensteinian approach to the psychophysical problem cannot help having toward designs to *reduce* M to B or, even worse, to *eliminate* M. If and when it becomes established that there are at least some features peculiar to the linguistic-conceptual-pragmatic universe M that are different and distinct from those of the linguistic-conceptual-pragmatic universe B, then it will have to be admitted that Davidson is right when he writes, in a passage already familiar to us, that the *identification* of M and B implies a categorial leap which can hardly be justified.

Wittgenstein had already pointed out the theoretical and historical origins of this leap in terms similar to those of Ryle. The entification of the mental, he said, derives mainly from a misguided 'con-formation' of the psycho-behavioral disciplines to the disciplines concerned with the bodily. "Psychology", he wrote in the

Philosophical Investigations, "treats of processes in the psychological sphere, as does physics in the physical". And yet on closer examination the similarity or symmetry is based on a "misleading parallel".

> Seeing, hearing, thinking, feeling, willing are not the subject of psychology in the same sense as that in which the movements of bodies, the phenomena of electricity, and so on are the subject of physics. You can see this from the fact that the physicist sees, hears, thinks about, and informs us of them, and the psychologist observes the external reaction (the behavior of the subject). (Wittgenstein 1953, para. 571)

If, for Wittgenstein, the mental is not assimilable to a physical 'thing', it can also not be considered (as some philosophers of mind have done) a state, a property, or an event. It is, rather, a *mode:* a certain mode *we have,* in which we look at ourselves and analyze ourselves. This mode, we should stress, is so far from being 'objective' that when we use it not only do we transform what we sought to grasp 'in itself', but we even create within ourselves a phenomenon *different* from the one we thought we were referring to. If this is true, it appears quite unreasonable to want to identify this *mode* with *physical processes.* We can at best recognize what Wittgenstein calls "characteristic accompaniments": the phenomena that seem to be connected with a certain regularity to what we live in our mental experience.

It would mean running the risk of committing another 'categorial error', however, to suppose that this (relative) regularity implies the existence of a causal relationship or, worse still, the reducibility of certain 'psychic' experiences to verifiable physical facts. How could I, for example, reduce what I feel, interpret, and experience as 'hope' to some neurophysiological or biochemical process? Anthony Kenny has observed that physical "characteristic accompaniments" may at best serve as some (of the many) of the identification marks of certain modes of the mental being. "The bodily expression of a mental process was a *criterion* for that process, i.e. it was a part of the concept of a particular mental process (e.g. the sensation of pain) that certain types of behaviour counted as direct and non-inductive evidence for its occurrence" (Kenny 1969, p. 258).

Seen from another angle, Wittgenstein considers the mental that with which we designate the *meaning* of what *happens,* or what we *suppose happens,* in a certain realm of experience. After all, meaning is itself something essentially *non-physical.* It is in large part, in fact, something *mental* – with all the enigmatic, elusive, indefinite features that characterize the mental. Indeed, meaning is an indescribable mental act, something definite but impalpable or intangible (Wittgenstein 1953, paras. 608 and 173–5). To speak of the mental then, or to constitute a certain class of meanings, involves the highly subjective-symbolic-conventional elaboration of certain terms and concepts which, in themselves, cannot be identified with, and much less exhausted by, a *fact* of any sort. "'Joy' designates nothing at all. Neither any inward nor outward thing" (Wittgenstein 1967, para. 487). That it is not external or externalized in some universal, objective sense is now, despite the behaviorists, generally agreed. Nor is it *internal,* however, or intelligibly mental or spiritual: *what do we mean* by internal? *What is* the mental/spiritual? These questions cannot be given, on a rigorously referential plane, an adequate and reliable answer. What we do know – though in rather approximate terms – is with what joy is more or less frequently *correlated* neurophysiologically. Yet, we have just pointed out that recognizing the existence of these correlations in no way implies that a certain way of being or feeling has been adequately understood. Of course, this does not mean that joy does not exist. It merely means that it exists within its own realm; it means, in particular and in fact, that "its meaning is its use in the language" (Malcolm 1970, p. 19).

Another characteristic of the mental, for Wittgenstein, is that it is in(de)finitely complex and plural, heterogeneous and polymorphous. Let us consider, for example, the mental 'fact' of remembering. Only a moment's reflection is needed to recognize that we are dealing with an act or event which could imply *n* completely different actions. "Remembering a word", notes Malcolm, "is different from remembering a face; and remembering a sensation is still different. Remembering your uncle is different from remembering that you have an uncle. Remembering to fix the radiator is different from remembering how to fix it" (ibid., p. 22).

In conclusion, Wittgenstein does not limit himself to rejecting the reification of the mental: he also refutes the claim that for each mental act or event there is *one* essence or *one* definition (the realist who insists on asking "what" with the aim of "understanding" a pain or something of the sort will receive "no answer" (Wittgenstein 1967, para. 678). He also strives to consider so-called mental phenomena as ways in which human beings act and speak. And he takes these ways quite seriously, without judging them on the basis of heteronomous criteria. Finally (we must repeat), Wittgenstein gives full recognition to the plurality and differences that exist among these various modes in relation to the subjects that use them and to the contexts and purposes for which they are used. Malcolm has observed lucidly:

> On Wittgenstein's view, philosophy should try neither to *identify* nor to *explain* the phenomena of the mind. What should it do then? It should *describe language.* It should remind us of what we say. It should bring to mind how we actually use the mental terms that confuse us philosophically. (1970, pp. 28–9)

BERNSTEIN AND THE DEFENSE OF PSYCHOLOGICAL LANGUAGE

As we have said, it was in the sixties that certain MBP scholars began to return, at times indirectly, to some of Wittgenstein's theses. Of particular significance, in this context, is the position of Richard Bernstein (1968, in Rosenthal 1971, pp. 200–22). Bernstein holds that the first, crucial choice a certain interpretation of the MBP must make is to abandon, unambiguously, an *ontological* perspective and to embrace a *linguistic* one. Now, if our approach to the world (including the human-mental world) is fundamentally linguistic, then it follows that a decisive function will be performed by *description.* We can describe reality, Bernstein writes, in many *different* ways. And we are quite free to substitute a mental description with a physical one. At this point, however, as we have often observed, the unavoidable question is, will the descriptions in my new language be as *rich* as the previous ones, and as *satisfying* as regards *all* the cognitive interests we might have concerning a given issue? We are familiar with the reductionist/physicalistic answer provided by the identity theory. Bernstein, for his part, has no intention of denying *in toto* the single prerogatives of physical language, although he is inclined to think that at least in certain cases it may prove to be less adequate than mental language. His aim is simply to defend – again from a Wittgensteinian perspective – the thesis that mental language also has its own autonomy and validity, even from a cognitive point of view.

In certain circumstances this mental system appears to Bernstein to be even irreplaceable. This is the case, in particular, of when I want to describe certain phenomena *as I experience them,* as part of my personal and private world (ibid., p. 218). "I claim that my present language for reporting and describing sensations is another, different, supplementary, legitimate mode of discourse for describing my experiences", he writes. (ibid., p. 220). Any other conception, he believes, could be extremely dangerous. If a certain language were eliminated, as the physicalists would like, we would risk losing (as other philosophers of mind have feared) an "entire mode of discourse including its *entire descriptive vocabulary"* (ibid. p. 219; italics mine).

No, we cannot do without this discourse. We must not give it up even if it might be (as different varieties of 'scientific' philosophers claim) inexact, vague, imprecise. There is an important reason for this: how can it be claimed that the world is made up of only exactness and precision? Or to put it differently, how can it be argued that men want to use and enunciate *only* exact and precise assertions? Some advocates of the identity theory and of the disappearance theory have, as we have seen, given priority to, or even absolutized, the criterion of *simplicity.* But for what reason? Why should our universe be deprived of the experience of the complex and the obscure? It is not true, Bernstein insists, that "the indeterminate and vague" is unreal (ibid., 221).

All these positions are explicitly derived, directly or indirectly, from Wittgenstein. It is not surprising, then, that Bernstein should conclude his attack on physicalism, eliminationism, and the identity theory (a polemic, we should note, based on a far more radical position than Davidson's) with an impassioned tribute to Wittgenstein (and the phenomenologists):

> It is Wittgenstein, perhaps more than any other contemporary philosopher who most deeply questioned and exposed the illegitimacy of three basic philosophical biases, perhaps because he was originally so profoundly affected by them. He has, or rather should have made us sensitive to the variety, complexity and non-reductiveness of different perspectives and life forms and the constant danger of giving in to the basic urge to impose a single paradigm or standard on the complex web of human life and discourse. . . . Nevertheless both the spirit and the letter of Wittgenstein and the contem-

porary phenomenologists should awaken us to an awareness that the consciousness of our own experience of the language in which we report and describe our sensations and feelings is different from and no less legitimate than the scientific discourse". (ibid., p. 222)

NORMAN MALCOLM'S ANTI-SUBSTANTIALIST REINTERPRETATION OF THE MIND

But the scholar who did the most to build upon the heritage of Wittgenstein within the context of the MBP – and from the theoretical perspective that interests us here – is Norman Malcolm. The problems surrounding the mental and its interpretability in physical terms is the subject of several significant articles and of an important monograph entitled *Problems of Mind: Descartes to Wittgenstein* (1971).

Malcolm's book launches a threefold polemic: against Cartesian dualism, against Australian materialism, and against logical behaviorism. This is not the place for a detailed analysis of the numerous criticisms Malcolm levels against these '-isms'. Suffice it to say, at a general level, that his Wittgensteinian perspective leads him to underwrite positions radically opposed to those of the identity theory and physicalism (positions, as in the case of Bernstein, well beyond the 'policy' of a Davidson). Malcolm brings to bear all the sophisticated methodology of his mentor to expose the insurmountable conceptual difficulties inherent in his adversaries' positions. He argues persuasively, just to give an example, that identity theorists must predefine the mental in autonomous terms if they truly intend (as they claim they do) to establish an *empirical and contingent* identity between mind and body. But we must be careful, warns Malcolm, since you can't have your cake and eat it, too. Either you define the mental in a way which is completely different from that of the bodily – and in this case it is not clear how we are to search for an *identity* between the two terms – or you give it a more or less markedly *physical* description, as though it were in some way *existent* and *given* in the brain – or even in the cranium. But in this case, Malcolm objects, we have already given a preinterpretation of the mental which tacitly (and incorrectly) attributes to it qualities that are *yet to be demonstrated*. Indeed, the foremost of these qualities is precisely that of *existence:* existing in a physical *way* and *place* (Malcolm 1971, pp. 66-8).

But the point that may be of even greater interest to us (perhaps not so much *in itself* as for some of its implications) is Malcolm's radical polemic against the reification of the mental. He stresses that the mental is in no sense a *thing,* and that the mental event is no *quid* to be grasped as it were *ab externo.* It is entirely absurd, for example, to suppose that *acts* like choices and decisions are clearly de-fined *facts* situated in a *space* called the 'mind' (or much less the 'brain'). "We cannot", insists Malcolm almost quoting Wittgenstein, "put our finger on *anything* occurring at the moment of understanding, which *is* the understanding. *The understanding itself is not anything we can single out or fix our attention on*" (ibid., p. 33). This is all the more true since – contrary to what the identity theorists claim – choices and decisions in no way constitute homogeneous classes of 'facts' with a common *essence* and common *norms.* Actually, in the phenomenological, experienced reality of the subject, every choice and every decision, which may appear to be 'general', constitutes a *single* and *particular* psychic event with its own peculiar genesis and meaning. And what about the *way* we examine these psychic events: what does the subject *really* do if and when he attempts to 'study' his own decision? Surely he cannot stand 'in front of' it and examine it as he would a *thing.* We should say, rather, that he assumes an *attitude,* which is, in fact, a *new mental act.* In other words, we are dealing with one 'part' (to use a questionable metaphor) of the mental – or is it of the *person?* – that contemplates another (ibid., p. 44).

Given these premises, it is quite superfluous to add that Malcolm forcefully rejects any attempt *to physicalize* the mental or, even worse, *to identify* the mental and the bodily. The flaw in certain conceptions, explains Malcolm, is that man conceives and models the mental in the image of the physical. Indeed, we must never tire of repeating that the 'things' we call mental have a dimension – or, better, perform a function – which is completely different from bodily determinations. "You could not', writes Malcolm, "explain to someone the concepts of decision, doubt, pain, or anger by referring him to cerebral processes" (ibid., p. 75). We can admit every conceivable *concomitance* and *correlation,* but the fact will *always* remain that decisions and doubts, pains and angers involve also and most importantly an order of *contexts, rules,* and *meanings* that clearly cannot be explained in neurophysiological terms.

MALCOLM: THE 'SUI GENERIS' FEATURES OF THE MENTAL ACT

Malcolm had already dealt quite effectively with the question of the features of the mental in the essay 'Scientific Materialism and the Identity Theory'. Is it possible to identity a mental act *an sich*? Is it possible, for example, to isolate and grasp a thought 'in itself' – as would be necessary if we wanted to identify it with a particular brain process? (Malcolm 1965, in Borst 1970b, p. 175). Malcolm answers with a firm 'no': a mental act is never – and could never be – a 'free', 'ab-solute' act. In a certain sense, this thesis might have pleased the materialists, persuaded as they were of the need to ground such acts on 'some-*thing*' physical (or even to identify them with that 'thing'). But Malcolm's perspective is completely different. For him mental acts are not 'ab-solute' only in the sense that they are always accompanied by, or included in, certain "practices", certain "rules", and certain "agreements" (ibid., p. 176). Certainly, the existence of these practices, rules, and consensuses implies not only that the interpretation of any mental act is, in fact, an *interpretation* – in the sense that it requires a hermeneutic understanding of what 'surrounds' the mental act under 'im-mediate' consideration. It also implies that the "brain conditions" of mental acts perform a function that is quite different from that claimed by the identity theorists. Predictably enough, this perspective leads Malcolm to state his opposition to physicalism with the utmost clarity: "There could not be an explanation of the occurrence of my thought . . . which was stated solely in terms of the entities and laws of physics" (ibid., p. 177).

Malcolm's (typically Wittgensteinian) sensitivity to categorial differences and to the different uses of the various human languages allows him to criticize the identity theory along more subtle and radical lines than those followed by the functionalists and the 'reformers'. The identity theory holds that the mental state (a thought, e.g.) is in the brain – or actually *is* (a part of) the brain. But how is it possible not to notice that this statement is logically (and semantically) incoherent? A little reflection will show that one of its implications – particularly evident in Smart – would appear to be that if a thought *is in* the brain, then the brain *has* (directly and concretely) a thought. Yet this connection and identification between *being* and *having* is groundless. It would be like saying, writes Malcolm, "that if my invitation to dinner is in my pocket, then my pocket has an invitation to dinner" (ibid., p. 180). This is not simply a more or less brilliant specimen of British humor: indeed, Malcolm touches here upon an issue of crucial importance. The point is that the *correlation*, or even (to use a risky metaphor) the *presence* of a thought in some particular *place* in no way implies a *belonging*, and much less an *identification* between that thought and the 'place'. It can at best imply a relationship between concomitants, functions, or vectors, in the sense that the thought is 'supported' by a certain physical structure – though it 'consists', from a phenomenological and cognitive standpoint, of many other components.

But let us return to Malcolm's text, and to the question with which we began. Can the *brain* 'have' a *thought* (or low spirits, or illusions)? The answer is again no, absolutely not. And the argument Malcolm presents in defense of this answer is, it must be admitted, quite suggestive. If the brain cannot have a thought, the "fundamental reason" is that "a brain does not sufficiently resemble a human being" (ibid., p. 180). The observation may appear to be paradoxical; actually, it is of capital importance. At last Malcolm extends the issue of the so-called 'mental' to include the role and figure of man as such. The *entity* that thinks is not a *thing* like the *brain*: it is a *human being*. *Only* the human being is that particular type of entity that has the prerogative to create those singular, unrepeatable figures we call human thoughts, and in ways that are equally singular and unrepeatable as they involve a *mélange* of cognitions and feelings, memories and projects, rules and exceptions, symbols and analogies, clarities and obscurities.

> *People* see, hear, think – not brains. A person can *look* attentive, surprised, or frightened (and so can a dog); but a brain cannot. Not only cannot a brain *display* interest or anger, but it could not have *objects of interest* or *occasions for anger*. It could not engage in any of the activities that are required for the application of those concepts. A brain does not have the right physiognomy nor the capacity for participating in any of the forms of life that would be required for it to be a subject of experience. (ibid., p. 77)

Anti-realism, anti-physicalism, anti-identityism, but, most importantly, a 'linguisticization' of the mental, a systematic analysis of this mental language, and the discovery that this language responds to precise *interests* of the subject – interests that are certainly not 'inferior', neither in quantity nor in quality, to interests of a *lato sensu* physical nature. These – along with the crucial reappraisal of the role of the subject (to which we shall return) and the claim that the subject cannot be reduced to the brain – are the essential points of the Wittgensteinian heritage which are taken up and developed in Norman Malcolm's stimulating, suggestive reflection.

RORTY: PSYCHOLOGY AS ''VOCABULARY'' AND THE NEED FOR 'MANY DESCRIPTIONS' OF MAN

We can hardly conclude this chapter without at least brief mention of Richard Rorty. Rorty is in fact rather close to the theses and positions of Wittgenstein and Ryle, which he picks up and develops from the standpoint of what he calls the 'linguistic turn' in the contemporary philosophy of mind (Rorty 1975). This might seem somewhat surprising if we recall his fierce 'eliminationist' battle against the mental and its science. But in this regard we should point out that Rorty's theory of the desirable ''disappearance'' of psychology was connected not so much with the existence of a *pre-dominant* bodily *reality* as with the thesis that it will ultimately be possible and necessary for the conceptual and expressive system of the physical to eliminate the by-now antiquated conceptual and expressive system of psychology. Indeed, in his essay entitled 'In Defense of Eliminative Materialism' Rorty explicitly criticized the myth of the 'given', and on other occasions he outlined an essentially 'linguistic' interpretation of the psychophysical relationship (Rorty 1965 and 1970). The limit of those papers (as we have argued) lay in their strong scientistic and physicalistic bent, which ultimately led to an unappealable condemnation of psychology.

In more recent years Rorty has developed his thought not only in a more markedly 'linguistic' direction but also with a more mature recognition of the plurality of languages – and of their pragmatic ''utility''. This orientation is clear both in the well-known volume *Philosophy and the Mirror of Nature* (1979; henceforth PMN) and in a couple of subsequent papers on the philosophy of mind (Rorty 1982a and 1982b). From the point of view of our present concerns what is most striking in these writings is Rorty's radical attack on philosophical realism. Explicitly declaring himself ''Wittgensteinian'', Rorty asserts in the most unambiguous terms that reality, in a certain sense, is ''discourse'' (PMN, p. 34): it is ''only a matter of seeing how various linguistic items fit together with other linguistic items" (1982b, p. 344). In the second place, the lesson of Wittgenstein leads him to assume a position that is also decidedly critical of any form of universalism or essentialism. General structures, 'deep' natures, forms in any sense transcendent or transcendental do *not* exist. Knowledge is made up exclusively of empirical acts, of particular acquisitions, and of the institution of *convenient* "inferential relationships" between propositions that use certain terms (ibid., p. 340).

Given these assumptions, it will hardly be surprising to find Rorty stressing that he is a "nominalist", an "epistemological behaviorist", and a "pragmatist" (PMN, pp. 174, 176, 320). The most interesting of these self-definitions may be that of pragmatism (see in this connection Rorty 1982c). Among contemporary American philosophers Rorty is one who has devoted considerable attention to the suggestive link between the 'linguistic turn' and the pragmatic perspective. If reality, and even more so our relationship with reality, is language, and if we lack the criteria to describe either the first or the second in an *objectively* verifiable way, then the *subject* will express himself according to certain *conventions* and his own *interests*. In and of itself, writes Rorty, the world "has no preferred way of being represented" (PMN, p. 300). It is men who must, in an autonomous and goal-oriented manner, construct these representations. If *nature*, Rorty continues, offers no suggestions, then the representations and definitions will appear as *"cultural* artefacts"": artefacts that must be judged "on the basis by their utility in accomplishing our aims" (1982b, p. 336).

Of course Rorty does not conceal the manifold implications that this thesis bears for the philosophy of mind. Every realist conception not only of the mind but also of the body is firmly rejected. The mental and the bodily are to be considered simply "labels". As for mental states, it is not that they do not exist, as the behaviorists claim: they are those states "whose descriptions occur in a *given* vocabulary used by psychologists" (1982b, p. 336). And asking ourselves if this is the *"right* vocabulary" is as pointless as asking whether such states are *really* mental or actually physical states in disguise (ibid.). Both neurophysiology and psychology are a certain language, a certain vocabulary: "and any vocabulary to describe anything is only one vocabulary among others, useful for certain purposes, useless for others" (PMN, p. 185). Consequently, all hegemonic and/or eliminationist claims must be rejected. Furthermore, writes Rorty in open conflict with certain utopian conceptions *à la* Feigl, it is simply false that a "completed neurophysiology" will help us to understand 'everything' about a man – why, for example, Galileo was superior to his contemporaries (PMN, p. 249).

Moreover, we find that Rorty's development of the pragmatist perspective brings him – Rorty, the former champion of the disappearance theory – to defend self-critically the rights and the "utility" of the specific language of psychology (PMN, pp. 118–19). Contrary to widely held opinion, psychology has its own "legitimacy", its own *raison d'être*. Even its most debatable instruments can, in certain contexts, prove to be concretely valid. In this connection, Rorty has no qualms about presenting the example of introspection (PMN, p. 219): this shows that, despite his sympathy for Ryle and for behaviorism, there are certain positions of a whole philosophical and psychological current which he does not embrace. If the discourse and procedures of psychology give expression to important aspects of man, it would be quite senseless to ban them – *a priori*, no less – from human conversation. In the final analysis, the languages of the mental and the physical simply reflect two possibilities, a choice between two analytical and expressive means of studying man – and this choice is simply a question of "convenience" (Rorty 1982a, p. 185; and 1982b, pp. 336–7).

The claim is at once sound and stimulating, but it would have been even more so if Rorty had recognized without reservation that psychology has a legitimate right to enter the citadel of knowledge. That is, if he had clearly acknowledged the *scientific* capacity of psychological inquiry: a position perhaps supported by a conception of Science as consisting of several diversified sciences. But this recognition is not granted – or at least not in a satisfactory way. Instead, Rorty argues that psychology offers precious data to man's self-image, to the awareness of the subject as such, and yet he tends to interpret these data as not belonging to a properly *cognitive* sphere. What psychology provides are essentially "descriptions", whereas only science provides "knowledge" – and, Rorty stresses, "the difference between 'description' and 'knowledge' is the essence of the matter". This is also confirmed by the fact that truly *scientific* knowledge is *materialistic:* indeed, "what other kind of science is there?" (Rorty 1982b, p. 345).

This position cannot pass unnoticed. In assuming it, Rorty distances himself considerably from an authentically Wittgensteinian matrix and reveals his ties to a 'scientific' tradition (now neo-materialistic, now neo-physicalistic): a tradition which in part persists, as we have seen, even in such sophisticated scholars as Fodor and Davidson. It is evident that Rorty's interpretation of psychology does not permit an adequate rehabilitation of the discipline from an epistemological point of view. And yet his reappraisal of psychological language is profoundly and convincingly positive. The *difference* between 'knowledge' and 'description' does not imply, at least for Rorty, that the latter is *subaltern* to the former. On the contrary, in Rorty's view so-called mental descriptions perform an essential and absolutely irreplaceable function within what might be called the practical (existential, decisional, ethical) sphere of human life. And this is a sphere to which man feels the need to pay considerable attention, not only on the emotional plane but also on that of reason and analysis. Correspondingly, Rorty sees in the language traditionally defined as psychological the instrument capable of answering this need. What *"further* descriptions" of man do we as human beings need? asks Rorty in his essay on the MBP, alluding to those already supplied by science. His answer seems inspired not only by pragmatic concerns but also by a 'humanistic' purpose: "we need *many different* descriptions of ourselves – some for some purposes and others for others, some for predicting and controlling ourselves and others for deciding what to do, what meaning our lives shall have" (ibid., 345).

But why is it, more exactly, that one might prefer to use the language of psychology? What do people *really* want to say when they use mental language? These are questions, as we shall see in due time, to which Rorty has provided some extremely important answers.

Chapter 8

Speaking in many different ways

The pluralization of descriptions and explanations in the MBP

THE PLURALITY OF DESCRIPTIONS AND
EXPLANATIONS IN THE ANALYSIS
OF THE MENTAL

The 'linguistic turn' produced many significant consequences in the debate on the MBP. One of the most important is the conviction that psychophysical phenomena can, and must, be given *different* descriptions and explanations. Ryle had argued explicitly for the rejection of notion of knowledge founded on a single type of explanatory procedure. As regards human phenomena, we read in *The Concept of Mind, two* equally legitimate kinds of question may arise: those concerning "rules" and those concerning "choices". When we observe a chess match, for example, we may ask ourselves why a particular bishop always ends up on a square of the same color, or why a player has moved his bishop in a particular way (Ryle 1949, p. 75). In the first case the question concerns the norms that objectively govern a certain system; in the second, the behavioral acts subjectively and decisionally performed by certain agents. Ryle also distinguishes two fundamental classes of explanatory models: those relative to "causes" and those relative to "reasons". Explanations by causes tend to identify the natural, general presuppositions underlying certain actions (as well as, obviously, the causes of phenomena that are not actions); explanations by reasons tend to identify the teleological, particular motives (and in certain cases the conscious, cultural motives) of the agents of those actions (ibid., pp. 86, 109, 305). There is no doubt that psychobehavioral events can belong to causal sequences of a physiological nature: but they also give rise to questions and answers that belong

195

to the domain of reasons and ends. "Not all psychological re-searches", Ryle writes in different context, "are searches for causal explanations" (ibid., p. 308).

In Malcolm's work there is an even clearer connection between the 'linguistic turn' and the pluralization of descriptive and explanatory schemes. If it is true that everything is in a certain sense language (or, better, languages), then man is called on not so much to describe or explain a *single* reality, as to elaborate a series of expressive, interpre-tive constructs that may serve his different needs and conditions. This implies that there must be *multiple* descriptions and explana-tions. Indeed, just as Malcolm rejects any *a priori* preference for one linguistic model over others, so does he reject a preference for any one particular descriptive, explicative procedure over others. As far as the MBP is concerned, we can certainly accept physicalistic descrip-tions and explanations of certain (psycho)cerebral processes, but we must also accept *non*-physicalistic descriptions and explanations (i.e., psycho-cultural, existential, social) of thought as such:

> In fact, an explanation of the one differs in *kind* from the ex-planation of the other. The explanation of why someone *thought* such and such involves different assumptions and principles and is guided by different interests than is an ex-planation of why this or that process occurred in his brain. These explanations belong to different *systems* of explanation. (Malcolm 1965, p. 179)

The awareness that it is possible/necessary to admit a plurality of descriptions and explanations in the context of the MBP is not always linked to the orientation we have called the 'linguistic turn'. In some cases it arises from different assumptions and objectives. For some philosophers of mind it is necessary (and at the same time sufficient) to stress the fact that *different* descriptions and ex-planations give adequate accounts of *different* properties and fea-tures, which take on specific meaning in relation to specific criteria and contexts. The error of many identity theorists is that they be-lieve that two descriptions of a mental state and a physical state respectively can be identified because they denote the same *desig-natum*. Actually, even if we were to admit that the *designatum* is indeed the same, it does not follow that the relative descriptive, explanatory statements can be considered identifiable. This objec-tion to the identity theory has been raised by D. M. Rosenthal, among others. In the collection of readings he edited on the MBP

Rosenthal juxtaposes the two descriptions 'Alaska is the largest state in the United States' and 'Alaska is the coldest state in the United States'. It is clear that we have here two equally legitimate and valid statements, each constructed in relation to a different semantic paradigm. It is also clear that these two statements, while referring to the same 'entity', are not reducible one to the other and require different explanatory procedures (Rosenthal 1971, pp. 3–4). The same is true for psychophysical reality. Pain, for example, can be described and explained both on a physiological plane, using physiological language, and on a mental plane, using mental language: and it can hardly be said that the two descriptions/explanations will cover each other completely, or that the latter can be reduced to the former (ibid.). From a different point of view, though comparable to Rosenthal's, Jaegwon Kim once stressed that events can be described "intrinsically" or "extrinsically". 'Intrinsically' Caesar was *stabbed;* 'extrinsically' he was *killed* (Kim 1976, pp. 166–7). For our purposes this example could be rendered even clearer by comparing the two descriptions of death 'X has died' and 'X has been murdered'. In this case, too, we have *two* descriptions of the *same event* that are equally legitimate and equally loaded with cognitive content; and these descriptions rest on explanations of a rather different nature. The point, once again, holds in the psychophysical sphere as well. If I describe a phenomenon on the one hand as 'an emotion' and on the other as 'a discharge of adrenaline', I produce two different linguistic-descriptive-cognitive statements, each of which probably offers a certain information that the other does not. Hence the advantage of preserving the autonomy of each.

'COMPLEMENTARY' AND 'DIFFERENT' KINDS OF KNOWLEDGE

Taking up and developing positions analogous to those just sketched, some scholars have used the expression (which also appears in Feigl) "twofold knowledge". But whereas Feigl (who eventually abandoned the term) was strongly attracted by the ideal of an ultimate unification of cognitive acts, these scholars are intent on preserving the *two* kinds of knowledge. This is the case, in particular, of Wilfrid Sellars, for whom the analysis of the psychophysical world has *two* different linguistic-conceptual-explicative apparatuses that are in some way not *antithetical* but *complementary* (Sellars 1971, pp. 269–89). In this connection, another position which, though in part different, deserves attention is that of Grover Maxwell. In an important essay on the MBP, which we have already referred to, Maxwell makes the point that *two* different descriptive-interpretive approaches to a *single* phenomenon may produce two characterizations of the same phenomenon which are *different* (and require different kinds of explanation), and yet not *antithetical;* they are, so to speak, *compatible.* An event, exemplifies Maxwell echoing Russell, can be *both* mental *and* physical, just as a man can be *both* 'a rational man' *and* 'a barber' (Maxwell 1978, p. 381; see also the debate in Maxwell 1976a).

What we have just described is not the only proposal concerning our problem, nor the most radical. There is another group of scholars that aims at something more than the mere recognition of the existence of two complementary types of description and explanation. Joseph Margolis, for example, in his important work *Persons and Minds,* to which we shall have occasion to return, insists that it is not only legitimate but also necessary to elaborate descriptions and explanations which are not merely *complementary,* but substantially *different.* Indeed, for Margolis, we cannot say the same things – or similar or homogeneous things – about brain states and mental states (Margolis 1978, pp. 34 and 35). On the contrary, the very way in which man constructs his descriptive and explanatory statements about psychic phenomena demonstrates that they cannot be unified in a single class with statements of a physicalistic nature. "No one", Margolis stresses in this connection, "has yet succeeded in reducing discourse about persons and sentient creatures to non-intentional discourse about the physical events and states of such systems" (ibid., p. 186). To admit this implies that "the methodology appropriate to physics and its allied sciences are inadequate for the explanation of the phenomena in question" – more precisely for the explanation of certain aspects of the human world (ibid., p. 225).

Positions in certain respects similar have been advanced, from a more 'linguistic' perspective, by Donald Davidson. Though he often seems tempted (as we have already suggested) by the seductive capacities of neo-physicalism, Davidson is quite explicit in admitting two types of description and explanation in the analysis of mind. For the 'categorialist' Davidson these two types derive from two different conceptual "schemes", that is, the mental and the physical (Davidson 1980, p. 222). These schemes, Davidson points

out significantly, have different uses and imply "disparate commitments" (ibid.). The two types of interest to which they respond
are *equally legitimate,* and even *necessary.* Thus, in particular, the
'physical' scheme selects and interprets a certain series of data in
relation to certain principles (physical, biological, neurophysiological) – and is quite right in doing so from a certain theoretical and
cognitive perspective. The *"mental" scheme,* on the other hand, has
entirely different frames of reference: psychological, subjective, and
private – and perhaps anthropological, sociological, cultural, and
political. When we use *this* scheme we want to place a certain state
in a context which prioritizes not its supposed physical correlates,
but rather its 'provenance' and its psychological and subjective content. In this case, in fact, "the attribution of mental phenomena
must be responsible to the background of reasons, beliefs, and intentions of the individual" (ibid.). This is especially true for intentional states, which "operate in a conceptual framework removed
from the direct reach of physical law by describing both cause and
effect, reason and action, as aspects of a portrait of a human agent"
(ibid., p. 225).

WEIMER: PSYCHOLOGICAL ANALYSIS AS THE COMPREHENSION OF SENSE

The third stage in our brief review of the debate on description and
explanation in the context of the MBP concerns a further development of the principle of the 'diversity' of the descriptive and explicative procedures connected to the mental. One of the most
significant representatives of this stage is Walter B. Weimer, a brilliant student of the epistemological problems of reduction with particular reference to the philosophy of mind (Weimer 1976, pp. 5–
30). Weimer, like Davidson and Margolis, is not satisfied with the
'weak' hypothesis that the descriptions and explanations of psychophysical phenomena are to be considered merely distinct and/
or complementary. On the contrary, he tends to radicalize the
difference between the analytical and interpretive models of the
mental and the physical. It would be superfluous to point out that
he has no intention of dusting off and re-presenting a metaphysical,
spiritualistic conception of knowledge. He is merely concerned to
clear up the serious and misleading ambiguities that have accompanied attempts to achieve a cognitive understanding of the mind–

body relationship. For Weimer, this approach to the problem is, and must remain, *twofold:* on the one hand there is what is called 'knowledge by description'; on the other, what is called 'knowledge by acquaintance' (ibid., pp. 1 and 8–9). It is true that neurophysiology has claimed (or claims) that it can explain in physicalistic terms both sentience and sapience – and even selfhood. But, Weimer stresses (referring to certain 'futurological' positions advanced by Feigl and the Australians), not even a "utopian physical science" that knows *everything* about the physical world will ever be able to say whether certain physical properties and events are the same as what subjects experience mentally. "Physicalistic doctrines fail", insists Weimer, "because they attempt to *translate* the mental into the physical, rather than admit both phases as distinct" (ibid., p. 23).

Why do they fail? It is in answer to this question that Weimer lays out one of his most interesting and original theses. Physicalistic doctrines are destined to fail because they seek (by description) something *different* from what is sought by acquaintance. Even if they were capable of grasping the physical *referents* of knowledge by acquaintance, still they would never grasp the *true objective* of this knowledge. The term Weimer uses to define this objective is somewhat foreign to the culture of many students of the MBP: "sense" (ibid., p. 9). What the subject's acquaintance (or the subject himself) looks for in a psychophysical event is the *Sinn* of the event itself. To look for the sense means to (try to) understand what a certain pain or a certain belief represents *for me*, for *my* experience, that is, what such events represent within a certain psychoexistential and sociocultural background and context.

At this point, clearly, analyses by description, though extremely useful from *another* cognitive perspective, have no role to play. They are superfluous because the principal goals of the investigation are no longer the 'data', in their (more or less reliable) objectivity and immediacy. Instead, they are the *ways* in which man experiences those data. And these ways lead us precisely to the individual, to man, to the 'titular' of the experiences and knowledge (ibid., p. 9).

Though not always convincing on other questions, Weimer is quite unambiguous and persuasive in his discussion of the problems that concern us here. The descriptions and explanations connected with knowledge by description proceed according to criteria and with objectives that are different from those of the descriptions and explanations connected with acquaintance. Furthermore, the criteria and objectives of acquaintance are in no sense 'non-cognitive' (as was argued, if in various ways, by Feigl, the Australians, and many neo-physicalists), nor are they cognitively 'inferior' to the criteria and objectives of description. Indeed, they are an expression of *subjectivity:* an absolutely central figure in the philosophy of mind which, for more than one reason, it is time to rehabilitate (and to which we shall return). Weimer's conclusion, then, is that we must admit what he calls the necessary "compossibility" of two radically different kinds of knowledge and explanation.

THE CRITERION OF RELEVANCE IN THE DESCRIPTIONS AND EXPLANATIONS OF PSYCHOLOGY

Few have spoken with greater efficacy of the dangers inherent in reducing and unifying different interpretations and explanations of the human world than Thomas Nagel. It may be, writes Nagel in his well-known essay on physicalism, that anything that can be explained in terms of water and its attributes can be explained in terms of molecules and their attributes. But it is very likely that "the two systems of explanation were so different in structure that it would be impossible to find a single attribute of the molecules which explained all and only those things explained by a particular attribute of the water" (Nagel 1965, in Rosenthal 1971, p. 105). This is (on closer examination) essentially the same point that the functionalists make, in a more strictly psychophysical context. Not every explanation, Putnam has written, must involve that sort of 'descent to the elementary' – that is, to the micromolecular components of phenomena – that the reductionists aim for. On the contrary, some particular kind of explanation "might have the property that the ultimate constituents don't matter, that only the higher level structure matters" (Putnam 1973, in Block 1980–1, p. 137).

'What matters': in other words, the criterion of *relevance.* The conviction is gradually spreading among the more updated philosophers of mind that *relevance* is the one category in a position to suggest, given a non-unitary cognitive perspective, which approach to explanation and description to choose, the physical or the mental, in relation to a given referent and context. A significant voice in this connection is that of Charles Taylor, one of the most important students of action theory (Taylor 1964), but at the same time (and the fact is worth pointing out) a careful analyst of the MBP. For Taylor the mental act and social behavior admit two different descriptions/explanations. Occasionally they may appear to be quite similar: but even in those cases they never 'say' the same thing, nor do they correspond exactly (Taylor 1967, p. 206). Taylor gives the example of a highway. I can talk about a highway as having a gradient x, a slipperiness y, a visibility z, and so forth; or I can say that it is 'dangerous'. Despite appearances, the two descriptions are not only different but also irreducible one to the other, since they have different meanings, resonances, and uses. Which is to be preferred? It is difficult to answer in the abstract. As Taylor writes, "It cannot be determined a priori which [explicative] level will yield explanations of the phenomena which will enable us to predict and control them, or which level will yield the most fruitful explanations" (ibid., p. 208). Once again it is the subject that must *decide*. It is the subject that must assess the relative fruitfulness of *this* or that model of description/explanation in relation to his own objectives and contexts (ibid., pp. 209 and 212). Only this criterion can determine the choice to be made. Clearly, all this is valid in the psychophysical sphere as well. There are cases in which certain phenomena can be better described and explained by physiological models; in other cases mental-based models will be more valid. An elementary feeling of pain can be efficaciously explained in physiological terms. In contrast, the analysis of a complex sensation like the suspicion of communists (the example is Taylor's) may bear more fruit if carried out with psychosociocultural instruments. From another point of view it should be added that explanations are connected not so much to the nature of the 'thing itself' as to what we want to know about a certain phenomenon on any particular occasion. In this sense, explanations are clearly products of pragmatic choices and goals.

PRIBRAM, WILKERSON, AND THE PRINCIPLE OF EXPLICATIVE PLURALISM

Taylor's argument, like the theses advanced by Weimer and Nagel, is quite persuasive. And yet a question arises. Why speak of just *two* descriptions? Why speak of just *two* explanations? Wouldn't it be more correct to say that there are, at least in principle, n possible descriptions and explanations? It is striking that one of the most strenuous defenders of this more genuine pluralism, in the MBP literature, is a scientist: the well-known neuropsychologist Karl Pribram. In a rather interesting essay Pribram approaches the issue from general and far-reaching premises. Reality, he writes, can and must be identified in many different ways. The study of a manuscript, for example, can concentrate on its physical composition, its cultural significance, or its historical importance. In some cases "some organizations of psychological states and processes are more readily understood by recourse to their environmental organizers than by delving into the responsible brain organization per se" (Pribram 1976, p. 100). In other cases, certain psychic acts and events require differentiated and specific heuristic strategies: some require prevalently physiological approaches, while others call for a prevalently psycho-cultural 'reading'. "There are those", concludes Pribram, "who label the [physical] organizations themselves as constituting mind. There are others who infer from the behavior of minding, as I have done here. And there are yet others who reserve for the mental, the subjectively experienced" (ibid., p. 110).

It was a philosopher, however, who dealt most efficaciously with the issue of the plurality of explanations within the sphere of the MBP. This philosopher is Wilkerson. The first point Wilkerson makes, in the context of what concerns us here, regards the nature itself of explanation and its relationship with reduction. For far too long physicalism and the identity theory have essentially considered coincident the *explicative act* and the *reductive act*: I can explain pain if and only if I reduce it to a certain brain event. For Wilkerson this approach to the problem is completely put off course, or at least extremely unilateral. Not always does explanation imply or lead to reduction. If someone runs into my car and I hurl insults at the driver responsible, there is no question that my anger can be explained (at least in large part) by the collision: but it does not follow that my anger is *reducible* to, or much less *identifiable* with, the collision. In contrast to the explanation/reduction 'match' Wilkerson advances what he calls the "theory of inductive generalization": what can be said about the relationship between the mental and the physical is only that "properties of the type B are regularly found to be associated with events of the type A" (Wilkerson 1974, pp. 99–100).

Wilkerson's second point addresses the problem at hand even more directly. It might be called the principle of *explicative pluralism.*

Any claim to give *the* explanation to a phenomenon, he says, belongs to an out-dated epistemology, often tied to a realistic ontology. Wilkerson proposes that realism with its assumption of 'truth-in-the-singular' be supplanted by a philosophy founded on the 'primacy' of cognitive *categories* over *things*, on the anchoring of these categories to *interests* and *goals*, and on the consequent multiplicity of cognitive practices. The truth is that the theoretical and practical needs of existence induce us to employ plural and diversified forms, functions, and languages. Presumably, "we employ different conceptual frameworks, different 'images', for different purposes" (ibid., p. 112).

Obviously, all this has decisive implications for the MBP debate. According to Wilkerson, the fifty-year-long battle between physicalists and anti-physicalists rested on a fundamental misunderstanding (caused mostly by the physicalists). This misunderstanding lies in the assumption that the two parties were speaking – and indeed could not help but speak – about the same subject. Actually, they were speaking about *different* things, or, better, they were constructing *different* linguistic-semantic universes. It should be added immediately (and Wilkerson makes this point) that, contrary to the theses of the physicalists, each of these two, or *n*, universes had (has) full *cognitive* legitimacy. Wilkerson goes on to stress that the two, or *n*, ways of speaking about certain phenomena are perfectly compatible *logically*. In *practical* terms, Wilkerson's position appears to be rather more rigid. He sees the two fundamental interpretations of the human sphere – the mental and the physical – as in competition, in conflict with one another. Both, we must repeat, are legitimate. But we must *choose*. It is something like cutting a pie. I can cut it in various different ways, but these ways (or at least some of them) are mutually incompatible: I can cut the pie *either* this way *or* that way (ibid., pp. 117–18). The same is true for the so-called psychophysical phenomena: I can interpret them in way *a*, or in way *b*, in way *c*, and so on. What I cannot do is interpret them in different ways *contemporaneously*.

Of course, this thesis does not invalidate the principle of explicative pluralism. At most, it will impose operational limits on its application, since we will have to take into account what epistemologists would call the mutual *incommensurability* of certain approaches or categories. Wilkerson's final word on the matter, in any case, supports a radically anti-reductionist and pluralistic orientation. Moreover, he expresses the conviction that at the present point in the theoretical debate one must defend above all the descriptive-explicative models of the *lato sensu* mentalistic type. Today, in fact, too much credit is given to the thesis that the *only* reliable knowledge is physicalistic, and that a *complete* knowledge of the mental and of man will be gained by gradually *adding* new data supplied by physicalistic inquiry. For Wilkerson this belief is entirely unfounded. Even admitting (though certainly not conceding) that a 'complete' knowledge of the human sphere is attainable, there is no guarantee that a *single* interpretive system (the physical system) will be sufficient to satisfy all of man's cognitive questions concerning the human universe. In many cases it will be necessary to draw on *new, different* systems: first and foremost in the case of the analysis of the mental and behavioral spheres. It would be a fatal error to presume that the heuristic toolbox of the neurosciences will be capable of explaining every aspect and meaning of human feeling, thinking, and acting. To understand some of these aspects and meanings it is necessary not to *increase the quantity of a certain kind of information* but to *transform certain analytical models*: in Wilkerson's words, "describing a set of physical events as an action, however, is to characterize them in terms of categories which are logically quite distinct from the categories of physicalism" (ibid., p. 172).

Chapter 9

The mind as a mode of
subjective experience

An interpretive model of the features of the mental

CHARACTERIZING THE MENTAL: SOME CRITIQUES OF THE MIND AND ITS TRADITIONAL ARTICULATION

"There is", a keen student of intentionality has remarked, "a growing body of opinion to the effect that mentalistic notions like *thinking, believing* and *desiring* belong to a primitive folk-theory which is either incoherent or false, or in some other way *flawed*" (Woodfield 1982, p. x). The scope of this observation should be extended. The movement of opinion Woodfield refers to actually includes not only *some* concepts belonging to the sphere of the mental, but the *whole* of the mental as such. Indeed the dimension of the 'mind', assailed from all sides by a certain brand of neo-physicalism, by recent versions of biologism (such as the sociobiology of E. O. Wilson), and by computer science and artificial intelligence, risks an eclipse similar to that which occurred during the heyday of behaviorism.

It must not be supposed, however, that all contemporary philosophers of mind have passively accepted this situation. On the contrary, many have shown that they have no intention of considering the game over so soon. Well aware that certain conceptions of the mind cannot be salvaged, some scholars have expressed the need for new interpretive models to represent the mental dimension. What are, Kim once asked, the "criteria" of the mental (Kim 1971)? What are, came the echo from another theoretical shore, the "marks" of the mental-subjective-conscious universe (Rorty 1970b)? The mind, Herbst had stressed even earlier, must not be *replaced* (and much less *eliminated*): it is to be "characterized" anew (Herbst 1967).

This last term (and the research program that may be correlated with it) is of capital importance. *Characterize* refers to something quite different from the more demanding *define*. It can mean searching – perhaps within an *episteme* that is not absolute, but relative and plural – for those traits that connote a referent in relation to a certain context and in connection with certain cognitive interests of the observer. When, from this perspective, Herbst advanced what he appropriately called a new "constructive theory of the mind", this is exactly what he was after (ibid., p. 64).

At the source of this need to 'characterize' the mental *ex novo*, there also arises a problem of terminology – which is very likely not only one of terminology. Some philosophers of mind have questioned the pertinence, or soundness, of the term/concept 'mind'. They might possibly accept, with reference to the formula 'MBP', the correlated notion 'body' – though 'body' is all too often interpreted as 'brain' (which is clearly something quite different). But 'mind'? And 'mental'? It has been pointed out that these terms seem to give precedence to specifically *intellectual* phenomena, whereas the figure of the mind, in the context of the issues that concern us, often alludes to a much vaster psychological (and psychoanthropological) dimension. Feigl himself was fully aware of this when he divided the 'mental' into sentience, sapience, and selfhood. We also know that many identity theorists have not taken this three-part division sufficiently into account, either neglecting selfhood or giving undue preference to sentience. The reason for this tendency is rather evident. For those who wanted to derive 'everything' from the corporeal, the dimension of sensations (in the broad sense) was obviously more susceptible than the others to being reexpressed in bodily or, more precisely, neurophysiological terms. For various reasons it is far more difficult to physicalize sapience. Even more arduous is the question of physicalizing selfhood.

Now, it is worth observing that scholars of rather diverse theoretical orientations have returned, by different paths, to the problem of giving a more comprehensive and articulate definition to the mental. In particular, Marjorie Grene has rejected in the firmest terms the priority position granted to sentience. This privilege derives from what Grene calls "the obsession with sensation" (Grene 1976, p. 117). This obsession is the offspring of the myth, typical of the (neo)positivistic tradition, of scientific exactitude and of the objective given. From one narrowly circumscribed philosophical perspective (which Grene considers completely misdirected), sensations are the most elementary and basic, the most real and indisputable *facts;* facts that appear to be susceptible to the most reliable and rigorous understanding. This explains the excessive significance attributed to sentience by many participants in the debate on the mental, at the expense of other equally important dimensions of the psychological universe.

Keith Gunderson has lucidly questioned the somewhat 'intellectualistic' message of the treatment reserved for the term 'mental'. In Gunderson's view, the so-called mental can in no way be reduced to exclusively cognitive functions – that is, to sapience alone – since it includes a series of *other* components, *other* functions of a very different nature (Gunderson 1971, p. 146). A specialist in the mind–machine problem (Gunderson 1964a, 1969, and 1971), Gunderson also devotes several pages of his most important essay to a critique of the attempt (made by many students of the mental) to identify sapience with mere problem solving. (He argues that the 'intelligent' function of man is far from reducible to the technical arrangement of data and questions – much less to something that can be physicalized and formalized in computable terms.) In a similar vein Roger Squires has also rejected a unilaterally 'intellectual' definition of the mental, proposing in its place a characterization of the mental that includes, alongside abstract thought, responsible behavior and the emotions as well (Squires 1970). Margolis, for his part, takes a promising step further: on the one hand he insists on the need to distinguish thematically and problematically sentience and sapience (which probably require different interpretive categories), and on the other – and most importantly – he stresses that greater attention must be paid to selfhood: that is, that an appropriate analysis must be devoted to individual and subjective awareness as a certain *way of being* of the human sphere (Margolis 1973b, p. 249).

All this does not mean that those scholars who openly oppose the identity theory and reductionism tend to neglect the dimension of sentience (thereby, in a sense, mirroring their adversaries). It only means that they are becoming increasingly aware that the mental must be interpreted as a broad, complex, unavoidably *sui generis* figure. And they are realizing that it is not possible, nor productive, to subdivide it into two or three rigid, in some sense 'factual', partitions – an operation which betrays the more or less conscious ambition to *reify* the mind. The reason for this is that the mental very likely is (or expresses) something more than, and different from, a *sum* of 'given', 'objective' components or performances. In this connection a thesis that has begun to emerge from various quarters is that the 'mental' alludes mainly to the subjective and conscious, individual and private, sociocultural and historical memorial dimension – or *quality* – of man's sensory, intellective, emotional, and existential experiences. It is a conception of this sort that seems to be the goal, though pursued in different ways, of scholars such as Wilkerson and Nagel, Malcolm and Margolis, Dreyfus and Grene. We shall deal with their positions toward the end of this essay. What concerns us here is to examine briefly in what way an autonomous characterization of the mental has begun to take shape – that is, a characterization immune to a reduction of the mental itself to a *lato sensu* physical referent. In other words, what are the principal features of the so-called mental which, from a certain cognitive (*not* ontological) perspective, some scholars have determined as specific and irreducible?

A 'FIGURE' WITHOUT PHYSICAL QUALITIES/FEATURES

A preliminary point to make concerns the admissibility, on a general plane, of asserting the existence of a possibly non-physical 'figure' like the mental. Actually, this admissibility seems to cause problems only for those who tend to identify 'existence' with '*physical* existence'. But logicians and linguists, scientists and epistemologists (as well as moral philosophers and sociologists) know full well that there may be entities – in the broad sense of the word – that *exist* but *not* in the same way that the 'things' of the natural world exist. Suffice it to mention the existence of rules and conventions, of theories and values, of myths and rites. Of course it may seem somewhat paradoxical, as Andrea Bonomi has observed, to defend the existence of "something that appears to correspond to nothing existent" (Bonomi 1983, p. 207). And yet, he adds, it must be recognized that there exist, aside from phenomenal facts, both "abstract entities" and 'things' "that frankly seem impossible to grasp" – that is, precisely mental events (ibid., p. 191). But certain paradoxes can be resolved if a distinction is made, as Bonomi suggests, between the *empirical factuality* of the objects and the *object* itself characterized by precise theoretical rules which alone constitute the referent (perfectly *existent* in its own way) of philosophical and scientific inquiry (ibid.).

Many philosophers of mind have stressed that it is possible and opportune to distinguish between existence and existence, between reality and reality. Or more precisely, as Margolis has written, we must admit different kinds of the *concrete, phenomenological appearing* of entities and experiences – including those which concern us here (Margolis 1973b, p. 282). "Mental processes are *real*", H. D. Lewis wrote rather emphatically (Lewis 1969, p. 43). But their reality, their existential modality – and this is the crux – is *different* from that of physical phenomena. On the other hand, the fact that they "exist differently" does not at all mean that such processes are less real, or even non-real. "My thoughts at the moment", writes Lewis, "are as real (they go on) as the movements of my hands. My thoughts are not abstractions". Lewis's conclusion, in short, is that mental events are real and existent, though not in a physical sense.

There have been many other scholars who, while not speaking of the mental in physical-materialistic (much less in metaphysical-spiritualistic) terms and not contenting themselves with a purely logical-theoretical analysis, have still underlined the evident *existence* – albeit *sui generis* – of the mental itself. This is the case of Peter Geach, who, in his classic *Mental Acts* (1957), insists on the one hand on the differences between *physical objects* and our *mental experiences* (of the objects themselves or of ourselves), and on the other on the status of existentiality enjoyed – in different terms – not only by the former but also by the latter (Geach 1971, pp. 111 and 126–7).

This insistence on the possible conjunction between *existence* and *non-physicality* was necessary because for many philosophers and psychologists the characterization of the mind (even independently of the *querelle* on the MBP) rests on the primacy of precisely the *non-physicality*, and with it the *non-corporeality* and the *non-spatiality*, of the mental universe. Since we are already familiar with the first two 'non's', we shall take a brief look only at the third. Ryle had already argued that the mind, if it is not a thing, can also not be a *space* or a *place:* in particular, it is not a sort of "repository" used to keep psychic states and 'facts' (Ryle 1949, p. 190). One of the scholars who has done the most to develop this point is Squires.

The mind, he writes, can by no means be thought of as a *spatial* dimension. Much less is it an "arena" (Ryle had spoken of a "private stage": ibid., p. 299), where certain events called psychic meet and clash (Squires 1970, p. 348).

The mind, or better the mental, is rather a *state*, a *way* of being of the subject. Another to insist on the 'non-extension' of the mind is G. G. Globus (Globus, Maxwell, and Savodnik 1976). For him, mental states and processes do not respond to any *topology*. If the question *'where is* the pain?' seems to be legitimate (though a moment's reflection should suffice to see how many ambiguities and how many *ubiquities* it entails), the questions 'where is the intention?' or 'where is the belief?' or 'where is the project?' appear, even intuitively, rather unreasonable. Of the same opinion as Globus is H. D. Lewis, who, in stressing the non-spatiality of the mental, invites us to reflect on certain singular and questionable expressions, such as 'my mind is elsewhere' or 'my thoughts are far away' (Lewis 1969, pp. 16–17 and 197–8). But 'elsewhere' with respect to what? Are we fully aware that these expressions are *metaphors*? Is it perfectly clear that they reflect a conception of reality anchored to things and spaces, which from many cognitive points of view (as we know) is hardly adequate to grasp mental experience?

Lacking spatiality, it should not be surprising that the mental, as Deutscher has written, also lacks *dimensions* (Deutscher 1967, pp. 76–7). How 'broad' is an understanding? How 'deep' a gratitude? How 'low' an envy? How 'sharp' a wit? Correspondingly, the mental is not (or is not wholly) *quantifiable* and *measurable*. 'How much' faith do I have? 'How much' is my jealousy? Or again, what does my thought 'measure'? What are the 'measurements' of my awareness? In this context it should be added that mental states and events are neither *sensorially perceptible*, nor *transferable*, nor *subdividable*. As regards the first point, Baier has pointed out that the mental is not something that can be grasped by means of one of the five traditional senses (Baier 1970, in Borst 1979, pp. 98–9). On the second, Deutscher has observed that I cannot, strictly speaking, 'move' an idea in the same way as I move an object or a part of my body (Deutscher 1967, p. 77). As for the last point, Fodor – as we have seen – has stressed on more than one occasion that a mental phenomenon cannot, generally speaking, be articulated into smaller parts. How could I distinguish a melancholy *in parts?* Nor is it thinkable that the psychic experience of an enthusiasm can be reduced to its single components (physical or metaphysical). A similar thesis was advanced by Wilkerson, who stressed the patent absurdity of any attempt to reduce a particular mental state to a sum of *n* smaller microstates (Wilkerson 1974, p. 100). From this point of view, Margolis seems to be perfectly right when he writes that the mind 'is' (knows, operates, perceives, suffers) in a *molar*, not *molecular* state (Margolis 1978, p. 173). This characterization is important not because it includes the concept of 'molarity' (so dear to Tolman) but because it implies that the events, states, and processes of the mind are relatively *irreducible*.

THE MIND AS A 'HOLISTIC' SYSTEM

Non-spatial, non-measurable, non-subdividable, non-reducible. . . . But is the mental at least *isolatable?* The answer to this question cannot be univocal. From one point of view it is possible to identify the mental *an sich* by means of a series of definitions or, better, of characterizations. I *identify* the mental by ascribing to it certain properties that distinguish it from the non-mental – I do this, of course, in a way which is not objectivistic, but observer-, or context-, or goal-dependent. From another point of view, however, the situation changes. It changes if, instead of identifying the mental in general, we attempt to identify a specific mental state or event. Indeed, the sensations, the thoughts, and the states of subjective awareness (to return to the tripartition dear to Feigl) always exist, or appear, according to *complex* structures and processes, which constitute the only psychic experiences we actually have. It is *we* who cut these structures up into a certain series of components, to which we attribute single and particular *names*. This operation is legitimate and *useful* – since we very often need to identify certain mental acts and states in relation to particular cognitive or practical objectives. We must only be aware (as William James already observed at the end of the nineteenth century) that the series of our mental terms/concepts does not express a corresponding series of objective things or processes. And we must also be aware that the act of identification is not legitimated by any ontological or epistemological assumption – of the sort complex psychic experience is constituted by a sum of *n* elementary, objective components which can and must be analyzed individually in order to grasp (by aggregation) the said experience *more scientifico*.

As regards the attempt to take and examine the single states or events of sentience, Marjorie Grene has written convincingly:

> That there are sensations, isolable, identifiable, single 'bits of consciousness' out of which experience gets built is just plumb *wrong*. Why so many intelligent people in the eighteenth century – even David Hume – believed in them I will never know. . . .But certainly our everyday experience just *is* not made up of such 'psychological atoms'. (Grene 1976, p. 117)

The same may be said about the states and events of sapience (and, *a fortiori*, of selfhood). Here too there is a widespread mechanistic and atomistic conviction according to which sapience can be understood as a sort of arrangement *composed* of various *elementary parts* that can be grasped *an sich* and successively *aggregated* so as to reproduce the overall arrangement. In recent years the results achieved by certain disciplines, especially artificial intelligence and computer science, seem to confirm the principle that certain functions of sapience can be isolated. But, as we have already pointed out, the alleged *reproduction* of these functions is in reality merely a *simulation* of them: the performance of thoughts, choices, and decisions on the part of a computer is something quite different from the processes that take place in the human being. The supposed ability of computer science to grasp specific *mental* functions can be identified only with the realization of certain *physical* operations organized *ab externo* by man according to criteria of analogy that are entirely *arbitrary* and *conventional* with regard to *actual* mental processes. The difference between the two types of process is due not only to the different nature of their 'agents' or 'means' (on the one hand a brain, or rather a man, and on the other an electronic circuit relay), but also to the fact that the states and events of sapience possess in the psychological sphere their own implications and significations (*inseparable* from these states and events, it should be stressed, if we consider them in their *effective* existence) which physical-computational performances can patently not have. Consequently, the testimony of artificial intelligence and computer science in favor of the isolatability of the acts of sapience bears rather little weight.

At a more general level (including sentience and sapience as well as selfhood) it has been said that mental states, in addition to being 'molar', that is, not reducible to elementary components, are also *organic.* That is, they are caught up in knots and cross-references that cannot be ignored by anyone who intends to investigate the real phenomenology of the mental universe. Indeed there is little to recommend the idea that *in* the mind there is a hope *here,* a belief *over there,* and an anxiety *down that way,* each independent of the other. Neurocerebral theories of the 'localizing' type, which are occasionally cited to support certain psychological conceptions, have not only been contested by various scholars on scientific and experimental grounds, but they also appear to have little relevance to the issue at hand. Indeed, even if we were to admit that a hope is bound *primarily* to a particular area of the brain, this does not imply that the psychic act 'hope' comes about and takes shape *exhaustively* 'alone'. In this connection H. D. Lewis once wrote that mental events never appear in isolation, one by one – and, more importantly, they can never be understood in their (improbable) separateness. To understand them we must analyze them in their reciprocal interaction (Lewis 1969, pp. 33 and 54). Mental properties, according to W. C. Wimsatt, are "configurational". This means that they are "specific 'relational properties' of parts, and not properties of parts apart from the whole" (introductory note to Wimsatt 1976, p. 199). To understand a mental event, then, I must necessarily understand the network, the irreducible complex of which it is a part. Wimsatt's 'systemic' thesis brings to mind the 'holistic' conception proposed by Davidson, who argued (as the reader will recall) that not only is a mental event not isolatable from a particular structure, but it is often generated, within that structure, by other mental events the analysis of which is indispensable to the understanding of the event under consideration.

It is, if we are not mistaken, in the light of Davidson's work that Christopher Peacocke, a scholar who embraces (neo-physicalistic) positions quite distant from those defended here, has elaborated his own "holistic" theory of mental events (Peacocke 1979). For him, every belief, every desire, and so on has certain characters and consequences only because the subject has – contemporaneously – *other* beliefs, *other* desires. Further, every belief cross-refers in some way to a desire, and vice versa. Consequently, when I attempt to individuate a belief on the basis of certain effects, I must take into account that these effects result also from some desire. "If an agent *desires*-that-*p*, then from this principle we cannot expect any particular kind of action until we know the agent's beliefs of the form 'If I Ø, then *p*'. Conversely, given knowledge of all his beliefs, we do not know which will issue in action until we know which *p*'s he desires" (ibid., p. 12). "What is *believed*", Peacocke observes, suggestively, in another passage, "may depend also on what is *remembered*" (ibid., p. 23; italics mine).

It is striking, finally, that another neo-physicalist (albeit 'liberal'), Kathleen Wilkes, also makes a point of stressing, in her analysis of the irreducible peculiarities of the mental, the fact that mental events are never *isolated* nor *isolatable*, nor are they ever produced *alone*. "Beliefs and desires", writes Wilkes, "do not come individually wrapped, but are all tied up together. No desire or belief of whatever kind can ever be attributed in isolation: each needs a background of related desires and beliefs into which it fits, against which it can be seen as rational" (Wilkes 1978a, p. 24). Accordingly, it may well happen that two apparently *identical* thoughts about something (a 'thought-about-Vienna') – and perhaps identical in their neurophysiological dynamics – may be profoundly *different* "because they are thought in different mental states" (ibid., p. 26). It is worth pointing out that it is in part on the basis of these 'holistic' premises that Wilkes takes an interesting stand in favor of the (relative) independence of the mental universe with respect to brain structures (ibid., p. 27).

THE MENTAL AS 'MODE' AND 'EXPERIENCE'

Brief mention was made of Davidson. It will be recalled that, in speaking of the monism that characterizes his philosophical perspective, Davidson uses the term "anomalous". This attribute could also be used in connection with the mental. Another scholar we have already mentioned, Weimer, has spoken of the constitutive "ambiguity" (but in a positive sense) of that which we indicate with the term/concept 'mind', alluding to the singular co-presence in mental events of the most diverse dimensions (Weimer 1976). H. D. Lewis, in the very title of his book devoted to the problem of the mind, has used the suggestive concept of the "elusiveness" of the mental (Lewis 1969).

Anomalous, ambiguous, elusive . . . In the light of what we have seen so far these somewhat singular characterizations of the mental should not be too surprising. Let us briefly summarize, although in absolutely provisional and partial terms, what we have said here and elsewhere about the mental itself. It exists, but not in a physical way. It has being, but we cannot perceive it. It is 'there', but it can be *placed* nowhere. Further, it acts in ways that are to a certain extent rule-governed, but which are relatively unpredictable and not very 'legal' (Margolis 1973b, p. 243). It expresses itself in complex figures, which can neither be simplified nor broken down into component parts. We speak about it as though it were composed of single tokens, of single isolatable 'occurrences': and yet our experience tells us that these occurrences imply one another indissolubly, and in the most varied ways.

There is more. We must include another particularly *sui generis* feature of the mental: the mental is not a unitary, internally homogeneous phenomenon. Indeed it appears to be organically composed of a 'factual' dimension and a 'modal' dimension. When the materialists and the identity theorists consider it only in terms of physical states and processes, they neglect its second dimension, thereby giving the mental a unilateral and partial characterization. Take a joy. It surely includes a neurophysiological (or biochemical, or bioelectrical) component; and it is certainly rooted in a particular area of the brain. But there is also the 'way' in which I experience that joy: deriving it from a certain *reason*, feeling it according to certain *forms*, interpreting it in the light of certain *principles*, making it the *matrix* of other states. This 'way', which is patently nonphysical, is by no means something *added* or *secondary* to some other *substantial* and ideally *precedent* thing. Indeed it has been asserted that the mental as such is *wholly* a 'way' (a mode). The 'rest' (the neurophysiological component, etc.) is to be considered essentially the *vehicle* of the state in question.

Though not going quite so far, various scholars have chosen to highlight this 'modal' specificity of the mental. C. I. Lewis, for example, has written that if a man were able to feel a pain and *contemporaneously* examine his brain with the most sophisticated instruments, "he would be conscious of *two* things, not *one*": of a way of being *and* of a certain *physical situation* (Lewis 1941, in Feigl and Sellars 1949, p. 63). Herbst has also insisted that in a psychophysical event there co-exist a dimension of 'things' and a dimension of 'experiences' (Herbst 1967, p. 63). When I examine a chromatic perception I can study physical mechanisms, or I can grasp features that do not coincide with these mechanisms – beginning with the way I experience this perception. There will be, once again, *two* objects of the inquiry – though closely linked one to the other. If, Herbst adds, I decide to devote myself to the second anal-

216

ysis, I will have to examine the perception essentially "in terms of *what is experienced*". It is impossible, he insists, to reduce the *experience* of a color to a *physical happening* devoid of *my* perception of the color (ibid.). "The further scientists go in reducing to uniformity the physical conditions of our experience, the less chance there is of identifying these physical uniformities with the multiformities of the experiences themselves" (Whiteley 1970, p. 199). These observations make an important contribution toward furthering the characterization of the mental. The mental is beginning to take shape (without sacrificing its relationships with the physical) primarily as *experience:* as subjectively, irreducibly, 'holistically' constituted experience.

THE CULTURALITY AND CONTEXTUALITY OF THE MENTAL

It is by analyzing this dimension of the 'mental as experience' that some philosophers of mind have singled out, from among the distinguishing features of the mental, 'culturality'. What, one might ask, does 'culture' have to do with the 'mental'? For some scholars – from Putnam to Margolis – quite a lot (Putnam 1973b, Margolis 1978 and 1983). And it is pertinent, though to varying degrees, to all levels of the mental itself: sentience, sapience, and selfhood (to return to the traditional tripartition). Obviously, if I consider a pain, a belief, or an awareness in exclusively *physical* and *factual* terms, 'culture' will clearly remain outside the scientific analysis of these phenomena. But if I consider these three mental states in *experiential* terms (or *also* in such terms), then the situation changes. Indeed pain as a specific *psychic experience* can be felt and experienced in many different ways. And it is clear that these different ways are strongly influenced by 'culture' (in the broad sense). Is it not *also* a cultural component that makes people feel pain in *different* forms and intensities? Let us leave aside the (overworked) example of the Indian fakirs with their beds of nails and certain Australian ascetics with their burning coals. Isn't it indisputable that even in our everyday Western experience we find that pain can be experienced in *many* ways: in ways – and this is the point – connected (or, again, *also* connected) on the one hand to our culturally constituted interior person, and on the other to the, again, culturally constituted symbolic and emotional context in which we experience it?

The same is true – indeed, even more so – for events belonging to the categories of sapience and selfhood. Belief – at least in appearance – is contained within certain convolutions of the brain (*where* else should it be, at least for those who do not believe in the existence of the soul?). And yet it has been observed that a neurophysiologist would not be able – *qua* neurophysiologist – to analyze a certain *convolution* to the point of grasping and illustrating a *belief*. Why? Because a belief, like a pain, is not only a *fact* – much less an exclusively physical fact; it is also an *experience*. This experience belongs to a sphere that cannot be explored by means of physical instruments because it is composed of figures and contents that can be properly defined as 'cultural'. Indeed it appears as a choice, a commitment that a subject makes on the basis of principles and criteria that are not in the least physical. Of course, empirical investigation will reveal that a belief *passes through*, or *is embodied in*, identifiable neurophysiological structures. But it is equally clear that this doesn't imply that it is *identical to* them, or *resolves into* them. It will remain an essentially *cultural* form, an understanding of which will require an appropriate *cultural* analysis. As Paul E. Meehl once wrote, Eisenhower is (or rather was) composed entirely of *physical* neurons and cells. But no investigation of these cells and neurons will reveal, and much less explain, the fact that Eisenhower had Republican beliefs: "none of Eisenhower's neurons", Meehl observes gravely, "was Republican" (Meehl 1970, p. 346). Republicanism is, evidently, something 'cultural'.

Without culture, in sum, we would understand very little about the psycho-subjective aspects of human action. Indeed the actions of individuals, when examined from a strictly psychological point of view, lead us necessarily to a series of causes, referents, and purposes that are not only independent of psychophysical mechanisms but also require an analysis in 'cultural' terms. Even typically psychic acts such as decisions necessarily involve principles, schemata, and criteria that only '*meta*-physical', 'cultural' disciplines can illuminate adequately.

Following an analogous line of reflection, some scholars have spoken of a 'contextualistic' dimension of the mental. Marjorie Grene, for instance, has stressed the "contextual nature" not only of the more complex mental events, but also of "almost all, if not all, so-called 'immediate' perceptions" (Grene 1976, p. 118). From this point of view, the context appears as an organic component of certain mental states or processes, or also as an indispensable referent of an appropriate analysis of such states and processes. Take jealousy, for example. Considered from one angle, it appears to be an exquisitely intrapsychic and individual phenomenon. But actually, we know quite well not only that it derives from an *external* source (which neither a neurophysiological, nor a psychological inquiry, could ever reveal), but also that it is interpreted as such *only* within a *meta*-psychic, a *meta*-individual system (i.e., a *context*). Indeed, one might go so far as to say that certain mental phenomena are literally un-thinkable without a context: a context in the twofold sense of a *complex of (exogenous) causes* that bring about a certain (endogenous) mental state or event, and of an *axiological-behavioral paradigm* with reference to which that state or event is interpreted and baptized in a certain way. Of the same opinion is the English philosopher Anthony Flew, who argues that a thought is or becomes a thought – that is it takes on the sense it has – not *alone*, not *in itself*, but only "in certain circumstances", that is in a certain context: in the same way that the act of putting a crown on a person's head is a 'coronation' only in a particular situation (Flew 1978, p. 133). Douglas R. Hofstadter, author of the celebrated *Gödel, Escher, Bach*, in discussing the psychic nature of the "beliefs" of an individual, asserts that studying the "chucks of symbols" that constitute them without making reference to the "context" would be "as silly as trying to describe the range of a single person's 'potential progeny' without referring to the mate" (Hofstadter 1979, p. 384). Even a phenomenon which may appear strongly 'personal' like selfhood is in reality very 'contextual'. Not only do I perceive myself as *others* perceive me from without (and force me to perceive myself). But even the way – the way in a formal, categorial sense – I perceive myself is, to a large extent, exogenous, contextualistic. Indeed, the way in which I feel my being is determined by perceptive and intellective structures whose origin and substance are largely social (Creutzfeldt and Rager 1978, pp. 311–18).

If what has been said thus far is true, the mental will have to be studied in a manner that is radically different both from the traditional approach and from orientations adopted by certain avant-garde research programs. As Paul Watzlawick has written, if "every man, even the most solitary, is placed in a *context* of relationships with others", then not only does the merely neurophysiological approach to mental/human phenomena appear to be insufficient, but also "any speculation on intrapsychic processes gradually loses meaning" (Watzlawick 1985, p. 35).

THE INTENTIONALITY OF THE MENTAL

But the peculiar feature of the mental which has drawn the greatest attention of a significant group of philosophers of mind is intentionality. One of the first to highlight the close relationship between this notion and the MBP was Sellars. Both in his essay *Empiricism and the Philosophy of Mind* (1956) and in the important debate with Roderick Chisholm (whose 1957 monograph *Perceiving: a Philosophical Study* is, along with Anscombe's equally famous essay 'Intention' (1957), one of the primary sources of a certain current of inquiry) Sellars has insisted that intentionality expresses a 'quality' of the mental which any reflection on the MBP must take seriously into account.

What is this quality? We could give an answer to this question that might at first sight appear paradoxical. Intentionality alludes, in fact, not to a *property* of the mental, but rather to what it *does not have*. It alludes to the circumstance that the mental is *not*, in many cases, truly self-sufficient – although this in no way implies that the mental itself requires the physical. What is this lack of self-sufficiency, and what does it derive from? It consists in the fact that a certain part of the mental cannot, constitutively, subsist *alone*. This is because it necessarily implies a sort of cross-reference to, or a tension toward, an 'otherness' – something else, something different from the mental itself. Thus, for example, a thought or a belief, or a hope, is nothing but an abstraction. It passes from abstraction to concreteness – that is to empirical, phenomenological reality – if and only if it can be determined *what it refers to*. The question of the necessary *reference* of the mental and the closely linked issue of its "aboutness" assume capital importance for the characterization and the understanding of a significant part of the mental. Sellars has written quite to the point: "Believing, desiring, intending, loving, hating, reasoning, approving – indeed, *all* characteristically human states and dispositions above the level of mere sensory consciousness – cannot be explicated without encountering such reference or *aboutness*" (Sellars and Chisholm 1958, p. 507; italics mine).

But why is this necessary 'pro-jection' of thought or of consciousness (mentalists would generalize: of the mental) toward the 'other-than-self' so important for the specific issue of the MBP? There are at least two reasons, both decisive: a) because the referent that the mental 'intends' is not something *physical*; b) because this 'projection' is *not* peculiar to all the processes of reality, but only to mental acts – or rather, as we shall see, to the human subjects that 'do' them (or that 'have' them). As for the first point, it should be noted that the 'intended' *otherness* of the mental can by no means be identified with physical-material determinations. The object of thought, belief, or hope is not a *bodily factuality* but an ideal *referent* ("noema" is Husserl's term). I think not a fragment of physical reality but an 'idea' of this fragment; I believe not a 'thing' but a symbolic scheme referring to a thing; I hope not a 'fact' but an essence/value relative to a fact.

But it is perhaps the second reason indicated above – the fact that only the mental (and not the physical) has intentionality – that has aroused the greatest interest among many philosophers of mind. Woodfield has pointed out that while intentional thought (or the intentional mental act in general) implies the existence of an ideal 'object' outside the intentional *thought* itself, "no *brain* state presupposes the existence of an external object" (Woodfield 1982, p. viii; italics mine). Indeed, whereas the *psychologist* who studies an act of intellection cannot avoid including in his analysis a referent 'different' from the mental event in the strict sense, the *neurophysiologist* who studies from his own point of view *the same* phenomenon (supposing that this is possible in a literal sense) will study it in and of itself, that is, in terms of a certain neuronal fact or process. What *else* (as we have already said) could a neurophysiologist *as* a neurophysiologist concern himself with anyway? In this connection, it is significant that Woodfield has no hesitation in asserting that it is precisely the intentionalistic doctrine – which aims at stressing the link between not the mental and the brain but between the mental and ideal ('*meta*-physical') figures and forms – that presents a radical refutation of any physicalistic and materialistic conception. Before Woodfield, another scholar we have mentioned on more than one occasion, Peter Herbst, had expressed himself on the relationship between an intentionalistic conception of the mental and the autonomy of the mental in even clearer and more precise terms:

> I myself do think that experiences, and particularly thoughts, cannot be identifyingly referred to except by references to their content, nor desires, ambitions, hopes, fears and expectations, except in terms of their objects. These objects need not be real existences, past, present, or future, and thus must stand in a peculiar internal relation to the alleged mental en-

221

tities, which does not occur in the material universe. (Herbst 1967, p. 64)

Given the importance of the question it is well worthy citing another position, which not only comes from one of today's most authoritative proponents of a review of the concept of intentionality, Roderick Chisholm, but also allows us to approach the problem from an analytic angle somewhat different from those mentioned thus far. "Some now believe", writes Chisholm, "that . . . the sentences we must use in describing psychological phenomena have certain logical properties that are shared by any of the sentences we use in describing non-physical phenomena, and that these properties are correctly called intentional" (Chisholm 1967, p. 203). He continues with an observation that cannot escape notice: *"If this is true, then the basic thesis of physicalism and of the unity of science is false"* (ibid.; italics mine).

It would be superfluous to underline the importance of this statement, which explicitly links the intentionalistic conception of the mental with the crucial battle waged by a part of contemporary philosophy against physicalistic and unitaristic conceptions of science. Some philosophers of mind, however, have proposed an even more pregnant, an even 'stronger' interpretation of intentionality than those mentioned so far. In particular Margolis, examining a circumscribed problem within a broad philosophical and anthropological context, expresses significant doubts about the theses of some rather innovative scholars. These doubts concern, in particular, the conceptions of Sellars. Despite his notable contribution to the rehabilitation of intentionality, Sellars (writes Margolis) occasionally gives the impression that he wants to limit himself to *adding* the intentionalistic property to what has been called by Margolis himself a "scientific theory of man" (Margolis 1984, pp. 15 and 17).

But for Margolis intentionality is not only *this*. Far from constituting one of the many functions that characterize the mental (susceptible, perhaps, to being reduced to another), intentionality is *the* property, *the* dimension par excellence – an *irreducible* dimension – of man as a mental/thinking/acting being. Man, in short, is fundamentally an intentional entity: and his every *modus essendi* and *operandi* – naturally beginning with mental acts – is 'qualified' by this characteristic. This is another reason, Margolis adds, why there cannot be (or there cannot be *only*) a "purely physical explanation" of the psychological capacities of human beings (Margolis pays particular attention to the communicative function; ibid., pp. 18 and 27. See also Margolis 1973b, pp. 218–20).

It is curious to note that a scholar like Margaret Boden, who is (as we have said elsewhere) one of the most determined supporters of the close kinship between men and computers, should insist not only on the specificity of intentional acts and statements, but also on the impossibility of reducing them to a class of events lacking certain pre-requisites. Indeed Boden's orientation is to give them, in linguistic terms, a rather specific and 'differential' characterization. In her book *Minds and Mechanisms* she writes: "the logical peculiarities of intentional sentences include indeterminacy, referential opacity, failure of existential generalization, no implication of any embedded clause (or its negation), and the non-extensional occurrence of embedded clauses". More to the point Boden adds that "the intentional object (the object of thought that is mentioned in the sentence) can be described only by reference to the *subject's* thoughts (purposes, beliefs, expectations, desires)" (Boden 1981, p. 43; italics mine).

As we see, in addition to presenting a rather rich and suggestive picture of the intentional universe of man, Boden concludes her reflection with an important connection between this universe and the pole of human subjectivity. It will soon be clear that this link, this potential identification of the mental in a 'strong' sense with human subjectivity, constitutes one of the most promising arguments to appear in the contemporary debate on the MBP. But we will get to this in due time. Here, instead, it should be pointed out that Boden, like Woodfield, insists on the fact that an appropriate interpretation of intentionality constitutes an additional, powerful lever to prevent the physicalization of the mental and the identification of the mental with the bodily. "There may be", she writes in *Minds and Mechanisms*, "no *actual thing* with which the *object of thought* can be sensibly identified" (ibid., p. 43; italics mine). In the same vein, though more closely tied to linguistic and cognitive concerns, she goes on to say: "to forbid the use of such intentional language would be to omit all mention of mental phenomena, since there is no possibility of saying anything about the mind using only the language of the body" (ibid., p. 46).

THE MENTAL AS IMMEDIACY AND PRIVACY

The question of intentionality – an absolutely crucial knot not only in contemporary philosophy, but also in contemporary human sciences – and its implications for the problems that concern us opens up a broad terrain for discussion. The remarks made thus far, however, should be sufficient to answer our immediate purposes. Indeed, not all champions of the autonomy and the specificity of the mental have played their high cards on its intentionalistic character. Various scholars have found other aspects of the mental universe to be its most characteristic and irreducible. Jaegwon Kim, for example, makes some striking observations on the 'true' differential features of the mental (Kim 1971), not that he represents an indisputably valid point of reference in the process which a part of the current philosophy of mind has initiated in an effort to achieve the full autonomy of the mental. It is for this reason that we shall not return to an analysis of his article on the "criteria of the mental". But there is a phrase in this essay that may serve as an ideal premise for a further stage in our itinerary. Kim states that "the concept of mental seems today more closely associated with such notions as 'privileged access', 'direct awareness', and 'privacy' than with the more abstract notion of intentionality" (Kim 1971, p. 336).

Whether Kim's thesis is completely or (as we are inclined to believe) only in part true, one thing is certain: quite a number of scholars who argue for the full emancipation of the mental have been concentrating their attention not so much on intentionality as on the "criteria" Kim proposes. In his essay, Kim goes into some detail particularly on "direct awareness" and "privileged access" – obviously of the subject with regard to his own *lato sensu* mental experiences (ibid.). The first "criterion" regards *several* characteristics of such experiences: many consider one of the most important of these to be so-called *immediacy*. The sense of this 'property' of the mental is rather clear. While my knowledge of an external datum is necessarily conditioned by many objective features of the datum itself, I grasp the existence of a mental event more quickly and in a *different* way: in other words more 'immediately'. This *immediacy*, it must be clear, does not allude to the possibility for the subject to experience a certain mental state or event in a 'pure' way: even such an experience necessarily passes through various filters.

But it is one thing to admit the existence of these filters and another to suppose – as some behaviorists do – that mental events are facts which can be understood and analyzed in the same (*mediated*) way as any other phenomenon. No, the way we grasp mental states or events is entirely different from the way we perceive other empirical states and events. "No one", Baier once wrote, "will ever say: 'from the [factual, external, verifiable] facts in my possession I can assert that I have a pain in my tooth'" (Baier 1970, in Borst 1979, p. 98). According to Baier, there is a definite "asymmetry" in our relationship with what happens *in our self* and *elsewhere* (ibid., p. 99): "for whereas it makes no sense to say 'I could see (or hear) that *I* had a pain', it makes quite good sense to say 'I could see (or hear) that *he* had a pain'" (ibid., p. 98).

The question of *immediacy* leads us to an even more relevant and more specific issue: that of *privacy*. This property of mental experience is a classic theme in the literature on the MBP. Reduced to its most essential terms, the problem is the following. Is the mental state/event something that can be rendered objective and 'public' (at least as far as scientific inquiry is concerned), or does it imply an *irreducibly* subjective and personal dimension which requires knowledge to equip itself with new and appropriate instruments (different from those of the physical sciences) in order to grasp it? As we know, for a long time scholars of diverse intellectual orientations have opted decidedly for the first answer: Feigl comes to mind, especially for the emphasis with which he makes his choice. But the party of adversaries has not lost heart: indeed its ranks have grown considerably. In the essay we have cited on more than one occasion, Baier lays great stress on the *private* dimension of both sentience and sapience. Of particular efficacy is his argument concerning sentience. If A and B have the 'same' pain (in the factual, scientific, or pathological sense of the term), this by no means implies that *A has B's pain* (and vice versa): in other words, it does not mean that A and B have the *same* experience of pain. Each of the two experiences *his own* – subjective and private – way of perceiving pain: a way which any science of psychology worthy of the name cannot ignore (Baier 1970, in Borst 1979, p. 98).

Of a similar opinion – though inspired by different motives – are scholars of rather different theoretical orientation such as H. D. Lewis, Harth, Globus, and Nagel. Harth focuses on the centrality, the "inviolability", and the "irrevocability" of the privacy of sentience in particular (Harth 1982, p. 29). Lewis extends this feature to all the functions of the mind (Lewis 1969). Globus stresses the *sui generis* and "privileged" access the subject has to his own private mental experiences (Globus 1972). Thomas Nagel vigorously contests the possibility that mental experiences can be 'de-privatized' to the point of considering them states freed of any subjective, personal dimension (and thus, in this sense, each substantially equivalent to the others), as is done with natural phenomena (Nagel 1974). Indeed, on closer examination it seems evident that a 'de-privatized', 'de-subjectivized' mental experience risks becoming a constitutively defective figure; and the contraposition of something that is ultimately 'real/objective/public' to *my* 'phenomenal/subjective/private' experience risks being quite misleading. "What sense is there", queries Nagel (in a passage we cited in the Introduction), "in asking what my experiences are *really* as opposed to what they *appear to be to me?*" (Nagel 1979, p. 178).

It is striking that even a neopositivist like Alfred Ayer, who is generally little inclined to give credit (at least from a certain point of view) to the notions of individuality and subjectivity, has defended the existence of *private* experiences, though striving not to set them in opposition ontologically to the others. "It is wrong", writes Ayer, "to say that there are no such things as private experiences. . . ; and it is wrong to say that when we describe them, we are describing something else, the condition of our bodies, whether inside or outside the skin". What is wrong, in short, is to believe that when we speak about our subjective states or events, we are actually speaking about "physical events": what we are talking about, Ayer emphasizes, is precisely the complex of *"our private* experiences" (Ayer 1955, p. 18; italics mine).

Immediacy and privacy, then, are properties peculiar and specific to the mental. Not that they must always be set in *opposition* to other (physical) properties, nor must one exclude the possibility of succeeding in grasping 'objectively' and 'publicly' some aspect of this more intimate and subjective dimension of *our* mental experience. But, without a doubt, the fact remains that when we speak of this aspect of the experience we are speaking not about *facts* but about *ways;* and not about ways that can be easily translated into objective *analoga,* but, on the contrary, about some of the more peculiarly qualitative, individual, and personal ways of the human experience.

THE 'INCORRIGIBILITY' OF THE MENTAL

Ideally connected to the question of immediacy and privacy is that of *authority* and *incorrigibility*. What is meant by the first of these two terms? While *objects* (and the description and evaluation of their properties, features, etc.) can in principle be subjected to different interpretations, opinions, and theories each with its own validity, in the case of *subjective/immediate/private experiences* the situation is quite different. Indeed, it hardly makes sense to organize a round table on the *modes* of *my* memory. It is not possible to legitimate B to experience the sensation of joy felt by A. Mental states and acts cannot be delegated and expressed indirectly – at least insofar as they are taken in their more personal sense. From a certain perspective, in sum, the individual is sovereign in the description of his *own* experiences. As Baier has written with customary flare, it would be rather absurd to say: 'I have a pain unless I am mistaken' (Baier 1970, p. 98).

It should be added that within the framework of an epistemology which tends to belittle an individual's statements concerning what he feels and thinks subjectively, it is important to erect defenses around precisely such statements. They have a meaning and a cognitive value that absolutely must not be ignored. They 'say', in fact, a mental experience actually possessed by the subject, the presence of which makes itself felt in various ways in his being and acting. Of course, appropriate analytical instruments will have to be devised. It will be necessary, that is, to recognize that such statements probably cannot be treated (or cannot always be treated) *in the same way* as statements concerning physical, natural phenomena. It will be necessary, in particular, to take into adequate account the *incontrovertibility* and *irrevocableness* of such statements. In this regard Deutscher, among others, has used these terms. Mental states, he writes, are characterized first of all by the fact that their possessor has a particular "authority" with respect to them. In the second place (and more importantly), such states are the object of what might be called the "incorrigible reports" expressed by those who experience them (Deutscher 1967, p. 76). "Incorrigible" does not imply, however, that they are true according to *any possible* criterion and in *any possible* cognitive sphere.

Among contemporary philosophers of mind no one has insisted more than Rorty on the theme of "incorrigibility" as a specific feature of the mental. "The thesis presented", writes Rorty in one of his most important essays on the MBP, "is that all and only mental events are the sorts of entities certain reports about which are incorrigible" (Rorty 1970b, p. 418). This position appears even more peremptory in that Rorty does not hesitate to demolish *all* the other traits usually considered peculiar to the mental. We shall not go into this merciless *destructio*: rather, we shall point out that for Rorty, the principle of incorrigibility is of particular importance, also because it appears to be the only valid principle that applies both to the intellective sphere and to the sphere of sensations. The objection that A may think and feel 'things' different from the *real* ones – that is, from those that *really* occur in him – is completely irrelevant: both because, in any case, whatever is thought and/or felt by A will always be *something that exists* and because it has in any case *its own validity* or *raison d'être*.

As for the fact that the subjective/private experiences expressed by A can be considered objectively *true* or *false*, here we must be very careful. First of all, it is not a question of a *fact* but of a *judgement*. Moreover, this judgement implies *shifting* what is under discussion from one plane – that of the concrete mental and existential phenomenology that *I* not only *live* but also *grasp cognitively* – to another one: that of another kind of experience, with its own principles and criteria, with its necessary codifications and delimitations, that end up by erecting a theoretical construct which is certainly legitimate and valuable, but (no less certainly) *different* from what is subjectively perceived by the individual. Unquestionably, I can demonstrate the truth or falsehood of what a man says about himself. On the other hand, however, his experiences and beliefs, insofar as they are *subjective* experiences and beliefs, preserve the right to a kind of knowledge that recognizes the irreducibility and the 'primacy' – that is, the incorrigibility – of the perception/analysis of the subject himself. Indeed Rorty points out quite appropriately that the significant expression "you are mistaken about what you are thinking" has fallen into disuse: it does not appear, at least from a certain point of view, to have a convincing foundation (the 'error', in fact, is not in the mental act of the thought but, if at all, in a possible interpretation of it in *other* terms and in another context).

THE INDIVIDUALITY, TITULARITY, AND
SUBJECTIVITY OF THE MENTAL

But the truly crucial question in connection with the issues we are discussing is what might be called the *individuality* and the *titularity* of the mental, as well as its relationship with *subjectivity*. The term, despite appearances, should not be too mysterious. It draws attention to the fact that feelings and thoughts are, to a large extent, *particular* states and events. As Rorty once wrote, it is not possible to talk about them *in general*. Or at least, when we talk about them in general, we are speaking at a level which is *not* that of a *concrete* experience. What is Joy? What is Suffering? What is Doubt or Belief? In a certain context – in *lato sensu* scientific discourse – these are undoubtedly important, irreplaceable concepts. Scholars of various fields – including philosophers – have made use of them to elaborate theoretical constructs of great importance, which in turn have contributed significantly to our understanding of the nature of the mental and of the human sphere.

At *another* level, however, Joy, Suffering, Doubt, and Belief *in general* in a certain sense *do not exist*. There exist instead (as we wrote in the Introduction) only *single* joys and *particular* sufferings, *single* doubts, and *particular* beliefs: single, particular – and, from a certain perspective, *irreducible*. On closer examination, no belief is *exactly the same* as another belief; no suffering *coincides without residue* with another suffering. When two individuals suffer (even contemporaneously and 'in the same' way), their pains cannot be identified with, or resolved into, the participation in *one single* general, objective form – nor, and most importantly, can those pains be fully understood through such an approach. 'A' feels *his own* pain and 'B' suffers *his:* and the two experiences will be characterized by precise subjective-personal peculiarities. If this is true, it becomes urgent to acquire a more mature awareness of the *psychoexistential individuality*, of the irreducible *particularity* of mental states and acts. From a certain perspective – and at least for certain cognitive interests – what exists in the concrete phenomenology of the living being is A's joy, B's suffering, C's doubt, and D's belief.

The phrase 'titularity of the mental' refers primarily to this reality, to this peculiar form of *possession* which expresses a peculiar form of *individuality* of mental acts and processes as well as a peculiar *theoretical position* of the subject with respect to them. "Many mental phenomena," Wilkes writes in this connection, "are such that their owner is in a privileged epistemological position in relation to them" (Wilkes 1978a, pp. 8–9). We might point out in passing that this characterization of mental states and events also provides further confirmation of the autonomy of the mental from the physical. As J. W. Yolton once noted, if I say 'this pain (of mine) is a brain state B', not only does the demonstrative adjective tie "my reference to something other than the brain-state", but if the expression 'this pain' is to have any meaning, it must refer to something which is identifiable by me: and "what is identifiable by me is not my brain but *my* pain" – that *personal, subjective* pain of which I am, so to speak, the only *titular* (Yolton 1967, p. 223). From an only slightly different perspective Wilkerson has observed that a physical object (an automobile, e.g.) can belong to me or to someone else – without this difference in the attribution of propriety altering the identity or the substance of the object. In contrast, a mental event (a particular thought, e.g.) is only *mine:* it cannot be shared with others (in a form absolutely unaltered, absolutely identical to itself), nor can it be yielded or lent (Wilkerson 1974, p. 31).

But, we said, together with the question of the individuality and titularity of the mental there is also the question of its relationship with subjectivity; and this question may be even more important. What has happened in this connection in certain sectors of the literature on the MBP is rather insignificant. Various scholars have been gradually approaching the conclusion that the phenomena of the mental sphere cannot be understood without referring to the pole of the ego, that is, to subjectivity. It should be stressed that this does not occur only at the level of greater and more evident psychic complexity: it also happens at the more elementary levels, at the level of simple sentience. As Baier once wrote, it is absurd to say: "it would be self-contradictory to assert the existence of unfelt pains which no sentient being has" (Baier 1970, p. 98). An analogous principle holds at the level of sapience. "Whether anywhere in the room there be a mere thought, which is nobody's thought", writes Eric Harth quoting James's *Principles of Psychology*, "we have no means of ascertaining" (Harth 1982, p. 195). Squires has also argued convincingly that it is impossible to identify both intellective and behavioral acts by connecting them exclusively with bodily organs while neglecting an indispensable reference to the persons that perform them (Squires 1970, pp. 352–3).

Sentience and sapience. Actually, the renewed attention that the philosophy of mind has shown for the subject has been developed largely in connection with the reflection on that sort of third component or pole of the 'mental' called 'self-consciousness', 'awareness', or, more often (and with a rather different and more ambitious label), 'selfhood'. This renewed sensitivity toward the question of self-consciousness is documented in numerous sources. From among these we might cite the severe judgement pronounced by Fodor concerning the "scarce or inexistent" role played by consciousness in twentieth century psychology (Fodor 1980, p. 44). This denouncement could be coupled with Margolis's attack, launched from another philosophical shore, on current philosophy's "arrogant rejection" of consciousness (Margolis 1978, p. 6). In other words, consciousness is *missing:* it is the absent figure, the dimension that has been censored and repressed in contemporary psychoanthropological reflection. Why is this? This question – and more generally the question of the peculiar reality of consciousness and its relationship with subjectivity – is one which has borne fruit in the reflection of Thomas Nagel.

NAGEL: THE 'CONSCIOUSNESS' DIMENSION OF THE MENTAL

After a debut on the MBP stage with an important article on physicalism (Nagel 1965), Nagel returned to the subject with an essay that for many has become an obligatory point of reference. The title is at once curious and, intentionally, provocative: 'What Is It Like to Be a Bat?' (1974, henceforth cited from Nagel 1979). The crucial question Nagel raises is the following: is it possible to be conscious of (or to grasp) what a bat feels? Nagel's ultimate answer is a resounding 'no': we do *not* know what it is like to be a bat. We do not know, and we cannot know by definition. As might be expected, bats in and of themselves play a relatively limited role in Nagel's argument. He brings them in only because they share certain physical features with humans, while at the same time they are extremely *different,* radically and significantly different from human beings (Nagel 1979, p. 168). Nagel begins with the following problem: "I want to know what it is like for a *bat* to be a bat" (ibid., p. 169). The first observation in this regard tends to underline the difficulty, indeed the substantial impossibility, of giving an adequate answer to the question. I cannot imagine the 'being' of a bat by *adding,* nor by *subtracting,* nor by transforming some aspect of *my* experience as a human being. At a more general level the theoretical (philosophical and psychoanthropological) issue that interests Nagel is of fundamental importance: what qualifies, what characterizes living beings – and, most importantly, man? And if this 'something' exists, what peculiarities does it possess – and, especially, why does it appear to be so difficult to grasp, to compare with other entities? Nagel's answer is unambiguous. This 'something' – leaving aside for the moment its claim to a rigorous conceptual legitimacy – *exists*. Yet it is connected to components that are not physical but of another type: and it can be called, with particular reference to man, *consciousness*. For Nagel, consciousness is an entirely *sui generis*, but indisputably existing, dimension of individuals as such. It exists as a way in which the living being – and in particular man – on the one hand connotes and delimits itself, on the other establishes relationships with – but also distinguishes itself from – the other, the world. From this perspective consciousness appears as a sort of "point of view": "whatever may be the status of facts about what it is like to be a human being, or a bat, or a Martian, these appear to be facts that embody a particular point of view" (ibid., p. 171). This return to the figure of the "point of view" (on which Nagel lays considerable emphasis) is quite suggestive. The historian of ideas will think of the outstanding theoretical role played by this notion in the period of crisis – of crucial importance for our modernity – at the turn of the century: an age in which philosophers, scholars, writers, and painters (from Nietzsche to the young Lukács and to Simmel, from Henry James to Proust and to Pirandello, from Cézanne to the cubists) found in concepts such as 'point of view' or 'perspective' an instrument to contest the supposed objective univocity of things and to highlight the existence of *a subjective, qualitative, differentiated way* of perceiving and experiencing them.

Of course, Nagel is distant, in many senses, from this historical framework. As regards the definition of consciousness as "point of view", his first concern is to determine its principal psychoanthropological and epistemological implications. We should say immediately that the intrinsic limits or, so to speak, the possible 'closure' of the "point of view" do not lead Nagel to suggest that the communication and comprehension between different subjects is impossible. On the contrary, he explicitly stresses that as long as certain fundamental affinities exist, communication and comprehension can exist between A's experience, B's experience, and C's experience. Rather, the existence of this 'consciousness-as-point-of-view' seems to him to differentiate clearly the status of *things* from that of (mental/existential) *experience*. The former are certainly conditioned by the perspective of the observer: nonetheless, says Nagel, they are still *relatively* autonomous from him (a stone enjoys an – albeit relative – *objectivity* that cannot be ignored). In the case of existential and mental experiences, the situation seems to be quite different: such experiences, in fact, are infinitely more *observer-* (or *subject-*) *dependent*. Here, Nagel writes: "In the case of experience, . . . the connexion with a particular *point of view* seems much closer" (ibid., p. 173). In a certain sense, man's experience *is*, or better *is constructed primarily by*, his subjectivity, his "point of view": it is, in other words, the peculiar and irreducible way in which the human being perceives/experiences himself and the world.

All this has fundamental consequences for an inquiry into cognition. In the case of *facts*, as Nagel stresses, knowledge is legitimated and encouraged to move in the direction of an increasingly less *subject-dependent* and more *observer-free* investigation. In the case of *experiences*, on the contrary, "it *appears* unlikely that we will get closer to the real nature of human experience by leaving behind the particularity of our human point of view" (ibid., p. 174). Indeed, "if the *subjective* character of experience is fully comprehensible only from one point of view, then any shift to greater objectivity – that is, less attachment to a specific viewpoint – does not take us near to the real nature of the phenomenon: it takes us farther from it" (ibid.). If, moreover, "every subjective phenomenon is essentially connected with a *single* point of view", and if the science preferred by physicalists, anti-subjectivists, and identity theorists leans toward a *general, nomological* knowledge, "it seems inevitable that an *objective, physical* theory will abandon that point of view": with clearly negative consequences for the knowledge of the *subjective* phenomena themselves (ibid., p. 167; italics mine).

Since we are discussing questions of an epistemological and cognitive nature, it is appropriate to add that the interpretation of consciousness as subjectivity and "point of view" also contains, for Nagel, definite implications for the way in which consciousness itself should be approached. Given that it is not a 'thing', and much less a physical entity, it is almost superfluous to point out that it cannot be examined by means of physical-natural instruments. But Nagel also stresses – in opposition to the functionalists (and their allies) – that an approach which considers consciousness in terms of functional states is ultimately impracticable. Indeed, it has been clearly shown that such states could also be attributed to robots that "behaved like people *though they experienced nothing*" (ibid., p. 167). Nagel does not mean that a functionalist analysis of consciousness is useless or impossible. But, he points out, it certainly does not give an exhaustive explanation of the peculiar features of consciousness, nor, in all probability, does it even touch upon the core of this dimension that matters most to man. If, in fact, *consciousness is essentially experience* – indeed experience from a particular subjective 'point of view' – then it follows that any attempt to reduce it to mere functions, which can be performed (by robots, etc.) even in the absence of a genuine *subjective experience*, will lead to the loss of one of its most decisive and specific features. Nagel draws some significant lessons from all this. An adequate philosophy of mind, he writes, must elaborate "*new* concepts" and a "*new* method". It will be necessary to pursue "a more objective understanding of the mental in its own right" (ibid., pp. 178–9). In line with these recommendations (which, it should be noted, are not adequately developed), Nagel is also prepared to rehabilitate the introspective approach to the phenomena of the mental and of consciousness.

An even more determined stance, on the issues that concern us, is that taken by Norman Malcolm (Malcolm and Armstrong 1984). Whereas Nagel seemed to admit, at least in principle, the existence of a consciousness in animals as well, Malcolm's refutation of this hypothesis is quite radical. More precisely, he stresses that consciousness as a dimension constituting an object of study for the philosopher of mind can be sensibly attributed only to man (ibid., p. 31). Indeed, it is not simply one mental (perceptive) state among many – as Armstrong, for example, had written. It is, rather, a particular *way of being*, which in its specificity can be ascribed only to human beings as *subjects*. When we say that 'X has the consciousness of. . . ' (or 'X is conscious of. . . ') we are fully aware that we are attributing rather peculiar and pregnant features to X. It is readily evident then that *consciousness*, in the strict sense, cannot exist in animals. If a fly takes flight, it does so for many reasons: but most certainly not because it is "frightened": that is, not because it has the "*consciousness* of some danger" in the way a man might (ibid., pp. 31–2). The truth is that when consciousness is attributed to living beings this is done on the basis of more or less useful "analogies" with human beings. But if by consciousness we mean the infinitely complex range of features and qualities that we all have in mind when we speak about being *conscious* of something, then we must attribute it to human beings alone. Only human beings, writes Malcolm recalling Wittgenstein, "are the paradigms of what can be said to be conscious or unconscious" (ibid., p. 31).

Chapter 10

The mind as 'subject' and as 'being-in-the-world'

Toward a non-mentalistic interpretation of the mental

PERPLEXITIES ABOUT MENTALISM AND 'CARTESIANISM' IN THE CONTEMPORARY PHILOSOPHY OF MIND

The portrait of the mental that emerges from the collaborative effort reconstructed in the preceding chapter is undoubtedly innovative and suggestive. For many philosophers of mind the features attributable to the sensory, intellective, and conscious universe of man constitute a dimension of the human world at once autonomous and different from that of the bodily. Correspondingly, there seems to be a discipline, a 'discourse', relative to that universe characterized by its own irreducible peculiarity. The claims advanced by the identity and eliminationist camps tending in various ways to penalize this discourse now appear to be even less valid than before. It also appears that the knowledge relative to this peculiar 'human' universe can and must be legitimately articulated into distinct cognitive spheres: spheres that, although certainly not in conflict, are accessible to non-coincident types of investigation implying distinct procedures and goals.

It must be pointed out, however, that not all the philosophy of mind committed to rethinking the mental in non-physicalist terms is completely satisfied with the new characterization of the mental we have described above. It is not merely a question of a difference of opinion concerning this or that aspect of the mind, or of its cognitive experience. Nor is it a question of adjusting the picture by *adding* or *subtracting* other marks of the mental. We are dealing, instead, with a dissatisfaction with the very way in which many have proceeded in their redefinition of the mental. In a certain area

236

of thought there lurks the suspicion that this approach was not radical enough and consequently not entirely convincing. Why and in what sense? In the view of many scholars the mental, although reinterpreted by its defenders in rather complex and sophisticated terms, has not been given a sufficiently credible characterization. It remains too ambiguous and lacks full self-sufficiency and legitimacy. It is still an entity (or, if one prefers, a theoretical construct) which could to some extent justify the attempt on the part of certain philosophical and scientific tendencies either to identify it with something else or to eliminate it.

But what is it about the 'mentalistic' perspective that raises doubts among so many philosophers of mind? Perhaps its underlying *vitium* has been that of having insisted too much on the *independence* – on the absolute independence – of the mental; of having believed that to demonstrate the irreducibility of M to B implies that M has a *completely* autonomous way of being; of having maintained, in short, that the mental is in some way *only the mental*, and that, therefore, when we speak about the mental, we speak about *strictly* and *exclusively* 'mentalistic' – that is, psychological – questions. Representative of this approach is the position of H. D. Lewis, undoubtedly one of the most acute analysts of the features peculiar to the mind (Lewis 1969). Lewis is not content to demonstrate the irreducibility of mental phenomena to physical phenomena. Indeed, he insists on the *complete autonomy* of the former. If on the one hand the mind "requires nothing beyond itself for it to be itself" (ibid., p. 231), on the other (and reciprocally) it also *expresses only itself.* And if that were not the case? What if the mental were in fact independent of the physical, and yet did not have a total 'apartness'? If it did not constitute in any meaningful and useful way a *separate* universe? If it referred, at least in part, to a 'further' *denotatum?* What if its language alluded, more or less metaphorically, *also* to different and more complex situations and problems than those described formally? What if, in a word, psychological discourse expressed (or *also* expressed) a world *above and beyond* that traditionally identified with sentience, sapience, and selfhood?

The path suggested by these and related questions has attracted a group of extremely significant scholars. Their objective is to 'read' the mental in a way that, without renouncing certain achievements gained in the mentalistic battle against the reduction of M to B, avoids the traps and risks of psychologism. It is also their aim, and priority, to carry out a critical examination of the assumptions that have led a conspicuous area of the philosophy of mind to elaborate an excessively 'mentalistic' interpretation of the mental.

These scholars have argued to the conclusion that one of the principal matrices of mentalistic assumptions lies in Cartesianism. This is hardly surprising. In certain periods, not a few adversaries of the identity theory have relaunched Descartes. The name of Popper comes to mind, who on more than one occasion has publicly acknowledged the influence of Cartesianism on his interpretation of the mental (Popper and Eccles 1977). But other names could be added: philosophers like H. D. Lewis, whom we have mentioned a few lines above, or Eric Polten (Polten 1973); scientists like Eccles and Penfield (Penfield 1975); scientist-philosophers like Chomsky and Fodor (Chomsky 1968 and Fodor 1983).[1] Further, in addition to those who make explicit reference to Cartesianism there are others who in refuting the identity theory manifest what could be called a *para*-Cartesian inclination (or temptation).

What unites the ranks of this (in part rather heterogeneous) camp is not merely the rejection of materialistic and physicalistic conceptions of the mental. It is also a markedly, even exasperatedly, 'independentistic' interpretation of the mental itself. It is the strong emphasis on the existence of a psychic dimension and of a psychological discourse which are absolutely *sui generis*. And it is, correspondingly, a lack of attention toward what 'else' or 'further' the mental might be as well as toward the possibility of a broader meaning of discourse on the mind. It is for these reasons that a whole lineup of scholars has attacked the Cartesian element in the modern philosophy of mind (and occasionally in modern philosophy in general).

An important source of inspiration for this assault comes, quite naturally, from Ryle: Ryle and his well-known polemic against the postulation of a "ghost in the machine", the misleading duplication of phenomenal experience in a mental experience which cannot be verified, and the constitution (more in general) of an invisible world, the generator of an abstract psychological metaphysics (Ryle 1949). But even without mentioning Ryle we could cite various scholars who subject the 'Cartesian' current of the contemporary philosophy of mind to severe criticism. Marjorie Grene, for exam-

---

1. Feigl, too, points out the existence of a solid Cartesian camp in the contemporary philosophy of mind. Among those he calls "present-day Neo-cartesians" he mentions Beloff, Ducasse, Shaffer, Popper, and Chisholm (Feigl 1967, 139n). See also Charles Landesman (1965).

ple, arguing on phenomenological-existential grounds, has attacked the "over-simple dichotomy" that Cartesianism, old and new, posits between the two traditional polarities of the human and the primacy it gives to an alleged mental/interior world *an sich* (Grene 1976, p. 124). This twofold operation is responsible for the extremely negative gap on the one hand between mind and body and on the other between the mind itself and the worldly context in which it exists and concretely works. In cognitive terms, moreover, the psychology – or science of the mental – that this approach leads to is rather unilateral (since the 'mental' cannot exist *alone*) and modelled on the example of the physical sciences (ibid.). Equally interesting is the position of the neo-physicalist Wilkes, whose main concern is to expose the epistemological implications and assumptions of Cartesian mentalism (Wilkes 1978a). But undoubtedly the most appropriate and significant analysis of certain questions has been carried out by Richard Rorty.

RORTY: THE POLEMIC AGAINST 'MENTALISM' IN MODERN THOUGHT

Rorty's anti-Cartesian and anti-mentalistic position is developed within the framework of an overall attack, launched in *Philosophy and the Mirror of Nature* (henceforth PMN), on a central pillar of Western speculative tradition. This tradition, says Rorty, has set itself three fundamental goals: a) to lay the groundwork for a universal objective knowledge independent of its subjective and linguistic dimension, of different particular/concrete ways of knowing, and of the goals and strategies worked out by man; b) to base practical life on certain principles or myths (Nature, Reason, Truth); c) to claim – in connection with the first two points – a hegemonic, leading role for philosophy. In order to attain these goals (and, at the same time, to strengthen and legitimate itself) this orientation of thought has made a series of 'moves', the most important of which are the following: a) the elaboration of a conception of thinking centered on the notions of foundation, essence, and universal (human reflection must begin with, and arrive at, *these* notions); b) the declaration that the things to be said about the notions listed above – and about other closely connected concepts – are *meta*-scientific, requiring therefore that they be asserted and controlled by a particular (a-scientific) discipline variously called, according to the intellectual context, 'gnoseology', 'epistemology', 'theory of knowledge', 'metaphysics' – or 'philosophy' *tout court*.

Within this framework this speculative orientation has made every effort, particularly in modern times, to underpin the *human* polarity with a special statute. If, in fact, the human sphere had been conceived as one 'thing' or 'phenomenon' among other things and phenomena, it would have been for knowledge just one 'object' among other 'objects'. Instead, for various reasons – beginning with the need for a privileged 'figure' in philosophical discourse capable of sustaining the above-mentioned system of foundations/essences/universals – the prevailing philosophical orientation in the West decided to make the human a largely *sui generis* entity or concept, an entity or concept that has been variously interpreted as cogito, subject, pure ego – or, in only apparently more empirical terms, as mind or consciousness.

It is at this point that the full import, and the theoretical responsibility, of Cartesianism clearly emerges. Indeed, after Plato and before Kant (but with greater emphasis than either) the principal promoter of the 'dilation' of the mental and the human – or better of the human as mental – was Descartes. It is to Cartesian thought that we owe the tendency to construct a metaphysical 'locus' dedicated to foundations and first principles. It is this thought that has given us a 'figure', equally metaphysical, considered capable of grasping these foundations and principles. And it is Cartesianism that has joined this locus and this figure to a definite epistemological design, according to which it is right and proper to distinguish a *knowledge as science* from a *knowledge as philosophy:* the former assigned to the study of empirical-natural phenomena by means of analysis; the latter destined (and legitimated) to perceive 'pure' mental/interior structures through intuition.

As to Rorty, he condemns not only this orientation in Western thought but also (and this is what concerns us here) the Cartesian conception of the mental. It is not that he denies any possible space or plausibility to some form of mentalistic discourse – the phase of the disappearance theory is to a large extent over (see the self-criticism in PMN, pp. 48–9). On the contrary, this 'second' Rorty makes a point of defending the universe of psychological propositions (PMN, p. 243). He frequently and explicitly recognizes the existence of intellectual interests requiring a non-physicalistic 'dictionary'. Rorty does not even hesitate to legitimate the use of a controversial heuristic instrument like introspection. But he is absolutely determined to refute all attempts not only to ontologize the mental but also to give it any form of special treatment. Taken in and of itself the mental is an "invention". It is an invention anchored to an anthropology of passivity and to a gnoseology of 'reflection': man as a being whose cognitive functions are reduced to the mere *representation* of reality by means of a cognitive organon (the mind) equated with a *mirror* (the *mirror of nature*). The mind – we read in an even more trenchant text – is essentially the "stain", the "obscurity" become "obsession" of Western philosophers "when they finally renounce that other obscurity that was the concept of God" (Rorty 1982a, p. 344). In the best of hypotheses the 'mental' is a term or a concept: indeed a "way" of "packaging" certain phenomena (PMN, p. 125). But it is a way which on the one hand designates "excessively heterogeneous notions" and on the other responds (poorly) to vastly different or, even worse, poorly formulated questions. It is possible that in Descartes's time the mind indicated a valid and plausible 'figure'. But today this is no longer the case: the concept is no longer "useful" or "convenient" (ibid., p. 343). Certainly, it is necessary to continue to reject the reductionistic absolutization of matter and body. But we must also reject, with equal firmness, the constitution of a *mental* dimension in a strict and 'separate' sense.

Rorty is fully aware, of course, that the more advanced tendencies in the philosophy of mind have abandoned any ontological interpretation of this dimension. He knows quite well that few contemporary philosophers of mind identify themselves explicitly with Cartesianism. But he is convinced that many adversaries of the identity theory often risk succumbing to a definite and misleading temptation. It is perfectly well and good to search for the marks of the mental – especially if this helps to articulate the overall picture of man. But this does not mean that we should accept the existence of a 'second nature' in man himself, and much less the myth of interiority (indeed it must be denied that "persons have more of an inside than particles": Rorty 1982a, p. 183). And we can also accept a language of the mental – which may enrich the ways of describing in certain ways the complex human world. But we must make sure that this language does not close itself off in a *mentalistic* account of the mind. Rorty's proposal is that we raise an entirely new, hermeneutical question: what do we really, or essentially, mean by 'mental'? What does psychological discourse really concern itself with? It is questions like these that have led Rorty and a handful of other scholars to advance what may be the most mature and sophisticated theses of the contemporary philosophy of mind.

FROM THE 'PHILOSOPHY OF MIND' TO THE 'PHILOSOPHY OF THE SUBJECT'

One of the first to investigate in the direction of the issues noted above was Thomas Nagel in the essay 'What Is It Like to Be a Bat?' His aim in this study is not (as some seem to think) to create a 'consciousness-entity' but to raise the question of what the *objectum*, the *effective* referent of psychological discourse actually is. Nagel's first assumption is that the mental cannot be identified with any physical component of man – nor can it be viewed as a separate entity. It is to be conceived, rather, as the *subjective dimension of his being and doing.* Consequently, if we want to provide a correct interpretation of the mind and its philosophy, it is indispensable to revisit the problems surrounding the "subjective". It is not incidental that consciousness – the main subject of Nagel's essay – reappears under the pregnant definition of "*subjective* character of experience" (Nagel 1979, p. 179). In this regard, Nagel emphasizes that this definition does not merely connote one of the many aspects of experience itself but individuates its *essential, central nature.* Thus subjectivity becomes the most peculiar trait of the mental/ 'personal' life of man. This position follows on what Nagel had already written in his essay on physicalism: "I cannot be a mere physical object, because I possess my mental states: I am their *subject*, in a way in which no physical object can possibly be the subject of its attributes" (Nagel 1965, in Rosenthal 1971, p. 108).

This is not a matter, of course, of simply clarifying the logical and linguistic terms of the problem. On the contrary, it is the lucid individuation of the 'pole' which concretely directs, or which is concretely referred to by, man's mental being/doing. On closer examination (and this is the crucial discovery made by Nagel and others), an investigation of the mental concerns the study not so much of certain *states* and *events* in themselves as of an *active being:* a being which is the *subject* of certain sentiences and sapiences, a being which qualifies in a particular way the whole of a definite experience. This being – as we saw in the passage cited above – is the *self*, the *subject* itself. Nagel's essay on bats is to a great extent inspired by this perspective. After all, an analysis of *mental* states and processes is impossible, or at the very least incomplete, if it is carried out without attributing to them a *subjective* referent. "Does it make sense", Nagel asks at a certain point (in a passage that has merited repeated citation in our essay), "to ask what my experiences are *really* like, as opposed to how they appear to be to me" (Nagel 1979, p. 178). Indeed, who if not *my self* constitutes *my* experience? What if not *my subjectivity* constitutes the modality by which I experience *my* mental states and acts?

It is possible to check, so to speak, the validity of this claim. If, observes Nagel, from an experience (sensory, intellective, affective, social) I eliminate the *subjective* dimension or point of view, what is really left? Actually, there remains (almost) nothing (ibid., p. 173). If I eliminate my *Erlebnis* of a perception, or an idea, or a feeling, what remains is purely and simply a certain neurophysiological and/or biochemical fact: but the *experience* – the experience as what I personally have lived, as the *inextricable* intersection of a certain situation and the way this takes form in me in the light of a thousand other psycho-subjective components of *mine* – *that* experience essentially vanishes.

Nagel is clearly not content merely to rehabilitate consciousness. Nor does he limit himself to restoring the features (however peculiar) of selfhood. Indeed, he goes on to identify in the self the essential 'constituent', the essential 'qualifier' of the mental world. Joy and pain, memory and thought, choice and intention are, it is true, *mental* events or states; but only in a certain sense, only on the basis of a very broad signification of 'mental'. Actually, when I speak of joys and pains, of memories and thoughts, of choices and intentions, I am not really speaking about particular *mental* states and events: I am speaking first and foremost about an individual who *is* – or who experiences – those states and events. What is a joy independently of a being that rejoices? What is a pain independently of a being that suffers? (Nagel 1965, in Rosenthal 1971, p. 98). When we say that depression is a psychic phenomenon we are actually using a somewhat reductive metaphor. It is not, after all, a *mind* that can be depressed but a *person*, as Margolis once wrote (Margolis 1978, p. 51). Only beings as subjects are entities of which we can meaningfully predicate *mental* states, properties, functions. In other words, *when we speak of the 'mental', we are actually speaking, at least to a large extent, about something that concerns the 'subject'.* Not always and not necessarily, but unavoidably within certain cognitive spheres, the philosophy of mind tends to take the form of philosophy of the subject.

It was a keen student of the MBP, Howard Robinson, who argued emphatically that a *new* philosophy of the mind must concentrate its attention essentially on the pole of the self, the subject. "It is subjectivity", he stresses, "that poses the problems [the *crucial* problems] for the physicalist" (Robinson 1982, p. 124). It is precisely the subject, the self that is left out of the materialistic perspective. The same opinion is expressed by Keith Gunderson, a philosopher of mind of quite a different theoretical inspiration. In his view the main problem for a certain kind of investigation of man lies precisely in the subject. The self, he says, constitutes above all "what seems to resist descriptions" of the physicalistic type. Gunderson's "perplexities" (the term used in the title of his article) concerning this situation are of no small account. If it is not possible "to show the ego installed comfortably at home in the sphere of the physical", its principal attributes – thoughts, feelings, and sensations (that is to say, everything that is normally referred to by the 'mental') – "will not seem to be at rest" in that domain either (Gunderson, in Rosenthal 1971, p. 112). It follows that a physicalistically constituted science of the mental can be neither constructed nor conceived. In Gunderson's opinion, in fact, the self will never be convincingly reduced to a physical entity. On the contrary, not only is it not susceptible of such reduction by objective science: it is also not susceptible (or not always) of an appropriate knowledge on the part of the subject itself (ibid., p. 147).

The limits of Robinson's and Gunderson's positions cannot go unmentioned. Robinson does not investigate the question of the self. He confines himself to a passing allusion and regards it as an abstraction, a sort of 'black hole' for materialism. Materialism, in fact, tends to barricade itself behind impenetrable theoretical walls for fear that a notion like that of the subject might reveal itself to be the Trojan horse of a renewed mysticism. As to Gunderson, he maintains that if the self cannot enter the citadel of knowledge, this is not such a great loss, since the concept appears to him "not needed in our descriptions of the world" (ibid., p. 126). Moreover, it can also be argued that as an entity, the ego is not completely autonomous and self-sufficient since there are significant traces in the egos of others: "each of us", he writes, "is then in a position to see and describe ourselves *via* an acceptance of how others see and describe us" (ibid., pp. 126–7). This conclusion, despite its Sartrian *allure,* is somewhat disappointing. Wasn't the problem, after all, the unsettling presence of a *different* perspective on our selves, that is, of a *subjective* point of view on the self which cannot be reduced to the point of view of *others?* And doesn't this proposal that our self-knowledge should be mediated by the knowledge of others bear some disturbing reifying, behavioristic implications?

On the other hand, however, the problems and exigencies expressed by Robinson and Gunderson are profoundly symptomatic: they attest, in some way, to the emergence of a new theoretical need. A certain area of contemporary thought has been quick to take a further step forward and save the concept group self-consciousness-subject from the danger of being imprisoned in an abstract mentalistic sphere, by 'expanding' what has traditionally been called 'the mind' into a broader, more complex, and more concrete figure: that of the human, of the person.

ON THE RELATIONSHIP BETWEEN THE
SUBJECT, THE PERSON-BRAIN,
AND THE BODILY

In relation to this line of research it is striking to find that certain highly esteemed scientists assume (often as self-evident) that the *brain* is *itself* the *subject,* the *self.* Indeed, on occasion the brain is even used as a *quasi-synonym* of the subject – as when the neurophysiologist Rodolfo Llinas contends, "We are capable, or . . . the *brain* is capable, of generating our feelings, hopes, loves, memories, etc." (Llinas 1979, in Piattelli Palmarini 1984). At other times the brain is even more radically *identified* with the self – a position which risks regressing to the problems inherent in the traditional identity theory. If this is how things stand, it is difficult to resist the temptation to recall once again the decisive objections raised by Malcolm:

> Could a *brain* have thoughts, illusions or pains? The sense-lessness of the supposition seems so obvious that I find it hard to take it seriously. No experiment could establish this result for a brain. Why not? The fundamental reason is that a brain does not sufficiently resemble a human being. (Malcolm 1965, in Borst 1979, pp. 179–80)

And in another passage, "*People*, see, hear, think – not brains . . . A brain does not have the right physiognomy nor the capacity for participating in any of the forms of life that would be required for it to be a subject of experience (Malcolm 1971, p. 77). As regards the neurocerebral system, what is important, as we have pointed out elsewhere, is to recognize that it performs an essential 'instrumental', mediating function in the realization of actual psychic *experience* on the part of the *subject*. As O. L. Zangwill wrote some years ago, "to say 'the person perceives the painting by virtue of his right hemisphere' is clumsy and *suggests only that the right hemisphere is necessary for that process*" (Zangwill 1977, p. 163; italics mine).

It should be added that similar theses are advanced by many philosophers of mind committed to the recognition and emancipation of the self as a psycho-existential subject. More generally, the recurring (and sometimes prevailing) theme in the texts of writers like Wilkerson, Malcolm, Margolis, Nagel, Weimer, and Robinson is that of the non-coincidence between the brain and the bodily, on the one hand, and the self and the subject, on the other. As Shaffer had written in the sixties, "at least *some* of the things we say about human beings" can – and probably must – be analyzed as "a set of remarks about a nonphysical entity (a body)" (Shaffer 1966, p. 59).

But Shaffer does not stop here. On closer examination, he observes, when we say that 'the body is the subject of something' (whether of a state or an act), what is actually meant is not the *body* as such, but rather its *owner:* that is, once again, a *self*, a *subject*. This distinction is particularly important because it holds only for entities that can effectively be *titulars* of *mental* events (in the usual broad sense of the term). When I say a man is happy, I must distinguish between his body (which at most may present certain *physical* conditions, expressions or implications generally connected with happiness) and his *self*, the only *subject* that really experiences the state of happiness. In contrast, when I speak about a rock, there is no need to separate the rock as 'subject' from the rock as 'body': the two predicates coincide.

On the basis of these and other considerations, Shaffer insists on what he calls the mere *contingency* of the relationship between the body and the subject (or the person). This means that the two 'entities' or 'figures' are linked, but only *usually* and *not necessarily*. An eloquent demonstration of this is provided by what happens as a consequence of death. It could be argued that this event concerns only the *body* and not the *subject*, since the latter remains as a referent of memories, meanings, and values. Conversely, one could argue – as Shaffer prefers to do – that what disappears is only the *subject*, while the *body* (though physically altered) continues to exist: however, it continues to exist – and this is the crucial point – not as *my* body (belonging to a particular subject), but as a mere physical entity (ibid., p. 64). "What makes me the particular person I am", Shaffer concludes, "is different from what makes my body the particular body it is" (ibid., p. 65).

RORTY: FROM THE MIND AS SUBJECT
TO THE MIND AS ACTING MAN

Working along similar lines, Rorty gives expression to some crucial, to a certain extent inevitable, theses. Let us accept that the mental is the subjective, and that speaking about the mind is, to a considerable extent, tantamount to speaking about the subject. But *why* is it that men talk about this mental sphere? What – if anything – is behind the debate on the subject? Rorty's answer to these questions is of capital importance. It must be admitted, he says, that man's preoccupation with the mental is not casual or unjustified. It is also true that there is 'something else' behind talk about the subject. In Rorty's view, men speak about the 'mental' *as a way of investigating the specificity and autonomy of the human sphere* (Rorty 1982b, pp. 323–37 and 343–4). What appears to be *psychological* discourse is in reality *humanological* discourse. More precisely (or more ambitiously), the 'mentalistic' inquiry aims at the allegedly more *certain* foundation of *being men,* or of *doing-as-men.*

If all this is true, then we have further confirmation of the principle that the bodily – or rather the relationship with the bodily – plays a relatively minor role in the debate on the MBP. It is not that we are a definite kind of entity (i.e., human beings) because of a particular relationship between the so-called mind and the so-called body. Nor does *being* human coincide *having* certain (psycho) physical properties. Actually, our peculiar way of *being* is to be identified with something quite different: not with "having additional faculties", but rather (and this is Rorty's main point) with *acting* in a certain way (Rorty 1982b, p. 322).

Of course this 'way', being anomalous and impalpable, creates formidable difficulties for a knowledge accustomed to reasoning in terms of what is substantial, or at least visible or visualizable. It was, for Rorty, with the aim of overcoming these difficulties in a reassuring manner that Western thought elaborated the figure of the Mind. It is the figure that gives consistency and dignity to the specific 'essence' of man. The strength of this elaboration lies in its capacity to transfer, by reducing the *quid proprium* of man to *mind*, an extremely complex anthropological and existential problem onto a theoretical plane which Western thought has always considered, so to speak, under control.

Rorty shares this interpretation of the problem and of the solution, respectively faced and proposed by Western thought. He is also perfectly aware that a proper understanding of the presumed essences, according to which a man is a *man*, creates serious problems. It is quite reasonable to think that man is not only his bodily organization. But it is not easy to respond convincingly to the question of "what more a human being is than his flesh", especially for those who are not willing to accept an answer that smacks of metaphysics or spiritualism (Rorty 1979, p. 34). Rorty's answer significantly shifts the question of the characterization of the human sphere from the *theoretical and metaphysical plane* to that of *praxis*. The 'human', he says, undoubtedly exists. But it does not exist in the form of an entity or property (not even as a 'mind' or a 'mental'). It cannot be sought, then, at the level of more or less visible essences, facts, or functions. Correspondingly, it does not belong to the analytical and descriptive terrain of science (ibid., p. 248). Rather, the 'human' is the matrix and the consequence of a series of *choices, decisions,* and *acts* (ibid., pp. 34–8). It must be sought, then, essentially on the plane of *evaluations, behaviors,* and *actions*. It can be reached not by *demonstration,* but by *belief, will, commitment.* Man, Rorty stresses, is first and foremost a *doing* and an *acting* – a *poiesis*. Man can be understood not by dissecting him into parts and properties, but by examining his concrete *operari*. In this *operari* sentience, sapience, and selfhood are inextricably intertwined, attesting to the irreducible, active nature of man. In a suggestive passage Rorty writes: "we are a poetic species, the one that can change itself by changing its own behavior . . . " (Rorty 1982b, p. 346).

The conclusion Rorty draws from these considerations is quite clear. Men are right in posing the question of their identity, of the peculiarity and specificity of their being compared with that of other entities and phenomena. However, they are mistaken in wanting to found this being on the figures of the mind and consciousness. The characterization of the human in psychological terms is weak: the mental only serves man as a means of expressing – in encoded, abbreviated form – far more complex situations. It follows, then, that if we study the mental *an sich*, we risk missing some of the most substantial meanings and implications of what we are studying. Consequently, a large part of the language of psychology should be reformulated or, at least, reinterpreted. What must be understood is that it 'says' not so much mental phenomena as aspects of a reality (human reality) which is less *'pure', psychic,* and *interior,* and more *'practical', existential,* and *worldly* than is generally believed. When I manifest a pain, a hope, or a design, I do not express certain 'facts' called mental events: I express, rather, the peculiarity of my nature as a man, the personal way in which I experience certain situations, characterized by my own subjectivity. For this reason an analysis of so-called mental phenomena becomes well-founded and credible only if I carry it out as an analysis of my concrete being, of my effective doing. As Ryle has written (in a passage we have already cited), only "human actions and reactions" and "what man says and does not say" constitute the "right and only manifestations to study: the only that might deserve . . . the grandiose title of 'mental phenomena' " (Ryle 1949, p. 302).

The reference to Ryle seems particularly appropriate, since he was the first to advance an interpretation of the human in 'poetic' terms and of the mental as a, perhaps indirect, way of describing this peculiar 'poetic' quality. Readers of *The Concept of Mind* have given too much weight to Ryle's broad anti-metaphysical and anti-Cartesian polemic. Actually, alongside this *destruens* argument, there unfolds a *construens* one of no lesser significance. The issue, for Ryle, is not merely to demolish what he calls the "intellectualistic legend" of Western thought. We must also rehabilitate the practical life of man and defend – but in the 'right' way – its theoretical foundations. If Western thought created a fetish called 'mind', this is in part because it quite rightly wanted to affirm a certain interpretation of practical life: an interpretation which gives priority, in the era of mechanization, to the figure of the subject as a conscious and responsible being (ibid., p. 73). For Ryle (and this is the point) the general intention was a serious one, even though some (or many) of the arguments were wrong. Indeed, something like an autonomous life, linked to definite human capacities, does exist despite the determinism that governs the world we live in. We have seen that not all the problems of human life are physical or reducible to physical terms (ibid., p. 74). There continue to exist ways of being and acting on the part of man that are bound not to *causes* but to *reasons*, not to *facts* (or to *laws*) but to *choices*. Correspondingly, the universe of mental language seeks to ground and express this nature, this teleological, axiological, decisional vocation of man. It seeks to ground and express the fact that man is not merely an acting animal but an animal that acts according to *aims* and *goals*. If the point is poorly argued, in that it refers to an irreal figure called 'mind', this does not imply that the topic of discussion is meaningless. We must then go back and look at the question carefully, salvaging the *message* and discarding the *medium*. Yet the admittedly singular metaphors of *psychology* express *humanological* qualities of crucial importance, which Ryle passionately defends. Speaking of the mental means reinterpreting "certain. . ." in such a way as to recognize their rational and moral characteristics (ibid., p. 171). It means speaking about what *man* as a *rational, acting person* "knows, tends. . ." (ibid., p. 206). It means highlighting the peculiar "commitments" and "evaluations" that man manifests (again as a person) when he faces the problems and dilemmas of reality. Not surprisingly, the concepts Ryle finds more adequate to talking about and judging the mental in its concrete acting are those of responsibility, merit, and demerit (ibid., p. 17). While firmly opposing any sort of "duplication" of the human world, Ryle steadfastly defends the absolutely *sui generis* features of man, which emerge *also* from the bizarre dictionary of psychology. "Men", wrote Ryle, in a passage that scarcely seems to have aged at all, "are not machines, not even ghost-ridden machines. They are men – a tautology which is sometimes worth remembering" (ibid., p. 79).

THE DISCOVERY OF THE 'PERSON'

When, in the heat of his attack on Cartesianism, Rorty writes that consciousness should be studied "like *any* other thing", indeed like any other "particle" (Rorty 1982b, p. 183), he assumes a position that may leave more than a few scholars perplexed. When, more generally, he tends to deny the mental its own autonomous foundation, his argument is too peremptory. It is also a pity that he does not carry out a thorough analysis of the *subject* of mental phenomenology. And it is surprising that notwithstanding the stress he lays on the exterior, worldly dimension of human and mental action, he does not examine what it is in the world that promotes, qualifies, and conditions this action.

This twofold task has, on the contrary, occupied various scholars of a rather different orientation: Wilkerson, Malcolm, Margolis, Grene, Dreyfus. While not willing to dissolve the whole mental universe, or to reinterpret it as a merely 'humanological' one, they fully agree with the thesis that the language of psychology concerns something far more complex than simply mental states or events. This explains why they direct their attention to this peculiar and *sui generis* 'something'. But it must not be supposed that in doing so they aim to resuscitate in some way a dualistic conception of the human being (roughly, an empirical and metaphysical conception of man). In this connection Malcolm has stressed that if, on the one hand, it is unfortunate that so many philosophers of mind "have lost sight of *the bearer* of mental predicates", this does not mean that one must fall back on forms of direct or indirect Cartesianism. "Today's philosophy", writes Malcolm, "has justifiedly turned its back on the Cartesian conception". And yet the rejection of this conception should not imply that the philosophy of mind can do without a subject to which psychic states and events can be ascribed. The nature, or the identity, of this subject certainly raises many problems, but Malcolm does not shirk his responsibility to propose a solution. Neither the brain, nor the mind, nor much less a 'machine', he emphasizes, is the true referent of psychological language, but only *man*. Man is the only being which may be described in psychological terms as "ignorant, timid, conceited, ambitious, affectionate, greedy, generous, honest, despairing, devoted, ungrateful, resentful, resolute" (Malcolm and Armstrong 1984, p. 101).

It is this referent, this central figure of psychological experience that is often given the name *person*. In underlining the need for a subject of psychic experiences, Nagel had already spoken of the existence of a "person" that lives such experiences. On closer examination, writes Nagel, the so-called MBP concerns a possible relationship not between sensations, thoughts and the like and brain processes, but rather between a *body* (not the pure and simple *brain*) and a *person*. The existence of pains, he adds, presupposes the existence of *individuals* that experience them (Nagel 1965, in Rosenthal 1971, p. 98).

It should be added that the use of the concept of person within a definite intellectual area does not lack significant precedents. At least as early as the sixties Anglo-American thought, both philosophical and socio- (as well as psycho-) anthropological, was rediscovering the 'person'. This revival had various sources – first and foremost of which was the need to reconsider the human universe from a non-reductionist, non-physicalistic perspective. Apart from rare exceptions, this discovery had absolutely nothing to do with the notion of the person defended by the spiritualistic orientation present in European thought between the wars. No Anglo-American scholar uses the concept 'person', while thinking, more or less secretly, of the concept 'spirit'. Moreover, if there have been some in the United States who have spoken of "personology" – for example, H. Murray (in Hall and Lindzey 1957, chap. 5) and W. P. Alston (in Harré 1976, chap. 4) – the label has never been confused with personalism. In other words, it is not metaphysical ambitions but definite empirical and interpretive needs (obviously underpinned by a well-determined philosophical and epistemological perspective) that urge many philosophers, anthropologists, and sociologists to highlight the notion of person. The elaboration of this notion, Wilkerson has written with admirable clarity,

> arises from one very simple and non-tendentious observation, namely that human beings appear to have many properties which the rest of nature (with the exception of some animals) do not. They can think, act, perceive, feel certain emotions, and so on; trees, stones, tables cannot. To analyse the concept of the person is essentially to analyse these peculiar properties. Whether we call them 'mental' properties (or more disastrously, lumping them together, 'a mind') or not matters very little. (Wilkerson 1974, p. 9)

It is well known that one of the principal points of reference for Anglo-American "personology" is 'Persons' by Peter Strawson. In this text, published toward the end of the fifties, the authoritative exponent of analytical philosophy faces the complex question of the primary referent of propositions concerning the human being. Strawson holds that we must distinguish between two types of predicate: those that ascribe "corporeal characteristics, a physical situation, etc.", and those which ascribe "states of consciousness" (Strawson 1959 p. 104). The first type of predicate is correctly applied essentially to material bodies; the second kind includes "all the other predicates we apply to persons" (ibid.). According to Strawson, it would be mistaken to infer from this division an argument in support of Cartesian dualism. It would be equally wrong to suppose that the 'subject' of utterances concerning the human sphere can only be consciousness. One reason for this is that since man unquestionably appears composed in a certain way (as much 'physical' as 'psychic'), "a necessary condition" in order that the states of consciousness can be ascribed to something as a human being is that they can be ascribed to entities also endowed with physical properties. "States of consciousness", Strawson adds, "could not be ascribed at all, *unless* they were ascribed to *persons*" (ibid., p. 102). In other words, it is the person, and only the person, that Strawson considers the fundamental referent of psychological, 'humanological' language.

Strawson makes a point of underlining that this concept is *irreducible* and *logically primitive*. It is irreducible in that it is in no way made up of parts such that their mere *sum* produces a person. To see oneself as a person, writes Strawson, means "a lot of things, but not a lot of separate and unconnected things" (ibid., p. 112). The figure of the person is also "logically primitive" in the sense that it precedes ideally that of consciousness as well as that of the bodily. An appropriate linguistic, conceptual analysis reveals, Strawson argues, that it is impossible to consider the person "as a secondary kind of entity in relation to two primary Kinds, viz., a particular consciousness and a particular human body" (ibid., p. 105). (On the primitiveness of the concept of person see the supporting arguments in Wilkerson 1974, p. 21, and the opposing ones in E. Wilson 1979, pp. 202–4.)

Many of the questions raised in Strawson's essay concern issues and problems of a strictly theoretical nature. However, the widespread interest in the concept of the person shown by contemporary thought is particularly evident within the framework of the problems posed by the human sciences, and especially in connection with the development of action theory and the MBP. This should not be surprising. The debate spurred in particular by action theory (a debate which is still in course) has shown in a number of ways that *subjective, individual action* cannot be reduced to *typologically and nomologically defined behavior*. If it is true that much of the discussion on action theory has focused on the structure and logic of action in itself (or on the structure and logic of its explanation), it is also true that many scholars have considered it equally important to identify the features which characterize the subject responsible for action. As Bruce Aune has written, limiting oneself to the analysis of *agency* alone may appear to be a rather unilateral enterprise: what is necessary is to correlate this analysis with an adequate study of the agent (Aune 1977). In this connection, the concept of person has made a valid contribution to the characterization of the agent and has served to stimulate action theorists to investigate the subjective and existential dimension of the 'producer' of action.

An example of this link and interaction between the concepts of action and person is provided in the classic book by Rom Harré and P. F. Secord on the explanation of social behavior (Harré and Secord 1972). On the one hand, the two scholars stress the specificity of human agency and its irreducibility to mere *physical movement* (cf., *contra*, Armstrong's theses summarized in Chapter 2). Action, they argue, cannot be separated from an intentional, goal-oriented, individual component, bound to a cultural and axiological matrix which is absent in the case of movement. On the other hand, Harré and Secord insist with equal force on the organic connection between agency and a subject-that-acts. And to the extent that the observer seeks to identify the *specific, particular* content of a definite action, this subject can be neither a *man* in a generic sense, nor much less a mere *body*. It can only be a *person:* a person in the sense of a being characterized existentially, culturally, and socially. Only a 'personological' inquiry will enable the observer to carry out an adequate examination of the action in question. It is essential, write Harré and Secord, "to conceive of human beings as *persons*" (ibid., p. 59). The implications of this suggestive formula are not limited to the anthropological and moral sphere. There is also an allusion to the need to promote the 'personal' subject to the role of protagonist of any investigation which aims to grasp and interpret (at least from a certain cognitive standpoint) psychic, behavioral, and social events. In the end, only this individual subject can provide the testimony essential to an understanding of what he himself feels, thinks, and does. This is one reason why Harré and Secord (and also Margolis) strive to rehabilitate the so-called first-person reports as a valid source of information about what the subject experiences psychologically, interpersonally, and socially (ibid., pp. 41–3, and chaps. 6 and 14; Margolis 1978, p. 72).

THE CENTRALITY OF THE 'PERSON'
IN THE PHILOSOPHY OF MIND

Action theory is far too complex a question to be treated within the boundaries of a discussion of the mind–body relationship. We shall have occasion to return to the problem in the near future. Here we should return to the concept of person and its implications for the MBP. We might begin by recalling what Aune says about the necessary connections between the agency and its agent. Just as Aune holds that an adequate study of action cannot do without an investigation of the figure of the *acting* person, in the same way it is indispensable for many students of the MBP to examine the figure of the *feeling, thinking* person as the subject of *mental phenomena.*

The determination with which various philosophers of mind focus their attention on the figure of the person is amply documented. A significant example is Tom Settle, who, in a critical examination of Mario Bunge's work, stresses the need to identify the subject of mental events "with the *person* rather than with the *mind*" (Settle 1981, p. 358). Even more to the point is the position of Herbst, who writes that the philosophy of mind must finally understand that, in reality, "there are no *mental entities*. . . , but only *mental modes of persons*" (Herbst 1967, p. 40; italics mine). Marjorie Grene is another: "I have suggested we take the 'person' rather than the 'mind' as our central concept" (Grene 1976, p. 124).

The pertinence of the concept of person in the context of the MBP is so clearly felt that, at least roughly speaking, 'person' is for some nearly synonymous with 'mind' (obviously in the more pregnant sense of the term). Thus, for example, in his search for an entity or concept which could appropriately sustain as predicates expressions relative to mental states and events, Margolis finds that "it is characteristic to speak of *persons* or of minds or of individuals as are thought to be persons or to be agents of some sort" (Margolis 1973b, p. 224). Isn't it true, moreover, that in everyday speech we say things like 'X is (or has) a good mind', or – the example is Squires's – 'the best heads around were at the conference'? Aren't phrases such as these rather imprecise, in that what is meant by 'mind' is really an *individual*, a *thinking being?* After all, it is not a *mind* but a *person* that can be considered 'good', or 'intelligent', or 'worthy'.

In the course of his argumentation Squires makes another crucial point: he maintains (and this is the second use or interpretation of the concept that concerns us here) that 'person' is a quasi-synonym of 'subject' – or more precisely of the *subjective totality* of an individual in a particular psycho-behavioral state. One cannot attribute to a *part* – much less to a *bodily* part – what *man* does: "it is a *person* that laughs, with his mouth; it is a *person* that gesticulates, with his arms" (Squires 1970, p. 353). And just as we do not speak of a mere *part* of the human being when we refer to his gestures or acts, in the same way we do not speak of only a *part* (the brain? the mind?) of someone when we say that he is suffering, thinking, or planning. It is always and exclusively a 'holistic', unitary entity (a *subject-entity*) that suffers, thinks, or plans. The *person* – and only the person – is the *irreducible* subject responsible for individual thoughts and interpersonal relationships.

It will not be surprising if, once the person is conceived as a quasi-synonym first of mind, then of the psychically and behaviorally acting human subject, many philosophers of mind point out the radical difference between the person itself and the body as an object of natural knowledge. A case in point is Sellars (1965, p. 443). Even more explicit is the position advanced by Herbst, one of the most acute proponents of the connection between the concepts of person and mind: "Persons have a multitude of characteristics which cannot conceivably be the characteristics of their bodies". Indeed, an analysis of the person "involves one in saying what he thinks, feels, desires": all properties that may be *connected* to, but can certainly not be *reduced* to, physical processes (Herbst 1967, pp. 38–9).

The irreducible heterogeneity between the person and the body has been investigated most thoroughly by Wilkerson. The issue on which he insists most is the necessary difference between the descriptions of entities called persons and those of bodily entities. At a general level descriptions – or at least an important class of descriptions – must be able to grasp the *specificity* of things. Thus, if I describe a soccer ball, for example, merely as a leather sphere I have not individuated many features which in our sociocultural society are considered essential of that 'sphere' (Wilkerson 1974, pp. 171–2). Similarly, if I describe a person as a mere bodily organism, I miss many properties which are rather important for certain cognitive interests. "An account of persons", Wilkerson adds, "should be concerned with those properties, P-properties, which tend to distinguish people from other material things" (ibid., p. 155). There is more. From a logical and semantic point of view it is empirically demonstrable that the categories used to refer to persons and their actions are "logically quite distinct from the categories of physicalism" (ibid., p. 172). Finally, an appropriate linguistic analysis reveals that the apparently common subject of statements (referring to a *lato sensu* human *denotatum*), though closely linked, may in reality be *two different* subjects. If I say, for instance, 'He is near the apple tree and he is eating', the first part of the statement refers to a *bodily entity*, while the second refers to an *acting* person or subject.

Given certain premises, the independence of the person from the bodily might seem in some sense obvious. A more delicate question, however, concerns the relationship between the 'personal' and the 'mental'. We have already seen that some scholars (Squires, e.g.) tend to consider – at least in certain cases – the two terms or concepts quasi-synonymous. Other philosophers of mind, instead, prefer to stress – as Ryle had suggested in the forties (1949, p. 161) – the 'surplus' of the 'personal' with respect to the 'mental'. This is the case of Wilkerson. Certainly, Wilkerson often assigns a special role to the relationship between person and mind, since the latter in many ways permits characterization and individualization the former (Wilkerson 1974, p. 60). Yet he is equally insistent on the autonomy (and the greater complexity) of the person. No commitment, however praiseworthy, to rehabilitating the mental must involve reducing the scope of the human. One thing is certain: the person does not consist exclusively of sensations and thoughts. The person, as concrete subjectivity, is also made up of *behaviors* and *actions:* behaviors and actions whose contents and modalities are often not intelligible when considered only within the sphere of the mental. The main reason for this, writes Wilkerson, is that behaviors and actions "may involve reference to human institutions, conventions, rules" (ibid., p. 57).

All this, while suggesting that the person cannot always be analyzed according to mental categories, certainly does not imply that it must be excluded from the inquiries of the philosophy of mind. It does mean, however, that basing these inquiries on the referent 'person' requires that the reflection on the mental continually expand its horizons to a broader, 'ultra-' or even 'extra-'psychological, plane. An approach which recognizes that the psychic state cannot avoid involving a subject/person that experiences it must necessarily connect the analysis of that state to an analysis of the *context* in which the subject lives his experience: not least because it is possible (indeed probable) that this context considerably affects the experience in question. In other words, it is precisely the unavoidable reference of the mental *experience* to an *experiencing* subject/person that makes it necessary to mediate the mental with the *Umwelt* in which it occurs. It follows, then, that psychology as a science of certain events and processes must link up with (through the science of the subject/person of these events and process) the science of their social, historical, and cultural context.

MARJORIE GRENE: THE MENTAL AS 'BEING-IN-THE-WORLD'

Of the scholars who have reconsidered the philosophy of mind from a non-mentalistic, 'humanological' perspective few have stressed more forcefully than Marjorie Grene and Hubert Dreyfus the need for an analysis of the mental capable of accounting for the influences that determine its being and acting in a concrete *worldly* situation.

Well-grounded in Heidegger, Sartre, Merleau-Ponty, and in contemporary *philosophische Anthropologie* (Plessner, Rothacker, etc.), Grene firmly rejects any sort of reified, reductionistic conception of man. Her scholarly commitment in a well-defined area of inquiry (the philosophy of life) leads her to be particularly adverse toward the biologistic tendencies in the human sciences. "I have been arguing", she writes in an essay on sociobiology, "against the reduction of the mental to the biological, in particular to terms of evolutionary biology" (Grene 1977, p. 221). Attacking the theses advanced by E. O. Wilson and other sociobiologists, Grene contends that biological knowledge can at best individuate certain "necessary conditions" of the genesis of higher psychic activities: but "to discover the biological conditions of mental development is not to say how, within those conditions, the mind *works*" (ibid., p. 219; italics mine).

Not surprisingly, then, Grene devotes considerable attention to the delicate question of the autonomy of the mental (and of the human). This does not mean that she is inclined to re-present some form of ontologistic, dualistic interpretation of man. On the contrary, she vigorously criticizes this orientation and stresses the "uselessness, if not the absurdity, of *any* concept of substance, *whether* mental *or* material" (Grene 1976, p. 118). Moreover, as we have already pointed out, she (like Rorty) is a relentless adversary of Descartes, whom she considers the main source of the abstract metaphysics of the human subsequently taken up by a certain area of modern thought. Descartes is contested both because he opposes men to beasts and because of his conception of the relationship between mind and body. Conceiving the living body, Grene writes, "as a machine with, in man, a completely incorporeal yet communicating entity mysteriously attached [to the body itself] raises all the insoluble problems of interaction that everyone has been pointing out for three centuries" (Grene 1974, p. 244). In the second place, Descartes is attacked for his 'separatistic' and privatistic conception of the mental: "it is important to insist", writes Grene in her article on sociobiology, "that 'mind' need not – indeed, should not – be understood either as substance or as subjectivity: as a separate entity, a *res cogitans*" (Grene ,1977, p. 215). This interpretation, in fact, has led many to absolutize the self, enclosing it in what is significantly called the "cage of subjectivity".

It is precisely this reaction against Cartesian mentalism that makes Grene one of the staunchest supporters of the concept of the person in the contemporary philosophy of mind. "I have suggested", she writes in an important passage we have already cited, "we take the *'person'* rather than the *'mind'* as our central concept" (Grene 1976, p. 124; italics mine). In effect, it is no longer possible to carry out an adequate psychoanthropological reflection on the sole basis of the notion of mind. What, after all, are mental events and processes if not acts and experiences of 'someone'? And who is this 'someone' if not man himself? One should be careful, however. When we evoke the notion 'man', we always run the risk of employing either a figure which refers to an all too generic theoretical background (which may even be crypto-metaphysical, as in man as Man), or a notion anchored to an excessively naturalistic domain (man as a bodily entity). This is why Grene insists not so much on the concept of man as on that of person: a concept which, from her point of view, contributes to a better defined and more sophisticated interpretation of the human being as a conscious, cultural, and social subject.

Grene acknowledges her debt to certain contemporary 'personologists' such as Strawson and, to some extent, Polanyi. At the same time, however, she quite rightly highlights the originality of her own theoretical contribution. Of particular importance is the distinction she draws between the 'subjective' and the 'personal'. The first term/concept is weaker, or at least in a sense more 'delimited'.

It indicates, writes Grene, "a very minor strand of experience, relatively 'inward', relatively passive, extremely evanescent" (ibid., p. 125). She uses the second term/concept – the 'personal' – to express a more concrete and pregnant figure. Only the person is the effective, context-dependent referent of mental and existential phenomenology. Only the person can express the *humanitas* at work in real psychoanthropological experience. "But it is precisely *not* the mind as subjectivity that is at issue here; it is the human mind" (Grene 1977, p. 215). For this same reason the person must be considered in its irreducible, holistic 'totality'. It would be seriously inadequate to interpret the person, unilaterally, as a merely intellective or pragmatic being. On the contrary, we must be fully aware of its inherent complexity, and indeed "complexify" the notion even further (Grene 1976, p. 126). This means that we must be able to read and analyze the person at the proper level: a level that can never be purely psychic and sensory, even when our interests are 'psychological' in nature.

> If one talks about the quality of a person's mind, one does not list his or her pleasures and pains or even long-term desires and emotions. One does speak, perhaps, of buoyancy or melancholy, vividness or lethargy, but primarily one speaks of quickness or slowness of thought, incisiveness or muddleheadedness – that is, of abilities related to the responsible use of humanly instituted symbol systems, whether in the sciences or the arts or in the worlds of practice or of theory, both of which are publicly and hence institutionally constituted – that is, artificially and therefore symbolically. (Grene 1977, p. 215)

Grene's observations are rather incisive and stimulating. The universe of the mental – which had appeared (and in large part *was*) so necessary to counter a physicalistic vision of the human – suddenly appears incomplete and one-sided. When we attributed certain characters and properties to a figure called the *mind*, we were actually speaking about another figure: the figure of the *person*; the person conceived as a complex subject, at the same time conditioned and enriched by its belonging to a system of events that are not merely *sensory* and *intellective* but *cultural* and *social*. In her attempt to explain adequately this figure of the person Grene turns to the Heideggerian notion of "being-in-the-world" (Grene 1976, p. 121). This suggestive expression indicates on the one hand that the subject of so-called mental matters does not coincide with the subject of the psychic universe, and on the other that this subject is embedded in a concrete worldly context. It is this embedment that makes it necessary for a study of the (so-called) mental to take into account all the components (the worldly and the social) that affect its being and doing.

M. GRENE: DIMENSIONS AND COMPONENTS OF THE MIND AS 'BEING-IN-THE-WORLD'

On this basis, the first of such components to attract Grene's attention is *culture*. In her view, it would be an error to consider the 'mental' and the 'cultural' as two absolutely independent and non-communicating worlds. In fact, they are organically related in many ways. And these relationships are, so to speak, reciprocal: not only in the cultural (in part) a 'projection' of the mental, but the mental is also (in part) a 'projection' of the cultural. It is this latter relationship that is of particular concern to Grene. She considers it quite essential to understand – to understand thoroughly – "the way in which the mind is an expression of culture" (Grene 1977, p. 220). In defining the latter concept Grene cites one of the major authorities in contemporary anthropology, Marshall Sahlins. According to Sahlins, culture can be defined as essentially "a construction by symbolic means", that is, an elaboration of theories and practices, concepts and objects through acts and operations "in which some things have been made to stand for others", not "necessarily or biologically, but in any of an indefinite number of possible ways" which are *arbitrary* (ibid., p. 221).

But if this is true, then the mental and the cultural appears to be substantially congruent and similar. For the mental, too, in Grene's view, is in large part the product of symbolic forms and figures. This, she stresses, "is precisely the characteristic that defines the mind from the point of view I support" (ibid., p. 221). In the second place (and more importantly) the mental is in many ways conditioned and occupied by culture. *Mental* acts do not consist purely and simply of *psychic* events and processes: they are also made up of memories and intentions, inspired by values and rules, projected toward aims and goals. And memories and intentions, values and rules, aims and goals are, quite clearly, *culture* and sociality. It is certain, concludes Grene, that "*culture* or human *society* and the individual's *mind* are not the same thing": but it is equally certain that any analysis of the effectively, phenomenologically existing mental cannot be separated from an analysis of the cultural. And it is no less certain that the mind is also "an expression, however unique and original, of the system of symbols of its society" (ibid.).

On the other hand, an investigation of the mental universe solely *sub specie cultural* is not sufficient. In effect, as a "being in the world" the subject of this universe does not enter into relationships only with the forms of culture: it is also related to the forms of what could be called practice. By this Grene means the concrete *situation* in which the subject actually realizes his sentience, sapience, and selfhood. "Practice" can also be interpreted as the complex of "uses" that promote, qualify, and condition the mental/existential life of the subject itself. Indeed, in a certain sense this life *is* those uses. This is precisely what Grene stresses when, illustrating the practical dimension of the mental, she writes (inspired in part by Wittgenstein) that human minds "are the *uses* made, in *cultural contexts*, of these pluralistically organized software machines [= brains]" (Grene 1976, p. 118; italics mine).

But this is not the last *facies* of the mental explored by Grene: there is another, perhaps more important, one. This she arrives at by way of what has just been said about practice. If man's being/doing is in fact the set of certain *uses* in certain *contexts*, then it is clear that an essential component of the psychic phenomenology of man is the *social*. Is it not, after all, *society* that constitutes the environment in which that phenomenology actually unfolds, independently of all the abstractions constructed by the philosophers of mind? Is it not there, promoted but also conditioned in certain ways, that man's feelings and thoughts actually occur? Correspondingly, just as Wilkerson had suggested, Grene insists upon the need to insert organically in the interpretation of the 'mental' the reference to "institutions". This connection is made quite explicitly in what is one of the most important pages of the essay under examination. For Grene, the "*mental* existence" of man is based – or is *also* based – on "the family structure, social and political institutions, languages, art forms, rituals": all social "artifacts" that have "both permitted this development to take place and prevented it from taking any of an infinite number of alternative, but no less human, forms" (ibid., p. 120). Moreover, "mental existence" is realized in manifold activities which include a strong social component: a component at work in the acts of giving meaning to 'things', of constructing intentional relationships, of interpreting/evaluating events and persons, of transforming situations – all this through *mental* operations, with *mental* instruments which are, however (and the point is worth repeating), also *socially* determined. In sum, the 'mind' is actually, to a large extent and in many ways, 'sociality'; and mental action is produced and realized by a range of social factors the analysis of which is essential to an adequate understanding of that action.

Culture, practice, society – but also *history*. This last element is also of considerable interest to Grene. Only the "historical development" of the subject-in-the-world, she stresses, "can identify a person as this person – and no other" (ibid., pp. 120–1). This position has some important consequences, beginning with the following: even from a 'mental' point of view the person must be interpreted first of all (which is not to say exclusively) in a way that Grene calls "historical" and "narrative" (ibid., p. 121). In fact, "story" and "narration" offer particularly useful hermeneutic models for grasping on the one hand the *human-likeness* of the 'mind-as-person' (only man has this peculiar *historical* origin, membership, and destination) and on the other the *individuality* of this 'mind-as-person': that is, while it is true that human beings clearly resemble each other in many ways, they also relate in infinitely diverse ways to an adventure-in-the-world (a *historical* adventure) which makes of each of them an irreducibly different individual.

DREYFUS: THE PRIMACY OF THE 'PUBLIC' IN THE PHILOSOPHY OF THE MIND AND PSYCHOLOGY AS WORLDLY 'HUMANOLOGY'

One of the more important of Grene's essays we have just examined was originally presented as a paper at an interdisciplinary conference on the relationships between medicine and philosophy (Spicker and Engelhardt 1976). The commentator of the paper (as well as of another by the neuropsychologist Karl Pribram) was the philosopher Hubert Dreyfus. Despite its brevity, this comment deserves mention here. In its substantial agreement with Grene's position, it witnesses a significant tendency within the contemporary philosophy of mind. Reference to this text will also give us the opportunity to refer, if fleetingly, to one of the more interesting and important exponents of 'new' American philosophy.

Deeply involved with, on the one hand, the problems of computer science and artificial intelligence and, on the other, phenomenological and hermeneutic thought, Dreyfus is the author of one of the most stimulating analyses available on the limits of computers and the differences between the mind and the 'machine' (Dreyfus, 1972, Dreyfus and Dreyfus 1986). He has also extended his inquiry in the direction of a philosophy alternative to the neoempiricist tradition and sensitive to certain positions expressed by contemporary European thought, from Heidegger to Foucault (see H. Dreyfus and P. Rabinow, *Michel Foucault: Beyond Structuralism and Hermeneutics,* University of Chicago Press, 1983).

As regards the questions of the philosophy of mind that interest us here, Dreyfus can be considered a harsh critic of reductionism, the identity theory, and physiologism. His critical perspective encompasses not only reductionists and 'classical' materialists but also more sophisticated doctrines such as cognitivism, functionalism, and information processing theory (Dreyfus 1972). In his view, all these conceptions (and their variants and subspecies) are invalidated, in different ways, by one fundamental error: the confusion between two different planes of human experience. The first plane is the physical and material one; the second is what Dreyfus calls the "phenomenological plane" (ibid., pp. 200ff.). The first refers to the mechanisms through which certain events take place; the second refers to these events from a phenomenological perspective: in what ways are they experienced by the subject? What are their possible meanings and 'origins' *beyond* physical factors? What references do we need to respond to certain cognitive interests concerning them?

In following this line of reasoning and research, Dreyfus points out that an inquiry into mental (and behavioral) phenomena must address two different kinds of question – both manifestly 'metaphysical'. On the one hand it is necessary to take into account all the cognitive functions – and they are many, heterogeneous, and not all formalizable – at work in the experience of man seen, so to speak, *a parte subjecti.* On the other hand it is no less necessary to analyze the components of that experience seen *a parte objecti.* But (his second, and crucial, observation) as regards these components it must be stressed that, far from being neutral and univocal, they are loaded with meaning, indeed carriers of many meanings – affective, intellective, social, historical. In real experience, Dreyfus writes, "We never encounter meaningless bits. . . , but only facts which are already interpreted [i.e., already meaningful] and which reciprocally define the *situation* we are in" (ibid., p. 200; italics mine).

It will not be surprising that in the years following the publication of *What Computers Can't Do* Dreyfus intensifies his analysis of the mental as active producer of 'subjective' meaning and at the same time continues his investigation of the notions of experience and worldly context – that is, of the 'place', already full of 'meaning', in which the mind/subject operates. This twofold search leads him to develop the issues that interest us from an even more radical personological, contextualistic, and sociocultural perspective than before. The comments he makes on Grene's *The Embodied Person* are an eloquent testimony of this. Grene is highly praised for her polemic against Cartesianism and, even more so, mentalism. *"Mind"*, writes Dreyfus, "has mattered too much....the mental does not have the role and the importance that has been attributed to it since Descartes" (Dreyfus 1976, p. 132). He also applauds Grene for having reestablished the corrected relationship between mind and culture. Not only is the first unthinkable without the second, but its activity is constantly oriented and conditioned by cultural patterns: consequently, "[Grene's] subordination of the mental to the cultural is on the right track" (ibid., p. 136).

But the point that concerns Dreyfus most is another: it is Grene's interpretation of the mind as self, person, "being-in-the-world". In answer to the question about 'where' mental events take place, Dreyfus suggests they "take place in a shared *world* in which we are surrounded by things and people external to us, and *not* in our *brains* nor in our *minds*" (ibid.; italics mine). As to the question about 'who' the agent, that is, the actual subject of mental acts, might be, the most appropriate answer seems to be *the person:* certainly not *the mind.* Reality, says Dreyfus, echoing one of the central theses of his book, is made of two "levels": the "physical" level consisting of physical bodies and the "phenomenological" level consisting of persons and their ways of perceiving the world. And "there is no place in this picture for a third level of mental states or processes shoved in between" (ibid.).

Having discarded any hypothesis of *three* dimensions or 'worlds' (something like the well-known Popper and Eccles model), Dreyfus sets out to characterize and define the mental as an intentionally acting subject in the world: in other words, as a *person*. What has traditionally been called 'the mental' is, roughly speaking, the unitary whole of conscious acts: in this sense, "to be a person is to be a unified consciousness" (ibid., p. 137). On the other hand, it must be added immediately that the universe of the realities and propositions concerning the mental goes well beyond the confines of the conscious and the subjective/private. Actually, one of the few critical remarks Dreyfus addresses to Grene regards the privileged role she assigns to this polarity (ibid., pp. 139–40). Indeed, the features Dreyfus attributes to the figure of the person are more markedly 'public' and social. Commenting on a passage in Grene's essay, he stresses that in an appropriate new philosophy of mind "the public is more basic than the private and that the 'psycho' refers to public, meaningful behavior, not mental states" (ibid., p. 140). In this context, the concept of the person is used to express on the one hand the relative independence of the 'mental' dimension from discredited psychic entities, and on the other its constitutive connection with man's 'being-in-the-world'.

The way indicated by Dreyfus leads in a more radical direction than one might expect. Not unlike the champions of the disappearance theory, who had sought to eliminate the conceptual and linguistic universe of psychology in favor of that of physical knowledge, Dreyfus too seems to aim for, if not the elimination, at least an equally radical deconstruction of the mental. He too, in effect, is convinced that certain concepts and ways of knowing are irreparably worn out. But instead of eliminating them in favor of a physicalistic epistemology, he would like to see them 'resolved' into an anthropological or socioanthropological perspective. Dreyfus, like Grene, maintains that psychology must ultimately become a science of a person/subject involved in a certain worldly and historical situation. Dreyfus finally concludes that "since words like 'private', 'subject', 'consciousness', and 'mental' are thoroughly corrupted by their Cartesian association, it might be best to follow Heidegger and introduce all new terminology when we speak of human being-in-the-world" (ibid.). A new terminology, in short, that would bring into relief the peculiar nature of the mind/person: existential, 'public', practical, interwoven with symbols and meanings, and with socially and historically determined needs and values.

Appendix

The mental as intentional/'personal' emergence

The psycho-personological perspective of Joseph Margolis

A "NONREDUCTIONIST" PHILOSOPHY AND THE NOTION OF EMERGENCE

In the course of this book, and particularly in the last two chapters, frequent mention has been made of the name and work of Joseph Margolis. Margolis is, in fact, one of the most important figures in the contemporary debate on the mental, the human, and their science. Already in *Knowledge and Existence* (1973b; hereafter KE), later in *Persons and Minds* (PM, 1978), and *Culture and Cultural Entities* (CE, 1983), as well as in many minor essays, he directs his attention with considerable efficacy to several of the themes which constitute the object of the present essay: the possibility of describing the real in exclusively physical terms, the role of functions or non-physical properties, the problems concerning the mental and its relationship with the bodily – and, most importantly, the notion of person as the central figure of a psychological (and psychoanthropological) reflection.

The only reservation one might have, from a certain vantage point, about Margolis's overall view concerns his allusion to a materialistic and, on occasion, monistic perspective. Actually, however, this reference is usually made at a rather general level and in a predominantly 'critical' context, as a rejection of any sort of spiritualistic or metaphysical position. Furthermore, it is clear that what Margolis is *really* saying can scarcely be characterized as materialistic or monistic (in the usual sense of the terms). What emerges from the above-mentioned texts – and especially from the fundamental essay *Persons and Minds* – is a reading of the world that is far from *unitary*, but quite to the contrary (and explicitly) *pluralistic*.

267

Indeed, Margolis's interpretation of reality insists on the need to articulate and distinguish – in *irreducible* terms, it should be stressed – different orders of entities, phenomena, and functions.

As regards materialism, one has the impression that Margolis's main concern is to define what it can *not* and must *not* be. One of his central and most valid theses, in fact, states that to say that everything exists is made of matter does not mean admitting that the *only* way things can 'appear' and present themselves (and much less the only terms we can use to talk about them) must be materialistic: this is only the essential assumption of *physicalistic* materialism, which Margolis rejects with particular force. The first (but not sole) error of certain materialists is that they confuse and identify the order of *things* with the order of *attributes*. In truth, although they are 'material', things can sustain or carry – if examined in a certain way – 'non-material' attributes. This is why Margolis makes a clear distinction between the two. And this is why he differentiates between the two notions "ontic dualism" and "attribute dualism". The former must be rejected without reservation. The latter, conversely, can and must be accepted: not least of all because, on closer examination, 'attribute dualism' "is not so much a dualism as the insistence or acknowledgement that the real properties of things are not reducible to being all and only physical properties or properties of some other single kinds" (CE, p. 2).

Just as Margolis rejects ontic and physicalistic materialism, so, within the more specific framework of the philosophy of mind, does he reject identity and eliminationist materialism. These conceptions are countered with another "nonreductionist" alternative: non-reductionist in the sense that it admits the existence of *qualities* and *properties* which, while connected in some way to the body, must be described in specific terms not belonging to the linguistic universe of the science of the body. From the same perspective, Margolis also speaks of a "compositional" materialism. As we read in an important essay on physicalism, "it could affirm, for example, that the *composition* of everything that exists – that of which everything that exists is composed – is matter, *but that not everything that exists is a physical object and/or that not all the attributes of that which exists are physical attributes*" (Margolis 1973a, p. 575; italics mine). It is in this context that Margolis introduces the concept of "emergence" (ibid., p. 577).

Certainly, in speaking approvingly of an "emergentistic" materialism, Margolis appears to link himself with that group of scholars (represented today by Mario Bunge, among others) who have seen in the notion of emergence the principle capable of founding a materialistic unitary, but not reductionist 'molecular', interpretation of the world (Bunge 1980). But, while these scholars stress the fundamental (*materialistic*) unity of reality, Margolis insists on its irreducible *articulation*. In his view of this world, *emergence* highlights above all the *plurality* of planes and their respective *differences* (PM, pp. 7ff., 20, 236–9). The point is clearly of particular significance within the psychoanthropological domain which concerns Margolis. Thus, for example, the person is defined as a "culturally emergent entity" (PM, p. 7) precisely in order to underline the existence in it of a dimension which, while not in itself a self-sufficient reality, can by no means be identified with the bodily organization of the person itself. The person becomes, then, a complex of "functions" at once irreducible to physiological structures and embodied in those structures.

THE CONCEPT OF 'EMBODIMENT' AND THE PERSON

One of the key notions in Margolis's writings – appearing as early as *Knowledge and Existence* and particularly stressed in *Art and Philosophy* – is in fact that of embodiment. Employed in various contexts of philosophical and scientific reflection, the concept has only recently gained a certain prominence in an important sector of the philosophy of mind. We find it, for example, in the work of a MBP specialist like Shaffer and in studies on the mental by Robinson (Shaffer 1966, p. 77; Robinson 1982, pp. 60 and 67). But the most important proponent of embodiment in the area which concerns us is unquestionably Margolis (see especially Margolis 1977, but also PM and CE, *passim*).

What is embodiment? In general terms, the concept alludes to a particular type of relationship between two dimensions or properties at once clearly *distinct* and closely *interconnected*. It refers, more precisely, to a relationship that mediates a 'dimension' or property not definable in physical terms with a physical 'dimension' or property in the second. Margolis gives such importance to the concept that it is applied not only to the issues of the mental and the person but also to the more general questions of society and culture. All artistic, intellectual, and social products, on his

view, are to be seen within the framework of the concept of embodiment. Take (as Margolis often invites us to) a work of art: a
sculpture or a literary text. What goes into Michelangelo's *David*?
Certainly a block of marble – a Martian would see nothing else in
it. But the sculpture is not made *only* of a block of marble. There is
'something else'. This 'something else' with respect to the materiality of the block of marble is the idea, the project of the sculptor
– with all his concomitant *cultural* assumptions and implications
(PM, p. 7). All this is that 'emergence' – irreducible to the (*material*)
components of the work and yet 'embodied' in them – to which
Margolis gives such importance. The same may be said of a poem.
From a certain point of view, it is made of ink marks or of graphic
symbols on a piece of paper. From another perspective, the poem
is also made of 'something else'. Indeed, a merely *physical* description of a poetic text would not allow us to grasp what we custom-
arily call its literary meaning and value. Ancient and modern
thought is marked, in Margolis's view, by a recurring oscillation
between two equally reprehensible extremes: between a *physicalistic
reductionism*, which regards the work of art as exclusively matter
(Neurath, for instance, has argued that a poem can be reduced to
purely material marks), and a *dualism* which *ontologically* separates
matter from meaning or from culture in general (and here come to
mind certain theses advanced by Popper and Eccles in their *The Self
and Its Brain*).

Now, Margolis uses the concept of embodiment precisely to
avoid these extremes. It permits him, in fact, to take into consideration, on the one hand, the need for a certain *bond* and, on the
other, the reciprocal *autonomy* of the two terms joined by that bond.
Despite everything – as he writes with particular reference to the
example of poetry – the poem "remains an entity whose identity
is necessarily linked to the identity of physical objects (or inscrip-
tions) and whose properties are at least a function of the properties
of those physical objects" (KE, p. 143). On the other hand, the object
'poem' (and any other cultural object) requires a characterization
and an analysis capable of grasping its specific peculiarities, those
which Margolis calls "(emergent) properties not otherwise ascribable", that is to say not ascribable in physical terms, such as "meaning", "symbolic import", "emotional quality", "purpose", and
"design" (KE, p. 144).

Although the notion of embodiment serves to give full recognition to the role of the 'cultural', Margolis employs it above all

in a certain interpretation of the 'mental' and the 'personal'. He sees the mind as a dimension irreducible to the neurocerebral and yet, at the same time, linked to it. 'Embodiment' makes it possible to consider this dual status of the mental on an empirical plane. For Margolis the mind exists, though not in a separate self-sufficient reality, and it must be conceived as a component of a more complex experience, which is to be investigated in various ways. The mind is certainly realized in a physical system: but this system, far from wholly including the mental, constitutes, as it were, only its 'vector'.

In certain respects this position is akin to functionalism. Indeed, Margolis's conception closely recalls the functionalist 'promise' to consider the bodily one of the possible 'embodiments' of the mental. But, as we saw, what the majority of functionalists proposed was too often a mere promise, and it was rarely kept: the bodily was all too frequently conceived not merely as the only *de facto* existing embodiment, but also as the (physical) dimension with which the mental could be *identified. These* positions are met with Margolis's radical dissent. While respecting the original theoretical nucleus of functionalism, he rejects certain of its developments. With particular reference to Fodor, Margolis does not share the latter's clear preference for hardware over software, that is the 'carrier' as opposed to the 'carried'. Moreover (and most importantly), he points out Fodor's own proximity to the position of identity theorists, albeit of the token–token rather than the type–type variety (PM, pp. 64ff.). Margolis's project is quite different. He does not extend credit to any form of the identity theory. His aim, instead, is to underline the *specificity* of the mental with respect to the bodily – and the notion of embodiment serves him quite well to this end. 'Embodiment', in fact, does not mean 'identification'. On the contrary, it also refers necessarily to a 'figure' that must be embodied and that requires an analysis *juxta sua principia.*

One of Margolis's preferred examples is that of the dream. The dream is a *mental* event that unquestionably passes through a *physical* system. An ideally exhaustive analysis of the dream could not, then, do without an exploration of that system. On the other hand, the dream itself can by no means be made to coincide with the physical system. There is a 'part' of the dream that, while *embodied* in certain neurocerebral mechanisms, cannot *be* those mechanisms. If in the course of a dream I have a nightmare, what I am afraid of is not a certain *physical* event but certain figures and happenings belonging to *another* order of reality (PM, pp. 34–5). No examination, however 'perfect', of the processes that take place in my brain would make it possible for me to grasp the 'whole' dream. To understand its symbolic, affective contents I must resort to *other* investigations and *other* instruments.

The specificity of the 'personal' is reinforced by the category of embodiment too. This category, writes Margolis in reference to the person, establishes and constitutes a "non-biological" and "sui generis" relationship which connects – while preserving a state of reciprocal independence – a "culturally emergent entity" and a body (CE, p. 13). If the physical polarity is obviously indispensable, it is equally necessary to maintain the other 'metaphysical' component. Indeed Margolis, taking into account certain significant theoretical orientations in psychoanthropology, shows that he wants to give particular importance to this component. On his view (not unlike Shaffer and Wilkerson), contemporary knowledge has an urgent need to reconsider the person and to highlight all its "functions" and irreducible components (PM, p. 24).

From this perspective, Margolis does not hesitate to criticize one of the most prestigious fathers of 'personological' reflection, Strawson, whom he accuses of ignoring the 'emergence' and the 'consistency' of the person – and slighting the radical difference between the person and mere "sentient animals" (PM, pp. 7–8). In the face of Strawson's 'conceptualism' Margolis seems to feel the need to outline a figure of the person at once more 'substantial' and more independent. This leads, among other things, to certain 'ontological' accents that may cause some uneasiness. His fundamental objective, however, clearly remains that of creating an adequate referent for a tenable phenomenology of the mental and the human.

'SENTIENCE', 'SAPIENCE', LANGUAGE: THE CRITICISM OF CHOMSKY

It is not essential to describe this phenomenology in all its stages and developments. Not only because various aspects of Margolis's positions have been mentioned in the preceding pages, but also for a more important reason. It is true that Margolis defines the person as an entity characterized by sentience, sapience, and selfhood – and by his linguistic, cultural, and social *operari*. But it is also true that in a significant passage in *Persons and Minds* he vigorously stresses the need to study the 'personal' (and the 'mental' as the 'personal') at the level of its greatest "ontological complexity" (PM, p. 230). The import of this appeal lies not only in its implicit criticism of the reductionistic, 'elementaristic' orientation of a certain philosophy of mind, but also in the weight given to the concept of 'complexity', which is firmly situated at the center of crucial debates in contemporary epistemology.

Given this premise, it will not be surprising that Margolis, both in *Knowledge and Existence* and in *Persons and Minds,* treats sentience with relative restraint. The analysis of this dimension of the mental and the person mainly serves to strengthen a direct attack on some positions advanced by identity theorists. Margolis is particularly concerned to stress the irreducibility of sentience to pure materiality. *Sensory* states are, at least in some sense, *functional* states – not identifiable, as such, with *one* particular *physical* referent. "No one", writes Margolis, "has yet succeeded in reducing discourse about persons and sentient creatures to non-intentional discourse about the physical events and states of such systems" (PM, p. 186). But of even greater importance may be the thesis of the 'unthinkability' of sentience as an autonomous component, isolated from the person. Indeed, man's sensory activity does not unfold – by means of a *specific* and *independent* neurophysiological mechanism – *alone*. On the contrary, it is organically connected to his intellective intentional activity.

> Living creatures, on the other hand, are said to be sentient insofar as they are also said to be intelligent: they are said to have certain sentient capabilities only insofar as whatever putative belief and knowledge may be ascribed to them conform ... to what would minimally cohere with putative intentions, desires, and behavior also ascribed to them. (PM, p. 178)

From this perspective – which Margolis calls "molar" as opposed to the "molecular" position of those who believe in the 'particle-based' reducibility of the human (PM, p. 173) – sentience in the strict sense refers directly to the more properly mental states constituting sapience. Among these, in addition to intellective processes, Margolis includes beliefs, intentions, linguistic activity, and other functions which in this context are of less interest to us. The reference to beliefs leads Margolis to assume a twofold position: against behaviorism and (once again) against physicalism. In the first place, Margolis argues persuasively for the *existence* of beliefs themselves (a term/concept to be uⅰderstood in a rather broad sense). They are neither fictitious nor reducible to something else (PM, p. 130). If anything, they refer to the figure and workings of those "cognitive agents" which are persons (PM, p. 134). In the second place, he stresses their irreducibility: "there is no plausible basis . . . for supposing that belief-states might be replaced by states lacking intensional features", according to the (unsuccessful) project of physicalists, old and new, nor that there are "causal correlations" between neural processes and beliefs so strict and meaningful as to permit the explanation of the latter in exclusively neurophysiological terms, and without reference to the overall mode of being of "persons" (PM, pp. 145 and 180).

But it is in cognitive and linguistic activity that Margolis identifies at once the most significant feature of the mental and one of the "most distinctive traits" of man as a person (KE, p. v). In this connection, it is by no chance that in *Knowledge and Existence* Margolis devotes considerable space to an analysis of the modes of human knowledge and that in *Persons and Minds* he develops an in-depth reflection on the sphere of language. It is especially this latter discussion that interests us here. Its interest lies both in the close relationship between the dimension of the mental (incomprehensible, for Margolis, without an adequate reference to language, which many philosophers of mind have neglected) and linguistic activity and in the way Margolis interprets this activity.

In a phase of our intellectual history increasingly dominated by a *bio*-linguistic orientation, Margolis does not hesitate to propose a completely different approach to the analysis of language. On his view, the *operari* of language must be interpreted as "a peculiarly *cultural* phenomenon" (PM, p. 97). It is a cultural phenomenon both because it expresses the *intentions* of the speaker (inseparable from 'provenances' and referents of a cultural nature) and because it manifests the property of "rule-following", the quintessential mark of culturally oriented human action (KE, p. 244). Long before being embodied in certain signs and structures, linguistic action is a cultural-conscious-mental activity. "To be able to use language", Margolis writes, "is to be able to reflect on the world experienced and on experience itself to the extent of being able to make reference to, and to make predictions of, selected elements in the world and in experience" (KE, pp. 243–4).

It is from the point of view of this 'cultural-reflective' interpretation of language (behind which one may glimpse various sources:

Cassirer, Wittgenstein, a certain 'lay' hermeneutics) that Margolis launches a radical critique of Chomsky (PM, pp. 98ff., 106ff.). In the first place, Chomsky is criticized for his conception of the innate character of the principal functions of language and for his emphasis on linguistic universals. This emphasis not only pushes into the background the individual component of linguistic expression, but is also connected with the identification of the mind with a sort of 'programmed machine'. This produces, in Chomsky's doctrine, an authentic vicious circle:

> We suppose that the most comprehensive linguistic generalizations are linguistic universals because we are already committed to the rationalist thesis that the mind is 'preset' to learn all possible languages; and we adopt the rationalist thesis because we suppose that the acquisition of language . . . cannot be accomplished unless the mind is appropriately supplied with linguistic universals. (PM, p. 113)

Even more explicit and radical, as one might have expected, is Margolis's polemic against Chomsky's conception of language as formulated in not so much *cultural* as *natural, biological* terms. This conception, he stresses, on the one hand "undermine[s] the thesis that persons are essentially cultural entities", and on the other ends up by downplaying the existing differences between persons themselves and merely sentient creatures (PM, pp. 98–9). From a different perspective Chomsky is accused of encouraging in various ways a reductionist approach both in the epistemological realm and in psychoanthropology. From a certain point of view, Chomsky's basic assumptions seem to be the fundamental self-sufficiency of man as a speaking being, the describability of his nature in physical (or physical-biological) terms, and the correlative possibility of determining in the human sphere *general laws* analogous to those operating in the natural world. From this standpoint, Chomsky seems to commit two errors: one which gives credence to the reducibility – even in the psychocultural universe – of the complex to the elementary; another which suggests that what is simply rule-like (or rule-dependent) can be reduced to what is – in a far more rigid, uniform, and binding way – law-like (or law-dependent). The attack against theses of this kind must be radical since Margolis (rightly) holds that they have been adopted not only by Chomsky, or by generative linguistics, but also by other disciplines, tendencies, and research programs:

The essential difficulty, linking Chomskyan linguistics, structuralism (Lévi-Strauss), and information-processing models,
lies in conflating molar and molecular levels of discourse –
and the terms are Tolman's (1932) – and in assuming that because nomic invariances occur on the molecular level and because, regarding machines, such invariances as well as
invariances of rulelike programming occur on both the molecular and molar levels, it must be the case that rulelike (intensional) invariances occur, among the higher sentient
creatures and persons, on the molecular and molar levels as
well, or that rulelike phenomena must be reducible to law-
like phenomena. (PM, p. 116)

In opposition to all this Margolis proposes, first of all, a rather
less uniform and generalizing conception of the linguistic functions
of men. *Real* languages, he writes, have features that violate the
supposedly natural *universalia*. In fact, certain *generalizations* carried
out by Chomsky have not been confirmed (and cannot be confirmed) at a *universal* level. In the second place, Margolis sets out
– again *contra* Chomsky – a non-innatist interpretation of language:
"the specific grammar of a given natural language is not innate to
the human infant" (PM, p. 102). Of even greater significance is his
proposal to counter 'internalism' and Chomskyan solipsism with a
contextualist, social interpretation of linguistic activity. Margolis –
who in this connection cites Vygotsky – lays considerable weight
on the notion of *context:* a notion of central importance for the
whole psychoanthropological issue under examination. Context,
Margolis stresses, is not accessorial but essential to an understanding of the meaning of words, to decoding the ambiguities and re-
dundancies of certain linguistic messages (PM, pp. 101ff.).

On a more general level, Margolis's alternative conception of language is based on a theory of the mental which is markedly different from that of Chomsky and his direct and indirect allies. For
Margolis, man's psycholinguistic activity is, as we have said, a *cultural* activity. Not *nature* but *culture* gives substance, meaning, and
distinction to mental and human activity. This is why Margolis
takes those scholars to task who have in one way or another neglected the cultural dimension in their analyses of the psychic and
the human. Culture, in fact, is an unrelinquishable "emergence":
an irreducible and specific dimension of man as a *mental* subject
acting according to *rules* and *purposes*. It includes many psychoso-

cial practices and activities, of which *Persons and Minds* offers a detailed inventory (PM, p. 239). There can be no questioning the existence of systems of ideas and symbolic universes, of ethical schemes and religious doctrines, of myths and rites, of practices and customs, of the planning and creation of artefacts, of communicative interaction and forms of social life. This existence, even taken in itself, contradicts the position of those – beginning with certain materialists – who would ignore or deny culture: "the bare admission of cultural phenomena shows at a stroke the inadequacy of all forms of radical or reductive materialism" (PM, p. 7). Culture – which is obviously not a *spiritual substance* in the metaphysical sense of the term – is also quite clearly not *matter*. It is not matter because it does not *coincide* with material entities and aggregates (the 'rule' of a game is not a *physical* component of the game; 'being-Christian' is not a property of any part of the human body), and because it cannot be grasped by the instruments, however sophisticated, of the bionatural sciences.

THE ROLE OF THE INTENTIONAL
IN MENTAL LIFE

This is not the place to analyze all the aspects of the universe of culture examined by Margolis. It is necessary, however, to examine certain modes and forms he considers essential to the connection between the cultural and the mental. While Margolis rejects a psychologistic *identification* of the latter with the former (which would be patently reductive), he insists on the organic, intimate relationship between these dimensions of the human. The mental, in a word, *is not* in itself the cultural: but it is *'pro-duced' according to cultural forms*. The principal function through which the mental, beginning with relatively elementary levels of existence, becomes manifest and culturally concrete is the *intentional* function.

If the intentional – which Margolis interprets (freely and at times critically) along the lines of Brentano, phenomenology, and recent American intentionalism – assumes in his perspective a privileged role, this is because it has, for him, the two absolutely decisive functions of rendering *human* and *personal* that typically *mental* property which is language, and of connecting the mental itself with human action and its rules, with the social and its institutions, with the historicity and its traditions. The intentional, then, is situated, so to speak, at the very heart of Margolis's conception of the person (and of the mental as personal).

The first of the two above-mentioned functions is particularly important. Margolis is well aware, in fact, that language as a transmission of information is not a prerogative of humans as persons. What is it, then, that makes linguistic activity specific and irreducible? Precisely intentionality, through which the individual confers meanings – polymorphous, ambiguous, over- and underdetermined – on words and propositions. A plan to reinterpret the human in terms not 'natural' but 'cultural', not machine-like but person-like, cannot do without intentionality: "only a creature that has mastered language and behaves in a way informed by such mastery acts in a culturally significant way. Such a creature behaves, we may say. . . , Intentionally; his real psychological states cannot be correctly described except in terms of intentional properties" (CE, p. 10).

In the second place, intentionality links the mental to a whole series of more complex and, consequently, more specifically human dimensions – beginning with the cultural. It may be useful to repeat, for the benefit of old and new psychologism, that for Margolis the *mental* as such is not the *cultural* – much less its *agency*, or the *social*, or the *historical*. Rather, the mental 'opens itself' to these 'different' dimensions: and it does so precisely through intentionality. In what way? First of all by 'relating' the mental itself to the 'other' by means of (intentionalistic) referents of a semantic or pragmatic kind; then by organizing this 'relationship' in the light of certain *norms*. The point is crucial. The intentional 'broadens' and 'gives substance to' the mental – in a cultural, social, historical direction – through the institution of *rules*. "I construe the intentional", writes Margolis, "in terms of the rule-governed. . . , which permits me to link the mental and the cultural, to link the analysis of language, belief, and action; the thesis suggests, also, a promising conception of what it is to be a person or a creature inferior to persons but possessing a mind" (KE, p. 281).

Opened to and linked in the direction of the cultural by means of the intentional function ("the cultural", we read in *Culture and Cultural Entities*, "is the intentional"; CE, p. 12), the mental is opened and broadened by the same mediator also toward '*action*' and the *social*. As regards the first direction, it is quite clear that *action* is organically connected with the *mental* – and that the mediator is intentionality. It is intentionality, in fact, that urges the mind (or better the mind-as-person) to act, to behave. Closed up in a unilateral, abstract vision of the mental, part of the traditional philosophy of mind has ignored the *pragmatic* implications of the mental and has made a serious mistake. As Rorty argues, the mental is not only a *being* and *having* but also a *doing.* Together with knowing, acting is one of the most direct manifestations of the mental and one of its most complex levels of expression.

Margolis does not commit the error that certain other philosophers of mind have fallen prey to. In his phenomenolgy of the mental and the 'personal' he devotes considerable attention to the analysis of action. His probe reaches as far as the primary (mental) sources of action: motives and interests. How can a serious psychology ignore the internal workings of motives and interests and their practical consequences? One of the most significant characteristics of the individual is precisely his 'living *interestedly'*, his directing himself (intentionally) toward certain goals and objectives worthy of a *practical commitment.* Another of his characteristics – which links even more closely doing and thinking, praxis and mind – is the ability to "change the interests and direction" of his own activity "for reasons of contingent and variable doctrinal conviction" (PM, p. 245). It is precisely *actions* that are the expression of this 'interested/intentional' life which unfolds in the light of *reason* and *knowledge.*

THE DIMENSION OF THE MENTAL: FROM ''LAWS'' TO ''RULES''

Not surprisingly, these considerations on the intentional as an opening of the mental toward the world and on action as a manifestation of the mental in the world lead Margolis to extend his reflection to the *social* dimension of the mental itself.

In this connection, it must not be forgotten that the forms and norms according to which the mental is and acts are to a large extent the fruit of the internalization of rules, values, and traditions originating in the outside social universe. In the second place, this complex whole of rules, values, and traditions – which is not completely internalizable – constitutes an 'objectivity' (the institution) which in itself exercises considerable pressure on the subject and on his being and acting. Hence, the mental states and the "behavior of human persons" are expressions, at times intentional and at times unintentional, which are in many ways (endogenous and exogenous, so to speak) conditioned by society (CE, p. 10). Margolis makes the same point in another context, when he writes that "relevant institutions play a causal role" in the psycho-behavioral domain as well, insofar as they "form, inform, groom, influence, habituate a population" in such a way that its members will tend to act in a functionally (intentionally) appropriate way, in virtue of having internalized the model of reasoning favored by those institutions (PM, p. 259).

All this does not merely lead to the conclusion that even in its more specifically 'psychic' manifestations the mental must be considered not *in abstracto* but in a *concrete* context. Nor does it stop at the further conclusion – to which Margolis argues with remarkable finesse – that the phenomenology of the mental is a *historical* and *relative* phenomenology: in the sense that the modes and imports of mental/'personal' events undergo continuous change in time (CE, p. 15; see also PM, pp. 25–7; KE, p. 145). It also leads to the third conclusion that, from a cognitive point of view, it is rather misleading to pursue, in a system as complex and fluid as the mental/'personal' world, laws and norms comparable in 'power' to those of the natural world. Rather than the rigid "covering laws" dreamt of by neopositivists as a means of governing cognitively the psychosocial world, we must think of less binding "covering institutions" capable of facilitating the analysis of mental/human phenomena (PM, p. 259).

It must not be supposed, however, that Margolis resigns himself to a non-scientific – or, much less, non-cognitive – approach to the mental/human world. He tends to stress rather the relative autonomy of the knowledge, the explanations, and the language concerning this world. What he does *not* believe can be achieved is that *nomological* science of the mental and social whose existence seems certain to so many – including the more recent Armstrong.[1] It is for this reason, among others, that he mistrusts (but so, it will be recalled, did the far more 'pro-science' Davidson) the generalized use of the concept of law in the domain of the human. 'Law' is explicitly contrasted with 'rule' – and, on occasion, with 'practice'. "Persons", writes Margolis in a significant passage in *Knowledge and Existence*, "are rule-following organisms or systems, or organisms

---

1. For Armstrong, not only is the unquestionable "regularity" of the world explained by the assumption that "there are laws" (*objective* and *universal* laws): but, once this is established, it seems to him "natural to go on to explain *all*

or systems capable of intentional states" (KE, p. 244; where he re-iterates the important connection between *rule* and *intention*). "The truth is", we read in the *Persons and Minds*, "that the 'laws' of the cultural domain are institutions and practices governing embodied phenomena" (KE, p. 259).

This limitation imposed on laws and the corresponding prefer-ence for rules does not imply – let us repeat – any tendency in Margolis toward epistemological 'anarchy'. Mental/personal/cul-tural phenomena are quite worthy as objects of study since they possess not only their own semantic properties but also their own order and coherence. It must simply be remembered that a certain act or event can be rule-following without necessarily being law-following. In this connection it is appropriate to recall Margolis's position in *Persons and Minds* in the context of his polemic against Chomsky: we must by no means suppose "that rulelike phenomena must be reducible to lawlike phenomena" (PM, p. 116).

What, for Margolis, is the sense of this distinction – and of the priority given to rules? Let us say, first of all, that the accent placed on rules suggests the existence – within the *lato sensu* human do-main – of constrictions, of bonds that are less rigid than those sug-gested by the notion of law: just consider the meaning (and intrinsic prudence) of an everyday expression like 'as a rule'. This is the point: for Margolis, the mental-cultural world is inhabited by phe-nomena about which one can at best say that they occur in certain ways 'as a rule' – but this does not exclude their occurring in *other* ways. Secondly, rules, at least as Margolis understands the concept, are more difficult to universalize than laws. Thus for example, in *Culture and Cultural Entities* he points out that while there are no universal norms governing language and cultural processes, they do show "regularities" traceable to particular identifiable and an-alyzable reasons (CE, p. 12). Thirdly, rules are far less anchored than laws to the causal chains and determinisms so dear to a certain style of thought. The "regularities" of mental-cultural phenomena, we read again in *Culture and Cultural Entities,* cannot be derived from "infra-psychological", and even less from "molecular", *causes* (ibid.). Fourthly, rules allude more directly to the world of experi-ence, of praxis, of society. We have already seen, in this connection, to what extent Margolis confers cognitive priority on what he calls

causality [at work in reality] in terms of laws". "My own bet", he adds, "is that these laws are in every case the laws of physics" (Malcolm and Armstrong 1984, pp. 166–7).

the social "covering institutions". Indeed, the structures which give direction to (though not deterministically) human phenomena and behavior derive in large measure, directly or indirectly, from "institutions" – and, more generally, from the social domain. And it is, among other things, precisely this connection with the social that explains another feature of the human which is of capital importance to Margolis, that is, its constitutive *historicity* – and consequently the continuous and non-casual transformations of the rules governing the human itself. Both reasons – the 'sociological' and the 'historical' – are vigorously underscored in a passage in *Culture and Cultural Entities*, in which Margolis writes that "rulelike regularities" operating *both* in the subset of the "psychological states" of persons *and* in that of their "actions and expressions" (note the parallelism) can be defined "societally". Correspondingly, he goes on to say, they change historically "under the causal influence of behavior similarly informed", that is, guided in turn by social regularities (CE, p. 12). At this point it will not be surprising that the emphasis on the impossibility of universalizing (and of axiomatizing) rules as well as the stress laid on the link between the rules themselves and the social domain ultimately leads Margolis to propose a suggestive encounter between his notion of rule-following and the notion of "life form" elaborated by Wittgenstein.

Bibliography

Abelson, R.
1977   *Persons: A Study in Philosophical Psychology.* London: Macmillan.
Agazzi, E.
1981   'Mind and Body: A Philosophical Delineation of the Problem', in Agazzi (ed.), pp. 3–20 (see below).
Agazzi, E. (ed.)
1981   *The Mind–Body Problem,* in *Epistemologia* 4 (monograph).
Alston, W. P.
1974   'Conceptual Prolegomena to a Psychological Theory of Intentional Action', in Brown (ed.), pp. 71–101 (see below).
1971   'Varieties of Privileged Access', *American Philosophical Quarterly* 8:223–51.
Anderson, A. R. (ed.)
1964   *Minds and Machines.* Englewood Cliffs, N.J.: Prentice Hall.
Anscombe, G. E. M.
1957   *Intention.* Oxford: Blackwell.
Aquila, R. E.
1977   *Intentionality: A Study of Mental Acts.* Philadelphia: Pennsylvania State University Press.
Arbib, M. A.
1972   *The Metaphorical Brain.* New York: Wiley.
Armstrong, D. M.
1961   *Perception and the Physical World.* London: Routledge.
1962   *Bodily Sensations.* London: Routledge.
1966   'The Nature of the Mind,' in *The Nature of the Mind and Other Essays* (see below).
1968   *A Materialist Theory of Mind.* London: Routledge.
1973   'Epistemological Foundations for a Materialist Theory of Mind', in *The Nature of Mind and Other Essays* (see below).

1976   'The Causal Theory of mind,' in *The Nature of Mind and Other Essays* (see below).

1977   'Naturalism, Materialism and First Philosophy,' in *The Nature of Mind and Other Essays* (see below).

1978a   *Universals and Scientific Realism.* 2 vols. Cambridge University Press.

1978b   'Between Matter and Mind,' *Times Literary Supplement*, 17 Feb., pp. 183–4.

1978c   'What Is Consciousness?' in *The Nature of Mind and Other Essays* (see below).

1980   *The Nature of Mind and Other Essays.* Brisbane: University of Queensland Press; and Ithaca, N.Y.: Cornell University Press, 1981.

1983a   'Recent Work on the Relation of Mind and Brain', in Fløistad G. (ed.), pp. 45–78 (see below).

1983b   *What Is the Law of Nature?* Cambridge University Press.

Armstrong, D. M., and N. Malcolm

1984a   *Consciousness and Causality.* Oxford: Blackwell.

1984b   'Self-profile', in Bogdan (ed.), pp. 3–53 (see below).

Aune, B.

1963   'Feelings, Moods, and Introspection, *Mind* 72:187–208.

1966   'Feigl on the Mind–Body Problem', in Feyerabend and Maxwell (eds.), pp. 17–39 (see below).

1967   *Knowledge, Mind and Nature.* New York: Random House.

Ayer, A. J.

1954   'Can There Be a Private Language? A Symposium', *Aristotelian Society Supplementary Volume* 28:63–76.

1955   'What Is Communication?' in A. Ayer (ed.), pp. 11–28 (see below).

1963   *The Concept of a Person and Other Essays.* London: Macmillan.

1955   (ed.). *Studies in Communication.* London: Sucker.

Baier, K.

1962   'Pains', *Australasian Journal of Philosophy* 40:1–23.

1970   'Smart on Sensations', in Borst (ed.), pp. 95–106 (see below).

Bakan, M.

        'Mind as Life and Form', in Rieber (ed.), pp. 131–54 (see below).

Bartley, S. H.

1967   *The Human Organization as a Person.* Philadelphia: Chilton Books.

Bateson, G.

1972   *Steps to an Ecology of Mind.* New York: Dutton.

Bateson, G., and R. W. Rieber

1980   'Mind and Body: A Dialogue', in Rieber (ed.), pp. 241–52 (see below).

Bealer, G.

1978   'An Inconsistency in Functionalism', *Synthesis* 38:333–72.

Beck, L. W.
1940   'The Psychophysical as a Pseudo-problem', *Journal of Philosophy*
        37:561–71.
Beloff, J.
1962   *The Existence of Mind*. London: MacGibbon.
1965   'The Identity Hypothesis: A Critique', in Smythies (ed.), pp. 35–53
        (see below).
Bergmann, G.
1940   'On Some Methodological Problems of Psychology', in Feigl and
        Brodbeck (eds.), pp. 627–36 (see below).
1955   'Intentionality', *Archivio di filosofia* 6:177–216.
Bernstein, R. J.
1968   'The Challenge of Scientific Materialism', *International Philosophical
        Quarterly* 8:252–75; rpt. in Rosenthal (ed.), pp. 200–22 (see below).
Bertalanffy, L. von
1963   'The Mind–Body Problem: A New View', *Psychosomatic Medicine*
        24:29–45.
1966   'Mind and Body Reexamined', *Journal of Humanistic Psychology*
        6:113 38.
Bianca, M., and D. De Martino (eds.)
1978   *La mente e la macchina*. Brescia: La Scuola.
Bianca, M., and P. Muzi (eds.)
1978   *The Mind–Body Problem: Philosophical and Psychosomatical Approaches*.
        Rome: Pozzi.
Bindra, D.
1976   *A Theory of Intelligent Behavior*. New York: Wiley.
1980   (ed.). *The Brain's Mind: A Neuroscience Perspective on the Mind–Body
        Problem*. New York: Gardner Press.
Binkley, R., R. Bronaugh, and A. Marras (eds.)
1970   *Agent, Action, and Reason*. Toronto: University of Toronto Press.
Bird, G.
1974   'Minds and States of Mind', *Philosophical Quarterly* 21:244–54.
Biro, J., and R. Shahan (eds.)
1982   *Mind, Brain and Function: Essays in the Philosophy of Mind*. Brighton:
        Harvester Press.
Blakemore, C.
1977   *Mechanics of the Mind*. Cambridge University Press.
Block, N.
1980–1 'Troubles with Functionalism', in Block (ed.), pp. 171–84 (see be-
        low).
1981   'Psychologism and Functionalism, *Philosophical Review* 90:5–43.
1980–1 (ed.). *Readings in the Philosophy of Psychology*. 2 vols. Cambridge,
        Mass.: Harvard University Press.

Block, N., and J. Fodor
1972   'What Psychological States are Not', *Philosophical Review* 80:159–81.
Boden, M.
1970   'Intentionality and Physical Systems', *Philosophy of Science* 31:200–
        14.
1972   *Purposive Explanation in Psychology.* Cambridge University Press.
1977   *Artificial Intelligence and Natural Man.* Hassocks, Sussex: Harvester
        Press.
1981   *Minds and Mechanisms.* Brighton: Harvester Press.
Boër, S., and W. Lycan
1980   'Who Me?' *Philosophical Review* 89:427–66.
Bogdan, R. (ed.)
1984   *D. M. Armstrong.* Dordrecht: Reidel.
Bonomi, A.
1983   *Eventi mentali.* Milan: II Saggiatore.
Borger, R., and F. Cioffi (eds.)
1970   *Explanation in the Behavioral Sciences.* Cambridge University Press.
Boring, E. G.
1933   *The Physical Dimensions of Consciousness.* New York: Century.
1946   'Mind and Mechanism', *American Journal of Psychology* 59:173–92.
Borst, C. V.
1970   'Perception and Intentionality', *Mind* 70:115–21.
1979   (ed.). *The Brain/Mind Identity Theory.* 5th edition. London: Macmil-
        lan; and New York: St. Martin's.
Boyd, R.
1980–1 'Materialism without Reductionism', in Block (ed.), pp. 67–106 (see
        above).
Braitenberg, V.
1984   *I veicoli pensanti.* Milan: Garzanti.
Brand, M.
1984   *Intending and Acting.* Cambridge, Mass.: MIT Press.
Brandt, R. B.
1960   'Doubts about the Identity Theory', in Hook (ed.), pp. 57–67 (see
        below).
Brennan, A.
1969   'Persons and Their Bodies', *Analysis* 29:27–31.
Brentano, F.
1874   *Psychologie vom empirischen Standpunkt.* Rpt. Hamburg: Meiner,
        1956–9.
Bridgman, P. W.
1959   'On the Fringes of Psychology', in *The Way Things Are.* Cambridge,
        Mass.: Harvard University Press.
1960   'Some Comments on the Dimensions of Mind', in Hook (ed.), pp.
        90–2 (see below).

Broad, C.

1925 *Mind and Its Place in Nature.* London: Routledge.

Brodbeck, M.

1966 'Mental and Physical: Identity versus Sameness', in Feyerabend and Maxwell (eds.), pp. 40–58 (see below).

Broughton, J.

1980 'Genetic Metaphysics: The Developmental Psychology of Mind–Body Concepts', in Rieber (ed.), pp. 177–222 (see below).

Brown, B. B.

1974 *New Mind, New Body.* New York: Harper.

Brown, J.

1977 *Mind, Brain, and Consciousness: The Neuropsychology of Cognition.* New York: Academic Press.

Brown, S. C. (ed.)

1974 *Philosophy of Psychology,* London: Macmillan.

Bunge, M.

1977 'Emergence and the Mind', *Neuroscience* 2:501–9.

1980 *The Mind–Body Problem: A Psychological Approach.* Oxford: Pergamon Press.

Buser, P. A., and A. Buser (eds.)

1978 *Cerebral Correlates of Conscious Experience.* Amsterdam: North Holland.

Callebut, W.

1982 'Reduction Reassessed', in Rose (ed.), pp. 151–74 (see below).

Campbell, K.

1967 'Materialism', in Edwards (ed.), V, pp. 181–8 (see below).

1970 *Body and Mind.* London: Macmillan.

Candlish, St.

1970 'Mind, Brain, and Identity', *Mind* 79:502–18.

Carnap, R.

1931–2 'Die physikalische Sprache als Universalsprache der Wissenschaft', *Erkenntnis* 2:43–65.

1932–3 'Psychologie in physikalischer Sprache', *Erkenntnis* 3:107–42.

1935 'Les concepts psychologiques et les concepts physiologiques sont-ils foncièrement différents?' *Revue de Synthèse* 9:43–53.

Castañeda, H. (ed.)

1967 *Intentionality, Mind, and Perception.* Detroit: Wayne State University Press.

Castell, A.

1965 *The Self in Philosophy.* New York: Macmillan.

Chappell, V. C. (ed.)

1962 *The Philosophy of Mind.* Englewood Cliffs, N.J.: Prentice-Hall.

Chiari, S.
1984   'Filosofia e scienza di fronte al problema mente-corpo oggi', *Cultura e scuola* 90:149–60.
1983   (ed.) *Il problema mente-corpo nel dibattito scientifico contemporaneo.* Arezzo: Università di Arezzo.
Chisholm, R. M.
1957   *Perceiving: A Philosophical Study.* Ithaca, N.Y.: Cornell University Press.
1967   'Intentionality', in Edwards (ed.), IV, pp. 201–4 (see below).
1975   *Person and Object: A Metaphysical Study.* La Salle, Ill.: Open Court.
Chisholm, R. M., and W. Sellars
1958   'Intentionality and the Mental', *Minnesota* 2:507–39.
1969   'The Loose and Popular and the Strict and Philosophical Senses of Identity', in N. Care and R. Grimm (eds.), *Perception and Personal Identity.* Cleveland, Ohio: Press of Case Western Reserve University, pp. 82–106.
Chomsky, N.
1968   *Language and Mind.* New York: Harcourt.
1980   'Mind and Body', in *Rules and Representations.* New York: Columbia University Press.
Choy, V.
1982   'Mind–Body, Realism and Rorty's Therapy', *Synthese* 52:515–41.
Chung-Ying-Cheng (ed.)
1975   *Philosophical Aspects of the Mind–Body Problem.* Honolulu: University Press of Hawaii.
Churchland, P. M.
1979   *Scientific Realism and the Plasticity of Mind.* London: Cambridge University Press.
1984   *Matter and Consciousness: A Contemporary Introduction to the Philosophy of Mind.* Cambridge, Mass.: MIT Press.
Churchland, P. M., and P. S. Churchland
1981   'Functionalism, Qualia and Intentionality', *Philosophical Topics* 12:121–45.
Clark, A.
1980   *Psychological Models and Neural Mechanisms.* Oxford: Oxford University Press.
Coburn, R.
1963   'Shaffer on the Identity of Mental States and Brain Processes', in Borst (ed.), pp. 130–3 (see above).
Cooper, D. E.
1970   'Materialism and Perception', *Philosophical Quarterly* 20:334–46.
Cornman, J.
1962   'The Identity of Mind and Body', in Borst (ed.), pp. 123–9 (see above).

1968   'On the Elimination of 'Sensations' and Sensations', *Review of Metaphysics* 22:15–35.
1969   'Mental Terms, Theoretical Terms and Materialism', *Philosophy of Science* 35:45–63.
1970   'Sellars, Scientific Realism, and Sense', *Review of Metaphysics* 24:417–51.
1971   *Materialism and Sensations*. New Haven, Conn.: Yale University Press.

Creutzfeldt, O., and G. Rager
1978   'Brain Mechanism and the Phenomenology of Conscious Experience', in Buser and Buser (eds.), pp. 311–118 (see above).

Critchley, M.
1979   *The Divine Banquet of the Brain*. New York: Raven Press.

Crittenden, Ch.
1970–71 'Ontology and the Mind–Body Problem', *Philosophical Forum* 2:251–70.

Crosson, F., and K. Sayre (eds.)
1967   *Philosophy and Cybernetics*. Notre Dame, Ind.: University of Notre Dame Press

Culberston, J. T.
1963   *The Mind of Robots*. Urbana, Ill.: University of Illinois Press.
1976   *Sensations, Memories and the Flow of Time*. S. Margarita, Calif.: Cromwell Press.
1982   *Consciousness: Natural and Artificial*. London: Libra Publ.

Cummins, R.
1975   'Functional Analysis', *Journal of Philosophy* 72:741–64.

Curi, U.
1973   *L'analisi operazionale della psicologia*. Milan: Angeli.
1985   (ed.). *La comunicazione umana*. Milan: Angeli.

Dascal, M.
1983–4 *Pragmatics and the Philosophy of Mind*. 2 vols. Amsterdam: J. Benjamin.

Davidson, D.
1970   'Mental Events', in *Essays on Actions and Events* (see below).
1971   'Agency', in *Essays on Actions and Events* (see below).
1973   'The Material Mind', in *Essays on Actions and Events* (see below).
1974   'Psychology as Philosophy', in *Essays on Actions and Events* (see below).
1980   *Essays on Actions and Events*. Oxford: Clarendon.

Delgado, J.
1969   *Physical Control of the Mind*. New York: Harper.

De Monticelli, R.
1985   'Immagini dell'anima. Per una lettura dei testi wittgensteiniani sulla filosofia della psicologia', *Teoria* 5:47–76.

Denes, F., and Umiltà, C. (eds.)
1978   *I due cervelli: Neuropsicologia dei processi cognitivi.* Bologna: Il Mulino.
Dennett, D.
1969   *Content and Consciousness.* London: Routledge.
1977a   Review of Fodor, *The Language of Thought,* in *Mind* 86:265–80.
1977b   'Why You Cannot Make a Computer Feel Pain', rpt. in *Brainstorms* (see below).
1977c   'Intentional Systems', rpt. in *Brainstorms* (see below).
1977d   'Conditions of Personhood', rpt. in *Brainstorms* (see below).
1978a   *Brainstorms: Philosophical Essays on Mind and Psychology.* Hassocks, Sussex: Harvester Press.
1978b   'Current Issues in the Philosophy of Mind', *American Philosophical Quarterly* 15:240–61.
1979   Review of Popper and Eccles, *The Self and Its Brain,* in *Journal of Philosophy* 76:91–8.
1982a   'How to Study Consciousness Empirically', in Ross and Roth (eds.), pp. 159–80 (see below).
1982b   'Comments on Rorty', in Ross and Roth (eds.), pp. 349–56 (see below).
Deutscher, M.
1964   'Mental and Physical Properties', in Presley (ed.), pp. 65–83 (see below).
Diamond, C., and J. Teichman (eds.)
1979   *Intention and Intentionality: Essays in Honour of G. E. M. Anscombe.* Brighton: Harvester Press.
Dreyfus, H.
1972   *What Computers Can't Do.* New York: Harper (rev. ed. 1979)
1976   'The Misleading Mediation of the Mental', in Spicker and Engelhardt (eds.), pp. 131–42 (see below).
Dreyfus, H., and St. E. Dreyfus
1986   *Mind Over Machine.* New York: Macmillan.
Dreyfus, H., and J. Haugeland
1974   'The Computer as a Mistaken Model of the Mind', in J. Brown (ed.), pp. 247–68 (see above).
Dreyfus, H., and H. Hall (eds.)
1982   *Intentionality and Cognitive Science.* Cambridge, Mass.: MIT Press.
Earman, J.
1975   'Physicalism: Ontology, Determination, and Reduction', *Journal of Philosophy* 72:551–67.
Eccles, J.
1963   *The Neurophysiological Basis of Mind.* Oxford: Clarendon.
1965   *The Brain and the Unity of Conscious Experience.* Cambridge: Cambridge University Press.

Bibliography

1966   *Brain and Conscious Experience.* Berlin: Springer.
1970   *Facing Reality.* Berlin: Springer.
1973   *The Understanding of the Brain.* New York: McGraw-Hill.
1979   *The Human Mystery.* Berlin: Springer.
1980   *The Human Psyche.* Berlin: Springer.
1982   (ed.). *The Mind–Body Problem.* Washington: Paragon House.
Edelman, G., and V. Mountcastle
1978   *The Mindful Brain.* Cambridge, Mass.: MIT Press.
Edwards, P. (ed.)
1967   *Encyclopaedia of Philosophy.* New York: Macmillan.
Elgin, C. Z.
1980   'Indeterminacy, Underdetermination, and the Anomalism of the
        Mental', *Synthese* 45:233–55.
Elihorn, A., and R. Banerji (eds.)
1984   *Artificial and Human Intelligence.* Amsterdam: North Holland.
Ellis, B.
1967   'Physical Monism', *Synthese* 17:141–61.
1975   'Physicalism and the Contents of Sense Experience', in Chung-
        Ying-Cheng (ed.), pp. 64–77 (see above).
Engelhardt, H. T.
1973   *Mind–Body: A Categorial Relation.* The Hague: Nijhoff.
Epstein, F. L.
1973   'The Metaphysics of Mind–Body Identity Theories', *American Phil-
        osophical Quarterly* 10:111–21.
Ewing, A. C.
1944–6 'Are Mental Attributes Attributes of the Body?' *Proceedings of the
        Aristotelian Society* 45:27–58.
1948   'Mental Acts', *Mind* 57:201–20.
Farrell, B.
1950   'Experience', *Mind* 59:170–98.
Feibleman, J. K.
1970   *The New Materialism.* The Hague: Nijhoff.
Feigenbaum, E. A., and J. Feldman (eds.)
1963   *Computers and Thought.* New York: McGraw-Hill.
Feigenbaum, E. A., and P. McCorduck
1983   *The Fifth Generation.* Reading, Mass.: Addison.
Feigl, H.
1934   'Logical Analysis of the Psychophysical Problem: A Contribution
        of the New Positivism', *Philosophy of Science* 1:420–45.
1945   'Operationism and Scientific Method', *Psychological Review* 52:250–
        9.
1950a   'Existential Hypotheses: Realistic vs. Phenomenalistic Interpreta-
        tions', *Philosophy of Science* 17:35–62.

1950b 'The Mind–Body Problem in the Development of Logical Empiricism', *Revue internationale de philosophie* 4:64–83 (rpt. in *Inquiries and Provocations*, pp. 286–301 (see below).

1951 'Principles and Problems of Theory Construction in Psychology', in W. Dennis (ed.), *Current Trends of Psychological Theory*. Pittsburgh: University of Pittsburgh Press, pp. 179–213.

1955 'Functionalism, Psychological Theory, and the Uniting Sciences', *Psychological Review* 62:232–5.

1958 'The "Mental" and the "Physical"', in Feigl, Scriven, and Maxwell (eds.), pp. 370–497 (see below); new ed. *The 'Mental' and the 'Physical': The Essay with a Postscript*. Minneapolis: University of Minneapolis Press, 1967.

1959 'Philosophical Embarrassments of Psychology', *American Psychologist* 14:115–28.

1960 'Mind–Body: Not a Pseudo-Problem', in Hook (ed.), pp. 33–44; rpt. in *Inquiries and Provocations* (see below).

1963 'Physicalism, Unity of Science, and the Foundations of Psychology', in P. A. Schlipp (ed.), *The Philosophy of Carnap*. La Salle, Ill.: Open Court.

1967 'Postscript after ten years', in *The 'Mental' and the 'Physical'*, new ed. (see above), pp. 135–69.

1971 'Some Crucial Issues of Mind–Body Monism', *Synthese* 22:295–312.

1975 'Russell and Schlick: A Remarkable Agreement on a Monistic Solution of the Mind–Body Problem', *Erkenntnis* 9:11–34.

1981 *Inquiries and Provocations: Selected Writings 1929–1974*, ed. by R. S. Cohen. Dordrecht: Reidel.

Feigl, H., and M. Brodbeck (eds.)

1953 *Readings in the Philosophy of Sciences*. New York: Appleton.

Feigl, H., and P. Meehl (eds.)

1974 'The Determinism–Freedom and Mind–Body Problems', in P. A. Schlipp (ed.), *The Philosophy of K. Popper*. La Salle, Ill.: Open Court, pp. 520–9.

Feigl, H., and W. Sellars (eds.)

1949 *Readings in Philosophical Analysis*. New York: Appleton.

Feigl, H., and M. Scriven (eds.)

1956 'The Foundation of Science and the Concepts of Psychology and Psychoanalysis', *Minnesota Studies in the Philosophy of Science*, 1:1–346

Feigl, H., M. Scriven, and G. Maxwell (eds.)

1958 'Concepts, Theories, and the Mind–Body Problem', *Minnesota Studies in the Philosophy of Science* 2:1–540.

Feyerabend, P. K.
1963a 'Materialism and the Mind–body Problem', *Review of Metaphsics* 17: 49–66; rpt. in Borst (ed.), pp. 142–58 (see above).
1963b 'Mental Events and the Brain', *Journal of Philosophy* 60:295–6; rpt. in Borst (ed.), pp. 140–1 (see above).
Feyerabend, P. K., and G. Maxwell (eds.)
1966 *Mind, Matter, and Method: Essays in Philosophy and Science in Honor of H. Feigl.* Minneapolis: University of Minneapolis Press.

Findlay, J.
1945 'On Mind and Our Knowledge of It', *Philosophy* 20:206–26.
1949–50 'A Linguistic Approach to Psycho-physics', *Proceedings of the Aristotelian Society* 60:43–64.

Flanagan, O. J.
1984 *The Science of Mind.* Cambridge, Mass.: MIT Press.

Flew, A.
1978 *A Rational Animal.* Oxford: Clarendon.
1964 (ed.). *Body, Mind and Death.* New York: Macmillan.

Flølstad, G. (ed.)
1983 *Contemporary Philosophy: A New Survey.* The Hague: Nijhoff.

Fodor, J.
1964 'Explanations in Psychology', in M. Black (ed.), *Philosophy in America.* London: Allen, pp. 161–79.
1968a *Psychological Explanation.* New York: Random House.
1968b 'The Appeal of Tacit Knowledge in Psychological Explanation', *Journal of Philosophy* 65:627–40.
1968c 'Materialism', in D. M. Rosenthal (ed.), pp. 128–49 (see below).
1974 'Special Sciences', *Synthese* 28:77–115.
1975 *The Language of Thought.* New York: Cromwell.
1978 'Computation and Reduction', in Savage (ed.), pp. 229–60 (see below).
1980 'Mente', in *Enciclopedia.* Torino: Einaudi, vol. IX, pp. 3–47.
1981a 'The Mind–Body Problem', *Scientific American*, pp. 124–32.
1981b *Representations: Philosophical Essays on the Foundation of Cognitive Science.* Cambridge, Mass.: MIT Press.
1983 *The Modularity of Mind.* Cambridge, Mass.: Bradford Books.

Frege, G.
1892 'Ueber Sinn und Bedeutung', *Zeitschrift für Philosophie und philosophische Kritik* 100:22–50.

Gallino, L.
1984 *Mente, comportamento e intelligenza artificiale.* Milan: Comunità.

Gardner, H.
1983 *Frames of Mind.* New York: Basic Books.

Garnett, A.

1952   'Mind as Minding', *Mind* 61:349–58.

1965   'Body and Mind: The Identity Thesis', *Australasian Journal of Philosophy* 43:77–81.

Gauld, A.

1966   'Could a Machine Perceive?' *British Journal for the Philosophy of Science* 17:44–58.

Gauld A., and J. Shotter

1977   *Human Action and Its Psychological Investigation*. London: Routledge.

Gava, G.

1977   *Mente versus corpus: Un errore logico-linguistico*. Padova: Liviana.

1979   'Il materialismo contemporaneo, ovvero la teoria dell'identità e due rilevanti tentativi di falsificazione: Penfield e Sperry', *Medicina nei secoli* 16:169–96.

1981a   'Some Remarks on Psychology and Neurophysiology', *Medicina nei secoli* 18:95–105.

1981b   'Tra gli ultimi baluardi di un dualista. . . : J. C. Eccles', *Medicina nei secoli* 18:335–51.

1982   'J. C. Eccles: Il mistero uomo', *Il progetto psicoterapico* 19:87–99.

1983   *Il problema mente-cervello. Genesi e sviluppo della teoria dell'identità*. Padova: Edizioni Libreria Cortina.

1984   'Fodor e il problema mente-cervello', *Storia e critica della psicologia* 5:29–42.

1980   (ed.) *La conoscenza della mente*. Verona: Bertani.

Gazzaniga, M. S.

1980   *The Bisected Brain*. New York: Appleton.

Geach, P.

1957   *Mental Acts*. London: Routledge; rpt. 1971.

1967   'Identity', *Review of Metaphysics* 21:3–12.

Gendron, B.

1971   'On the Relation of Neurological and Psychological Theories', *Boston Studies in the Philosophy of Science* 8:483–95.

Gibson, J. J.

1966   *The Senses Considered as Perceptual Systems*. London: Allen.

Globus, G.

1972   'Biological Foundations of the Psychoneural Identity Hypothesis', *Philosophy of Science* 39:291–301.

Globus, G., G. Maxwell, and I. Savodnik (eds.)

1976   *Consciousness and the Brain: A Scientific and Philosophical Inquiry*. New York: Plenum Press; 2nd ed. 1977.

Glover, J. (ed.)

1976   *The Philosophy of Mind*. Oxford: Oxford University Press.

Goldberg, B.

1968   'The Correspondence Hypothesis', *Philosophical Review* 77:438–54.

Goodman, N.
1984   *Of Mind and Other Matters*. Cambridge, Mass.: Harvard University Press.

Granit, R.
1977   *The Purposive Brain*. Cambridge, Mass.: MIT Press.

Gregory, R.
1966   *Eye and Brain*. New York: McGraw-Hill.
1970   *The Intelligent Eye*. London: Weidenfeld-Nicolson.
1981   *Mind in Science: History and Explanations in Psychology and Physics*. London: Weidenfeld-Nicolson.

Grene, M.
1974   *The Understanding of Nature: Essays in the Philosophy of Biology*. Dordrecht: Reidel.
1976   'Mind and Brain: The Embodied Person', in Spicker and Engelhardt (eds.), pp. 113–29 (see below).
1977   'Sociobiology and Human Mind', in M. S. Gregory (ed.), *Sociobiology and Human Nature*. San Francisco: Jossey-Bass, 1980.
1971   (ed.) *Interpretations of Life and Mind*. London: Routledge.

Grice, H. P.
1941   'Personal Identity', *Mind* 50:330–50.

Griffin, N.
1977   *Relative Identity*. Oxford: Clarendon.

Grossmann, R.
1965   *The Structure of Mind*. Madison: University of Wisconsin Press.

Gunderson, K.
1964a   'Descartes, La Mettrie, Language and Machines', *Philosophy* 39:193–222.
1964b   'The Imitation Game', *Mind* 73:234–45.
1968   'Robots, Consciousness, and Programmed Behavior', *British Journal for the Philosophy of Science* 39:193–222.
1969   'Cybernetics and the Mind–Body Problem', *Inquiry* 12:406–19.
1970   'Asymmetries and Mind–Body Perplexities', *Minnesota Studies in the Philosophy of Science* 4:273–309; rpt in Rosenthal (ed.), pp. 112–27 (see below).
1971   *Mentality and Machines*. New York: Doubleday; new ed. Minneapolis: Minnesota University Press, 1985.
1977   'Content and Consciousness and the Mind–Body Problem', *Journal of Philosophy* 69:591–604.

Gunner, D. L.
1967   'Prof. Smart's 'Sensations and brain processes' ', in Presley (ed.), pp. 1–20 (see below).

Gustafson, D. F.
1963   'On the Identity Theory', *Analysis* 24:30–2.

1964   (ed.) *Essays in Philosophical Psychology.* Garden City, N.J.: Double-day.

Hall, C. S., and G. Lindzey

1957   *Theories of Personality.* New York: Wiley.

Hampshire, S.

1959   *Thought and Action.* New York: Viking Press.

1971   *Freedom of Mind and Other Essays.* Princeton, N.J.: Princeton University Press.

1966   (ed.) *Philosophy of Mind.* New York: Harper.

Hanson, N. R.

1958   *Patterns of Discovery.* Cambridge University Press.

Harney, M. J.

1984   *Intentionality, Sense and the Mind.* The Hague: Nijhoff.

Harré, R.

1983   *Personal Being: A Theory for Individual Psychology.* Oxford: Blackwell.

1976   (ed.) *Personality.* Oxford: Blackwell; 2nd ed. 1979.

Harré, R., and P. Secord

1972   *The Explanation of Social Behavior.* Oxford: Blackwell.

Harris, E. E.

1966   'The Neutral Identity Theory and the Person', *International Philosophical Quarterly* 6:515–37.

Harth, E.

1982   *Windows on the Mind.* Brighton: Harvester Press.

Haugeland, J.

1982   (ed.) *Mind Design: Philosophy, Psychology, Artificial Intelligence.* Cambridge, Mass.: MIT Press.

Healey, R.

1978–9 'Physicalist Imperialism', *Proceedings of the Aristotelian Society* 79: 191–211.

Hebb, D.

1959   'Intelligence, Brain, Function and the Theory of Mind', *Brain* 82: 260–75.

1974   'What Psychology Is About', *American Psychologist* 29:77 ff.

1980   *Essay on Mind.* Hillsdale, N.J.: Erlbaum.

Heidelberger, H.

1966   'On Characterizing the Psychological', *Philosophy and Phenomenological Research* 26:529–36.

Hellman, G., and F. Thompson

1975   'Physicalism: Ontology, Determinism and Reduction', *Journal of Philosophy* 72:551–64.

1977   'Physicalist Materialism', *Nous* 11:309–46.

Hempel, C. G.

1935   'The Logical Analysis of Psychology', in Feigl and Sellars (eds.), pp. 373–84 (see above).

Henle, P.
1942   'The Status of Emergence', *Journal of Philosophy* 39:486–93.
Herbst, P.
1967   'A Critique of the Materialist Identity Theory', in Presley (ed.), pp. 38–64 (see below).
Hinton, J. N.
1967   'Illusions and Identity', in Borst (ed.), pp. 242–58 (see above).
Hirsch, E.
1982   *The Concept of Identity*. Oxford: Oxford University Press.
Hirst, R.
1968   'Mind and Brain: The Identity Hypothesis', in *The Human Agent*, Royal Institute of Philosophy Lectures. London: Macmillan, pp. 160–80.
Hockutt, M.
1967   'In Defense of Materialism', *Philosophy and Phenomenological Research* 27:366–85.
Hoffman, R.
1970   *Language, Minds, and Knowledge*. New York: Humanities Press.
Hofstadter, D. R.
1979   *Gödel, Escher, Bach: An Eternal Golden Braid*. New York: Basic Books.
Hofstadter, D. R., and D. Dennett
1981   *The Mind's I*. New York: Basic Books.
Hollis, M.
1977   *Models of Man: Philosophical Thoughts on Social Action*. Cambridge: Cambridge University Press.
Hook, S. (ed.)
1960   *Dimensions of the Mind*. New York: New York University Press.
Horgan, T. E.
1978   'Supervenient Bridge Laws', *Philosophy of Science* 45:227–49.
Hoy, R. C.
1980   'Dispositions, Logical States and Mental Occurrents', *Synthese* 44: 207–39.
Irani, K. D.
1980   'Conceptual Changes in the Problem of the Mind–Body Relation', in Rieber (ed.), pp. 57–78 (see below).
James, W.
1890   *Principles of Psychology*. New York: Holt.
1904   'Does Consciousness Exist?'; rpt. in *Essays on Radical Empiricism*. New York: Longmans, 1912.
Jaynes, J.
1976   *The Origin of Consciousness in the Breakdown of the Bicameral Mind*. Boston: Houghton.

Jervis, G.
1984   *Presenza e identità*. Milan: Garzanti.
Kalke, W.
1969   'What is Wrong with Fodor and Putnam's Functionalism', *Nous* 3:83–94.
Kenny, A.
1969   'Philosophy of Mind in the Anglo-American Tradition', in R. Klibansky (ed.), *La philosophie contemporaine*. Florence: La Nuova Italia, vol. III.
Kenny, A., Lonquet-Higgins, A. C., Lucas, J. R., and Waddington, C. H. (eds.)
1973   *The Development of Mind*. Edinburgh: Edinburgh University Press.
Kekes, J.
1966   'Physicalism, the Identity Theory and the Doctrine of Emergence', *Philosophy of Science* 33:360–75.
Kim, J.
1966   'On the Psycho-Physical Identity Theory', *American Philosophical Quarterly* 3:227–35; rpt. in Rosenthal (ed.), pp. 80–95 (see below).
1967   'Psychophysical Laws and Theories of Mind', *Theoria* 33:198–201.
1968   'Reduction, Correspondence and Identity', *Monist* 52:424–38.
1971   'Materialism and the Criteria of the Mental', *Synthese* 22:323–45.
1972   'Phenomenal Properties, Psychological Laws, and the Identity Theory', *Monist* 56:177–92.
1976   'Events as Property Exemplification', in M. Brand and D. Walton (eds.), *Action Theory*. Dordrecht: Reidel, pp. 159–77.
1978   'Supervenience and Nomological Incommensurables', *American Philosophical Quarterly* 15:149–56.
Kim, J., and R. B. Brandt
1967   'The Logic of the Identity Theory', *Journal of Philosophy* 64:515–37.
Kirk, R.
1979   'From Physical Explicability to Full-blooded Materialism', *Philosophical Quarterly* 29:229–37.
Kitcher, P.
1982   'Two Versions of the Identity Theory', *Erkenntnis* 17:213–28.
Klein, D.
1984   *The Concept of Consciousness: A Survey*. Lincoln: University of Nebraska Press.
Kneale, M.
1949–50 'What Is the Mind–Body Problem?' *Proceedings of the Aristotelian Society* 50:105–22.
Kneale, W.
1959   'Mental Events and Epiphenomenalism', in P. A. Schilpp (ed.), *The Philosophy of C. D. Broad*. New York: Tudor, pp. 437–55.
1962   *On Having a Mind*. Cambridge: Cambridge University Press.

1969   Review of Armstrong's *A materialist theory* . . . (see above), *Mind* 78: 292–301.

Koestler A., and J. R. Smythies (eds.)

1969   *Beyond Reductionism: New Perspectives in the Life Sciences.* London: Macmillan.

Kosslyn, S.

1980   *Image and Mind.* Cambridge, Mass.: Harvard University Press.

Kraut, R.

1980   'Indiscernibility and Ontology', *Synthese* 14:113–35.

Kripke, S.

1971   'Identity and Necessity', in Munitz (ed.), pp. 135–64 (see below).

1980   *Naming and Necessity.* Oxford: Blackwell.

Landesman, Ch.

1965   'The New Dualism in the Philosophy of Mind', *Review of Metaphysics* 19:329–45.

Langer, S.

1972   *Mind: An Essay on Human Feeling.* 2 vols. Baltimore: Johns Hopkins University Press.

Laslett, P. (ed.)

1950   *The Physical Basis of Mind.* New York: Macmillan.

Levin, M. E.

1975   'Kripke's Argument against the Identity Theory', *Journal of Philosophy* 72:149–69.

1979   *Metaphysics and the Mind–Body Problem.* Oxford: Oxford University Press.

Lewis, C. I.

1941   'Some Logical Considerations Concerning the Mental', in Feigl and Sellars (eds.), pp. 385–92 (see above).

Lewis, D. K.

1966   'An Argument for the Identity Theory', *Journal of Philosophy* 63:17–25.

1972   'Psychophysical and Theoretical Identifications', in Block (ed.), pp. 207–15 (see above).

Lewis, H. A.

1985   'Is the Mental Supervenient on the Physical?' in Vermazen and Hintikka (eds.), pp. 159–72 (see below).

Lewis, H. D.

1969   *The Elusive Mind.* London: Allen.

1982   *The Elusive Self.* London: Macmillan.

Linguiti, G. L.

1980   *Macchine e pensiero.* Milan: Feltrinelli.

Llinas, R., and A. Pellionisz

1979   'La mente in quanto proprietà tensoriale dei circuiti cerebrali', in M. Piattelli Palmarini (ed.), 1984. *Livelli di realtà.* Milan: Feltrinelli.

Lloyd, B.

1972   *Perception and Cognition.* Harmondsworth: Penguin Books.

Locke, D.

1971   'Must a Materialist Pretend He's Anaesthetized?' *Philosophical Quarterly* 21:217–31.

Lucas, J. R.

1961   'Minds, Machines, and Gödel', *Philosophy* 36:112–27.

Luccio, R.

1983   'Monismo emergentista e rapporto mente-corpo', in S. Chiari (ed.), pp. 9–16 (see above).

Luce, D. R.

1960   'The Action of Mind on Body', *Philosophy of Science* 27:171–82.

Lurie, Y.

1979   'Inner States', *Mind* 88:241–57.

Lycan, W.

1969   'On "Intentionality" and the Psychological', in Marras (ed.), pp. 97–112 (see below).

1974a   'Mental States and Putnam's Functionalist Hypothesis', *Australasian Journal of Philosophy* 52:48–62.

1974b   'Kripke and the Materialists', *Journal of Philosophy* 71:677–89.

1981   'Form, Function, and Feel', *Journal of Philosophy* 78:24–50.

Lycan, W., and G. Pappas

1972   'What is Eliminative Materialism?' *Australasian Journal of Philosophy* 50:149–59.

Mace, C. A.

1966   'The Mind–Body Problem in Philosophy, Psychology, and Medicine', *Philosophy* 41:153–64.

MacKay, D. M.

1952   'Mentality in Machines: A Symposium', in *Aristotelian Society Supplementary Volume*, pp. 66–86.

1978   'Selves and Brains', *Neuroscience* 3:599–606.

1980   *Brains, Machines, and Persons.* London: Collins.

MacKenzie, B. D.

1977   *Behaviourism and the Limits of Scientific Method.* London: Routledge.

Malcolm, N.

1965   'Scientific Materialism and the Identity Theory', *Dialogue* 3:115–25; rpt. in Borst (ed.), pp. 171–80 (see above).

1968   'The Conceivability of Mechanism', *Philosophical Review* 77:45–72.

1970   'Wittgenstein on the Nature of Mind', *American Philosophical Quarterly*, Monograph no. 4, pp. 9–29.

1971   *Problems of Mind: Descartes to Wittgenstein.* New York: Harper.

1977   *Thought and Knowledge.* Ithaca, N.Y.: Cornell University Press.

Malcolm, N., and D. M. Armstrong
1984   *Consciousness and Causality: A Debate on the Nature of Mind*. Oxford: Blackwell.

Margolis, J.
1966   *Psychotherapy and Morality*. New York: Random House.
1971   'Difficulties for Mind–Body Identity Theories', in Munitz (ed.), pp. 213–31 (see below).
1973a   'Perils of Physicalism', *Mind* 82:566–78.
1973b   *Knowledge and Existence*. Oxford: Oxford University Press.
1976   'Persons and Psycho-Surgery', in Spicker and Engelhardt (eds.), pp. 71–84 (see below).
1977   *Art and Philosophy*. Atlantic Highlands, N.Y.: Humanities Press.
1978   *Persons and Minds*. Dordrecht: Reidel.
1980a   'Persons: Notes on Their Nature, Identity, and Rationality', *Southern Journal of Philosophy* 18:463–72.
1980b   'The Trouble with Homunculus Theories', *Philosophy of Science* 47: 244–59.
1983   *Culture and Cultural Entities*. Dordrecht: Reidel.
1984   *Philosophy of Psychology*. Englewood Cliffs, N.J.: Prentice-Hall.

Marks, Ch.
1980   *Commissurotomy, Consciousness, and Unity of Mind*. Cambridge, Mass.: Bradford Books.

Marras, A. (ed.)
1972   *Intentionality, Mind, and Language*. Urbana: University of Illinois Press.

Martin, M.
1971   'Neurophysiological Reduction and Psychological Explanation', *Philosophy of the Social Sciences* 1:161–70.

Matson, W. I.
1966   'Why Isn't the Mind–Body Problem Ancient?' in Feyerabend and Maxwell (eds.), pp. 92–102 (see above).
1976   *Sentience*. Berkeley: University of California Press.

Maxwell, G.
1975   'Russell on Perception and Mind–Body', in Chung-Ying-Cheng (ed.), pp. 131–53 (see above).
1976a   'The Role of Scientific Results in Theories of Mind and Brain', in Globus et al. (eds.), pp. 317–28 (see above).
1976b   'Scientific Results and the Mind–Body Issue: Some Afterthoughts', in Globus et al. (eds.), pp. 329–57.
1978   'Rigid Designators and Mind–Brain Identity', in Savage (ed.), pp. 365–403 (see below).

McCorduck, P.
1979   *Machines Who Think*. San Francisco: Freeman.

McCulloch, W. S.
1965   *Embodiments of Mind*. Cambridge, Mass.: MIT Press.
McDougall, W.
1911   *Body and Mind: A History and Defense of Animism*. London: Methuen.
McGinn, C.
1980   'Philosophical Materialism', *Synthese* 44:173–206.
1982   *The Character of Mind*. Oxford: Oxford University Press.
Mecacci, L.
1977   *Cervello e storia*. Rome: Editori Riuniti.
1984   *Identikit del cervello*. Bari: Laterza.
Medlin, B.
1960   'Ryle and the Mechanical Hypothesis', in Presley (ed.), pp. 94–150 (see below).
Meehl, P.
1966   'The Compleat Autocerebroscopist', in Feyerabend and Maxwell (eds.), pp. 103–80 (see above).
1970   'Psychological Determinism and Human Rationality', in Radner and Winokur (eds.), pp. 310–72 (see below).
Meehl, P., and W. Sellars
1956   'The Concept of Emergence', *Minnesota Studies in the Philosophy of Science* 1:239–52.
Meiland, J. W.
1970   *The Nature of Intention*. London: Methuen.
Melzack, R.
1973   *The Puzzle of Pain*. New York: Basic Books.
Miles, T. R.
1963–4 'The "Mental–Physical" Dichotomy', *Proceedings of the Aristotelian Society* 64:71–84.
Miller, G., E. Galanter, and K. Pribram
1960   *Plans and the Structure of Behavior*. New York: Holt.
Miller, J. (ed.)
1983   *States of Mind*. London: BBC Ed.
Millikan, R. G.
1984   *Language, Thought, and Biological Categories*. Cambridge, Mass.: MIT Press.
Moor, J. H.
1978   'Three Myths of the Computer Science', *British Journal for the Philosophy of Science* 29:213–22.
Moravia, S.
1984   'Realismo epistemologico e universali della natura umana', *Paradigmi* 2:189–214.
Morick, H. (ed.)
1970   *Introduction to the Philosophy of Mind*. New York: Humanities Press.

Morris, Ch. W.
1932   *Six Theories of Mind.* Chicago: University of Chicago Press.
Morton, A.
1980   *Frames of Mind.* Oxford: Oxford University Press.
Munitz, M. K. (ed.)
1971   *Identity and Individuation.* New York: New York University Press.
Nagel, Th.
1965   'Physicalism', *Philosophical Review* 74:339–56; rpt. in Rosenthal (ed.), pp. 96–110 (see below).
1970   'Armstrong on the Mind', *Philosophical Review* 79:394–403.
1971   'Brain Bisection and the Unity of Consciousness', in *Mortal Questions* (see below).
1974   'What Is It Like to be a Bat?' *Philosophical Review* 83:435–50; rpt. in *Mortal Questions* (see below).
1979   *Mortal Questions.* Cambridge: Cambridge University Press.
1980   'The Limits of Objectivity', in S. McMurrin (ed.), *The Tanner Lectures on Human Values.* Cambridge: Cambridge University Press.
1986   *The View from Nowhere.* New York: Oxford University Press.
Neisser, U.
1963   'The Imitation of Man by Machine', *Science* 139:193–7.
1976   *Cognition and Reality.* San Francisco: Freeman.
Nelson, R. J.
1976   'Mechanism, Functionalism, and the Identity Theory', *Journal of Philosophy* 73:365–85.
Neurath, O.
1931   'Physikalismus', *Scientia* 25:97–303.
1931–2 'Soziologie im Physikalismus', *Erkenntnis* 2:294–431.
Norman, D. A. (ed.)
1981   *Perspectives on Cognitive Science.* Norwood: Ablex.
Nozen, St.
1970a   'Identity, Materialism, and the Problem of the Danglers', *Metaphilosophy* 1:318–34.
1970b   'Smart's Materialism: The Identity Thesis and Translation', *Australasian Journal of Philosophy* 48:54–66.
O'Conner, J. (ed.)
1969   *Modern Materialism: Readings on Mind–Body Identity.* New York: Harcourt.
Odegard, D.
1970   'Persons and Bodies', *Philosophy and Phenomenological Research* 31:225–42.
Oliverio, A.
1981   'An Evolutionistic Approach to the Mind–Body Problem', in Agazzi (ed.), pp. 73–96 (see above).

1984a   *Storia naturale della coscienza*. Turin: Boringhieri.
1984b   'Cervello e mente', *Prometeo* 2:38–47.
Oppenheim, P., and J. G. Kemeny
1956   'On Reduction', *Philosophical Studies* 7:6–17.
Oppenheim, P., and H. Putnam
1958   'Unity of Science as a Working Hypothesis', in Feigl, Scriven, and Maxwell (eds.), pp. 3–36 (see above).
Ornstein, J. H.
1972   *The Mind and the Brain: A Multi-aspect Interpretation*. The Hague: Nijhoff.
Pap, A.
1952   'Semantic Analysis and Psycho-Physical Dualism', *Mind* 61:209–21.
1954   'Das Leib-Seele Problem in der analytischen Philosophie', *Archiv für Philosophie* Bd. 5, Hft. 2, pp. 113–29.
Parisi, D.
1984   'La simulazione della mente e del corpo', *Teoria* 2:15–36.
Peacocke, T.
1979   *Holistic Explanation*. Oxford: Oxford University Press.
Penfield, W.
1975   *The Mystery of Mind*. Princeton, N.J.: Princeton University Press.
Perkins, M.
1965   'Two Arguments against a Private Language', *Journal of Philosophy* 57:443–59.
Perry, J. (ed.)
1975   *Personal Identity*. Berkeley: University of California Press.
Philipp, R. L.
1967   'Descriptive versus Revisionary Metaphysics and the Mind–Body Problem', *Philosophy* 42:105–18.
Pitcher, G.
1970a   'Pain Perception', *Philosophical Review* 79:368–93.
1970b   'The Awfulness of Pain', *Journal of Philosophy* 67:481–92.
1971   *A Theory of Perception*. Princeton, N.J.: Princeton University Press.
Place, U. T.
1956   'Is Consciousness a Brain Process?' *British Journal for the Philosophy of Science* 47:44–50; rpt. in Borst (ed.), pp. 42–51 (see above).
1960   'Materialism as a Scientific Hypothesis', *Philosophical Review* 69:101–4; rpt. in Borst (ed.), pp. 83–6 (see above).
1966   'Consciousness and Perception', *Aristotelian Society Supplementary Volume* 40:101–24.
Polanyi, M.
1958   *Personal Knowledge*. London: Routledge.
Polten, E.
1973   *Critique of the Psycho-physical Identity Theory*. The Hague: Mouton.

Popper, K.

1953   'Language and the Mind–Body Problem', *Proceedings of the XI International Congress of Philosophy* 7:101–7.

1972   'On the Theory of the Objective Mind', in *Objective Knowledge*. Oxford: Clarendon.

Popper, K., and J. Eccles

1977   *The Self and Its Brain*. Berlin: Springer.

Pratt, J. B.

1963   'The Present Status of the Mind–Body Problem', *Philosophical Review* 65:144–56.

Presley, C. F. (ed.)

1967   *The Identity Theory of Mind*. St. Lucia: University of Queensland Press.

Preti, G.

1984   *Logica e filosofia*. Milan: Angeli.

Pribram, K.

1971a   'The Realization of Mind', *Synthese* 22:313–22.

1971b   *Languages of the Brain*. Englewood Cliffs, N.J.: Prentice-Hall.

1976   'Problems Concerning the Structure of Consciousness', in Globus et al. (ed.), pp. 297–313 (see above).

Puccetti, R.

1964   'Science, Analysis, and the Problem of Mind', *Philosophy* 39:249–59.

1967   'On Thinking Machines and Feeling Machines', *British Journal for the Philosophy of Science* 18:39–51.

1968   *Persons: A Study of Possible Moral Agents in the Universe*. London: Macmillan.

1973   'Brain Bisection and Personal Identity', *British Journal for the Philosophy of Science* 24:339–55.

1974   'Physicalism and the Evolution of Consciousness', *Canadian Journal of Philosophy* 1:171–83.

Puccetti, R., and R. Dykes

1978   'Sensory Cortex and the Mind–Body Problem', *Behavioral and Brain Sciences* 3:337–76.

Putnam, H.

1960   'Mind and Machines', in Hook (ed.), pp. 138–64 (see above).

1961   'Brain and Behavior', in Block (ed.), pp. 24–36 (see above).

1964   'Robots: Machines or Artificially Created Life?' *Journal of Philosophy* 61:69–91.

1967   'The Mental Life of Some Machines', in Castañeda (ed.), pp. 177–200 (see above).

1967b   'The Nature of Mental States', in Rosenthal (ed.), pp. 150–61 (see below).

1969   'Logical Positivism and the Philosophy of Mind', in P. Achinstein and St. Barker (eds.), *The Legacy of Logical Positivism*. Baltimore: Johns Hopkins University Press.

1970   'On Properties', in N. Rescher (ed.), *Essays in Honor of C. G. Hempel.* Dordrecht: Reidel, pp. 235–54.

1973a   'Reductionism and the Nature of Psychology', *Cognition* 2:131–46.

1973b   'Philosophy and our Mental Life', in Block (ed.), pp. 134–43 (see above).

1975   *Mind, Language, and Reality.* 2 vols. Cambridge: Cambridge University Press.

1981   *Reason, Truth and History.* Cambridge: Cambridge University Press.

1982a   'Machines with a Point of View', *London Review of Books*, Feb. 4–18.

1982b   'Why There Isn't a Ready-made World', *Synthese* 51:141–67.

Pylyshyn, Z.

1973   'What the Mind's Eye Tells the Brain's Eye', *Psychology Bulletin* 80:1–24.

Quine, W. V.

1960   *Word and Object.* Cambridge, Mass.: MIT Press.

1966   'On Mental Entities' (1950), in *The Ways of Paradox.* New York: Random House.

Quinton, A.

1965   'Mind and Matter', in Smythies (ed.), pp. 201–33 (see below).

1973   *The Nature of Things.* London: Routledge.

Radner, M., and St. Winokur (eds.)

1970   'Analyses of Theories and Methods of Physics and Psychology', *Minnesota Studies in the Philosophy of Science* 4:1–429.

Reeves, J.

1958   *Body and Mind in Western Thought.* Harmondsworth: Penguin Books.

Rhees, R.

1954   'Can There Be a Private Language? A Symposium', *Aristotelian Society Supplementary Volume* 28:77–94.

Rieber, R. W. (ed.)

1980   *Body and Mind: Past, Present and Future.* New York: Academic Press.

Ringle, M. D. (ed.)

1979   *Philosophical Perspectives in Artificial Intelligence.* Atlantic Highlands, N.Y.: Humanities Press.

Robinson, H.

1982   *Matter and Sense: A Critique of Contemporary Materialism.* Cambridge: Cambridge University Press.

Rollins, C. D.

1967   'Are Mental Events Actually Physical?' in Presley (ed.), pp. 21–37 (see above).

Rorty, A. O. (ed.)

1976   *The Identities of Persons.* Berkeley: University of California Press.

Rorty, R.

1965   'Mind–Body Identity, Privacy, and Categories', *Review of Metaphysics* 19:24–54; rpt. in Borst (ed.), pp. 187–213 (see above).

Bibliography

1970a 'In Defense of Eliminative Materialism', *Review of Metaphysics* 24:112–21; rpt. in Rosenthal (ed.), pp. 223–31 (see above).

1970b 'Incorrigibility as the Mark of the Mental', *Journal of Philosophy* 67:399–424.

1972 'Functionalism, Machines, and Incorrigibility', *Journal of Philosophy* 69:203–20.

1979 *Philosophy and the Mirror of Nature*. Princeton, N.J.: Princeton University Press.

1982a 'Comments on Dennett', in Ross and Roth (eds.), pp. 181–7 (see below).

1982b 'Contemporary Philosophy of Mind', in Ross and Roth (eds.), pp. 323–48 (see below).

1982c *Consequences of Pragmatism*. Minneapolis: University of Minnesota Press.

1975 (ed.) *The Linguistic Turn*. Chicago: University of Chicago Press.

Rose, S.

1972 *The Conscious Brain*. London: Weidenfeld.

1982 (ed.) *Against Biological Determinism*. London: Allison.

Rosenblueth, A.

1970 *Mind and Brain: A Philosophy of Science*. Cambridge, Mass.: MIT Press.

Rosenberg, A. L.

1978 'The Supervenience of Biological Concepts', *Philosophical Review* 45:368–85.

Rosenthal. D. M.

1976 'Mentality and Neutrality', *Journal of Philosophy* 73:386–415.

1984 'Armstrong's Causal Theory of Mind', in Bogdan (ed.), pp. 79–120 (see above).

1971 (ed.) *Materialism and the Mind–Body Problem*. Englewood Cliffs, N.J.: Prentice-Hall.

Ross, S. A., and P. A. Roth (eds.)

1982 'Matters of the Mind', *Synthese* (monograph) 53:157–356.

Routley R., and V. Macrae

1966 'On the Identity of Sensations and Physiological Occurrences', *American Philosophical Quarterly* 3:87–110.

Rubinstein, B. B.

1965 'Psychoanalytic Theory and the Mind–Body Problem', in N. Greenfield and W. Lewis (eds.), *Psychoanalysis and Current Biological Thought*. Madison: University of Wisconsin Press.

Ruddick, W.

1971 'Physical Equations and Identity', in Munitz (ed.), pp. 233–50 (see above).

Russell, B.

1921 *The Analysis of Mind*. London: Allen.

1927   *The Analysis of Matter.* London: Kegan Paul.

1948   *Human Knowledge: Its Scope and Limits.* London: Allen.

Ryle, G.

1949   *The Concept of Mind.* London: Hutchinson; rpt. London: Penguin, 1986.

1950   'The Physical Basis of Mind', in Laslett (ed.), pp. 79–96 (see above).

1954   *Dilemmas.* Cambridge: Cambridge University Press.

Sahlins, M.

1976a   *Culture and Practical Reason.* Chicago: University of Chicago Press.

1976b   'Colors and Culture', *Semiotica* 16:1–22.

Sartre, J.-P.

1939   *Esquisse d'une théorie des émotions.* Paris: Harmann.

Savage, C. W.

1976   'An Old Ghost in a New Body', in Globus et al. (eds.), pp. 73–98 (see above).

1978   (ed.), 'Perception and Cognition: Issues in the Foundations of Psychology', *Minnesota Studies in the Philosophy of Science* 9:3–502.

Sayre, K.

1969   *Consciousness: A Philosophical Study of Minds and Machines.* New York: Random House.

1976   *Cybernetics and the Philosophy of Mind.* Atlantic Highlands, N.Y.: Humanities Press.

Schank, R., and K. Colby (eds.)

1973   *Computer Models of Thought and Language.* San Francisco: Freeman.

Scher, J. (ed.)

1962   *Theories of Mind.* New York: Free Press of Glencoe.

Schlick, M.

1918   *Allgemeine Erkenntnislehre.* Berlin: Springer, 1925; English trans., New York: Springer, 1974.

1935   'On the Relations between Psychological and Physical Concepts', in Feigl and Sellars (eds.), pp. 393–407 (see above).

Scriven, M.

1953   'The Mechanical Concept of Mind', *Mind* 62:230–40.

1960   'The Compleat Robot', in Hook (ed.), pp. 113–33 (see above).

1966   'The Limitations of the Identity Theory', in Feyerabend and Maxwell (eds.), pp. 191–7 (see above).

Searle, J. R.

1980   'Minds, Brains and Programs', *Behavioral and Brain Sciences* 3:417–57.

1982   'The Myth of the Computer', *New York Review of Books* April 29.

1983   *Intentionality: An Essay in the Philosophy of Mind.* Cambridge: Cambridge University Press.

1984   *Minds, Brains and Science.* Cambridge, Mass.: Harvard University Press.

Bibliography

Segall, M. E., and Campbell D. (eds.)
1966   *The Influence of Culture on Visual Perception*. Indianapolis: Bobbs-Merrill.
Sellars, W.
1952   'Mind, Meaning and Behavior', *Philosophical Studies* 3:83–94.
1953   'A Semantic Solution of the Mind–Body Problem', *Methodos* 5:45–94.
1956   'Empiricism and the Philosophy of Mind', *Minnesota Studies in the Philosophy of Science* 1:253–329.
1962   'Philosophy and the Scientific Image of Man', in *Science, Perception, and Reality* (see below).
1963   *Science, Perception and Reality*. London: Routledge.
1964   'Notes on Intentionality', *Journal of Philosophy* 61:655–66.
1965   'The Identity Approach to the Mind–Body Problem', *Review of Metaphysics* 18:430–51.
1967   *Philosophical Perspectives*. Springfield, Ill.: Ch. Thomas.
1971   'The Double Knowledge Approach to the Mind–Body Problem', *New Scholasticism* 45:269–89.
Sellars, W., and R. Chisholm
1958   'Intentionality and the Mental', *Minnesota Studies in the Philosophy of Science* 2:507–39.
Settle, T.
1981   'Letter to Mario [Bunge]: The Self and Its Mind', in J. Agassi and R. Cohen (eds.), *Scientific Philosophy Today*, Dordrecht: Reidel, pp. 357–79.
Shaffer, J.
1961   'Could Mental States be Brain Processes?' in Borst (ed.), pp. 113–22 (see above).
1963   'Mental Events and the Brain', in Borst (ed.), pp. 134–9 (see above).
1965   'Recent Work on the Mind–Body Problem', *American Philosophical Quarterly* 2:81–104.
1966   'Persons and Their Bodies', *Philosophical Review* 75:59–77.
1967a   *Philosophy of Mind*. Englewood Cliffs, N.J.: Prentice-Hall.
1967b   'Mind–Body Problem', in Edwards (ed.), vol. V, pp. 336–46 (see above).
1972   'Mind, Bodies and Theoretical Entities', *Ratio* 14:83–6.
1983   'Recent Work in the Mind–Body Problem (II)', in K. G. Lucey and T. R. Machan (eds.), *Recent Work in Philosophy*. Totowa, N.J.: Rowmand and Allanheld.
Shoemaker, S.
1963   *Self-knowledge and Self-identity*. Ithaca, N.Y.: Cornell University Press.
1975   'Functionalism and Qualia', *Philosophical Studies* 27:291–314.
1981   'Some Varieties of Functionalism', *Philosophical Topics* 12:93–119.

Shoemaker, S., and C. Ginet (eds.)
1983   *Knowledge and Mind.* Oxford: Oxford University Press.
1984   *Identity, Cause and Mind: Philosophical Essays.* Cambridge: Cambridge University Press.
Shoemaker, S., and R. Swinburne
1984   *Personal Identity.* Oxford: Blackwell.
Shotter, J.
1975   *Images of Man in Psychological Research.* London: Methuen.
Simon, M.
1969   *The Sciences of the Artificial.* Cambridge, Mass.: MIT Press.
Simon, M. H.
1970   'Materialism, Mental Language, and the Mind–Body Identity', *Philosophy and Phenomenological Research* 30:514–32.
Skinner, B.
1953   *Science and Human Behavior.* New York: Macmillan.
Sloman, A.
1974   'Physicalism and the Bogey of Determinism', in Brown (ed.), pp. 283–304 (see above).
1978   *The Computer Revolution in Philosophy.* Brighton: Harvester Press.
Smart, Br.
1977   'How Can Persons Be Ascribed M-Predicates?' *Mind* 86:49–66.
Smart, J. J. C.
1959a   'Sensations and Brain Processes', *Philosophical Review* 68:141–56; rpt. in Borst (ed.), pp. 52–66 (see above).
1959b   'Ryle on Mechanism and Psychology', *Philosophical Quarterly* 9:349–55.
1960   'Sensations and Brain Processes: A Rejoinder', *Australasian Journal of Philosophy* 38:252–4.
1961   'Further Remarks on Sensations and Brain Processes', *Philosophical Review* 70:406–7; rpt. in Borst (ed.), pp. 93–4 (see above).
1962   'Brain Processes and Incorrigibility', *Australasian Journal of Philosophy* 40:68–70; rpt. in Borst (ed.), pp. 107–9 (see above).
1963a   'Materialism', *Journal of Philosophy* 60:651–62; rpt. in Borst (ed.), pp. 159–70 (see above).
1963b   *Philosophy and Scientific Realism.* London: Routledge.
1964   'Comments on the Paper', in Presley (ed.), pp. 84–93 (see above).
1971   'Reports of Immediate Experiences', *Synthese* 22:346–59.
1972   'Further Thoughts on the Identity Theory', *Monist* 56:346–59.
1975   'On Some Criticism of a Physicalist Theory of Colors', in Chung-Ying-Cheng (ed.), pp. 54–63 (see above).
1985   'Davidson's Minimal Materialism', in Vermazen and Hintikka (eds.), pp. 173–82 (see below).
Smith, J. W.
1984   *Reductionism and Cultural Being.* The Hague: Nijhoff.

Smythies, J. R.

1969 'Aspects of Consciousness', in Koestler and Smythies (eds.), pp. 233–57 (see above).

1965 (ed.) *Brain and Mind: Modern Concepts of the Nature of Mind*. London: Routledge.

Somenzi, V.

1965 'Dalla materia inerte alla materia vivente e pensante', *De homine* 15/16:143–86.

1967 'Mente, vita, materia', *Giornale critico della filosofia italiana* 46:343–51 and 520–7.

1972 'Intelligenza naturale e intelligenza artificiale', *Filosofia* 23:17–21.

1978 'Mind–Body, Mind–Brain and Brain–Body Problems', in Bianca and Muzi (eds.), pp. 33–6 (see above).

1977 'Sui rapporti mente-cervello', *Medicina nei secoli* 1:61–9.

1980b 'Mente-cervello secondo Popper-Eccles', in Gava (ed.), pp. 165–74 (see above).

1983 'Tra "fisico" e "mentale"', in Chiari (ed.), pp. 17–22 (see above).

1965 (ed.) *La Filosofia dagli automi*. Turin: Boringhieri.

1969 (ed.) *La Fisica della mente*. Turin: Boringhieri.

Sperry, R. W.

1952 'Neurology and the Mind–Body Problem', *American Scientist* 40: 291–312.

1965 'Mind, Brain, and Humanistic Values', in *Science and Moral Priority* (see below).

1968 'Disconnessione emisferica e unità della coscienza', in F. Denes and C. Umiltà (eds.), pp. 215–35 (see above).

1969 'A Modified Concept of Consciousness', *Psychological Review* 77: 532–6.

1970 'An Objective Approach to Subjective Experience', *Psychological Review* 77:585–90.

1973 'Mental Phenomena as Causal Determinants in Brain Function', in Globus et al. (eds.), pp. 163–77.

1980 'Mind–Brain Interaction: Mentalism, Yes, Dualism, No', *Neuroscience* 5:195–206.

1983 *Science and Moral Priority: Merging Mind, Brain, and Human Values*. New York: Columbia University Press.

Spicker, St., and H. T. Engelhardt, Jr. (eds.)

1976 *Philosophical Dimensions of the Neuro-medical Sciences*. Dordrecht: Reidel.

Spilsbury, R. J.

1952 'Mentality in Machines: A Symposium', *Aristotelian Society Supplementary Volume* 26:27–60.

Squires, R. J.

1970 'On One's Mind', *Philosophical Quarterly* 20:347–56.

Stanzione, M.
1975 'Le teorie dell'identità mente-cervello', *De homine* 53/6:157–94.
Sternbach, R. A.
1968 *Pain: A Psychological Analysis*. New York: Academic Press.
Stevenson, J. J.
1960 'Sensations and Brain Processes: A Reply to Prof. Smart', *Philosophical Quarterly* 69:505–10; rpt. in Borst (ed.), pp. 87–90 (see above).
Stich, S. P.
1983 *From Folk Psychology to Cognitive Science*. Cambridge, Mass.: MIT Press.
Strawson, P. F.
1958 'Persons', in Feigl, Scriven, and Maxwell (eds.), pp. 330–53 (see above); rev. ed. in *Individuals* (see below).
1959 *Individuals*. London: Methuen (rpt. 1974).
1966 'Self, Mind and Body', rpt. in Morick (ed.), pp. 89–108 (see above).
Sutherland, N. S.
1970 'Is the Brain a Physical System?' in Borger and Cioffi (eds.), pp. 97–137 (see above).
Swinburne, R.
1973–4 'Personal Identity', *Proceedings of the Aristotelian Society* 74:231–48.
1982 'Are Mental Events Identical with Brain Events?' *American Philosophical Quarterly* 19:173–80.
Taylor, Ch.
1964 *The Explanation of Behavior*. London: Routledge.
1967 'Mind–Body Identity, a Side Issue?' in Borst (ed.), pp. 231–41 (see above).
1969 'Two Issues about Materialism', *Philosophical Quarterly* 19:73–9.
Taylor, R.
1969 'How to Bury the Mind–Body Problem', *American Philosophical Quarterly* 6:136–43.
Teichman, J.
1961 'Mental Cause and Effect', *Mind* 70:36–52.
1967 'The Contingent Identity of Minds and Brains', *Mind* 76:404–15.
Thompson, D.
1965 'Can a Machine Be Conscious?' *British Journal for the Philosophy of Science* 16:33–43.
Thomson, J. J.
1964 'Private Languages', *American Philosophical Quarterly* 1:20–31.
1969 'The Identity Theory', in S. Morgenbesser, P. Suppes, and N. White (eds.), *Philosophy, Science and Method: Essays in Honor of E. Nagel*. New York: St. Martin's Press, pp. 219–34.

Thorp, J.
1980   *Free Will: A Defense against Neurophysiological Determinism.* London:
        Routledge.
Tolman, E. C.
1935   'Psychology vs. Immediate Experience', *PS* 2:356–80.
Tomkins, S., and S. Messick (eds.)
1963   *Computer Simulation of Personality.* New York: Wiley.
Tormey, A.
1973   'Access, Incorrigibility, and Identity', *Journal of Philosophy* 70:115–
        28.
Townsend, J.
1975   'The Mind–body Equation Revisited', in Chung-Ying-Cheng (ed.),
        pp. 200–17 (see above).
Trigg, R.
1970   *Pain and Emotion.* Oxford: Clarendon.
Troyer, J., and S. Wheeler (eds.)
1974   'Intentionality, Language, and Translation', *Synthese* 23:123–456.
Turbayne, C. M.
1972   'Metaphors for the Mind', in R. Rudner and I. Sheffler (eds.), *Logic
        and Art: Essays in Honor of N. Goodman.* Indianapolis: Bobbs-Merrill,
        pp. 58–77.
Turing, A. M.
1950   'Computing Machinery and Intelligence', in Somenzi (ed.), *La filo-
        sofia degli automi*, pp. 116–56 (see above).
Uttal, W. R.
1978   *The Psychobiology of Mind.* Hillsdale, N.J.: Erlbaum.
Van Peursen, C. A.
1966   *Body, Soul, Spirit: A Survey of the Mind–Body Problem.* Oxford: Ox-
        ford University Press.
Vendler, Z.
1972   *Res Cogitans.* Ithaca, N.Y.: Cornell University Press.
1976   'Thinking of Individuals', *Nous* 10:35–46.
Vermazen, B., and M. Hintikka (eds.)
1985   *Essays on Davidson.* Oxford: Clarendon.
Vesey, G. N.
1965   *The Embodied Mind.* London: Allen.
1974   *Personal Identity: A Philosophical Analysis.* Ithaca, N.Y.: Cornell Uni-
        versity Press.
1964   (ed.) *Body and Mind.* London: Allen.
Watson, J. B.
1919   *Psychology from the Standpoint of a Behaviorist.* Philadelphia: Lippin-
        cott.
1924   *Behaviorism.* Chicago: University of Chicago Press.

Watzlawick, P.
1985   'Comunicazione e scienze umane', in Curi (ed.), pp. 31–40 (see above).
Weimer, W.
1976   'Manifestations of Mind: Some Conceptual and Empirical Issues', in Globus et al. (eds.), pp. 5–30 (see above).
Weiner, H.
1980   'Contemporary Research and the Mind–Body Problem', in Rieber (ed.), pp. 223–40 (see above).
Weizenbaum, J.
1976   *Computer Power and Human Reason*. San Francisco: Freeman.
White, A. R.
1967   *The Philosophy of Mind*. New York: Random House.
Whiteley, C. H.
1944–5 'The Relation between Mind and Body', *Proceedings of the Aristotelian Society* 45:119–29.
1970   'The Mind–Body Identity Thesis', *Philosophical Quarterly* 20:193–9.
1973   *Mind in Action*. Oxford University Press.
Wiggins, D.
1967   *Identity and Spatio-temporal Continuity*. Oxford: Blackwell.
1980   *Sameness and Substance*. Cambridge, Mass.: Harvard University Press.
Wilkerson, T. E.
1974   *Minds, Brains, and People*. Oxford: Clarendon.
Wilkes, K.
1978a   *Physicalism*. London: Routledge.
1978b   'Consciousness and Commissurotomy', *Philosophy* 33:184–99.
1981   'Functionalism, Psychology, and the Philosophy of Mind', *Philosophical Topics* 12:147–67.
Williams, B. A.
1956–57 'Personal Identity and Individuation', *Proceedings of the Aristotelian Society* 57:229–52.
1960   'Mind as a Matter of Fact', *Review of Metaphysics* 13:203–25.
1970   'Are Persons Bodies?' in S. Spicker (ed.), *Philosophy of the Body*. Chicago: Quadrangle Books.
1979   Wilson, E. *The Mental as Physical*. London: Routledge.
Wilson, E. O.
1975   *Sociobiology: The New Synthesis*. Cambridge, Mass.: Harvard University Press.
1978   *On Human Nature*. Cambridge, Mass.: Harvard University Press.
Wilson, E. O., and Ch. Lumsden
1981   *Gene, Mind, and Culture*. Cambridge, Mass.: Harvard University Press.
1983   *Promethean Fire*. New York: Powell.

Bibliography

Wimsatt, W. C.

1976 'Reductionism, Levels of Organization, and the Mind–Body Problem', in Globus et al. (eds.), pp. 205–67 (see above).

Wisdom, J. O.

1949–50 'The Concept of Mind', *Proceedings of the Aristotelian Society* 50:189–204.

1951–52 'A New Model for the Mind–Body Relationship', *British Journal for the Philosophy of Science* 2:295–301.

1952 'Mentality in Machines: A Symposium', *Aristotelian Society Supplementary Volume* 26:1–26.

1959–60 'Some Main Mind–Body Problems', *Proceedings of the Aristotelian Society* 60:187–210.

1965 *Other Minds*. Oxford: Blackwell.

Wittgenstein, L.

1953 *Philosophische Untersuchungen*. Oxford: Blackwell.

1967 *Zettel*. Oxford: Blackwell.

1980 *Remarks on the Philosophy of Psychology*. 2 vols. Oxford: Blackwell.

Woodfield, A.

1976 *Teleology*. Cambridge: Cambridge University Press.

1982 (ed.) *Thought and Object: Essays on Intentionality*. Oxford: Oxford University Press.

Woolridge, D.

1968 *Mechanical Man: The Physical Basis of Intelligent Life*. New York: McGraw-Hill.

Yolton, J. W.

1967 Review of A. Campbell Garnett and R. Grossmann, *Synthese* 17: 223–9.

Zaner, R.

1971 *The Problem of Embodiment*. The Hague: Nijhoff.

Zangwill, O. L.

1976 'Thought and the Brain', *British Journal of Psychology* 67:301–14.

1977 'Consciousness and the Brain', in G. Butts and J. Hintikka (eds.), *Foundational Problems in the Social Sciences*. Dordrecht: Reidel.

Ziedins, R.

1971 'Identification of Characteristics of Mental Events with Characteristics of Brain Events', *American Philosophical Quarterly* 8:13–23.

Name index

Alston, W. P., 252
Anscombe, G. E. M., 220
Apel, K. O., 6
Armstrong, D. M., 6, 14, 88–103, 105, 123, 126, 141, 145, 150, 181, 251, 254, 280 and n.
Aune, B., 254
Ayre, A. J., 226

Baier, K., 20–1, 211, 225, 227, 230
Bain, A., 1
Beloff, J., 76 n., 238 n.
Bergson, H., 1
Bernstein, R. J., 76 n., 116, 123, 126–7, 129, 178, 185–7
Bettelhein, B., 29
Binswanger, L., 24
Block, N., 95, 132, 145, 149, 201
Boden, M., 10, 143–5, 223
Bogdan, R., 89, 94, 98
Bonomi, A., 209
Borst, C. V., 62, 69, 72, 79, 80, 83 n., 108, 116, 118, 119, 245
Boyd, R., 145
Bradley, M. C., 62
Brandt, R. B., 154, 156
Brentano, F., 277
Bridgman, P. W., 177
Broad, Ch. 115–16
Bunge, M., 13, 255, 269

Campbell, K., 73–5
Cassirer, E., 275
Castañeda, H., 131, 137
Cézanne, P., 232
Chisholm, R. M., 5, 220, 222, 238 n.
Chomsky, N., 152, 238, 275–6, 281

Churchland, P. M., 10
Cooper, De. E., 76 n.
Cornman, J., 115–16
Creutzfeldt, O., 219
Curi, U., 177

Davidson D., 15–17, 27, 153, 156–9, 162–74, 176 and n., 178, 182, 186, 194, 198–9, 214–15, 280
Delgado, J., 10
Dennett, D., 6, 111, 143, 145
Descartes, R., 3, 6, 22, 96–7, 132, 238, 240–1, 259, 265
Deutscher, M., 61–2, 114–15, 211, 227
Diderot, D., 119, 132
Dreyfus, H., 23, 209, 251, 258, 263–6
Ducasse, G., 38 n.

Eccles, J., 45, 96, 123–4, 160, 238, 265, 270
Eisenhower, D. D., 218
Elgin, C. Z., 167
Engelhardt, H. T., 263

Feibleman, J. K., 9
Feigl, H., 2, 4, 11, 14, 30–60, 60 n., 61–2, 68, 84–5, 105, 123, 168, 178, 193, 197, 200–1, 207, 212, 216, 225, 238 n.
Feyerabend, P. K., 14, 90, 101, 118–19, 122
Flew, A., 219
Fløistad, G., 123
Fodor, J., 15, 22, 130, 134–43, 145, 148–51, 152 n., 176, 194, 211, 231, 238, 271
Foucault, M., 264
Frege, G., 108–9

Name index

Gall, F. J., 22, 152 n.
Gava, G., 126
Geach, P., 107, 210
Geschwind, N., 41
Globus, G., 211, 225
Grene, M., 23, 207–8, 213, 218, 238–9, 251, 255, 258–65
Gunderson, K., 146, 208, 244–5
Gunner, D., 62

Habermas, J., 5–6, 125
Hall, C. S., 250
Hare, R. M., 157
Harré, R., 250, 252, 254
Harth, E., 9, 156, 225, 230
Hebb, D., 85
Heidegger, M., 7, 23, 258, 264, 266
Herbst, P., 20, 62, 109, 112–14, 206–7, 216, 221–2, 255–6
Hirsch, E., 106, 111
Hofstadter, D. R., 143, 219
Horgan, T. E., 158
Husserl, E., 221

James, H., 232
James, W., 1, 26, 212, 230

Kalish, D., 110 n.
Kant, I., 166, 240
Kenny, A., 183
Kim, J., 15–16, 114–15, 153–60, 162, 176, 197, 206, 224
Kitcher, P., 94–5, 149
Kneale, W., 92, 105
Kripke, S., 111
Kuhn, Th., 90, 101

Landesman, Ch., 238 n.
Leibniz, G. W., 1, 32, 58, 110–11
Lévi-Strauss, Cl., 103, 276
Levin, M. E., 9–10, 111, 161
Lewis, C. I., 171, 216
Lewis, D. K., 12
Lewis, H. D., 210–11, 214, 215, 225, 237, 238
Lindzey, G., 252
Llinas, R., 245
Lukács, G., 232

Maine De Biran, M.-F.-P., 1
Malcolm, N., 25, 91, 93, 99–100, 106, 108, 125–6, 129, 145, 181, 184–5, 187–91, 196, 209, 235, 245–6, 251, 280 n.

Margolis, J., 13, 19, 96, 112, 126, 129, 149, 198–9, 208–10, 212, 216, 217, 222–3, 231, 243, 246, 251, 254–5, 267–82
Martin, C. B., 61–2
Martin, M., 149
Maxwell, G., 113–14, 198, 211
Medlin, B., 62
Meehl, P. E., 218
Melville, H., 174
Merleau-Ponty, M., 258
Miller, J., 141 n., 152 n.
Montague, R., 110 n.
Moore, G. E., 157, 180
Murray, H., 252

Nagel, Th., 26, 95, 112–13, 201–2, 209, 225, 231–4, 242–3, 246, 251
Neurath, O., 128, 270
Nietzsche, F., 13, 17, 232

Oliverio, A., 7–8
Oppenheim, P., 133
Orwell, G., 51

Peacocke, T., 27, 149, 214
Penfield, W., 238
Piattelli Palmarini, M., 245
Pirandello, L., 232
Place, U. T., 14, 61–9, 81, 83 n., 85, 91–2, 105, 107
Platone, 240
Plessner, H., 258
Polanyi, M., 259
Polten, E., 109, 238
Popper, K., 13, 19, 34, 45, 96, 123–4, 160, 238 and n., 265, 270
Presley, C. F., 61 and n., 109
Preti, G., 107
Pribram, K., 202–3, 206, 263
Proust, M., 25, 172, 232
Putnam, H., 9, 15, 57, 113, 130–7, 142, 145–6, 156, 161, 176, 201, 217

Quine, W. V. O., 111

Rabinow, P., 264
Rager, G., 219
Robinson, H., 36, 123–4, 129, 244–6, 269
Rollins, C. D., 76 n.
Rorty, R., 4, 14, 17, 22, 25, 95, 111, 116, 118–24, 126, 128–9, 148, 191–4, 206, 227–9, 239–41, 247–8, 250, 258, 279

318

Rosenberg, Al., 158
Rosenthal, D. M., 88, 113, 116, 122, 123, 127, 138, 155–6, 179, 185, 196–7, 201, 242, 243, 244, 251
Rothacker, E., 258
Russell, B., 198
Ryle, G., 21–2, 25, 62, 73, 163, 179–82, 191, 195–6, 210–11, 238, 249–50, 257

Sahlins, M., 261
Sartre, J.-P., 6, 258
Savodnik, I., 211
Schopenhauer, A., 1
Searle, J. R., 146
Secord, P., 254
Sellars, W., 5, 58, 116, 156, 197–8, 216, 220, 222, 256
Settle, T., 255
Shaffer, J., 178, 238 n., 246–7, 269, 272
Shoemaker, S., 140
Shotter, J., 5, 10
Simmel, G., 232
Skinner, B., 103
Smart, J. J. C., 14, 61–2, 69–88, 91–2, 95, 105, 119, 136, 150, 189
Sperry, R. W., 158
Spicker, S., 263
Spinoza, B., 1

Squires, R., 208, 210–11, 230, 255–6
Strawson, P. F., 252–3, 259, 272

Taylor, Ch., 6, 100, 201–2
Taylor, R., 11
Thomson, J. J., 156, 160
Tolman, E. C., 212, 276

Vesey, N. A., 1
Vygotsky, L., 276

Watson, J. B., 91
Watzlawick, P., 219
Weimer, W. B., 199–200, 202, 215, 246
Whiteley, C. H., 110, 217
Wilkerson, T. E., 2–3, 123, 126, 129, 177, 179, 202–4, 209, 212, 230, 246, 251–3, 256–7, 262, 272
Wilkes, K., 11, 149, 215, 229–30, 239
Wilson, E., 9–11, 94, 253
Wilson, E. O., 9, 103, 206, 258
Wimsatt, W. C., 214
Wittgenstein, L., 17, 62, 181–7, 191–2, 235, 275, 282
Woodfield, A., 206, 221, 223
Wright, G. H. von, 6, 25, 100

Yolton, J. W., 230

Zangwill, O. L., 246

NATIONAL UNIVERSITY
LIBRARY SAN DIEGO

NATIONAL UNIVERSITY
LIBRARY
SAN DIEGO